How New
Technologies Will
Change the
Way We Shop and
What We Buy

FUTURE SHOP

AN AUTHORS GUILD BACKINPRINT.COM EDITION

Future Shop
How New Technologies Will Change The Way We Shop and What We Buy

AN AUTHORS GUILD BACKINPRINT.COM EDITION
Published by iUniverse

iUniverse books may be ordered through booksellers or by contacting:

iUniverse
1663 Liberty Drive
Bloomington, IN 47403
www.iuniverse.com
1-800-Authors (1-800-288-4677)

Originally published by St. Martin's Press

Because of the dynamic nature of the Internet, any Web addresses or links contained in this book may have changed since publication and may no longer be valid.

ISBN: 978-0-595-50363-6 (pbk)

Printed in the United States of America

To our parents and grandparents,
who made this project possible

KNOWLEDGE IS POWER.

—Francis Bacon

CONTENTS

Preface to the 2008
Reprint of *Future Shop*

The history of the marketplace has been one of accelerating product complexity, especially since the advent of the Industrial Revolution. This growing complexity has led to growing consumer confusion. *Future Shop* addressed the economic and moral consequences of this consumer confusion.

The economic consequence was inefficiency, including the absence in the marketplace of many potentially useful products. The moral consequence was opportunistic behavior, including misleading claims about the price and quality of goods. *Future Shop* called for public policies to reduce such consumer confusion, which it defined in terms of asymmetric information between buyers and sellers.

Future Shop's key intuition was that emerging information technologies could significantly reduce those information asymmetries. In the colloquial words of *Future Shop*, "This book tells why in today's market, despite the huge amount of money spent on consumer information, it's impossible to shop wisely. It also tells why we believe this situation can and will change, if we can only continue to build an information infrastructure that will revolutionize the economics of providing consumer information."[1]

Future Shop framed itself as a manifesto predicting that the advent of new information technologies would facilitate both an economic and moral revolution in the marketplace. The economic revolution would entail a vast change in the production and distribution of products that would lead to the creation of new types of businesses and the explosion of product choice. The moral revolution would entail better informed consumers who would reduce the economic incentive for sellers to engage in puffery and deception.

Future Shop envisioned that the potential of this revolution would only partially be realized as a result of the workings of the private marketplace. The growth of online shopping, for example, would depend on the cost and quality of the telecommunications infrastructure, which the government heavily regulated. Similarly, public policy would influence the development of efficient online transactions mechanisms, including low cost signals of trustworthiness from product information sources and access to comparative product information in online clearinghouses (now often described as "information aggregators").

In retrospect, *Future Shop*'s success at prediction was a mixed bag. It got many of the big trends right, including the huge growth of online shopping, product choice, independent consumer reviews of products, and product information clearinghouses. On the other hand, many of its specific predictions were far off the mark, including the growth of paid independent consumer reviews, the decline of retailing relative to manufacturing, and the need for government disclosure mandates to facilitate online product information clearinghouses.

Future Shop's public policy recommendations were mostly ignored. In the case of some policy areas, such as the management of the electromagnetic spectrum, its recommendations remain as relevant today as they did back in the late 1980s.[2] In other areas, such as the specific proposals for government to take a greater role in setting up product information clearinghouses, Terra Ziporyn and I wish we could take back most of our words because new private companies such as Google, eBay, and Amazon have succeeded in creating such clearinghouses in ways that exceeded our grandest imaginations.

The parts of *Future Shop* that remain most relevant today are its Preface and Chapters, 6-10, and 14. These are the chapters that broadly describe the problem and consequences of consumer confusion and outline the way new information technology, with the help of public policy, could and would play a major role in alleviating that confusion. The rest of the book is a mere historical curiosity.

Successful Predictions

During the last two decades, information technology has radically changed how consumers shop and what they buy. When *Future Shop* was written, online sales represented less than .01% of retail sales and the World Wide Web, which was to popularize the Internet, hadn't even been invented. In the Fourth Quarter of 1999, near the peak of the dotcom boom, the U.S. Department of Commerce began collecting statistics on online retail sales. In that quarter, they had grown to .63% of total retail sales. By 2007, they had increased to 3.5% (up from 2.9% in 2006), a more than 500% increase over the preceding eight years.[3] Recasting the Department of Commerce's e-commerce numbers to exclude products that are unlikely ever to be sold online, such as products sold at restaurants, gas stations, and convenience stores, Forrester Research estimates that online retail sales constituted 6% of total retail sales in 2007 and projects this number will increase to 10.7% in 2012 (a 14% annual growth rate versus only a 2.6% growth rate for shopping in physical stores).[4] According to a Pew/Internet survey, 20% of U.S. Internet users on a typical day "have used the Internet to do research about a product they are thinking about buying."[5]

The same growth in e-commerce is happening worldwide. According to a report by Cisco's Internet Business Solutions Group, by the end of 2007, more than 875 million people had bought a product online, an increase of over 40% in the last year.[6] A report by Wall Street Transcripts found that 11% of retail sales in South Korea in 2007 were purchased online--making the U.S. an e-commerce laggard in comparison.[7]

The number of products readily available to consumers has exploded.[8] Consider the book market. In the late 1980s, the average book buyer could purchase with a modicum of search time at most tens of thousands of books. Since books were not conveniently available online, they had to be acquired through travel to a physical book store. By the end of 2007, thanks to online book sellers such as Amazon, Barnes & Noble, and Borders, book buyers could readily access millions of books for purchase without even leaving their homes. Thanks to Google Books, even books out of print are now available to the public with a click of a button. A similar explosion in consumer choice has played out in many other markets including movies, music, news, dating, and jobs. According to a Pew/Internet survey, 76% of Internet users agree that "the Internet is the best place to buy items that are hard to find."[9]

Not only are consumers purchasing online, they are also getting product information online, even when they ultimately purchase from a physical store. According to a Pew/Internet survey, "On a typical day, 20% of Internet users use the Internet to do research about a product they are thinking about buying."[10] According to a

Cisco survey, "51 percent of U.S. shoppers research products online before they purchase in stores."[11]

The type of product information consumers are using has also radically changed. Online price-comparison services of identical products have become a major force in the marketplace. These include services that cover vast sections of the marketplace such as Amazon's Marketplace, eBay's Shopping.com, and Google's Froogle.

Online retailers also make comparisons between similar products easier than ever before. Consumers specify what features they are looking for and then all the products with those features show up, thus facilitating comparison shopping. These retailers include travel sites such as Expedia, Travelocity, and Orbitz; consumer electronics sites such as Newegg.com, Buy.com, and Tiger.com; and job search sites such as Monster.com, USAjobs.com, and CareerBuilder.com.

Future Shop was prescient in predicting that product information clearinghouses/aggregators would come to play a central place in the marketplace and that they would help consumers wade through historically unprecedented numbers of products. Today, private aggregators such as Google, eBay, Amazon, Expedia, Match.com, Morningstar, and IMDB.com provide such functionality—often very profitably

Services that provide expert online product quality ratings have also thrived, especially in financial services. Financial rating companies include Moody's (which rates bonds and had revenue in 2006 of $2 billion), Morningstar (which rates mutual funds and had revenue in 2007 of $3 billion), and Fair Isaac (which rates consumer creditworthiness and had revenue in 2007 of $825 million). Other rating companies include Metacritic (games), Edmunds.com (cars), creditcards.com (credit cards), avvo.com (attorneys), zagat.com (restaurants), ViaMichelin.com (travel), cnet. com (consumer electronics), Match.com (dates), Consumers Union's ConsumerReports.com (consumer products), and the New York Times' ConsumerSearch.com (consumer products).

Given *Future Shop*'s focus on the growth of independent consumer reviews of products, the most remarkable development has been the explosion of such reviews.[12] According to a study by Shop.org, a division of the National Retail Federation, during the 2007 Holiday season 58.7% of consumers used online customer product reviews.[13] According to a joint study by The Kelsey Group and comScore, "Nearly one out of every four Internet users (24 percent) reported using online reviews prior to paying for a service delivered offline." For product categories such as restaurants, hotels, and travel, more than 79% of review users "reported that the review had a significant impact on their purchase."[14] Amazon alone has more than 10 million consumer reviews. Other prominent websites with consumer reviews include eBay.com (used product sellers), TripAdvisor.com (hotels and other travel destinations), AngiesList.com (home service companies such as plumbers, electricians, and landscapers), Digg.com (news and opinion articles), Yelp.com (restaurants and nightlife), Martindale.com (attorneys), ratemyteacher.com (teachers), and IMDB.com (movies).

Another less formal type of free consumer review comes from the explosion of groups that have formed online.[15] An example would be the countless groups that have formed for sufferers of diseases who share their problems and the remedies they have found effective in solving them. Examples of such sites include crohns.org (for sufferers of Crohn's disease) and dlife.com (for people with diabetes).

Thanks in part to trusted user reviews of sellers, there has been an explosion of small companies serving national markets. Examples include the tens of thousands of small merchants that sell via Amazon and eBay.

Some consumer reviews have undoubtedly been planted by sellers. But in the vast majority of cases the consumers doing the reviewing receive absolutely no direct or indirect compensation from sellers.

One of the most interesting developments is that consumers now often trust peer product reviews more than expert product reviews— perhaps because they believe that experts are less likely to be truly independent. According to the 2007 Edelman Trust Barometer, more than 50% of consumers trusted peer reviews more than expert reviews.[16] This is a major change in just the last five years. In 2003, Edelman found that only a fifth of the respondents picked their peers as their most-trusted source.[17] An Avenue A | Razorfish survey found that when researching products, only 21% of consumers relied on expert opinions the most whereas 55% relied on user reviews the most (22% also relied on comparison charts the most).[18]

Another striking development is that the relative importance of advertising versus independent product reviews has declined. According to a study by Universal/McCann, advertising expenditures as a percent of GNP has declined from 2.52% in 2000 to 2.05% in

2007, with declines in 7 of the 8 years studied.[19] Writes Jonah Bloom in *Advertising Age*:

> It doesn't matter how loud or often you tell consumers your ``truth," few today buy a big-ticket item (or switch allegiance on a regular purchase) before they know what existing users have to say about the product. This is a low-trust world. Even if the marketer they're considering buying from hasn't lied to them, another marketer has--and it takes just seconds to find a host of opinions on any product or service.[20]

Forrester Research, a leading researcher of online consumer behavior, is promoting its 2008 Consumer Forum by highlighting the decline of marketing self-promotion: "Step by step, consumers have less trust in brands; consumers find their own information and entertainment— globally—rather than relying on what TV, print, and radio feed them; they support each other with online reviews and advice and skip ads; and they take control."[21]

Deloitte, one of the world's largest accounting and consulting firms, summarizes its own study on the changing consumer marketing landscape:

> To build their knowledge arsenals, consumers are turning to online reviews in large numbers – and those reviews are having a considerable impact on purchase decisions. According to a recent survey by Deloitte's Consumer Products group, almost two-thirds (62 percent) of consumers read consumer-written product reviews on the Internet. Of these, more than eight in 10 (82 percent) say their purchase decisions have been directly influenced by the reviews, either influencing them to buy a different product than the one they had originally been thinking about purchasing or confirming the original purchase intention.... In the past, clever marketers and advertisers shaped brands, but now consumers are increasingly empowered, everyone has a voice, and information and opinions are instantly dispersed.[22]

Amazon CEO Jeff Bezos has made his own prediction about the decline of advertising: "I'm not saying that advertising is going away. But the balance is shifting. If today the successful recipe is to put 70 percent of your energy into shouting about your service and 30 percent into making it great, over the next 20 years I think that's going to invert."[23]

At least in some areas, the ready availability of better consumer information has reduced the incentive to engage in misleading advertising. For example, *Future Shop* focused on the prevalence of misleading lowest price guarantees and sales in the consumer electronics retailing industry. The growing ease of online comparison shopping has made these claims far less effective. As a result, the major consumer electronics retailing firms now rarely make such outlandish price claims.

From today's vantage point, such predictions of dramatic change in the marketplace may seem self-evident. But in the late 1980s, the close linkage between changing information technology and shopping behavior was harder to fathom. The average household had dialup telephone data service at 2,400 bits/second (compared to millions of bits/second today), paid 35 cents/minute for long distance telephone service (compared to unlimited long-distance service via the Internet today), and had never heard of the Internet (which was viewed as an esoteric text-based tool used for highly specialized, non-commercial purposes). In its *Digital Design Outlook 2008*, interactive marketing and technology agency Avenue A | Razorfish reflects on the telecommunications developments over the past decade:

> Once upon a time there was dial up…. Remember, say, 1999? Just pause for a moment, close your eyes, and recall what it was like to watch a Web site load onto your computer screen chunk… by… chunk… by…this better be worth it… chunk…. Broadband, and the unprecedented tidal wave of innovation that followed it, changed everything—most especially, human behavior online.[24]

In the late 1980s, plans were afoot to build out a much improved telecommunications infrastructure, but the conventional wisdom was that the primary effect on shopping would be to merely shift the locus of sales from physical to online stores, not radically change the structure of the marketplace. Also widespread was the belief that online shopping would be a poor substitute for shopping in physical stores where consumers could see, touch, smell, and test products in their full richness. The notion that online shopping would have many information advantages over shopping in physical stores came across to many as a pipe dream.

Failed Predictions

Those who make predictions about the future often rue them when history reveals their flaws for the world to see. From the vantage point of almost two decades since *Future Shop* was written, history has revealed many flaws, both of commission and omission.

Future Shop predicted the growth of independent product reviews, but it thought those reviews would be created by professional, paid, product reviewers such as *Consumer Reports*, Morningstar, and Fair Isaac. Instead, as we have seen, most of those reviews have been voluntarily contributed by millions of Americans based on their personal experience with products.

Future Shop predicted that government would take major steps to make product markets more transparent, with the practical effect of creating product information clearinghouses. In the last 15 years, a radical shift in government philosophy regarding the regulation of private product markets has indeed occurred.[25] There is less emphasis on regulating product inputs (e.g., occupational licensing) and outputs (e.g., product features such as safety standards), and more emphasis on empowering consumers with product information via laws mandating that sellers disclose product information, often to government sponsored information clearinghouses. For example, at the federal level of government, the Securities & Exchange Commission, Department of Transportation, Department of Education, and Environmental Protection Agency have mandated the disclosure of many types of new information in centralized clearinghouses available online to the public. According to a study by Harvard's John F. Kennedy School's Transparency Policy Project, the federal government alone passed 133 targeted transparency rules between 1996 and 2005. Summing up this shift in regulatory philosophy, Mary Graham, the head of Harvard University's Transparency Policy Project, writes: "During the last decade, government's authority to compel the disclosure of information has taken a legitimate place beside its authority to set rules and redistribute financial resources as a means of furthering public priorities."[26] Nevertheless, such government clearinghouses have not become a major force in the vast majority of product markets.

Future Shop predicted that new technology would reduce the amount of asymmetric information between buyers and sellers, and it hailed this reduction for its economic and moral effects. (Asymmetric information occurs when one side to a transaction has material information that the other side lacks.) But it failed to anticipate that new information technology would also facilitate many new markets characterized by asymmetric information. Partly as a result, its utopian vision of a world where people could not exploit asymmetric information between buyers and sellers was fundamentally flawed. The book was correct in predicting that new information technology would allow consumers to cope better with the marketplace complexity that traditionally caused conditions of asymmetric information between buyers and sellers. But it overlooked the possibility that this new information technology would also create the conditions that would lead that marketplace to become ever more complex.

Future Shop predicted that retailers would be superseded by small, independent agents as product information sources. It didn't anticipate the extent to which a new type of giant, diversified retailer would have an incentive to become independent agents themselves. Amazon.com, for example, now sells many millions of products from tens of thousands of different vendors. It cares relatively little if consumer reviews alienate a particular vendor because any one vendor represents such a tiny percentage of its overall business. More important to Amazon is preserving its general reputation among consumers as a clearinghouse of unbiased product features and consumer reviews. In contrast, retailers with small product lines cannot afford to have negative consumer reviews because the effect is to lead consumers to competitors' websites rather than different parts of their own.

Cisco found that 52% of the e-commerce sites it surveyed provided customer reviews, which it said "are becoming a fundamental expectation." But it also found that few retailers "are allowing the unedited, self-policed, shopper-generated content that appears to drive increased sales, but can create significant operational and PR nightmares."[27] One of the exceptions was Amazon, which "provides the best and most extensive offering of product reviews" and "has become the destination for consumers conducting product research."[28]

Future Shop also didn't anticipate the extent to which small retailers would want to operate under the umbrella of these giant retailers, in part because the giant retailers could provide the credible, unbiased reputation systems necessary to generate consumer trust in small retailers. The result has been standardized disclosure systems and giant product information clearinghouses without government involvement.

Future Shop predicted the decline of all traditional advertising, most of which, like the typical 30 second TV commercial, was intrusive and unwanted.[29] But it failed to distinguish between ads consumers wanted and didn't want, and ads they did and didn't find intrusive. Partly as a result, it failed to anticipate the extent to which desired ads could be efficiently targeted to consumers via search engines and other newfangled technologies.

Public Policy Recommendations

Future Shop's policy recommendations focused on three main areas: how to improve America's telecommunications infrastructure, foster the development of trusted and independent sources of product opinions, and foster the development of factual databases of product information that would facilitate comparison shopping. These remain worthy and often underappreciated goals, but *Future Shop*'s specific recommendations were often wanting. More effort should have been devoted to developing a broader and more rigorous analytical framework.

The relationship of telecommunications policy to the development of e-commerce remains as important today as it was several decades ago. Good telecommunications policy spurs the deployment of telecommunications networks, which spurs the development of e-commerce. Some of *Future Shop*'s specific criticisms of telecommunications policy, such as the federal government's management of the electromagnetic spectrum—the wireless broadband network—continue to be relevant today. Other specific recommendations have held up less well. A notable example was the recommendation to allow telephone companies to accelerate the rate at which they could depreciate their investments to give them an incentive to build out a high speed optical fiber-based broadband network. These were the policies the government was already beginning to pursue. But instead of using the money to build out their networks, the telephone companies used most of it to increase profits and subsidize their monopolistic and highly inefficient operations. In 2006, Bruce Kushnick estimated that the government wasted more than $200 billion on such subsidies to the telephone industry.[30] The result is that the telecommunications networks evolved much more slowly than *Future Shop* predicted.

More central to *Future Shop*'s public policy vision was a new way to think about creating more transparent and efficient consumer product markets. *Future Shop* disparaged the old model of consumer regulation, which it called the "old consumerism." The old consumerism evolved as an ad hoc response to product scandals and special interest pleadings. It featured local, occupation specific licensing; prohibitively expensive, centralized government enforcement; and regulation of products rather than product information. The "new consumerism," in contrast, was based on creating a simple, universal regulatory framework based on principal-agent theory; national, high visibility principal-agent occupational certification; enforcement via well-structured private sector checks & balances; and consumers empowered to protect their own interests with better product information.

An example of the type of consumer regulatory philosophy *Future Shop* opposed was the local licensing of approximately 800 occupations. The regulations attached to these licenses were scattered in countless obscure laws, whose obscurity made them ideally suited for special interest abuse. Ostensibly designed to protect consumers, the occupational licensing laws often smacked of ad hoc, ill-conceived responses to scandal and the machinations of occupational lobbies seeking to reduce competition.

A special focus of *Future Shop* was on conflict of interest regulation. *Future Shop* opposed the huge number of obscure, occupation- or industry-specific laws either mandating the disclosure of or banning conflicts of interest by information providers. Examples of such laws include mandates that doctors disclose their referral fees; that cable, satellite, and over-the-air broadcasters disclose paid product placements within their advertising; and that mutual fund managers disclose their stock trades. Instead, *Future Shop* wanted a simple certification system that would allow all independent information providers, not just those in particular politically salient occupations or industries, to make a credible and affordable claim that they were indeed independent. Such a certified unbiased information provider (called an I.C.I.C. in the language of *Future Shop*) would have to disclose all material conflict of interests, with materiality defined as a conflict of interest that a reasonable consumer might use to discount the quality of a provider's product information. In the language of principal-agent theory, government should make it possible for an information agent (the information provider) to signal at low cost to a principal (the consumer) that it has no material undisclosed conflicts of interest.

The Securities & Exchange Commission (SEC), with its focus on empowering investors with better information, was a regulatory model for much of what *Future Shop* proposed. The SEC's laws were primarily developed in response to financial scandals that had collectively cost Americans trillions of dollars over the decades. The loss of so much money in the financial markets had caused Americans great pain and led to unusually thoughtful public discussions of financial market failure. This had led to the creation of a strikingly different and original type of consumer protection system. An independent board designed financial accounting standards. Independent auditors then used these standards to report the financial condition of public companies. The companies, in turn, disclosed this information in a well-structured format to a centralized, publicly accessible database. Independent financial analysts then used the resulting public database of financial information to issue opinions about the companies. Most of the accountability mechanisms relied on checks and balances among well-structured private entities, with a focus on ensuring that individual investors got timely, accurate, unbiased financial information.

Future Shop envisaged that this type of regulatory scheme would become more affordable as a result of emerging information technologies, and thus could be extended to product markets where they had previously been prohibitively expensive.

However, *Future Shop* itself was torn on the extent to which the private sector could create institutions of transparency and trust to facilitate a more efficient and moral marketplace. Its contribution to that debate was not the specific recommendations it made but its general sensibility that a major rethinking of the government's role in facilitating e-commerce should become a priority. That message is still as relevant today as it was then. It will probably take the public policy community many decades to think through how not only to mitigate the potential harms created by e-commerce, but also to fully exploit the opportunities it creates.

Conclusion

In its concluding paragraph, *Future Shop* observed: "The way consumers go about gathering information and making decisions today is closer to the eighteenth century than the twenty-first century.

As the twenty-first century progresses, the consumer's growing information power will transform the marketplace and many of the values currently associated with it." Despite the many failed predictions it made, *Future Shop* nailed this one. The way consumers shop has indeed changed monumentally since *Future Shop* was written close to twenty years ago. If I were to hazard one more prediction about the future of shopping, it is that the next twenty years will see even greater changes than we've seen in the last twenty.

--J.H. Snider
May 31, 2008
Cambridge, Massachusetts

(Endnotes)

1   J.H. Snider and Terra Ziporyn, *Future Shop: How New Technologies Will Change the Way We Shop and What We Buy*, 1st ed. (New York: St. Martin's Press, 1992), 14.

2   J.H. Snider, "The Art of Spectrum Lobbying: America's $480 Billion Spectrum Giveaway, How It Happened, and How to Prevent It from Recurring," (Washington, DC: New America Foundation, August 2007), ———, "Spectrum Policy for the Emerging Ultrabroadband World: Should Spectrum and Tangible Property Rights Be Bundled?," (New York, NY: Columbia University's Institute for Tele-Information, June 22, 2007).

3   See U.S. Census Bureau, "Quarterly Retail E-Commerce Sales," (Washington, DC: U.S. Census Bureau, February 15, 2008).

4   Sucharita Mulpuru, "Us Ecommerce: 2008 to 2012," (Cambridge, MA: Forrester Research, January 18, 2008).

5   John Horrigan, "Online Shopping," (Washington, DC: Pew Internet & American Life Project, February 13, 2008), iv.

6   Danein Dunne, et al., "Third Annual Cicso Ibsg E-Commerce Survey," (San Jose, CA: Cisco Internet Business Solutions Group, May 2008), 2.

7   "Internet Retail Report," (New York, NY: Wall Street Transcript, June 18, 2008).

8   For an depth discussion of this phenomenon, see Chris Anderson, *The Long Tail : Why the Future of Business Is Selling Less of More*, 1st ed. (New York: Hyperion, 2006).

9   Horrigan, "Online Shopping," 13.

10 Ibid., iv.

11 Dunne, "Third Annual Cicso Ibsg E-Commerce Survey," 12.

12 For an in depth discussion of this phenomenon, see Yochai Benkler, *The Wealth of Networks: How Social Production Transforms Markets and Freedom* (New Haven [Conn.]: Yale University Press, 2006).

13 "2007 Shop.Org/Shopzilla Eholiday Study," http://www.shop.org.

14 Press release, "Online Consumer Generated Reviews Have Significant Impact on Offline Purchase Behavior," (Reston, VA: comScore and The Kelsey Group, November 29, 2007).

15 For an in depth discussion of this phenomenon, see Clay Shirky, *Here Comes Everybody: How Digital Networks Transform Our Ability to Gather and Cooperate* (New York: Penguin Press, 2008).

16 Cited in Joan Voight, "Getting a Handle on Customer Reviews," Adweek, July 5, 2007.

17 Ibid.

18 "Digital Consumer Behavior Study," (New York, NY: Avenue A | Razorfish, 2007), 7.

19 Robert J. Coen, "Insider's Report: Robert Coen Presentation on Advertising Expenditures," (New York, NY: Universal McCann, December 2007), 4.

20 Jonah Bloom, "The Truth Is: Consumers Trust Fellow Buyers before Marketers.," *Advertising Age*, February 2006.

21 "Forrester's Consumer Forum 2008: Keeping Ahead of Tomorrow's Customer, October 28-29, 2008, Dallas Texas," http://www.forrester.com/events/eventdetail?eventID=2235.

22 Press release, "New Deloitte Study Shows Inflection Point for Consumer Products Industry: New Technologies Provide Consumers with a Wealth of Information to Make Purchase Decisions, While Also Empowering Them to Shape Company Reputations," (New York, NY: Deloitte, October 1, 2007).

23 Chris Anderson, "The Zen of Jeff Bezos," *Wired*, January 1, 2005, 167.

24 "Digital Outlook Report 2008," (New York, NY: Avenue A/Razorfish, 2008).

25 Archon, Mary Graham, and David Weil, *Full Disclosure : The Perils and Promise of Transparency* (New York: Cambridge University Press, 2007), Mary Graham, *Democracy by Disclosure : The Rise of Technopopulism* (Washington, D.C.: Governance Institute/Brookings Institution Press, 2002).

26 Ibid., p. viii.

27 Dunne, "Third Annual Cicso Ibsg E-Commerce Survey," 12.

28 Ibid., 8.

29 E.g., see Julie Bosman, "Advertising Is Obsolete. Everyone Says So," *New York Times*, January 23 2006.

30 Bruce Kushnick, *$200 Billion Broadband Scandal* (TeleTruth, 2006).

Preface:
The Dawn of a
New Consumerism

In 1927 Stuart Chase and Frederick Schlink published *Your Money's Worth*. Often called the *Uncle Tom's Cabin* of the consumer movement, this book charted the corruptions and inefficiencies in the marketplace and called for the formation of an impartial non-profit organization to test products scientifically. This led to Schlink's 1928 founding of Consumers Research, which was superseded in 1936 by the newly formed Consumers Union (publishers of *Consumer Reports*).

Unfortunately, there hasn't been a fundamentally new idea in consumerism in the more than fifty years since *Your Money's Worth* first appeared. Worse, despite increased government regulation and the success of publications such as *Consumer Reports*, the old consumerism simply isn't working. Blatant deception and gross inefficiency may be phenomena of the past, but thanks to the proliferation and increased complexity of products, underlying consumer confusion has actually increased. Today, in fact, we are facing an epidemic of consumer confusion far greater than at any time in history.

This book attempts to bring consumerism into the information age. Over the years, many observers have looked at the marketplace and concluded that widespread consumer confusion was morally and economically harmful. Most of these observers have been pragmatic cynics, recognizing that this imperfection was just one of the many problems with which we would have to live in this flawed world. More idealistic types sought remedies, some through increased government control of the marketplace, others through the intervention of virtuous non-profit organizations. This book, in contrast, argues for a radically new type of consumerism—a consumerism based on building an information infra- structure that will radically alter the economics and logistics of providing and using consumer information. The New Consumerism is about information power; it's about consumers empowered by information; it's about the information infrastructure necessary to bring this about; it's about all those forces that would prefer that this didn't happen. It could, most accurately, be called an information movement.

This book also aims to enrich the discussion of the emerging informa- tion age: the long-term shift from an industrial to an information-based society. Over the years, conventional wisdom has held that the key to understanding this change lies in production ("supply") rather than consumption ("demand"). That is, conventional wisdom has paid much attention to how new information technology could affect the production of goods and services, but relatively little to how that same technology could eliminate the inefficiency, loss of innovation, and deception that is an inevitable consequence of the way consumers now find out about products. Here we argue that better consumer access to information will revolutionize not only consumer decision making and buying, but also—indirectly—production, distribution, media, and even values.

In short, this book deals with the problem of growing consumer confusion and how new technology can help alleviate it. It provides a theory of consumer knowledge—a theory of how our access to informa- tion profoundly affects the moral, social, and economic world around us. And it forecasts how improved consumer access to information will radically change that world.

This book is, as such, a visionary manifesto. It puts consumption (defined as "life-style decisions") in the central place of our economy and civilization, and it sees in information technology the dynamo that will alter the whole social and economic edifice built upon our current consumption patterns. Moreover, the book contends that these changes will be beneficial. They will lead to much greater prosperity and happiness, and the reconciliation of ethics and the profit motive. The hope is that the ambitious and thoughtful reader will see the economic and moral opportunities enunciated here and help bring them to fruition.

The idea for this book came to me out of a mixture of faith and mundane consumer experience. Back in 1978 when I was an undergraduate at Harvard, I was gripped by "information religion," the belief that new information technology could dramatically improve human life. One day, while reading Daniel Bell's *Coming of Post-Industrial Society*, which deals with the importance of good information to a healthy society and economy, I happened to be shopping for a stereo system. Although Bell's book didn't specifically discuss consumers and the problem of their ignorance about purchases, my frustrating search for the right equipment led me to my own conclusion: one of the biggest changes the "Information Age" would bring in years to come would have to do with the way in which consumers make purchasing decisions. I also was inclined to believe that anything that profoundly affected consumption—the life-style decisions that fill a large portion of our time—must be something very important to our economy and civilization.

Of course, given my tender age and the vagueness of my ideas, I couldn't expect to interest anyone in such a concept. In fact, after spending that summer working as an intern for the Congressional Clearinghouse for the Future, the most future-oriented organization in the U.S. government at the time, I quickly gave up the idea as impractical. The world simply wasn't ready for immediate overhaul. One reason was that the technology required to implement my idea just wasn't very plausible in 1978. Sure, scientists such as Alan Kay had envisioned an inexpensive, book-sized personal computer that had the power of the largest and most expensive computers of his day—as well as a host of other remarkable features. But in the real world, the personal computer had only just been invented, the telecommunications industry was lost in the doldrums of AT&T's monopoly, and high-definition TV and optical fiber networks weren't even topics of conversation.

But as the years went by, my frustrations as a consumer kept nagging at me. The idea that there might be a solution to the problem of consumer ignorance had drawn my attention to the problem of consumer ignorance itself. And I began to reflect: Did other people share such ignorance? And if so, what would be the effects of this ignorance multiplied millions of times over? Gradually, I began to see that the primitive way we got information about products profoundly affected not only consumers but the entire structure of the marketplace.

In 1985 I proposed this idea as an essay to an editor at the *Harvard Business Review*. Once again the idea was shot down: the technology just wasn't far enough along to make the ideas relevant or interesting. Afterwards, my co-author and soon to be wife, Terra Ziporyn, suggested that instead of merely predicting this revolution in consumer buying habits, we could do something to bring it about. As a professional science and technical writer (with a doctorate in the history of science), Terra had years of experience translating complex ideas into understandable language, and she saw no reason why we couldn't apply this skill to the confusing world of product selection. Convinced, I got a job at *Consumer Reports*, widely regarded as the leading consumer-product rating organization in the world, and Terra did some writing for them. My hope was to spearhead the organization's transition to the twenty-first century. Instead, I found myself wading through the tens of thousands of reader letters it gets every year and trying to devise a computerized system to categorize and respond to them. The experience of reading these letters left me with one simple insight: the ambition to do absolutely everything, to cover more than a million consumer products—and to do so within the limitations of 110 short printed articles per year and a product-evaluation budget significantly smaller than the budget a major candymaker would use to promote a popular candy bar—was not a formula that could succeed in the next century.

So what type of formula would succeed? Late in 1986, while I was finishing my studies at the Harvard Business School, Terra and I decided to find out. We hoped to form a company that would be a model for an entirely new industry. We hoped to prove that in the new era of information, it would be the private sector, not government or the non-profit sector, that would and should be the consumer's best friend. Part of this effort led us to an in-depth study of the selling practices of the major appliance, consumer electronics, and personal-computer industries, an experience which provided us with vivid and often surprising examples about the extent and significance of consumer confusion.

No sooner had we finished this study, however, than we realized that the time had finally arrived for us to incorporate our vision in a book. There was a feeling in the air that the 1990s would finally be the decade that would revolutionize consumer access to information. The Baby Bells in the United States and NTT in Japan were on the verge of launching a campaign to introduce fiber-optic networks into every American and Japanese home. Two major American computer companies, Apple Computer and IBM—along with a slew of Japanese consumer-electronics companies—had announced multimedia computers. And Congress, spurred on by Japan's imminent introduction of high-definition TV, was treating the development of a U.S. version with a sense of national shame and purpose not seen since the Soviets launched Sputnik into space in the 1950s. Meanwhile, consumerism was back in vogue. The 1980s excesses of deregulation had renewed American awareness that corruption, inefficiency, and deregulation often go hand in hand. Ralph Nadar had been resurrected, and business ethics was once again a respectable topic. At the same time, the rapid advances in information technology during the 1980s had given Americans a basic sense of confidence in that industry's future. Multimedia computers, flat-screen computers, wireless computers, affordable home computers, high-definition TV, integrated services digital network (ISDN), voice recognition, optical fiber, digital cellular telephones, personal communication networks, microcomputers with supercomputer power—all these technologies were beginning to be part of the vocabulary and strategic planning of even the most hard-headed businessman. And not of least importance, some of this technology was even beginning to trickle down to the consumer. Electronic shopping, primitive and flawed as it was, was beginning to emerge. There were, for example, the Home Shopping Network, Prodigy, Main Street, and 15,000 information kiosks scattered throughout the United States. Foreign governments, such as those of Canada and France, had taken the lead in encouraging the massive development of state-of-the-art consumer information services. And even *Consumer Reports* was taking a step into the future with an innovative computerized information service. Finally, the time had come for information technology to tackle the problem of consumer confusion.

It has often been said that the underlying technological structure of a society determines its economic and moral structure. For example, the electric light, the telephone, the automobile, the TV, and the birth control pill have all left their mark on our society. Likewise, the information technology that is about to reach consumers will change our lives and our world fundamentally. One of the most important changes will be a new awareness of problems that have always existed but, for want of a solution, have never been noticed. At the same time, with the problems in clearer focus, we can work more rapidly and effectively toward their solution. This book hopes above all to begin this process by igniting interest in the problem of consumer ignorance and by pointing to what can, should, and will be done to remedy it.

—JIM SNIDER
March 1991
Smugglers' Notch, Vermont

PART I

THE PROBLEM:

THE CONFUSED CONSUMER

CHAPTER 1

Why You Can't Be a "Smart Shopper" Anymore

Pick up a pamphlet from your local consumer-protection agency, a copy of a consumer magazine, or a book by a consumer advocate, and you'll get plenty of lessons on how to shop smart and protect yourself. But what none of these sometimes well-intentioned sources tells you is that their list of instructions is about as easy to follow as tips on how to simultaneously win Wimbledon, the World Series, *and* the National Football League Championship: practice tennis, baseball, and football every day; find good tennis, baseball, and football coaches; and refrain from all distractions such as alcohol, sex, employment, family, and friends. It's humanly possible, perhaps, but only if you're willing to sacrifice years of your life.

As the twentieth century draws to a close, people in modern countries face a dizzying array of choices, and each choice makes shopping and life in general that much more complicated. For most of history, people have led much simpler lives, with consumer choices limited to a few basic matters: for example, do I plant beans or corn, do I buy sugar or honey, or do I sew with wool or cotton? Until quite recently, in fact, many people didn't even have to choose whom they would marry, where they would live, or how they would earn their living; various customs and rituals decided these issues for them.

DECISIONS, DECISIONS, DECISIONS

The number of choices consumers faced actually didn't start to skyrocket until the beginning of the Industrial Revolution. Even in the late eighteenth century, most people were still self-sufficient, living in rural areas, and making very few consumer decisions. Just think for a moment about the way Americans lived throughout most of our country's history. Before this century, average citizens had no cars or electrical appliances. Their diet consisted of perhaps twenty-five different foods. Their furniture was simple. They had maybe a couple of choices for evening entertainment. If they were uncertain about the specific product they wanted, they could turn to a family member or a friend for impartial and valuable advice. Products didn't change much, and peers would surely have experience with whatever they wanted to buy.

Similarly, until relatively recently consumers chose from relatively few vendors. They probably bought most goods from the perhaps fifty "stores" in a local village market. They knew all the owners. They trusted them because community members would soon boycott any vendor who tried to cut corners. And, again, if for some reason consumers didn't know a vendor, they could turn to a knowledgeable family member or friend for advice.[1]

With our increasingly complex civilization, the world is becoming more confusing and intimidating to the consumer every day. Caught up in what futurologist Alvin Toffler has termed "a fire storm of change," we must choose between hundreds of thousands of goods, services, pursuits, and life-styles, many of which demand large amounts of time and energy to understand.[2] Often, friends and family can no longer provide any useful advice. At the same time, the salesperson from whom we purchase is likely to be an unknown face—and probably someone we don't trust very much.

" 'When my father was young, he used to take a horse-drawn carriage to the railroad station,' " Ralph E. Gomory, senior vice-president for science and technology at IBM, was quoted as saying in *Fortune* magazine. " 'There were no automobiles, no telephones, no movies. No airplane had ever flown. There was no television, no atomic bomb, no man on the moon. But by the time he died, he had flown in a jet and had seen all those other things happen. No generation had ever been through a transformation like that.' "[3]

Many economists and sociologists believe that the world is now changing faster than ever before. In fact, in *Future Shock*, Toffler quotes economist Kenneth Boulding as saying that human history can be divided into two equal parts, with the dividing line "well within living memory." Boulding contends that today's world "is as different from the world in which I was born as that world was from Julius Caesar's. . . . Almost as much has happened since I was born as happened before."[4]

Toffler adds that the average annual rate of increase in gross national product during the 1960s for twenty developed nations suggests

> nothing less revolutionary than a doubling of the total output of goods and services in the advanced societies about every fifteen years—and the doubling times are shrinking. This means, generally speaking, that the child reaching teen age in any of these societies is literally surrounded by twice as much of everything newly man-made as his parents were at the time he was an infant. It means that by the time today's teen-ager reaches age thirty, perhaps earlier, a second doubling will have occurred. Within a seventy-year lifetime, perhaps five such doublings will take place—meaning, since the increases are compounded, that by the time the individual reaches old age the society around him will be producing thirty-two times as much as when he was born.[5]

Although Toffler's fifteen-year doubling rate is probably exaggerated given today's slower-growing economies, looking at some broad numbers representing changes in consumer choice over the past two centuries tells a similar story. Two hundred years ago, for example, only 9 percent of Americans lived in urban areas.[6] Most lived in rural villages or farms, and lacking flexible means of transportation and communication, were primarily restricted to shopping in a single general store located in the nearest village. American historian Jack Larkin estimates that the average American home in 1800 probably contained only about fifty to seventy-five store-bought, non-work-related products (e.g., food inventory, furniture, books, kitchenware, clothing materials, and miscellaneous tools) that members of the household themselves had purchased.[7]

An early-nineteenth-century farmer would be overwhelmed if he or she could step into a time machine and see today's average American home, which could easily consist of several thousand purchased items. And many of these items would be much more complex and confusing than any known in the previous century. Today a typical household may possess hundreds of books; numerous pieces of furniture, such as chairs, tables, lamps, bureaus, rugs, bedstands, trash cans, laundry bins, and baby equipment; dishware, including cookware, serving dishes, pots, pans, plates, bowls, cups, glasses, china, silver, flatware, measuring devices, carving knives, spatulas, ladles, and special tools; various types of paper and writing instruments; electronic equipment, including clocks, security devices, audio and video hardware, telephones, answering machines, and computers and computer peripherals; appliances, including washer, dryer, microwave oven, refrigerator, snow blower, automobile, air conditioners, electronic can opener, blender, food processor, hair dryer, vacuum cleaner, hot-water heater, electric water pump, home-heating system, space heaters, humidifier, dehumidifier, electric fans, electric iron, electric shaver, and electronic pencil sharpeners; numerous toys and games; food, including spices, canned goods, dry goods, refrigerated goods, and frozen goods; outdoor camping gear; computer software programs; compact discs, records, and tape cassettes; bathroom items, including pills, ointments, first aid, cosmetics, brushes, combs, and soaps; hardware, including light bulbs, screws, pliers, hammer, screwdriver, wrench, wire cutter, and electric drill; various soaps and cleansing agents; tools for gardening, lawn care, and tree maintenance; apparel, such as shirts, ties, pants, blouses, skirts, dresses, shorts, underwear, pajamas, robes, shoes, coats, hats, jewelry, socks, and eyeglasses; sports equipment; financial instruments, such as credit cards, bank accounts, stocks, bonds, and life insurance; and knickknacks, sheets, towels, umbrellas, photographs, posters, and paintings.

Beyond what we *do* buy, the number of things that we *can* buy today in contrast to the American of two hundred years ago is just as mindboggling. A typical American in 1800 had access to less than 300 products on sale in his or her hometown, one retail establishment (a country store), and approximately 500 square feet of retail space.[8] For example, in 1809 the Miner Grant store, which served as the primary retail establishment for residents of Stafford Springs, Connecticut, stocked 262 different products in its 563 square feet of shopping space.[9] In contrast, a typical American today in a metropolitan city of 1 million people has access to more than a million consumer products, thousands of merchants, and 15 million square feet of selling space. Just at Wal-Mart's HyperMart alone, one of the country's largest retail stores, consumers can select from among nearly 110,000 different products in 130,000 square feet, while an average supermarket carries 25,000 items in 40,000 square feet. Many large modern malls contain over 350,000 types of merchandise.[10]

In the single year of 1988, moreover, manufacturers introduced a record 8,183 new food products, doubling the number of new offerings since 1983. In this one year new products included 1,608 condiments, 1,130 candies and snacks, 968 bakery foods, 936 beverages, 854 dairy products, 613 entrées, 548 processed meats, 402 side dishes, 55 baby foods—and even 97 new breakfast cereals.[11]

Our choices extend beyond goods and services to fundamental decisions that determine our overall life-style. Many Americans today, unlike most people throughout human history, must choose their own schools, occupations, locales, and spouses. It may at first seem unsettling or even offensive to lump such activities as choosing a spouse or choosing an occupation together with choosing a toaster or choosing a box of cereal. Yet each of these choices is a consumer choice as well, not in the sense that it necessarily costs us cash money, but in the sense that it costs us time and/or energy. Looking for a spouse, for example, can involve taking classes, attending parties, conducting in-depth conversations, meeting families, and arranging dates; looking for an employer can involve treading pavements, reading advertisements, buying clothes, writing résumés, and attending interviews. All these activities involve time and energy. Moreover, the growing number of employment agencies, career counselors, and dating services—businesses hired to help make these agonizing decisions—only make it even easier to think of them as consumer decisions.

As the number of life-style possibilities from which we have to choose has increased overwhelmingly, so has the time and energy increased. Many of us no longer feel compelled to go to one of the three hometown colleges or marry a hometown sweetheart. Many of us no longer feel compelled to work in the family business or vacation no farther from our home than a day's walk. The entire world is ours to choose from. But while the expanded choices are welcome, the poor-quality information we presently have on which to make decisions means the actuality must necessarily fall far short of the promise.

Toffler observes that the addition of each option creates "the need for more information, more decisions and subdecisions." While shopping for a car, he found himself giving up days shopping for and reading about the various brands, models, lines, and options. Car buyers are equally baffled by the sheer multiplicity of options. " 'Figuring all possible combinations of styles, options and colors available on a certain new family sports car,'" Toffler quotes Marshall McLuhan as saying, "'. . . a computer expert came up with 25,000,000 different versions of it for a buyer. . . . When automated electronic production reaches full potential, it will be just about as cheap to turn out a million differing objects as a million exact duplicates.'" Toffler believes that our society is "racing toward 'overchoice'—the point at which the advantages of diversity and individualization are cancelled by the complexity of the buyer's decision-making process."[12]

In short, today's consumer faces a wholly unprecedented number of choices, and the number and complexity of choices facing consumers is increasing at an exponential rate. And, unfortunately, until now our information tools, the tools from which we can learn about these choices, have not kept up with the growth and complexity of the products and services. Thus, whether it is choosing a doctor, a college, a spouse, an employer, a locale, a life insurance policy, a home, or, as we shall be particularly concerned with in this book, choosing high-tech household equipment, the factors to be considered are now beyond the powers of even the most intelligent and tireless consumers.

CONSUMER ELECTRONICS: A CASE STUDY IN CONFUSION

One of the most vivid illustrations of the problems faced by modern consumers comes from the world of consumer electronics. Here just in the past quarter century the number of consumer choices have increased phenomenally. The 1964 electronics industries yearbook lists only three main consumer products: radios, phonographs, and televisions. Such a small number of color television sets were sold that it wasn't even thought worthwhile to record it. Today this same yearbook lists dozens of different product categories, including radios, monochrome TVs, color TVs, projection TVs, phonographs, tape players, compact-disc players, VCRs, camcorders, cellular telephones, corded telephones (only rented through AT&T in 1964), cordless telephones, telephone answering machines, facsimile machines, personal copiers, personal computers, computer software, computer printers, satellite earth stations, portable audio players, videodisc systems, electronic keyboards, electronic watches, electronic toys, home-security alarm systems, and electronic home-health-care products. A typical superstore selling consumer electronics, major appliances, and home office equipment carries approximately four thousand different pieces of merchandise.[13]

Furthermore, the products that existed in 1964 were much simpler than their counterparts today. Buying a TV back then merely involved selecting one out of about a dozen different models in a typical store. The choice was based on a few basic features, such as type of tuner and picture tube (black-and-white or color), a simple mechanical channel switcher accessing VHF channels, and a choice of various furniture styles.[14] Today's televisions include more than a hundred different features, and the typical dealer now offers more than 150 different models.

This is how one writer in *Video Review* described the situation to his fellow videophiles:

> In the next 20 seconds you will learn everything you need to know about today's high-tech video equipment. Ready? Here we go: SP, LP, EP, SLP, SAP, MTS, VCR, DNR, VNR, CAV, CLV, VCP, CATV, NTSC, HDTV, A/V, RF, AFT, VHF, UHF, MPX, FST, LCD, CTL, LED, CCD, VCP, PIP, MOS, HD, HQ, CD, LV, CD-V, VHS, VHS-C, S-VHS.
>
> There, now you're an expert. What's the matter, did I go a little too fast for you?[15]

If hobbyists have this much trouble keeping track of what's going on, how is the average consumer expected to cope?

It's not just that there are a lot of things out there to choose from that makes it so hard to shop smart for consumer electronics. It's also that a lot of the options have become terribly complicated. Most people can't just walk into an electronics store and squeeze a television the way they can a melon, nor can they just eyeball a refrigerator and decide how well the motor has been constructed, nor can they just read the hundreds of thousands of lines of code in a software program to discover all its bugs. You can look at a TV and decide you like the picture, but you can't know whether that picture will maintain its quality over the next five years or whether the remote control makes an annoying little squeak every time you try some of its more esoteric programming functions. You can read consumer magazines and decide you want certain features, but when you walk into a store and see that each TV boasts thirty features, all described in completely different terminology than those in the magazine article, you'll end up buying a favorite brand or a "sale" model. In short, there are just too many internal parts—and too many external features—for any one person to make a truly informed decision.

Worse still, even if you learn a little something about computers or stereo systems, chances are high that what you know will be completely outdated next year—or even next month. It seems that almost every day, computer manufacturers and software developers are hailing some breakthrough. And the fact is, despite all the hype and false starts, they're right for the most part. The major personal computer systems of just five years ago, once lauded by companies, are now considered toys fit for grade-schoolers. And customers can be fairly certain that in another five years their computers of today will be similarly regarded.

Even after you have made a decision, you have no basis on which to determine if it was the best. One washing machine may last ten years on average, another fifteen, but most consumers will never be able to reasonably infer that a particular washing machine is worth 50 percent more because it lasts 50 percent longer. The same can be said for most goods and services in our country—including auto repairs, insurance policies, credit cards, ethical drugs, and VCRs. For the most part, Americans purchasing these items are no more able to tell after their purchase than before whether they got a good deal.

Not surprisingly, then, shopping wisely for high-priced consumer electronics, major appliances, and computers today is a full-time sport. Even the most well-informed shopper feels intimidated by the hundreds of computers, software programs, TVs, and microwave ovens on the market. No matter how much you read, how many stores you visit, and how many friends you talk to, it's nearly impossible to get unbiased, timely, and accurate information. You may even put off the purchase of a novel kind of product entirely because you're intimidated by the options available and afraid of making a mistake. And when you do buy, you probably walk out of the store with a vague sense of confusion and unease, never suspecting that these feelings, multiplied millions of times, result in a huge cost to our society.

The reason for this cost is not that manufacturers and retailers are making huge profits. Nor is it that manufacturers, retailers, consumer media, and consumer-protection organizations don't necessarily have the consumer's best interests in mind. Although these explain the situation in part, the core of the problem—in both consumer electronics and all other areas where consumers must make choices—resides in the primitive technological and corresponding institutional structure which determines the economics of disseminating and utilizing product information. In other words, the number, complexity, and rate of change of products has increased, but the methods of informing consumers about these developments have not kept pace.

NO SERVICE, NO TIME

These trends leading to more consumer confusion will undoubtedly continue: products will keep proliferating, changing faster and faster, and our choices will become increasingly complex. In turn, consumers will have to depend more on the service of others for information about the items they buy. But so far there are few signs that service can keep up with product proliferation.

Unfortunately, for a great number of our purchasing choices, it's simply uneconomical to provide decent service: talented help is too difficult and expensive to find. Take aspirin. You would almost certainly prefer to spend $4.00 total for a brand-name bottle of aspirin that costs $0.50 to produce, than pay $1.00 for a generic brand plus $20 for a consultant/salesperson to assure you that the generic brand is equally potent and reliable. Or take a $150 CD player. You'd probably prefer to spend an extra $30 for a Sony and be confident of getting a reliable, high-quality product, than spend $60 gathering information that tells you that a less expensive, less well known brand is of equivalent quality.

This basic inefficiency in providing service has helped spawn a major discount industry in the United States in the last twenty years. From 1960 to 1987 this industry grew from $2.0 billion to $74.6 billion in annual sales, about 4.5 times the comparable growth in gross national product.[16] Discount businesses are characterized, among other things, by less service than the department stores and mom-and-pop shops they superseded.[17] Most extreme are the warehouse clubs which offer absolutely no service. In most of these operations, members pay an annual fee for the privilege of cruising huge bare-bones floors to buy boxed goods at sometimes rock-bottom prices and haul them home themselves. This segment of the retail industry has grown from zero sales in the late 1970s to $21.1 billion in sales in 1990 and is now the fifth-largest form of mass merchandising in the nation.[18]

The growth of discount mail-order firms also fits this trend. Firms like 47th St. Photo, J&R Music World, and PC Connection, which provide comparatively little buying information, allow shoppers to pick up a phone, dial a toll-free number, and order products such as telephone answering machines, CD players, camcorders, and computers. In their advertisements and other promotional statements, these firms claim that cutting back on service and retail rent saves consumers money.

While discounters have been a great boon to the consumer, allowing much more value for the dollar, they have done nothing to alleviate the inefficiency that results from consumers buying aspirin for $4 that costs 50 cents to produce and distribute. And, as we shall see later, they do nothing to alleviate the stifled innovation that results when consumers are confused about their purchases.

Furthermore, in some respects—as full-priced retailers love to argue—the growth of the discount industry has actually hurt consumers. In particular, sometimes consumers would not only love more service but be willing to pay for it. But for various structural reasons, they will never get that service. The problem is that stores that provide high levels of service and charge high prices find it very difficult to compete with poor-service stores that offer the same products at much lower prices. Consumers shop the high-service stores but buy from the low-priced ones; they would like more service, but because they have not been willing to pay for it in the past, it is no longer available.[19] Retailers try to get around this problem by participating in certain questionable practices such as fixing prices or offering derivative models (to keep prices uniformly high or keep exclusive inventories), but such tactics, besides adding inefficiencies of their own, only partially solve the problem: consumers know that a brand-name camcorder that sells for $1,500 at a full-service retailer is likely to be very similar to a brand-name $1,000 camcorder with identical features sold at a warehouse club or mail-order house. Thus, the previously full-service store is forced to cut service and prices to compete with the discounter.

Difficulty in recouping personal selling costs combined with decreased product costs (resulting from improved methods of production) relative to higher labor costs (resulting from a generally higher standard of living) have led stores in all retailing segments to cut supervision and sales personnel such that by 1982 "poor retail store service had become the rule rather than the exception."[20] Much of the information consumers are getting from the salespeople is actually incomplete or false, brought about by the simple ignorance of the people whom the consumer must trust. Not surprisingly, consumers report frustration after dealing with salespeople, wishing they could talk to people bright enough to understand the technology and to help them make difficult decisions.

And indeed, even if salespeople had the time to explain complex products, most of them are too confused themselves to educate consumers adequately. People sufficiently trained and intelligent enough to understand these products are very hard to come by and usually unaffordable. "How many consumers know, much less understand, those terms and initials already in use [for consumer electronic products]?" asks an article in a recent trade publication. "How many salespeople can provide a helpful, truly convincing story about the products such terms identify? . . . [T]he so-called salesmanship at the retail level not only in electronics but virtually all products leaves a great deal to be desired."[21]

In short, for a number of deep-seated reasons, service has deteriorated almost across the board. With the highly complex and fast-changing items featured in this book, such as major consumer electronics, major appliances, and personal computers, the trend is particularly evident. For example, an industry educator at one major consumer-electronics convention told dealers never to let their salespeople spend more than twelve minutes with each customer. Twelve minutes is just too much to give away if a store wants to make any money. Unfortunately, it's also far too little time to even begin explaining anything to a consumer choosing between today's complex consumer electronics and appliances.

Unfamiliar goods and poor service are not the only factors underlying inadequate consumer information and dissatisfied consumers. Another is the increasingly limited shopping time of consumers themselves. Concluding that "time may well have become the most precious commodity in the land," a 1988 Harris poll found that the number of leisure hours in a week available to Americans has dropped from 26.2 in 1973 to 16.6 in 1987. "The decline in leisure time is steady and unending," says the study. "It is perhaps even more revealing about a harried frame of mind that exists in most Americans as the 1990s approaches. . . . The levelling out of the work week has not added up to more leisure time, indicating real problems most Americans have in coping with the time shortage and the responsibilities that cannot be ignored." In 1990 a *Business Week* survey found that Americans were "shopping less and hating it more." Compared to five years ago, the survey found that 54 percent of Americans had less time for shopping compared to only 21 percent with more such time. In 1991, a survey by MAS Marketing, a Chicago-based market research firm, found that 80 percent of women shoppers viewed shopping as annoying but necessary. Says Janet Coats, a thirty-four-year-old free-lance writer and mother of two in Plainsboro, New Jersey: " 'Ten years ago, I could shop alone, and it was a leisurely thing. Now, I have two toddlers with me, and it's a nerve-shattering experience.' "[22]

The time shortage's effect on shopping is best evidenced in the booming "convenience industry." Non-store retailing, including catalogs, direct-response mail stuffers, and television shopping shows, is now a $56 billion a year industry, having doubled in size in ten years to include everything from food to housewares, toys to electronics. As *Business Week* put it,

> as the proportion of two-income families in the U.S. approaches the 50% mark, time is becoming increasingly scarce for millions of people. When both partners work, obviously, there is little time left for chores. . . . What used to be a time crunch has become a time famine."[23]

But the "time famine" stems not only from the growth of two-career families and the resulting shrinkage of leisure and shopping time. The other side of the equation is that as a result of technological progress and a rising standard of living, more and more leisure-time activities compete with shopping, including family, travel, sports, education, dining out, diverse broadcast and cable programming, and easily available pre-recorded videotapes. With more leisure activities to choose from, but less leisure time in which to undertake them, our time to shop wisely for consumer goods and services obviously shrinks.

THE WAY TO SHOP SMART

There are hundreds of books and magazines on the market today telling you how to be a "smart shopper." This book isn't one of them. This books tells why in today's market, despite the huge amount of money spent on consumer information, it's impossible to shop wisely. It also tells why we believe this situation can and will change, if we can only continue to build an information infrastructure that will revolutionize the economies of providing consumer information.

Unfortunately, there are a lot of people who still like to believe that all this complexity can be overcome with mere individual effort. In this world view, if consumers must settle for second best, it's their own fault, not the system's. In other words, we blame the victim. Unfortunately, most of the media, corporations, and public figures in this country still take this position, and it underlies all the advice floating around about how you can become a better consumer: you, the individual, supposedly have the answer in your hands, and if you don't make good choices it's nobody's fault but your own. Given our present information system, however, it's clear that unless we make some changes at a societal level, nobody's ever going to have the superhuman resources necessary to be a "smart shopper."

1. See, for example, Stuart Chase and F. J. Schlink, *Your Money's Worth: A Study in the Waste of the Consumer's Dollar* (New York: Macmillan, 1927), pp. 27–28.

2. Alvin Toffler, *Future Shock* (New York: Bantam Books, 1970), p. 9.

3. "Technology in the Year 2000," *Fortune*, July 18, 1988, p. 92.

4. Toffler, p. 12.

5. Toffler, p. 24.

6. Mary Norton et al., *A People and a Nation: A History of the United States* (Boston: Houghton Mifflin, 1986), p. 270. The figure is from the year 1800. At that time the United States had a population of about 5 million, only thirty-three towns had populations of over 2,500, and only three towns had more than 25,000.

7. Phone interview with Jack Larkin, author of *The Reshaping of Everyday Life—1790–1840* (New York: Harper and Row, 1988), as well as estimate made at the Pliny Freeman farmhouse at Old Sturbridge Village, Massachusetts, November 1988. Note that clothes were made from simple purchased cloth and that such items as baskets and bread were made from scratch from materials grown on the farm. For a related description of the possessions and life-style of even earlier New Englanders, see Kenneth A. Lockridge's description of a farmer's possessions in Dedham, Massachusetts, in *A New England Town: The First Hundred Years* (New York: W. W. Norton, 1970), pp. 69–70. Things weren't so different across the ocean; in fact, according to historians Neil McKendrick and John Brewer, in preindustrial Europe, "the purchase of a garment, or the cloth for a garment, remained a luxury the common people could only afford a few times in their lives." See McKendrick and Brewer's *Birth of a Consumer Society: The Commercialization of Eighteenth-Century England* (Bloomington, Ind.: Indiana University Press, 1982), p. 31. See also John S. Moore, *The Goods and Chattels of Our Forefathers: Frampton Cotterell and District Probate Inventories 1539–1804* (London: Phillimore, 1976), p. 34; John Demos, *A Little Commonwealth: Family Life in Plymouth Colony* (New York: Oxford University Press, 1970), p. 30; Carlo M. Cipolla, *Before the Industrial Revolution: European Society and Economy 1000–1700* (New York: W. W. Norton, 1976), pp. 29–31; and Fernand Braudel, *Civilization and Capitalism 15th–18th Century*, vol. 1: *The Structures of Everyday Life* (New York: Harper and Row, n.d.) pp. 104, 106, 283.

8. These numbers were provided by the research staff at Old Sturbridge Village, a replica of an early-nineteenth-century American town located in Sturbridge, Massachusetts.

9. Gerald Carson, *Country Stores in Early New England* (Sturbridge, Mass.: Old Sturbridge, Inc., 1955), p. 3. At that time, many Americans didn't even have access to a country store, but had to purchase consumer goods from the occasional wandering peddler. However, the 262 figure doesn't include the significant amount of food and other products likely to be traded between neighbors and relatives. The floor space of the Miner Grant country store was calculated from an architectural floor plan in the archives of the Old Sturbridge Village library.

10. Richard Halverson, "K mart Opens 2nd Hypermarket," *Discount Store News*, April 9, 1990, p. 1; *Discount Merchandiser*, September 1988, p. 92; and Anthony Ramirez, "Will American

Shoppers Think Bigger Is Really Better?" *New York Times*, April 1, 1990, p. 11. We determined the number of merchants by examining metropolitan yellow pages. To determine the square feet of retail selling space, we multiplied 15, the number of square feet of retail selling space for the average American (compiled by the National Research Bureau and published in *Shopping Center World*), by the number of Americans in a typical city (1,000,000). To determine the number of consumer products, we first considered the Burlington Mall, one of the largest New England shopping malls, which has 1,178,000 square feet of leasable space (excluding all common areas). Most stores in malls have unique merchandise; the products sold in each store are different from the products sold in other stores in the same mall. If we assume roughly the same product density as in a typical modern hypermarket of one product per three square feet (a conservative estimate), we calculate that a large modern mall has about 350,000 different products in it. This is, then, what many consumers confront in a typical shopping experience. If we hypothesize that a given mall only has about 20 percent of the consumer products available on the market—including those available from specialty mail-order companies—then there are well over one million comsumer products available on the market today. In fact, if you add up the total number of books, videocassettes, audio cassettes, and software programs, you'd probably have well over a million items in just these categories alone. In 1942 Neil Borden estimated that "more than a million brands have been advertised simultaneously in the U.S."—see Neil Borden, *Advertising in Our Economy* (Chicago: Richard D. Irwin, 1942), p. 29.

11. Paul Angiolillo, Jr., "So Many Choices," *Boston Globe*, August 9, 1989, pp. 69–70.

12. Toffler quoting Marshall McLuhan, p. 269. Original quotation can be found in Marshall McLuhan and George B. Leonard, "The Future of Education," *Look*, February 21, 1967, p. 23. See also Paul Ingrassia and Gregory Patterson, "Is Buying a Car a Choice or a Chore?" *Wall Street Journal*, October 24, 1989, sec. B, p. 1.

13. "Silo Heads for $1 Billion," *Discount Merchandiser*, August 1988, p. 50. See also *Fortune*, "Technology in the Year 2000," July 18, 1988, p. 92.

14. See "All-Channel TV Sets," *Consumer Reports*, January 1964, pp. 22–25.

15. James Meigs, "VCR Fans Choke on Another Serving of Alphabet Soup," *Video Review*, 1988, p. 30. For similar sentiments, see "The A–Z of TV," *Video Review*, June 1989, p. 36, and Earl Lifshey, "If You Ask Me," *Home Furnishings Daily*, July 17, 1989, p. 88.

16. Store growth figures are from "Growth in Stores and Volume Since 1960," *Discount Merchandiser*, June 1988, p. 28. In inflation-adjusted dollars, the growth would be from $2.0 billion to $20.1 billion in annual sales. GNP figures are from the *1988 Statistical Abstract of the United States* published by the U.S. Department of Commerce, p. 52. Discount stores did 9.4 percent more business than department stores in 1987. According to "A Decade of Change: 1978–1987," *Chain Store Age Executive*, November 1988, p. 64: "During the last 10 years department store retailing has suffered a 2% *reduction* in inflation adjusted sales per square foot of selling area. . . . Meanwhile, full-line discount store sales per square foot jumped an inflation adjusted 46.6%."

17. "Growth in Stores and Volume Since 1960," *Discount Merchandiser*, June 1988, p. 28. A discount store is defined as "a departmentalized retail establishment utilizing many self-service techniques to sell hard goods, health and beauty aids, apparel and other soft goods, and other general merchandise. It operates at uniquely low margins. It has a minimum annual volume of $1 million, and is at least 10,000 square feet in size."

18. See Cathryn Jakobson, "They Get It for You Wholesale," *New York Times Magazine*, December 4, 1988, p. 57, and Arthur Markowitz, "Membership Clubs Consolidate and Expand," *Discount Store News*, March 18, 1991, p. 49.

19. See Bill Donaldson, "Losing Sales on Price Is a Reseller's Dilemma," *Computer & Software News,* November 14, 1988, pp. 125–126. A more analytical treatment of this idea can be found in Douglas Greer's *Industrial Organization and Public Policy,* 2nd ed. (New York: Macmillan, 1984), p. 85. Because information is a very easy product to steal, private enterprise provides less of it than would be optimal for society.

20. Robert Parket, *Retailing for the 1980's: A Strategic and Financial Analysis* (New York: Dun & Bradstreet, 1983), p. 27. See also "Holiday Shoppers' Season of Discontent: Depleted Stock and Scarce Help Make Spirits Sag," *Wall Street Journal,* December 22, 1988, sec. B, p. 1; "Responding to the Changing Retail Store," *Marketing Communications,* February 1988, p. 48; Froma Joselow, "Why Business Turns to Teen-Agers," *New York Times,* March 26, 1989, sec. 3, pp. 1, 6; and Richard Stevenson, "Watch Out Macy's, Here Comes Nordstrom," *New York Times Magazine,* August 27, 1989, p. 40.

21. Lifshey, p. 88.

22. Louis Harris and Associates Staff, *Americans and the Arts* (New York: American Council for the Arts, January 1988), pp. 3, 20–22, and "Shoppers Are a Dwindling Species," *Business Week,* November 26, 1990, pp. 140, 144. The *Business Week* study also found that 63 percent of Americans said they got little or no pleasure from shopping.

23. "Presto! The Convenience Industry: Making Life a Little Simpler," *Business Week,* April 27, 1987, p. 86. See also "A Decade of Change," p. 56; Alix Freedman, "Most Consumers Shun Luxuries, Seek Few Frills but Better Service," *Wall Street Journal,* September 19, 1989, sec. B, p. 1; and Francine Schwadel, "Shoppers' Blues: The Thrill Is Gone," *Wall Street Journal,* October 13, 1989, sec. B, p. 1.

CHAPTER 2

The 365-Day Sale
to End All Sales

Although this book is about consumer choice as a whole, about how people go about making many of the most important decisions that affect their lives, and about how consumer ignorance affects these choices, the following four chapters focus specifically on consumer electronics, appliances, and computers. One reason we focus on these items is that the products themselves, complex and high-tech, represent the beginnings of an ever more pervasive form of merchandise in our society. Another reason is that high-tech retailing is at the vanguard of future selling tactics. Finally, unlike some more subtle effects of ignorance, the impact of these selling tactics is something most people can immediately relate to their daily lives.

These chapters specifically concentrate on the way the retailers of these items, rather than the manufacturers, have reacted to consumer confusion. Much of the material may therefore be surprising, since most people, including many top economists, think that modern retailers have relatively little flexibility in this area. After all, two retailers selling the same item (e.g., a package of Oreo cookies or a Sony 13-inch TV) must primarily compete on price and service, seemingly simple things for consumers to evaluate. In contrast, manufacturers can differentiate their merchandise with all sorts of mysterious ingredients, striking packages, and exotic features. Nevertheless, as we shall see, today's retailers have tremendous power not only to exploit but to increase consumer confusion. Indeed, as the retailing industry has become more concentrated over the last few decades, its powers to generate and then abuse consumer ignorance have grown proportionately.

What is important to understand from these details, however, is that our discussion is not only about "not getting the best toaster" but about how people go about getting the information necessary to make the decisions that direct their lives, decisions that go beyond electronics, appliances, and computers and include choices as large as choosing a doctor, a college, a spouse, a life insurance policy, an employer, and a home.

If there were only one TV left in the world, quip consumer-electronics folk, it would still be sold at a discount. Like most jokes, this one is funny because it touches on the truth. And it touches closer now than ever before.

To survive and attract consumers today, most stores must run sales virtually every day. They must also keep a good proportion of the merchandise "on sale" most of the time. And to keep up that special meaning of "sale," they must claim that these sales are unique, one-time events.

"To get [their customer] in the store at all—even during the one season of the year when shoppers *must* buy—merchants have to offer sales and bargains. These clearances train the customer never to pay full price," noted Susan Caminiti in *Fortune* magazine.[1] One trade publication aptly described the current situation facing retailers:

> Sometime during the last 10 years a new calendar was printed *just* for retailers. It was a calendar that had "sale" written on every month, every week, every day. Textiles had white sales every month. Price breaks for bathing suits Memorial Day instead of Fourth of July. Double, no triple, coupons to rope the customers in. The reasons for the plethora of price promotions may have seemed justifiable when they began, but the net result is that today customers are conditioned to buying on sale. Indeed, studies have shown that anything less than 25% off is not considered a sale.[2]

Studies have also shown, said a retail analyst for Goldman Sachs, that 100 percent of merchandise now sells for below list price.[3] Thus, list price has become nothing other than a marketing tool, a farcical figure used to set off the "sale" or discount price. In fact, these list prices have become so ridiculously inflated that some manufacturers don't want them readily available for comparison with more realistic prices in consumer publications. Not surprisingly, then, public-relations departments of many major manufacturers, especially certain computer manufacturers, refused to give their list prices once they thought we might publish them.

There was a time when running constant sales and distorting regular prices in this way would have resulted in a loss of credibility and profits. A hundred years ago, for example, it would have been hard to imagine the little corner shoe store you walked by daily running constant "once-in-a-lifetime" sales on most of the merchandise in the store. You'd have become numb to all the claims very quickly and realized that what the merchant called "a great deal" was really just the price the shoes sold for every day of the year. You'd have started quickly ignoring just about everything the merchant claimed and would have taken your business to a more reputable shoe store. But that no longer seems to be the case. In fact, for the major superstores and discounters selling consumer electronics and major appliances, the reverse is now true: merchants who don't run once-a-year sales three or four times a week don't seem to be able to survive. In fact, it's only those chains that can afford to run sale ads day in and day out that seem to be thriving. They realize that people like to buy on sale, and so they provide sale opportunities as often as they can.

If you think about how often you actually buy a television or washing machine, you'll quickly understand how this situation arose. Retailers rightly assume that most people don't spend their lifetime studying advertising and prices. They figure that most people will spend at most one or two days every year shopping for a specific large purchase and that these people will prefer a store that at least claims to have rock-bottom prices. You may notice the price of eggs in the supermarket every week and know if Friendly Market's "sale" price is really genuine, but you'll have no idea that Sony KV1963 has been selling at Major Discounter for the so-called sale price every three weeks for the past year.[4] So, when you do happen to look closely at the ads, and they tell you that this is the "Sale to End All Sales," you take the bait and run quickly to the store to take advantage of this great opportunity. Everyone feels good—except that you may very well have spent less money and made a better purchase if you had known what was really going on.

What is really going on? For several years we scrupulously collected and analyzed the ads running in various local newspapers. For example, one year Fretter, a national superstore that has fifty-seven stores, advertised in Boston an "Operation Cleanout" sale on August 23, a "Now or Never Sale" on August 30, a "Clean-Out Sale" on September 11, "The Most Electrifying Sales Event in History" on October 1, and a "Drastic Price Reductions Like Never Before!" sale on October 21—and many smaller sales in between. Those who missed the "now or never" sale in late August may have been comforted to know that in just over a month they could experience "the most electifying sales event in history." On the other hand, those who rushed out to buy in late August may have been mortified.

WHEN'S A SALE NOT A SALE?

What's wrong with having so many sales? Isn't it actually good for consumers, giving them more opportunities to buy at better prices? Well, yes; if sales really represented genuine reductions in price and presented truly unique opportunities, the more sales the better. Unfortunately, the kind of sales we're talking about do neither. In fact, they seriously mislead consumers into buying the wrong model at the wrong price from the wrong store at the wrong time.

First of all, the ads often lead consumers to believe that they have to buy the advertised item then and there if they want to save money. In most cases, this idea simply isn't true. The fact is that items that do go on sale, do so frequently. In fact, at Zayre we found that all you have to do is pick up the price tag on a TV set, and you'll find the future sale price underneath it; every few weeks the management tells salespeople that certain items are "on sale," and they move the regular price tag to the back. Chances are if you see a TV selling at regular price, you can wait a few weeks until someone turns over the sale tag. Conversely, it's hardly crucial to buy a TV while it's "on sale," since you can be fairly certain it will be on sale again in a month or so.

One Highland Superstore ad running on October 25, 1988, warned shoppers that "You've only got one day to save big," and urged, "And hurry, after Wednesday at 9 pm it's all over, Baby." And yet, some of the prices advertised were hardly worth rushing out of the house for. A 40-inch stereo remote Mitsubishi TV shown at the top of the ad, for example, was selling for the supposedly not-to-be-missed price of $2,199. And yet, Highland ads in the same newspaper on October 14, September 18, September 15, September 9, August 26, and August 4, 1988, all advertised the very same model for the very same price of $2,199!

Often retailers will repeatedly extend the dates of the so-called limited sale, thereby violating consumer-protection laws. For example, in 1988 the New York City Department of Consumer Affairs alleged that Sears had engaged in deceptive and/or misleading practices including repeatedly advertising the same sale offer by using such phrases as "Hurry! Call by . . . ," thus suggesting that the sale was about to end, when in fact the deadline was constantly changed. (Without admitting wrongdoing, Sears agreed to pay New York City $10,000 in costs of the action and promised to comply with the city's consumer-protection laws in the future.)

Furthermore, in late 1987 the same New York City department requested an injunction against Autoland, a car dealer, alleging "that the company's ads indicating that the offer is available for a limited time only are deceptive in that the offer had been repeated or extended immediately after its announced expiration date. For example, an ad that appeared in a daily newspaper on November 20 stated 'Now through Monday only!' The same ad appeared again on November 27, stating 'Now through Monday only!'" No wonder, then, that chief counsel of Missouri's attorney general's office, Henry Herschel, in an unrelated case, cited a salesperson who defined "sale" as "nothing more than offering goods in the stream of commerce."

Even if a sale means real discounts lasting only two days, sales' short, cyclical nature means that if you miss one week's sale, you can catch one the next week. When we looked at a year of Fretter ad headlines, for example, we picked up the two-week sales cycle: the first Friday, Saturday, and Sunday are sale days. Then Monday and Tuesday were regular-price days. Wednesday is a sale day. Thursday is a regular-price day. The second Friday is a one-day sale, often a "midnight madness" sale. Saturday is a regular-price day. Sunday, Monday, and Tuesday are sale days. Wednesday is a regular-price day. Thursday is either a regular-price or a sale day, and then the cycle begins anew.

Sears also rotates its sale items, but on a monthly basis. A retired Sears salesman, who sold appliances there for over twenty-five years, told us that a given piece is on sale about once every other month. "We always had a representative group of merchandise on sale," he told us. "For each product category in major appliances, there would always be at least three items on sale per week. For example, there would be three dryers on sale. A low-end dryer. A mid-level dryer. And a high-end dryer."

One way Sears rotated its sale items didn't please New York's attorney general, who sued Sears in late 1989 over a phony price-advertising scheme. Sears was accused of offering four comparable Kenmore vacuum cleaners at a "regular price" of either $299.99 or $319.99 and a sale price of either $189.99 or $199.99. According to a press release issued by the attorney general's office, "Sears continuously rotated these products on sale, so that it would appear that the vacuum not on sale at any given time was honestly being offered at a 'regular' price which Sears later discounted. In reality, Sears made very few sales at the regular price because consumers would naturally buy the product that had been marked down $100 or more compared to a nearly identical vacuum." The result was that while Sears sold only 6 vacuums of one model at the regular price, it sold 1,512 at the sale price, and while it sold only 56 of another vacuum at the regular price, it sold 4,301 at the sale price.

Lechmere, the largest consumer-electronics and major-appliance chain in the New England area, has a slightly different approach. Every week it issues a large circular of items on sale. But in addition, every month it runs a "two-day event," at which time everything in the store is on sale. One salesperson there explained that Lechmere had been forced into this approach by the advent of constant sales by superstores. Before August of 1988 Lechmere had sales only four times a year. Now they have two-day sales once a month, and every Sunday the local newspapers carry a circular advertising a "Lechmere Sale."

In many cases, the so-called sale price is no great bargain. Some items in these "sale" ads aren't even on sale. For example, one Service Merchandise flyer has the word "sale" plastered all over the front of the cover, including the letters "S-A-L-E" in huge print in the upper-right-hand corner of the first page plastered in a vibrant red, white, and blue circle of stars. The top third of the ad is filled with a giant picture of a 19-inch color TV. Two stars, similar in shape to the ones around the word sale, are placed on the TV image. However, the TV is not on sale. It's just selling at its regular catalog price. Nor, for that matter, is the VCR below it on sale. In fact, the only items on sale in the catalog are marked with a plain little marker that says "sale" below the price. But at the same time, on every page of the catalog is a big colorful slogan that says "Anniversary Sale."

We've found similar tactics in the ads for computer hardware by Computer Factory. For several months in early 1989, this major chain alternated sales, running an "Apple Sale" one week, a "Commodore Sale" the next, and so on. During the "Apple Sale," the ad listed the Macintosh Plus computer as selling for a certain "sale" price. And yet the next week, during the "Commodore Sale," this same Macintosh was listed at the bottom of the page, this time not "on sale," but for the very same price. Whether or not the headline said sale, the price remained the same.[5]

Perhaps even more deceptive is the almost-universal retailing practice of marking items up before marking them down. Amazingly, some classroom texts describe this practice as standard and acceptable. In *Retailing: New Perspectives,* Dorothy S. Rogers and Mercia M. T. Grass observe that

> most stores use a system called promotional markup (PMU) to establish a comparative price for advertising purposes. After the item has been on the selling floor for perhaps ten days and had a 10 to 20 percent sell-off, it is permanently ticketed at a low, or sale, price.[6]

This test defines PMU as a "higher price used during a short, initial sell-off period and then later in comparative advertising."[7] A "management aid" distributed at a seminar on retailing by the National Association of Retail Dealers of America (NARDA) offers a similar philosophy: "Our so-called 'sale' or outright best price . . . is the price that we would really like to obtain on most products."

Evidence is overwhelming that retailers put this textbook advice into practice. "[Some department store sales are] unrealistically based on initially marking up private label goods and then giving it, say, a month or so before they drastically mark it down. They still get a pretty good markup with that markdown," notes Isadore Barmash in the trade publication *Stores.*[8] "In recent years merchants have been so caught up in the craze [to have sales] that they marked up goods just so they could put them on 'sale' and still keep their average profit margins," agreed an article in the *Wall Street Journal.*[9]

"Two months ago Highland marked up everything by 5 percent," one Boston retailer, now selling at Highland, explained. "Two weeks later they had a 5 percent to 40 percent markdown sale. I believe they only had one or two items in the store at the 40 percent off price, and they were dogs." He added that before the spring of 1988 Highland used to put merchandise on sale for just 98 cents off, "reducing," for example a $999 camcorder to $998.[10]

Two other Highland salespeople we interviewed confirmed these scenarios: "At our 'Midnight Madness Sales' the only thing that goes down more than 5 percent are floor models and dreck—stuff we can't get rid of—and the advertised stuff," said one.

The retired Sears salesman added that Sears's advertised "lowest price ever" on an expensive major appliance is often just five or ten dollars off its previous lowest price. "Sears—and everybody else, too—raises prices and then takes $30 to $50 off, figuring that's the price we really want and expect to sell the merchandise at."

The pervasive rebate represents just a more subtle version of this practice. In 1989 the *Wall Street Journal* recently reported that rebates from the Big Three automakers now average more than $1,000 per vehicle. Although manufacturers boast about all the money they're "saving" consumers, to finance these savings they have to aggressively raise prices. Time and again, the company offering an impressive rebate is chalking up record earnings, and consumers who think that they're saving money on their purchase are actually just getting back part of the extra money they spent on the jacked-up sales ticket.[11]

Often sale advertisements don't tell you what the original price has been, so you have no way to tell whether you're getting a good deal or not. Ads will simply proclaim "sale," and you'll just have to assume that the price listed is a lot better than the usual price. The New York City Department of Consumer Affairs has charged Sears for advertising a range of discounts, such as "Save 15% to 30% and more!" without disclosing the basis from which the advertised reduction was taken (original price? list price?) in violation of Consumer Protection Law regulation 13.9. They also cited Sears for advertising the lowest price in a range of prices, such as ". . . as low as $34.99" without also disclosing the highest price in the range, in violation of Consumer Protection Law regulation 207. (As noted above, Sears settled these charges, without admitting wrongdoing, by paying $10,000 to the city and promising to comply with city consumer laws in the future.)

Such nondisclosure is not just potentially misleading: it is unquestionably abused. In fact, we've quite frequently found that the so-called sale price was actually higher than the average price we had seen the item selling for over the past several months. For example, on August 24, 1988, we saw the Sears-Kenmore microwave oven number 88329 "on sale" at the Sears store in Auburn, Massachusetts, for $180. The price tag claimed that this price was $100 off the regular selling price of $290. And yet when we looked up this microwave oven in our database, we found that the average selling price over the past nine months had been $178—two dollars *less than* the so-called sale price. Many times the sale tag had claimed that the "regular" price was $290 or even $300 rather than $280. Furthermore, of the thirty-six times we had seen that model in catalogs, ads, or store shelves from late 1987 until the end of September 1988, we had seen it selling for $280 (and never for more) only three times (in stores on April 5, August 9, and August 31) but selling for $170 six times and for $180 twenty-five times. We even saw it selling as low as $160 once!

The attorney general's office in Missouri found a similar practice going on at Best Buy superstores. In its lawsuit against the chain, the attorney general's office charges that Best Buy "has offered consumer goods in weekly advertising as sale merchandise, when, in fact, the prices shown are the prior, regularly offered price." The suit also charges that the chain divides its merchandise into three distinct pricing categories: Every Day Low (EDL), Lowest Price Guaranteed (LPG), and Best Buy (BB). Contrary to a shopper's probable expectation, the investigators found that goods "designated at EDL have had little or no profit margin or sales commission added to their price. Profit margins and sales commissions increase in the pricing of LPG and BB goods."[12] Thus, you probably get a better deal on the non-sale items, if these charges prove true. (Best Buy is countersuing and claiming that they will "further lower the regular price of over a thousand items, regardless of the damage it may inflict on our profits"!)

The concept of a sale price is even made farcical, because on any day of the week you often can negotiate down to the sale price without any official sale going on. Salespeople at several superstores told us that they're given two or three prices for each item; the higher price they get the consumer to pay, the better commission they get. Sometimes these prices actually are encoded into the price tag. Look, for example, at this Highland tag for a videocassette recorder:

Row 1: 316.00
Row 2: SHP VC7995   4 S   104
Row 3: #S01000#A0059996 #B053800
Row 4: L 90 DY—P 1 YR—O NONE
Row 5: SL#35088 E 53188 P062488

When you, the consumer, look at this tag, you probably just see the price, $316, and a bunch of nonsense numbers. But when Highland salespeople look at this tag, they see something very different. In Row 1 they see what they call the "X" line price of $316. That's the price they'd prefer you spend on the TV because it will yield them the best commission. In Row 2, they recognize an abbreviated version of the

VCR's brand (SHP = Sharp) and then the model number (VC7995). This row also tells them a little bit about some basic features: here the "4" stands for a four-head VCR, the "S" stands for standard tuner and features (i.e., there's nothing particularly special about this VCR to push). The "104" is the inventory code for VCRs. Row 4 tells the salespeople some warranty information. The "L 90 DY" stands for ninety-day labor warranty. The "P 1 YR" stands for parts warranty of one year. The "O" stand for other, the "NONE" tells them there is no other warranty category. (Some products have a special warranty in addition to parts and labor warranties. In the case of a refrigerator, the special warranty might be on the compressor.) Row 5 merely represents some inventory codes for this specific model.

"It's Row 3, though, which reveals how negotiable prices really are. Scanning down to this row, the salesperson find out the details of how much they can make selling this VCR to you. Each piece of information is separated by a "#" sign, and the zeros before numbers are garbage, meant to complicate the code. Thus, the first "S" stands for "spiff," the extra bonus the salesperson will get for selling you the VCR at the X-line price. In this case the "1000" following the zeros stands for $10 (just move the last decimal point over to the left two places to get "10" from "1000"): if the salesperson sells the VCR for $316, he or she will get not only the standard 2 percent commission on the selling price but also the $10 spiff.

In the same row, the salespeople can now look at the next section beginning after the next "#". The "A" stands for "the A commission at the A selling price." Again, skip the following zeros. Now look at the number "59996." That stands for $599.96 (again the salespeople just move the last decimal point over to the left by two). If they divide that number in half to get $299.98 they know the "A" selling price. If they sell the VCR at this price instead of the $316 X-line price, the salesperson still gets the $10 spiff but loses the 2 percent commission. The last section in Row 3 is called the "B" section. Here the logic is the same. Divide $538.00 by two to get $269.00, the B selling price. If the salesperson sells it at this price, he or she gets half the spiff. In this case, it would be just $5.

It's easy to see from these codes that a sale of 5 percent usually isn't going to get you any better deal than you could have already had by paying the A or B line price. In fact, what stores advertise as the "sale price" is usually nothing other than the A or B line price that they fully intended to sell the item for in the first place. True enough, more than 75 percent of customers pay at the X line price when there's no sale, simply because they don't realize that they can bargain. But any day of the year, sale or no sale, a salesperson can sell at the A line price at his or her own discretion, and the only real limit is the B-line price, which a salesperson can't go below. All you have to do to "bargain" is just threaten not to buy until the item comes on sale again, and the salesperson is instructed to drop the sale price (the real price anyway) to get the sale.

The fact that only a small percentage of a store's items ever go on sale also indicates that these sales have virtually no meaning. There are so many sales and so few items to "reduce" that the sale price of these items basically becomes their regular price. And everything else in the store keeps selling for its regular high price despite the constant sales.[13]

We found the GE 8–2503 TV featured in Fretter "sale" ads for an entire year, for example. The same model numbers—such as the Sony CCDV3 camcorder—keep appearing in the mail-order ads week after week at "bargain" prices. Nor are such exclusive sales restricted to these upstarts. Even at venerable Sears, out spotters found the same model, washing machine model 28721, on sale for five months in a row.

Generally only a few preselected "promotional pieces" ever really get discounted significantly. In fact, certain brands don't allow their merchandise to go on sale. "Mitsubishi and JVC will never go on sale for more than 5 percent," a Highland salesperson told us. "Every day, customers ask me, 'Is this on sale?" The customer thinks everything will go on sale. But lots of merchandise never goes on sale more than 5 percent."

Is it fair to condemn these constant sales as unethical and morally repugnant? Readers can draw their own ethical conclusions, but our concern here is the more objective one of showing the economic and social consequences of ignorance. If constant sales genuinely provided important comparative pricing information to consumers, in fact, we'd praise them as a useful allocation of resources. Our gripe, however, is simply that we think that these sales serve no useful economic function and, in fact, squander valuable resources. That retailers themselves are beginning to recognize this cost is apparent in the words of Sears chairman Edward Brennan: "Over the years we began to sell a substantial percentage of our merchandise on sale—much of it on a low gross margin. These off-price promotions result in duplicative merchandise inventory which takes up valuable warehouse and floor selling space."[14] In fact, Michael Bozic, chairman of Sears's merchandising group, announced to retail analysts that the chain expected to lower costs by

$200 million as a result of eliminating inefficiencies born of constant sales, which required the constant reticketing of items and the stocking of duplicate merchandise. Without constant sales, Sears would be using salespeople more efficiently by motivating and scheduling them to sell all day every day, rather than just during sales events.[15]

By providing false information, running sales constantly also encourages the success of inefficient manufacturers and retailers. We suspect, too, that this is one reason that pseudo-sales are generally considered unethical: their inefficiency reduces the standard of living of the American people, and this very real harm leads people to think that such actions should be viewed as unethical.

THE "EVERY-DAY LOW PRICE" VERSUS THE CONSTANT SALE

In the late 1980s a number of major retail stores began promoting "every-day low prices" in lieu of frequent sales. The most prominent of these was Sears, Roebuck and Company, the largest retailer in the world. In early 1989 Sears announced its new pricing policy. The idea was to become the kind of store known for its low prices, a discounter of sorts, rather than the kind of store with relatively high prices but good sales. A full three-quarters of Sears prices reputedly were lowered 35 to 50 percent, and Sears even guaranteed customers that it would "meet or beat the competition's current advertised price on the identical item."[16] The change to the new policy generated significant national media attention and the release of normally secret pricing information.

One reason for this switch may have been to prevent some of the costly legal problems brought on by constant sales. As Edward Weller, a senior retail analyst at Montgomery Securities, put it: "The percentage of business [Sears does] at regular prices has declined almost every year since the mid-1970s. . . . Now, I would guess that they sell less than a third of their merchandise at regular prices. That means the sale prices are becoming the regular prices, and that creates legal problems."[17] Sears retailing practices are by no means unusual, as we have seen, but they have become a highly visible and convenient target for some of this country's most aggressive state attorneys general. The fact that Sears has been singled out, however, means that continuing a sales-based approach to selling would have put Sears at an unfair disadvantage.[18] One Sears representative even complained that the New York State attorney general's office's "strict" policy on preventing constant sales would have required Sears to print special promotional materials just for that state, at great extra expense to itself.

Despite the special problems of Sears as a large and conspicuous national retailer, retail analysts argue that the pendulum among other retailers also is swinging back from constant sales to "every-day low pricing," especially as consumers become immune to the pervasive word "sale." As Francine Schwadel wrote in the *Wall Street Journal*, "Month-long specials and constant price promotions, even during Christmas and other peak shopping seasons, sapped the meaning from the word 'sale.'"[19]

Schwadel, who considers this shift in tactics a *fait accompli,* quotes Morris Saffer, chairman of both Saffer Advertising, Inc., and the Retail Advertising Conference, a trade group, as saying that "'Customers no longer thought of regular prices as being real prices, because they weren't.'" Schwadel also adds that two years ago, 55 percent of the one thousand people surveyed by New York retailing consultant Walter K. Levy said they believed that the "sale" price of merchandise was the "real" price and that the "regular" price was artificially inflated. "Although he hasn't repeated the survey," writes Schwadel, "Mr. Levy says the proportion of people who believe they shouldn't pay 'regular' prices probably has risen."

Nonetheless, it would be premature to say that we're seeing the end of constant sales. Consider, for example, that Sears's "new prices" have been at or above its old "sale prices." What's really happening is not that Sears (or anyone else) is suddenly selling everything at a lower price than before—that just wouldn't make sense if they expected to keep up their profit levels—but rather that they're selling merchandise for the same prices they did before: it's just that what was once called the "sale" price—and once made up most of the store's revenue—is now the "every-day low price." In fact, in 1988 only 45 percent of Sears's revenue came from merchandise sold at "regular" prices.[20] What seems to have happened is that Sears simply switched from unofficially selling everything at a certain price (once known as the sale price) to officially selling everything at the same or even slightly higher price (now known as the new every-day low price). Not surprisingly, then, in December 1989, the New York State attorney general accused Sears of "creating the false impression that its 'everyday low prices' represent substantial discounts from its former prices," when it "actually has offered consumers no significant savings."[21]

What is remarkable is that this shift to every-day low prices should be considered so novel. Fifteen years ago there were far fewer sales than today, and though no one made a promotional brouhaha about it, stores generally had a fixed price on merchandise, which you were supposed to assume was reasonably "low." We can expect that once consumers get used to "every-day low prices" again, more sales will begin to creep back, and the pendulum will once again swing to today's position. Already, in fact, Sears is increasing the amount of merchandise on sale, or as they prefer calling it, offered as "special purchases." Thus, consumers now have to reconcile that what Sears likes to call its "sale that never ends" can still be bettered by an even lower price. "Who's fooling who?" asks Tony Lisanti, a writer for *Discount Store News*. "Does the average consumer believe that today's price is the lowest price? And what happens when a particular item is offered at a lower price under the guise of a 'special purchase'?"[22] What happens, as the next chapter will show, is that to have any meaning, an "every-day low price" must become some type of "guaranteed *lowest* price."

1. Susan Caminiti, "What Ails Retailing," *Fortune*, January 30, 1989, p. 61.

2. "A Decade of Change: 1978–1987," *Chain Store Age Executive*, p. 57. See also Teri Agins, "As Retailers' Sales Crop Up Everywhere, Regulators Wonder If the Price Is Right," *Wall Street Journal*, February 13, 1990, sec. B, p. 1, and Andrew Gaffney, "Everyday Pricing Challenges Sales," *TWICE*, October 23–27, 1989, p. 8.

3. Actually, this analyst may be overstating the case: we have found many *discount* chains selling consumer electronics *above* manufacturers' list price. On the other hand, the analyst may be right in the sense that even though those products are at least temporarily displayed in the store above list price, we're not sure that they actually sell at those prices.

4. See Thomas Nagle, *The Strategy and Tactics of Pricing* (Englewood Cliffs, N.J.: Prentice-Hall, 1986), p. 184.

5. See also Computerland ads running in *The Sunday New York Times* business section from 1987 through 1989.

6. Dorothy S. Rogers and Mercia M. T. Grass, *Retailing: New Perspectives* (Chicago: Dryden Press, 1988), pp. 374–375.

7. Ibid., 374.

8. Isadore Barmash, "Private Label: Flux," *Stores*, April 1987, p. 2.

9. Francine Schwadel, "The 'Sale' Is a Fading Retailing Tactic," *Wall Street Journal*, sec. B, p. 1. See also "Discounter Curbs: A Strong Protest," *New York Times*, May 24, 1988, sec. D, p. 2, and Schwadel's "Store's Concept of 'Sale' Pricing Gets Court Test," *Wall Street Journal*, May 15, 1990, sec. B, pp. 1, 7.

10. Many similar instances in other retail industries are noted in Paul Blumberg, *The Predatory Society: Deception in the American Marketplace* (New York: Oxford University Press, 1989).

11. Joseph B. White, "A Rebate Debate: How Much Further Can Detroit Go?" *Wall Street Journal,* February 17, 1989, sec. B, p. 1. In recent years automakers in particular have regularly raised list prices on their cars, only to increase their so-called rebate. See Lisa H. Towle, "As Profits Slide, a Struggle to Survive," *New York Times,* October 22, 1989, p. 15; Bradley Stertz, "Rebates Are Now Beating Some Cars to Showrooms," *Wall Street Journal,* September 25, 1989, sec. B, p. 1; and Joseph White, "GM Follows Ford by Boosting Car Prices, Creating Big Opportunity for Japanese," *Wall Street Journal,* August 15, 1990, sec. B, p. 1.

12. "State of Missouri, ex rel., William L. Webster, Attorney General of the State of Missouri, Plaintiff v. Best Buy Co. Inc., a Minnesota Corporation . . . Petition for Permanent Injunction, Civil Penalties, Restitution and Ancillary Relief," pp. 4, 6. Best Buy paid $200,000 to settle the case.

13. There are a number of reasons why many items don't go on sale: (1) Many items, such as no-name brands or inexpensive, infrequently purchased goods, do not draw customers into the store and therefore don't work well as sale items, (2) putting an item on sale alienates buyers who purchased it at the regular price, thus hurting the store's image, and (3) stores with price-protection policies may be forced to refund money if they don't segregate the sale items from the non-sale items.

14. Tony Lisanti, "Sears Awakens with Vengeance," *Discount Store News,* March 20, 1989, p. 14.

15. "Will the Big Markdown Get the Big Store Moving Again?" *Business Week,* March 13, 1989, p. 110.

16. David Mehegan, "To Do or Die: Sears Retags Its Future," *Boston Globe,* February 28, 1989, pp. 25, 34.

17. Michael deCourcy Hinds, "New York and Sears Battle over Ads," *New York Times,* September 10, 1988, p. 52.

18. See Kate Fitzgerald, "Sears Battles New York Regs on 'Sale' Ads," *Advertising Age,* July 4, 1988, p. 35, and Michael deCourcy Hinds, "New York and Sears Battle Over Ads," *New York Times,* September 10, 1988, p. 2; and "Everyday Low Pricing Tack on the Wane?" *Home Furnishings Daily,* January 8, 1990, p. 100.

19. Schwadel, "The 'Sale' Is a Fading Retailing Tactic," sec. B, p. 1.

20. Francine Schwadel, "A Look Behind Sears's New Approach," *Wall Street Journal,* March 1, 1989, sec. B, pp. 1, 6.

21. Francine Schwadel, "Sears Calls It 'Low Prices,' New York Calls it Misleading," *Wall Street Journal,* December 22, 1989, sec. B, p. 1.

22. Tony Lisanti, "Sale or No Sale: Fashion, Not Price, Is the Issue," *Discount Store News Home Market Trends Supplement,* November 13, 1989, p. 3; " Everyday Low Pricing Tack on the Wane?" *Home Furnishings Daily,* January 8, 1990, p. 100; Joseph Pereira, "Discount Department Stores Struggle Against Rivals That Strike Aisle by Aisle," *Wall Street Journal,* June 19, 1990, sec. B, p. 7; and Francine Schwadel, "Who Wins With Price-Matching Plans? Not Shoppers, For Few Bother Ever to Collect," *Wall Street Journal,* March 16, 1989, sec. B, p. 1.

CHAPTER 3

How Everyone Can Have the Lowest Price

"NOBODY, BUT NOBODY, SELLS FOR LESS!"

"LOWE$T PRICE$—WE WILL NOT BE UNDERSOLD"

"ABSOLUTELY NOBODY SELLS FOR LESS!"

"NOBODY SELLS FOR LESS!"

"GUARANTEED—LOWEST PRICES IN TOWN"

"WE BEAT THEM ALL"

How can everybody have the lowest prices? When retailers make mutually exclusive claims like these, even the most trusting soul has to wonder. Clearly, the stores are bluffing, and yet every day they plaster such promises all over the newspapers. And despite our "truth in advertising" laws, nobody seems to mind.

How in our modern world of consumer-protection laws can they get away with such claims? Is there some subtle scam going on? Or are we consumers today just so skeptical that we shrug off these truly ridiculous promises filling pages of respectable publications?[1]

The reason a retailer would want to guarantee a lowest price is simple, of course: customers are more inclined to make a purchase if they feel they're getting a good deal. It's the same principle that leads retailers to have constant sales. In fact, a lowest-price guarantee is the principle of constant sales carried to its logical and ultimate extreme: it's not enough to claim to best your own price, you can claim to best *everyone's* price, and not only claim it, but *guarantee* it. Making a profit with such a policy is no problem either: guaranteeing a set price simply represents a common retail strategy of setting prices not to reflect cost but to reflect what consumers are willing to pay. Even if the promised prices really turn out to be the best around—which they rarely do—a guaranteed lowest price doesn't necessarily mean a price as low as it could be if consumers knew more about real value.[2]

WHY STORES MUST GUARANTEE LOWEST PRICES

Shoppers feel good knowing that they don't have to run around town looking for the best price. The price guarantees play on this emotion; by handing you one of their gilt-edged guarantees, a retailer suggests that you need look no further (See Figure 3–1). Retailers make these claims in advertisements as well, primarily to get you into the store. Since most people only go to two or three stores before they buy, retailers know that a large part of the sale is just getting you in the door. And if you really believe all the items are selling for the lowest price in town, you'll be willing to "Buy now and shop later."

Of course, if comparison shopping weren't so often painful and fruitless and if consumers weren't so confused, overwhelmed by choices, and busy, price guarantees wouldn't be necessary. People would know beforehand a good product and a good price and wouldn't be swayed by meaningless promises. But in today's market, these guarantees are essential. In fact, as one salesperson pointed out to us, they actually do positive good by relieving people's stress.

Even established retailers who never had such guarantees before have been forced to add them in response to an influx of major superstores with their garish headlines. In the Boston area, for example, the major local electronics chain, Lechmere, took to guaranteeing the lowest price just about the time that Highland entered the local market. "People are much more price conscious today than they used to be," says a former Lechmere salesman. "They expect you to have the lowest price." In fact, today in Boston, this reputable discounter is promising "Guaranteed Price Protection"; a well-established appliance store promises "LOWE$T PRICE$"; a mid-sized electronics dealer promises "Nobody Sells For Less!"; a local superstore moving into the area promises "Lowest Prices Ever . . ." and "Ain't No Better Price"; and major superstores, who

FIGURE 3–1A. LOWEST PRICE GUARANTEES FROM 3 MAJOR CONSUMER
ELECTRONICS SUPERSTORES

FIGURE 3–1B. LOWEST PRICE GUARANTEES FROM 3 MAJOR CONSUMER
ELECTRONIC SUPERSTORES

FIGURE 3–1C. LOWEST PRICE GUARANTEES FROM 3 MAJOR CONSUMER ELECTRONIC SUPERSTORES

have just recently entered the market, promise "Our prices are untouchable" and "Nobody but Nobody Beats Our Best Price."[3] Even an upscale audio store that pushed service over price for years has switched from image advertising to price advertising. "Look at their ads," a superstore salesperson pointed out. "It's no longer 'We are for the Yuppies who drive BMWs and Porsches' . . . . People don't buy from people who give them the information, but from the person who has the lowest price." The only major seller of electronics in that market to resist the temptation to promise or guarantee lowest prices we've found to date is the department store Jordan Marsh.

Similar promises are being made all over the country by superstores, discounters, and even local merchants. Some superstores take these guarantees to ridiculous extremes, reflecting a basic contempt for the intelligence of the American consumer. Some, like New Jersey–based Tops, promise a $100 reward if they can't beat a competitor's price.[4] And the "lifetime" guarantees so common a few years ago (and still appearing now and then—what in the world does a price guarantee for "life" mean?) or statements promising "It's yours free if we don't meet your best price"—are merely clever and meaningless turns of phrase. Yet they work. Whenever we've hesitated to purchase a particular item at Highland, for example, the salesperson whips out the fancy "certificate" that guarantees us the lowest price—or the merchandise is free. "Obviously, we wouldn't be dumb enough to give our stuff away for nothing," the salesperson says, winking. "So, clearly, we must have the best prices."

This logic may seem impeccable, but as we will soon show, it neglects a few facts. Even at face value, the promise to meet or beat a price says nothing about the actual price of the merchandise as stands.[5] For many customers, however, the assurance that the prices are the best in town is all they have to hear to take out their charge plates. As one seminar leader noted to the audience in his "Basic Retail Survival Course" at the National Association of Retail Dealers of America's (NARDA) 1987 show, "A lie repeated often enough will be believed."

"Of course it's absurd," admitted a Fretter salesperson discussing his store's promise to give customers free merchandise if it refused to meet a competitor's price. "Everybody is going to beat your best price before they give it to you for free. There's no way in hell anybody's going to lower our price more than a few dollars. Imagine this scenario. It's a $300 TV. You go to Highland and they knock it down to $299. You go back to Fretter, and we knock it down to $298. You go back to Highland, and they knock it down to $297.95. You got to Fretter, and we knock it down to $297.90. It'll never happen. It'll never be worth anyone's time. We have [the promise] on the ads because people like the word *free*."

HAVING YOUR CAKE AND EATING IT

The problem, of course, is that it's impossible for everyone to have the lowest price. So, although retailers bombard consumers with these guarantees, they undercut them to make them virtually meaningless.

How do they do so? There are many different methods, each one mixed and matched depending on the current practices of competition and regulatory emphasis. Thus, although we found five methods dominating the consumer-electronics scene as we researched this book—(1) vertical price-fixing, (2) derivative models and brands, (3) the fine print, (4) the inconvenience factor, and (5) the game of averages—it's not the specifics of these methods that matter as much as noting the diverse bag of tricks that retailers can choose from to establish a profitable "marketing mix."

Vertical Price-Fixing

More than seventy years ago Congress passed antitrust laws to prevent both horizontal and vertical pricing-fixing. Horizontal price-fixing occurs when different companies in the same business get together to fix prices. For example, if all the steel or oil companies decide that all oil or steel would sell for one predetermined price, that would be horizontal price-fixing. Vertical price-fixing occurs when a manufacturer demands that at least one retailer sell its products for some preset price. Historically, the American government has opposed both forms of price-fixing because they inhibit price competition and encourage the formation of large monopolistic types of retailers and manufacturers.

Vertical price-fixing (also called "retail price maintenance") has been quite common in the consumer-electronics and major-appliance industries—although, as we write this book, it looks like the government may be clamping down once again. Typically, retailers are required to advertise the manufacturer's merchandise above a preset minimum. In reality, this price is often the minimum at which the merchandise can be sold without alienating the manufacturer and getting cut off from the supply. The result, as far as consumers are concerned, is that prices increase, and price guarantees become farcical: although you may not find a price *lower* than the one in front of you, that price might not be very low at all, since it's the same everywhere.[6]

Although vertical price-fixing remains strictly illegal, it's been a rampant problem for some years now, primarily because the requirements for proving it are unreasonably strict. Specifically, it's illegal for a manufacturer to force a retailer to sell an item at a specified price. But a Supreme Court ruling during the late 1980s dramatically increased the evidence required to prove this "official" arrangement, thereby making it extremely difficult to obtain convictions. In fact, the Justice Department did not file a single vertical price-fixing suit during the entire Reagan administration.[7]

The ruling actually lets manufacturers fix prices fairly blatantly. In fact, an article in *Home Furnishings Daily* in July 1988 went so far as to state the following:

Seeking to shore up shrinking profit margins and prevent major appliances from becoming "commodity" products, Whirlpool Corp. will implement a retail pricing program withholding advertising co-op monies from dealers who advertise most Whirlpool-brand appliances for below certain price points established by the company. With this "minimum advertised retail pricing program," as the company calls it . . . Whirlpool becomes the first American maker of major appliances to do what some consumer electronics players such as RCA already have done . . . : to attempt to exercise a greater degree of control over how products are sold. In both cases, the goal is the same: to encourage higher retail prices, and thus higher profit margins.[8]

Similarly, an article of January 23, 1989, in the same publication about GE's price "regulation," quotes Steve O'Brien, vice-president of sales and distribution for GE Appliances, as saying, "In order for a dealer to collect co-op advertising reimbursement from GE, the advertisment must show no pricing on GE models lower than the established minimums." The fall 1988 version of this "no-price" program specified the withholding, in extreme cases, of specific models from dealers.[9] Other companies we found written up in trade magazines as having minimum pricing policies included Zenith, Hitachi, Mitsubishi, Infinity, RCA, and Sanyo.[10]

Manufacturers are loath to acknowledge these practices, and, in fact, apparently have since abandoned any such official policies. But there's no question that at least unofficial vertical price-fixing was aiding and abetting lowest-price guarantees at least through 1990. One RCA representative admitted to us, "We ask dealers to maintain a minimum advertised price." Furthermore, countless retailers have confirmed that certain manufacturers effectively fix prices by "punishing" retailers who don't advertise and sell merchandise at predetermined prices. In January 1989 the New York State attorney general's office charged Panasonic with fixing the prices for certain Panasonic and Technics merchandise, resulting in a settlement that required Panasonic to refund up to $16 million to qualified consumers.

Other companies named by one or more retailers as engaging in unofficial price regulation include Sony, NEC, Mitsubishi, RCA, Hitachi, Sharp, Whirlpool, Hotpoint, and GE. One retailer from Sacramento, California, told us, "Every time I advertise, I must look at these companies' pricing guidelines to make sure that I'm not advertising something at a price I'm not supposed to." This dealer further claimed that if he violates RCA's pricing guidelines, his outfit won't share in the co-op advertising for that month, and RCA will rebill him for it next month. He added that other companies were copying RCA's lead. And, according to Montgomery Ward's vice-president and general manager of its Electric Avenue operations, "They all basically have done and still do it."[11]

A manufacturer can also "punish" a retailer who doesn't sell at the fixed price by removing "bad guys" from its allocation list. Again, this cut can be accomplished subtly but firmly. The president of a mid-sized Boston-area electronics store, for example, told us that Sony "cut him off" because "we advertised stuff at a lower price than they wanted to see it advertised for."

"Sony's biggest thing is that they want stuff advertised at a certain price," he continued. "If you don't, they shut you off. Goods become 'back-ordered.' Or your credit gets put on hold. Or you're a 'suspended dealership pending outcome of problems.'" He referred to a sheet Sony issued called "Suggested Profit Picture Guidelines," which suggests amounts for which dealers should advertise and sell certain products. According to a former Sony representative, Sony and Panasonic have "detailers" who are assigned to go into stores and report the selling prices to their branch managers. He added that Hitachi and Magnavox merely survey ad prices to make sure products are selling at the right price.

Price-fixing works to the advantage of certain retailers: those who want to "guarantee" the lowest price but have to sell at high margins to compete. Thus, as one retailer told us, an upscale audio shop can carry Mitsubishi, a brand very careful to control retail price, and not have to worry about being undercut by some neighborhood discounter.

But price-fixing can also handicap a discounter selling itself on aggressively low prices. For example, a mail-order firm that is an authorized dealer for Panasonic has to follow Panasonic's rules. Meanwhile, the shady firm down the street can pick up Panasonics through transshipping or through the gray market (unofficial distribution channels) and sell them for whatever price it chooses.

Derivative Models and Brands

Another way retailers manage to have the "lowest" price—especially if vertical price-fixing is difficult—is to carry different models than everyone else so that they have the lowest price by default. Manufacturers encourage this practice by offering a large variety of models with virtually the same features. One model may be described in the promotional literature; the other "derivative" model may look the same, sound the same, and work the same, but has a different model number. Thus, you can't find any of them selling at a lower price because each derivative is available at only one store in the area.[12] As one Highland salesperson explained, the Sony KV2080R TV and the KV2093R TV are identical, but one is sold at Fretter and the other at Highland. "This way, we can both sell them for whatever we want," he told us. Alluding to this practice, some advertisements of Circuit City, the nation's largest specialty consumer-electronics superstore, mention—albeit in small print—that their "Plus 10 Low Price Guarantee" may be difficult to implement because "comparisons of some exclusive Circuit City brands and models may not be possible."

According to most of the industry people we've interviewed, retailers have strong-armed manufacturers into offering these derivative models, so that the superstores don't "bash each other," as one salesperson put it. Sony, RCA, Philips, Magnavox, Fisher, and Sharp are manufacturers mentioned numerous times to us and represent just some of the brands known among retailers for selling essentially the same piece of equipment under more than one model number. Manufacturers may also make slight cosmetic changes to justify a different number. For example, the RCA's VR270 videocassette recorder is a derivative model of the standard VR280. According to the president of a large Boston-area retailer, the two models differ only in that the buttons are located in different places and they're of slightly different sizes.

"I love derivative models," agreed a Fretter salesperson. "We had one GE refrigerator. We were the only one in the country with it. They gave us a special little black strip on the front door. I loved it. I was making good money on it."

Sometimes a manufacturer will make one version of the model for large superstores and another for smaller specialty stores. The smaller stores insist on this practice so that the high-volume superstores don't squeeze them out of the market. Thus, one "small guy" we interviewed got the KV2780 television from Sony, whereas his local "big guy" competitor got the derivative model KV2795. The two televisions were identical, but the small retailer could keep his price high to survive and still "guarantee the lowest price." Of course, department stores and even superstores are just as demanding about getting their own versions.[13]

Stores generally don't advertise these derivative models but try to "step up" shoppers to them once they're in the store (see the next chapter), a former Sony distributor told us. Consumer-electronics manufacturers often advertise "selective distribution," "sell up," and "higher profits" in their advertisements to the trade press. Thus, even if all the major superstores in the area are advertising the same model in the newspaper and all claiming the lowest price on it, they know that no one will hold them to their price guarantees. "The thing [on the advertised model] is not the comparative price," explained a Highland salesperson. "Nobody is going to buy a refrigerator with cheap, nonadjustable wire shelves except the landlord or someone with a summer home. And any woman who has owned a dryer won't buy one without a lint filter or a delicate cycle." Once you step into the store, you will almost certainly want the much nicer derivative model, which happens to be available nowhere else around.

Some manufacturers placate retailers by changing model numbers frequently. The vice-president of a mid-sized electronics store, for example, has observed that for certain lines, Sharp and Fisher change model numbers—without changing the actual features—every six months. Meanwhile, some retailers keep selling the "old" models. Some manufacturers keep selling them, too. "Manufacturers have a lot of old product they still ship," the vice-president continued. "We can buy TVs from RCA that are one and a half years old. The bad rap goes to the retailer, but it's the manufacturer." Each competing superstore will also claim that its particular model is the "new" one, when, of course, new and old models are identical and both new and old are being sold at the lowest price by default.

Another way manufacturers help all the retailers in the same area carry different models is by limiting distribution. For some manufacturers, this practice means restricting certain pieces in their line of select retailers. A Highland salesperson told us, "Sony has restricted distribution on some pieces, such as its projection TVs. If you're good with Sony's stuff, then they'll let you sell the high-profit top-of-the-line stuff."

Alternatively, a manufacturer may slap several different brand labels on virtually identical models and sell each brand to a different retailer. For certain items, Kenmore and Whirlpool, Maytag and Magic Chef, and GE and Hotpoint, for example, are virtually identical (although consumers often end up paying a lot more just for the most prestigious name). "Big guys carry Hotpoint, small guys carry GE," a Fretter salesperson explained. "The idea is, 'We don't hurt them, they don't hurt us.'"

Although GE and Hotpoint washers and dishwashers differ rather significantly, he said, dryers and refrigerators are very similar.

This salesperson added that this limited distribution pattern makes it possible for his Fretter outlet to thrive just several blocks away from a Lechmere outlet, which also guarantees the lowest price. "Why do we want to be near Lechmere?" he asked. "We've got this unique GE line, you see, and Lechmere doesn't carry any GE. They've got only Hotpoint. The consumer can't find anything close." As Richard Schulze, president of Best Buy, put it, referring to Sears Brand Central's GE line, "Clearly, if we would share a brand with Sears Roebuck, it would have to be with products that would be exclusive for us."[14]

An extreme example of these "derivative brands" involved Daewoo, one of South Korea's four largest companies, which produces models under the brand names of Daewoo, Daytron, and Portland. Whatever the brand label, these models are so completely identical that Daewoo doesn't even bother printing up separate literature for each of them. It merely sells the identical model (with the same model number) under three different brand labels. Other companies do much the same thing more subtly. For example, North American Philips sells four brands: Philips, Magnavox, Philco, and Sylvania—with much of the merchandise under the different labels virtually identical.[15]

There are also dozens of tiny brands that are sold to retailers in a specific region on an exclusive basis or as private labels. These are almost invariably just relabeled merchandise from other manufacturers so that a given retailer won't have to compete on that item. Large department stores sell as much as 25 percent of their merchandise (mostly apparel) with private labels.[16]

The Fine Print

Of course, all price-fixing and derivative models aside, there are still models left that you can find selling at different prices at more than one store. Once you consider the price demands by the manufacturers and consumers, the difference between two retailers often amounts to a few dollars—hardly worth fighting over. But there can indeed be a significant price difference between a superstore, for example, and a New York mail-order firm, or a high-end audio store and a warehouse club, and retailers here must find a way to guarantee the lowest price and still maintain a viable business.

That's where the fine print comes in. Retailers can cover their promises on an individual basis simply by including multiple exceptions to the price guarantee—such as not meeting prices of mail-order firms, warehouse clubs, or nonauthorized dealers; not comparing prices with stores more than some specified distance away or without "similar service"; or not matching prices if the other store is selling the item in limited quantity or claims it's out of stock. A retailer may also insist that you document a competitor's price with some sort of written proof such as an ad or a signed testimonial from the other seller.

For Fretter to beat a price before a sale or up to thirty days after it, for example, you have to present written proof that the identical model is in stock and selling for a lower price at a local authorized dealer. You can't expect Fretter to match the price if you find the model selling for less in some limited-quantity sale. Leiser superstores, a New England chain, will guarantee prices only against those *advertised* by competitors located within twenty-five miles of one of its stores, requires that the item be in stock, and excludes floor samples and damaged, discontinued, or limited-quantity items. Tweeter won't match a price from a nonauthorized, nonlocal dealer; furthermore, it requires that the store selling the lower-priced model have "equivalent services," although the fine print does not define what this term means. Presumably, a warehouse club with no service or even a discounter with untrained sales help would not qualify for the price guarantee.

Certain brands are excluded from these guarantees as well. Mitsubishi, for example, refuses to authorize any retailer that discounts its models below a certain level. Thus, when the superstores advertise Mitsubishi, they neglect to put the little asterisk that promises lowest price next to the Mitsubishi models. No matter that headlines at the top of the ad claim that these stores will beat all prices and give away models free if they don't. No matter that these promises implicitly apply to all advertised merchandise. By leaving out the asterisk, the retailers can make their promise but cover themselves with the manufacturer, too. Most annoying to the consumer, of course, is to go into a store believing yourself entitled to a refund or matched price, only to find yourself confronted with these exceptions. Worse still, you can be told one thing over the phone only to find that when you go there, the store slips into some obscure little rule and refuses to meet your price.

Every so often, as part of the consumer-information service we ran, we tested a store's price guarantee and saw exactly how these exceptions work. "Spotters" visited stores on a monthly basis to collect availability and pricing information. In addition, we entered into our computer the prices and models from local advertisements and catalogs. As a result, we undoubtedly had the most comprehensive, up-to-date database around in the consumer-electronics/major-appliance world; we actually knew what everyone had out on the sales floor, what everyone was advertising, and what prices they were asking. We were therefore in a unique position to put these price guarantees to the test.

Thus, one day after going through the newspaper, we noticed Highland advertising the GE 82568 television for $466. We had seen it selling at BJ's Wholesale Club just a few days earlier for only $400, so we went into Highland to see if they would truly meet this much lower price. When we got into the store, however, and found the GE 82568, we noticed that the pricetag was offering the model for $499—with no indication whatsoever that the TV had been advertised for $466 that very day.

The salesperson we consulted admitted that someone had forgotten to change the tag but that, of course, the price was only $466. We then asked him if Highland would meet prices with a membership warehouse club. When he said, "Yes, of course," we told him about the BJ's price and asked if Highland would match it. "Sure," he replied. He'd just have to call BJ's to verify the price. He walked away smiling.

When he returned from the phone call, however, he was no longer smiling. "I've got good news and bad news," he told us. "The good news is that BJ's has the TV in stock and is selling it for $400. The bad news is that we can't sell it to you for $400."

"Why not?" we asked. "You just told us that you'd meet a warehouse club's price, and when we looked at your price guarantee, we also saw that it doesn't specifically exclude wholesale clubs. So, what's the problem?"

The salesman explained that his manager had told him that Highland "no longer" matches prices with warehouse clubs. Handing us what was supposedly Highland's latest price-guarantee terms, he offered to sell us the TV for $410. Of course, if we had been serious buyers, we would have accepted the offer because BJ's is fifteen miles away and offers much less service than Highland. But we truly wanted to see if Highland would fulfill its own price guarantee, so we simply left.

It was only once we got home and scrutinized the "new" price guarantee that we noticed that there was still no mention of excluding warehouse clubs.

Specifically, the certificate he had given us said: "BEFORE YOU BUY: If you see a lower price offered by any local stocking merchant (verifiable written proof required) on the same brand name and model number that Highland sells, we promise to beat that price or it's yours FREE!" A few paragraphs later the certificate also said:

> Naturally, this Price Guarantee does not apply to mail orders, manufacturer's rebates, dealers' going-out-of-business sales, merchandise offered as floor samples, one-of-a-kind or limited quantities, nor does it apply when the purchase involves premiums or trade-ins, or when the purchase price includes special items, such as carrying cases, installation or delivery charges, nor to any offers where merchandise is not readily available for immediate delivery.

Again, nowhere could we find any mention of warehouse clubs.

So, knowing that Highland guaranteed to give the merchandise "free" if they wouldn't beat the best price, we phoned the manager. At first the operator reported that Mark, the manager, was "out," but when we explained our difficulty, she somehow found him. We told him that we had seen the GE 82568 at BJ's for $400—a price verified over the phone—and that there was no printed exclusion for warehouse clubs but that the salesperson refused to sell it for less than $410. We added that according to Highland's price guarantee, we were entitled to the television for free. At that point Mark replied that he wouldn't give us the TV for nothing but that he would beat BJ's price by one dollar if we'd drive back to the store. We then asked him if he had ever given away a TV for free, and he had no comment.

The Inconvenience Factor

Fortunately for the retailers, customers only rarely end up pushing a store manager to this extreme, mainly because no one has a database like ours. And without this kind of armamentarium, you may not actually know that someone out there has a better price. In fact, when retailers neglect to include the model number on the ad and/or the display, they make comparison shopping difficult, if not impossible. Obviously, if you don't know the model number on the TV you're interested in, you can't find out if anyone else is selling the very same model number for less. And, as a corollary, even if you do know the particular model number you're after, if you can't find any model numbers on the competition's merchandise, you'll never know if you're getting the best price either.

Leaving out this crucial information may make it impossible for you to satisfy certain conditions of the guarantee.[17] Many retailers guaranteeing the lowest price, for example, insist that you document your claim with "written proof." If you can actually persuade a salesperson from a rival store—who is also, incidentally, claiming the lowest price—to put his or her price in writing, you may actually be able to get someone to enforce this policy. But don't expect to get your written proof in the form of an advertisement, since many of these lack either price or model number. After collecting ads and price-shopping stores for over three years, we found that many stores guaranteeing the lowest price either fail to list any model numbers at all in their ads or displays, or they may use parts of model numbers.[18] The New York City Department of Consumer Affairs noted this problem when they characterized Chase and Citicorp's price guarantee as being "impossible to satisfy." To promote their Visa card, these banks promised consumers "points" with which they could purchase selected merchandise at a "guaranteed lowest price." After reviewing eighty newspaper ads, however, Bureau researchers found that only forty-four contained both model numbers and brand names—both necessary to meet the conditions of the guarantee. Thus, the Department concluded that the conditions necessary to prove another merchant's price were virtually impossible to fulfill, given the prevalent lack of labels and prices.

Most shoppers don't have the New York City Department of Consumer Affairs—one of the few truly active government watchdogs in the country—protecting them against impossible-to-satisfy guarantees, however. Instead, they have to contend with all the improperly labeled merchandise every day as they circulate sales floors and clip advertisements and nonetheless try to match prices. One large retailer we know, for example, routinely leaves out the first few digits of a model number in its ads, so that, for example, the Sony KV1967 TV becomes "1967." The retailers may know the TV's the same, but the average consumer, who doesn't spend her or his life studying model numbers, will simply assume that this model can't be compared to the KV1967 selling across the street.

Even if you don't need written proof, you may not even be able to recognize a model number and use it to speak up for your rights. First of all, many of today's superstores have so many samples sitting on the floor that you may have to wander about squinting at cards for fifteen minutes before you find a specific model number you're after. By the time you've done that, moreover, you probably don't have the energy to run all over town to several other superstores just to save a few bucks.

Furthermore, even if you do actually have the time and energy to pinpoint specific model numbers, you may not be able to identify them.

Most merchandise in stores today is littered with numbers, including sale price, "list price," various codes to salespeople regarding commissions (see previous chapter), SKU (stock-keeping unit) number, and, finally, the model number itself. Unless you decide to make a career out of consumer electronics, you probably won't know how to tell a model number from any other number on these cards. Only rarely will a retailer (who is genuinely selling price-competitive merchandise) clearly label this number as "model number."

If the model number is visible, furthermore, the price may not be. And, obviously, you can't directly comparison shop without both a model number and a price. Such shoddy labeling isn't always an across-the-board policy and sometimes may simply result from oversight or stealing (salespeople routinely snitch tags from other stores, they tell us, to study the commission schedules, etc.). Frequently, however, retailers purposely leave off tags. In fact, in an instructional manual for retailers a member of the NARDA's Advisory Board noted three possible systems to tag items:

1. Prominently placed tags on every item.
2. All tags semi-hidden.
3. A split system where leader models, ADV [advertised] specials and close-outs would have visible tags. All other merchandise would have semi-hidden tags which the customer can locate as they [sic] look through the product, and/or the salesman can pull out to show the customer.

Whether purposeful or not, the bottom line is that as a consumer you will find it nearly impossible (a) to learn if two stores in the area both have a certain model number and (b) to compare the prices. In fact, before vertical price-fixing came into fashion, almost every store we visited had incomplete model numbers or prices on at least 10 percent of the merchandise. Some had missing model numbers and prices on virtually everything in stock.

The Game of Averages

Sophisticated retailers know that selling is at least partly a game of averages. They have legitimate loss leaders to get consumers into the store, but then they hope that the consumers will buy other, more expensive merchandise. The loss-leader item is then written off as a form of advertising expense. Supermarkets, for example, routinely advertise fantastically priced produce or beverages in the expectation that when you're in the supermarket you'll also fill your cart with more-expensive groceries. Similarly, computer dealers routinely advertise the core computer unit at cost, expecting that they can make it up on peripherals. Consumer-electronics and major-appliance chains, which less frequently have peripherals (except for service contracts), often figure that—despite all the selling strategies described above—they'll just have to take a loss on a certain percentage of their goods. For example, according to reports in the trade literature, Crazy Eddie in New York routinely figured it would have to sell 10 percent of its merchandise at a loss to maintain its low-price image.[19]

Thus, many retailers of consumer electronics and major appliances genuinely sell certain items at rock-bottom prices but compensate by selling others at or above list price. Certain discounters have a reputation for being the "best price in town," and many people buy everything there out of habit, assuming that if they got a good deal once or twice before, they will always get a good deal. The database in our consumer-information service, however, documented the specific merchandise various stores had and the specific prices they were offering it for. And from this database we have been able to confirm that the same discounter that promised and indeed had the lowest price in town on one model would also sell another model at above list price. Consumers who don't routinely study best prices and just assume a certain store gives them fair prices need to be aware of this extremely common phenomenon.

Some retailers that promise the lowest price simply lower the prices on the specific items advertised by other stores—since consumers are most likely to compare these items. Then they leave everything else at its original price, which may or may not be lower than anyone else's. "We read Lechmere ads in the morning and change all our tags immediately to undercut them," said a Fretter salesperson. "So, we take a hit. Big deal. We've made our market impression." Highland salespeople report a similar practice, in which they lower all advertised models to $1 below the advertised price to "prove" that they always meet the competition. Retailers know that as long as the most obvious items are low-priced, most consumers will never check every item around.

To reinforce the profitability of this practice, a retailer can make the low-priced items extremely hard to find by placing them above eye level or surrounding them with hundreds of other models. Or they can simply neglect to put the low advertised price on the item in the store, hoping that most customers won't know it's on sale. We've documented this practice many times at Boston-area Fretter and Highland stores. We come in with a newspaper advertising a particular television at a particular price. When we finally locate that model, we notice that the price on the tag is $50 to $100 higher than the advertised sale price. Nowhere is there any mention of a sale.

Another common practice is to display the same model at two or more different prices. Several superstores we frequently visit employ the practice of routinely selling the same model on the same day for different prices. One salesperson we interviewed gave a reason for this: stores use one of the models to make a profit and one to prove the store's low prices. Strategic positioning on the sales floor allows the same model to serve both purposes.

THE MIX-AND-MATCH PRINCIPLE

The tactics described above for making price comparison shopping difficult for consumers are not mutually exclusive. Stores like to mix their selling strategies to match the needs and vulnerabilities of as many different types of consumers as possible: a little vertical price-fixing here, a little inconvenience factor there; a little fine print here, a little average-playing there. It's hard for us to imagine, for example, that a store could get away with all derivative models or all models with vertically fixed prices: the store would lose all credibility in the consumer's eye, and, of course, at times regulatory authorities are particularly attuned to one particular practice. A far better strategy is to have a few highly visible and competitive models, but keep 80 percent or more of the merchandise under close protection. For the remaining 20 percent, you can then rely on fine print, the inconvenience factor, or the game of averages so that you're not hurt too badly by price competition.

A good analogy is the way stores display their merchandise. A common attitude is that it is good to have a little bit of merchandise for each type of person: some like name brands, some don't recognize them; some like lots of features, some don't know the difference; some like to buy floor models, some only "A" grade models; and some like only models on sale, while others will buy at full price.

P L A Y I N G   O N   I G N O R A N C E

In the summer of 1988 the *Wall Street Journal* reported that pitches guaranteeing the lowest price "increasingly are coming under fire." In particular, the newspaper discussed a case in which the National Advertising Review Board, an industry self-regulating panel, branded Montgomery Ward's price guarantee as "inaccurate" and "confusing." As a result of this action, Ward's agreed to modify its "lowest prices guaranteed" claim within three months.[20] Interestingly, however, this article—and the NARB report itself—didn't even mention the frequent claims by major superstores. We suspect the explanation lies in the fact that the National Advertising Review Board has jurisdiction only over *national* advertising. Thus, at the moment, only national mail-order or catalog houses will be taken to task.

Even so, we expect that at some time lowest-price guarantees will be banned or severely restricted. As the most extreme form of special price or sales claim, they can't help but be attacked. Our real concern, however, is not with the bizarre price guarantees, but the underlying practices that foster consumer confusion and reduce competition and hence efficiency in the marketplace, the same practices which will disappear once we have a new information infrastructure in place.

Many retailers we talked to pointed out that uninformed consumers— who fall for low-price claims and ignore good service and quality merchandise—are asking for this kind of treatment. They object to the many customers who seem to think they deserve to buy at cost and assume that retailers are running a charity. The retailers add that very few consumers are stupid enough to take these low-price claims literally; most consumers, if pressed, would have to acknowledge that no one retailer could really have the lowest prices consistently. The lowest-price guarantees are merely a code, understood by American consumers to mean that the store is serious about selling at fair prices.

These arguments are all true. Consumers demand low prices and buy at stores promising them, even if they know deep down that there might be a better price around. It's simply too much trouble to investigate every claim and a lot easier to believe an ad when you really want that new camcorder. Nonetheless, we maintain that consumers do not really want to be deceived, nor do they want the inefficient market that such deceptions produce. We also believe that, emotionally, most consumers do not really know that these claims are merely a code—even if they would eventually realize this if they thought about it long enough. After all, if consumers really knew what was going on, retailers wouldn't go to such great lengths making price guarantees and inventing exceptions to them.

Consumers, unfortunately, are overly obsessed with price because it is all they understand—the products themselves are too confusing. In return, the stores spend a huge amount of energy and money focusing on appearing to have the lowest price. Thus, consumers in turn, have indirectly paid a lot of money for this advertising and promotion, and in return they get none of the education which would be most useful for them and the economy. As we shall see in the last part of this book, everyone would benefit if stores could focus more money on the merits of their goods and services rather than on trying to fool consumers into thinking they have the lowest prices anywhere. And everyone would benefit, too, if consumers were less intimidated by their purchases so that they might be influenced by more substantial things than low price—or, rather, the appearance of low price.

1. Francine Schwadel, in her *Wall Street Journal* article "Who Wins with Price-Matching Plans? Not Shoppers, For Few Bother to Collect" (March 16, 1989, sec. B, p.1), provides excellent coverage of many of the issues developed in this chapter.

2. Barry Berman and Joel Evans, *Retail Management: A Strategic Approach* (New York: Macmillan, 1986), p. 427, and William Davidson, Daniel Sweeney, and Ronald Stampfl, *Retail Management* (New York: John Wiley, 1988), pp. 408–409.

3. These were the claims made in newspaper ads as of late 1988. Occasionally the ads are modified.

4. Peter Hisey, "Aggressive Advertising Puts Tops on Top of the Competition," *Discount Store News*, August 21, 1989, p. 3. See also Mark Harrington, "Sears Again Tests Software Waters," *Home Furnishings Daily*, February 12, 1990, p. 93.

5. Francine Schwadel, "Lowest-Price Claims in Ads Stir Dispute: Guarantees Seen as Inaccurate And Misleading," *Wall Street Journal*, August 12, 1988, sec. 2, p. 15, and Mark Harrington, "N.Y.C. Hits Newmark & Lewis Again; Says Rebuttal Ads Deceptive," *Home Furnishings Daily*, November 13, 1989, p. 80.

6. Julie Cohen, "Price-Fixing Bill Gaining in Congress," *Home Furnishings Daily*, March 5–9, 1990, p. 28.

7. Ken Rankin, "A New Breeze Is Blowing Through Justice, FTC," *Discount Store News*, November 27, 1989, p. 6. See also Michael Waldman and Jonathan Cuneo, "The Court Is Winking at Price Fixing," *New York Times*, May 15, 1988, sec. F, p. 2, and "A Big Win for Price-Fixers," *Consumer Reports*, August 1988, p. 492.

8. Ted DuPont, "Whirlpool to Deny Co-op Ad Funds to Price Slashers," *Home Furnishings Daily*, July 18, 1988, pp. 1, 116.

9. "GE Appliances Broadens Program Regulating Prices Advertised by Dealers," *Home Furnishings Daily*, January 23, 1989, pp. 145, 148; and "GE Changes Policy on Co-op Ads," *Home Furnishings Daily*, November 13, 1989, p. 107.

10. Bob Gerson, "Zenith Plans Profit Revamp," *TWICE*, May 9–13, 1988, p. 1; Marc Berman, "Two Suppliers Suggest 'Suggested Retail' Tags, *TWICE*, January 25–29, 1988, p. 1; Gerson, "2 Firms Take Profit Track," *TWICE*, May 16–20, pp. 1, 22; "Sanyo Keeps Distribution Limits as It Broadens Lines; Suggests Retail Prices," *Home Furnishings Daily*, September 12, 1988, p. 171; and Gerry Beatty and David Jones, "GE Shift Gets Mixed Reviews," *Home Furnishings Daily*, November 20, 1989, p. 107.

11. "Vendor Price Control Under Fire by NY AG," *Consumer Electronics*, February 1989, p. 10.

12. See Peter Hisey, "Brand Central Hits the Big Time," *Discount Store News*, March 20, 1989, p. 43, and Cliff Roth, "Tricks of the Trade," *VideoMaker*, January 1990, pp. 58, 62, 64.

13. See "How Sharp Keeps Its Edge," *Home Furnishings Daily*, January 9, 1989, p. 155. Note that most retailers belong to buying groups, and it is these buying groups rather than individual retailers themselves that order the derivative merchandise. Buying groups are composed of noncompetitive (geographically dispersed) retailers that use their collective buying power to wring better deals from manufacturers.

14. Quoted in Mark Harrington, "Sears Sees 120 Free-Standing Brand Central Units," *Home Furnishings Daily*, February 20, 1989, p. 115.

15. "Putting the Power Behind Magnavox," *Home Furnishings Daily*, January 2, 1989, p. 14.

16. "Marketing Private Label," *Stores*, June 1989, p. 20; Muriel Adams, "Private Label: Now Trump," *Stores*, June 1988, p. 18; and Roth, p. 13.

17. See Francine Schwadel, "Who Wins with Price-Matching Plans?"

18. In April 1990 Massachusetts began requiring model numbers on all ads, and to date most of the chains seem to be complying—at least in their newspaper ads.

19. "The E.Z. Way" (an interview with Elias Zinn), *Venture Magazine*, May 1988, p. 55.

20. Francine Schwadel, "Lowest-Price Claims in Ads;" also, "Report of NARB Panel 44: Disposition of Appeal by the National Advertising Division Regarding Advertising by Montgomery Ward & Co., Inc." (New York: National Advertising Division, Council of Better Business Bureaus, July 1988).

CHAPTER 4

Bait and Switch
The "Legal" Way

A store has two fundamental goals: (1) to get you into the store, and (2) to make a profitable sale. Achieving both these goals may conflict, and when it does, the result is "bait and switch." Pure bait and switch, in which the store advertises goods it has no intention of selling, is strictly illegal, but more subtle forms are pervasive in the consumer-electronics, major-appliance, and computer businesses.

In the most basic and grossest form of bait and switch (which we refer to as "pure," "classic," or "old-fashioned" bait and switch), you come into a store and ask for a specific advertised model, and then the salesperson switches you to a different model by claiming that the advertised model is out of stock. In a less rigorous variation, one that is more difficult for consumers and consumer-protection agencies to detect, the retailer keeps a few of the advertised models in stock but disparages them when you come in to buy them. Such disparagement can involve the model itself, as well as its warranty, availability, service and parts, or credit terms. After hearing the pitch, you, anxious to buy something, readily agree to buy another model on which the store makes a better profit.[1]

Occasionally, stores still practice this strictly illegal form of bait and switch. Right after New Year's Day, Ms. G.,[2] a woman from Connecticut, and her father made the two-hour trip into Manhattan to a store where they thought they could get the Panasonic PV220 or PV300 camcorder at the best price. Although they had already looked at these models in other stores, they had little confidence in their knowledge of camcorders, so when the salesperson drew their attention away from the Panasonic models, they listened. He overtly disparaged the PV220 and PV300 by saying that they had no AC adapter cords, which would cost

$100 extra. That said, the salesperson had little trouble persuading Ms. G. and her father to buy, for $1,050 (tax included), the Hitachi VM2000A. This camcorder reputedly could record indoors with no additional lighting and included a case as well. When Ms. G. asked about the warranty, the salesperson told her to bring the camcorder back to him if there were any problems. She'd just need her receipt.

What makes Ms. G.'s story sound like a classic bait and switch are the events unveiled after she took the camcorder home. What became clear is that the salesperson not only falsely maligned the advertised item, but switched her to an inferior one. First of all, she noticed the receipt— necessary for warranty repairs—was incorrectly dated as "1/2/86" rather than "1/2/87." Moreover, she found that the camcorder had no original box or packaging and no warranty information and that the case had obviously been used—the strap was frayed, the inside was torn, and there were ink marks all over it. Four accessories were missing, including those needed to hook the camcorder to a TV. Furthermore, the camcorder didn't work right: recorded pictures had almost no colors, even when recording outside in bright sunlight. What really clinched things, however, was the report from several other stores that the AC adapter cord was standard equipment on the two Panasonic models she had originally asked about; in other words, the salesman misrepresented the Panasonic camcorders, presumably to make the Hitachi sound better in comparison.

When Ms. G. and her father took the two-hour trip back to Manhattan eight days later to exchange this defective camcorder, she had to explain everything to a new salesperson. He gave her the name of a service center but refused to help her further, claiming that the Hitachi was " 'too good a deal' " for him to exchange it. Only after Ms. G.'s many letters of complaint to the New York City Consumer Frauds Bureau was she allowed to exchange the Hitachi for a full refund or for a Magnavox camcorder. The store never offered her the Panasonics despite its advertisements!

We have found that mail-order houses most frequently practice this rather unsophisticated form of bait and switch. When a man from Columbia, Missouri, called to order the Matsushita VCR he had seen advertised in *Video,* a New York firm claimed that the model was out of stock but that he could buy a Lloyds VCR for the same price. It turned out that this Lloyds not only had inferior features but was only a player—not a recorder at all. And despite what the salesperson had told him, the firm advertised the same "out of stock" Matsushita VCR in the next month's *Video.* Similarly, a physician from White Plains, New York, reported seeing several ads in local newspapers for the Nikon Tele Touch Camera, but each time he called the mail-order firm, he was told that this model was not readily available and then was asked to consider a new "highly rated" model.

Such stories are hardly surprising. When we started our research, in fact, we actually presumed that in any market with such confusion on the part of consumers and temptation on the part of retailers, bait and switch must not only exist but flourish. What surprised us, however, was how extraordinarily resistant to *pure* bait and switch the stores appeared to be. This old type of bait and switch, as described in consumer guidelines put forth by the Better Business Bureaus and attorneys general, didn't seem to be a major problem. Except for a few sleazy operations and a few occasional slips like the ones just mentioned, retailers seemed to be obeying the law.[3]

But then we made this extraordinary discovery: it's the consumer confusion itself that has nearly killed off the old bait and switch. In other words, today's consumers are too confused for this type of game to work! The old concept of bait and switch and all the laws around it were based on the principle that consumers were fairly familiar with the advertised commodity. When there weren't that many products to choose from, consumers had little difficulty staying moderately well informed; for example, a TV had two or three features, and many of them could be understood intuitively (such as the size of the screen or the quality of the paneling). Thus, a store could advertise a specific high-quality model at below cost and assume that a knowledgeable consumer would take the bait. Today stores can wave gold camcorders and diamond TVs all they want, but consumers won't even recognize the value.

THE MODERN WAY TO BAIT AND SWITCH

Mail-Order Switching

Consumer ignorance has led stores to more sophisticated—and, conveniently, less blatantly illegal—forms of bait and switch. Along with a few unusually shady walk-in retailers, consumer-electronics mail-order firms occasionally still employ the more brazen tactics, mainly because they lack some of the persuasive sales and promotional tools available to mainstream retail stores. Nevertheless, they also share the remarkably subtle variations on bait and switch with their walk-in competitors. There are literally dozens of companies nationwide that all sell the same merchandise. Moreover, when it comes to this type of mail order, most consumers primarily shop price. So how do many mail-order firms stick their head out in front of the pack? The answer is clear: *appear* to have the lowest prices. The problem is that stores cannot always make money on the prices they need to advertise to get consumers to call their order lines. When claiming to have the lowest price may affect profitability, some rather clever forms of bait and switch can follow.

SWITCHING FROM GRAY-MARKET MERCHANDISE.

The store advertises gray-market merchandise—merchandise generally intended for other countries, obtained through unofficial distributors—without saying so and then tells you over the phone that it doesn't come with a U.S. warranty. If you want the warranty you have to pay $40, $50, even $200 more than the advertised price. Suddenly the price stops being so good, but many people will be intimidated enough—or tired enough of calling—that they'll buy anyway. We actually had this experience ourselves with a New York firm when we purchased a camcorder. We saw the Panasonic PVS150 advertised in *Video* magazine at this firm for $1,199, an excellent price. When we called to order it, however, the operator told us that if we wanted a U.S. warranty, we'd have to pay $170 more. In other words, they enticed us to call by advertising a gray-market model, but once they had us on the line they disparaged the warranty and tried to lure us into buying a different version of the model. Not all that different from classic bait and switch.

A more virulent form of this kind of gray-market bait and switch occurs when a firm actually sells you the gray-market goods without telling you. In this case, you don't literally get switched from what was advertised; instead, you get switched from what you *thought* you ordered. Only upon opening the package and finding out that you need an adapter for U.S. circuitry or that the instructions are in Japanese do you possibly discover that something went awry; on the other hand, like many people, you may never realize that such problems just weren't part and parcel of the confusing way electronics are sold in this country today.

DELAY AND SWITCH.

In this form of bait and switch, a mail-order firm makes the switch to another model *after* you hang up the phone. This apparently happened to

Mr. B. from Cleveland when, on October 14, 1986, he called a New York firm to order the Panasonic RX-C20 audio system. Without a hitch, he was able to order the system on a credit card and he was assured he'd have it "within 10 days." Approximately two and half weeks later, however, a representative from the firm called him to say that the Panasonic system was on back order and had been discontinued by the manufacturer. At that point, he attempted to induce Mr. B. to buy an Aiwa CA-R80U system. Mr. B. said he wasn't interested.

No matter what Mr. B. said, however, the firm was determined to sell him something. On November 8, he received papers which stated that he had to respond before they could send him the Aiwa. Even though he had already refused to buy this model, to oblige the company he checked the box marked "No—please cancel order and send refund," and signed and dated the form. However, when he received his charge card bill, he saw that he had been charged $174.90 for the Panasonic on the first day he had ordered it—despite the fact that the Panasonic was indefinitely out of stock. Furthermore, on December 10 a package arrived which he assumed to be the Aiwa he had expressly *not* ordered. On December 12 his next charge-card statement showed that the firm had added another $7.05, presumably representing the additional cost of the Aiwa system. It took months of letter writing to people including the commisioner of the New York City Department of Consumer Affairs and the assistant attorney general before Mr. B. could get the firm to take off the charge and take back the merchandise.

ADVERTISING A COMPARABLE MODEL.

Here the company advertises a model, say, the Panasonic PVS150 camcorder, for a very low price. Baited by this great offer, you call up, only to discover that the real model for sale at that price isn't the PVS150 at all but a "comparable model" by Magnavox. However, the store does have the PVS150 you wanted and will sell it for a higher price. Thus, you either end up paying more than you planned for the model you wanted or you end up buying something you didn't intend to buy.

This "comparable model" advertising isn't as deceptive as it sounds, however, for there may be a little notation like "equiv." next to the model number advertised. Not that many people will know what this "equiv." means, but at least you were supposed to be put on guard. Once you know about this practice, you can avoid it by reading ads carefully.

STOCK SPLITTING.

This is unfortunately a rampant form of bait and switch. The company advertises a standard model number, but removes items that are usually sold with it. The customer is then strongly advised or even required to purchase these items with the basic model. In the case of camcorders, for example, this is frequently done with the carrying case. Sometimes the price charged for the carrying case can be two or three times its regular retail price, so that, in the end, you actually end up paying much more than you would have paid at the place advertising the camcorder for more money! In another variation of stock splitting, the salesperson might simply try to sell you a bunch of accessories with your basic purchase. If no accessories are purchased, you might find that the main item you wanted suddenly seems to be out of stock.

We consider this a form of bait and switch because the price and product that bait you are not the price and product that you end up with. This practice is particularly common with personal computers, where most of the profits are made on peripherals and training rather than on the basic unit.[4] For example, Computer Factory, one of the largest walk-in computer retailers in the United States, routinely advertises various Apple computers at extraordinarily low "sale prices" (which rarely change from week to week), only to mention in almost unreadable fine print that the sale price is invalid unless you also purchase several highly priced peripherals necessary to make the machines run.

Sometimes such splitting can be carried to ludicrous extremes. For example, when Dr. L., a public relations executive, purchased an NEC MultiSpeed laptop computer for $1,499 from a mail-order firm in New York City, the salesperson told her (she bought the computer in person) that the computer would not operate without a DOS 3.2 operating system, which would cost an additional $180. He then wrote up a sales slip for $1,806.58, tax included. When Dr. L. got home, however, she discovered that a DOS 3.2 was already in the box as part of the standard equipment and that the DOS sold to her was a copy (the label was hand-printed), even though unauthorized duplication is a violation of copyright. As it happened, the Chicago office of her company had actually handled the introduction of this computer, so Dr. L. called a colleague to see if DOS was standard equipment. It was.

The extent of the stock splitting grew, moreover, when Dr. L. went back to the mail-order firm to complain. This time the clerk told her that he had *given* her the DOS as a backup, free of charge, and claimed that the additional $180 covered not the DOS but the cost of the AC adapter (at $100) and the U.S. warranty (at $80). Again, however, both of these items had come inside the original box. And, indeed, when Dr. L. checked in the users manual and with NEC management, she confirmed that (1) the warranty is provided directly and (2) the DOS and the AC adapter are part of the standard equipment; they are *not* options and are not priced or sold separately.

Not everyone has time or connections to investigate these matters as well as did Dr. L., and consequently stock splitting can be quite difficult for consumers to uncover. Occasionally, however, enough complaints are made that government agencies crack down. In 1988, for example, Grand Central Camera in New York City was fined by the New York City Department of Consumer Affairs for stock splitting.[5]

CHANGING THE PRICE AFTER THE CALL IS MADE.

Sometimes the store will "switch" you from what you called to buy simply by telling you that the price has gone up since the last advertisement was placed. Of course, it's hard for you, the consumer, to argue, since in any particular instance, they might be telling you the truth based on changing market conditions. A much more sophisticated variant of this practice is to call you up *after* the sale is made with the news that the wrong price was given because the price has since increased. If the salesperson is friendly and you know you are still getting a good deal anyway, this approach can be very effective. The store gets you to call but still switches you to the going mail-order price.

EXCESSIVE HANDLING EXPENSE.

Handling expense can vary tremendously. At one extreme it may be only 1 or 2 percent of the cost of the merchandise. At the other extreme it may be 10 percent or more (which is a lot on a $2,000 camcorder, for example). By combining postage and handling as an all-encompassing amount, a firm may subtly suggest that the entire fee is some nonnegotiable charge by United Parcel Service or the Postal Service, when actually the firm has tacked on a vague handling charge to the actual shipping costs. Some firms even claim that their charge covers insurance as well. What they don't usually tell you is how much of the fee is actual postage, how much is some arbitrary handling charge (which can easily eclipse the low price you thought you were getting), and how much of your $1,500 camcorder the "insurance" will be covering.

We consider these elusive charges a form of bait and switch, too, because they lead you to pay more than the advertised price for an item plus a reasonable shipping charge; these charges make the advertised price false and misleading. Here's one way this kind of switching works: a man from Texas saw an RCA TV advertised by a New York firm in both the *New York Times* and in *Modern Photography*. Over the phone, he was told that shipping costs would be about $40. He checked this cost again, since he lived in a small and out-of-the-way town, and the operator repeated $40 and guaranteed that charges would be under $50 in any case. But the actual bill came to $72.43. Since the firm claimed that the original estimate was $60 to $70 and reflected the actual cost of shipping and handling, however, the man had no recourse but to pay it or sue. Similarly, the same firm charged a corporate president from Clearwater, Florida, $63 for shipping a Canon PC24 Copier and accessories. When he called UPS, however, he found that the actual UPS charge was a third less. He called up the mail-order firm, only to be informed, contrary to what he had been told when he bought the merchandise, that the rest of the cost reflected a "handling" charge. Only well-documented complaints on company stationery led the firm to change its mind and send the executive a check for $38!

CHARGING EXTRA FOR CREDIT CARDS.

Some mail-order companies will attempt to charge you more for ordering with credit cards. In certain states, including New York, this practice is illegal. But in other areas it's quite common to see a tantalizing price in an ad, only to call, charge it to your credit card, and find yourself paying up to 5 percent more—which can mean $75 more on a $1,500 computer disk drive.

This kind of bait and switch has also been reported in mail-order companies' walk-in operations. When Mr. W. of New York City was about to purchase a Smith-Corona 1000 typewriter from one of these firms, for example, he noticed that the tag on the typewriter read: "$169.99 (cash)." When Mr. W. said he'd be paying by American Express, the salesman tacked on an additional $8.50 (5 percent), to make a total cost of $178.49. Had Mr. W. paid by check, he learned, the salesperson would have tacked on 3 percent. As Mr. W. noted, if the store had stated that the actual price of the typewriter was $178.49 with a 5 percent discount for cash and a 2 percent discount for checks, consumers would have been able to make a sensible decision. As it stood, however, they were baited into buying the typewriter by the low price, only to be switched to the higher price just for using a credit card.

MIXING CHEAPER PARTS WITH THE ORDERED MERCHANDISE.

Mail-order firms sometimes bundle name-brand merchandise with no-name merchandise. A fancy camera, for example, may be repackaged with a cheap lens from another company. Alternatively, a brand-name computer may be packaged with a no-name hard drive, graphics card, and so forth. You may be told that all the parts aren't from the prestigious manufacturer, in which case the practice is perfectly acceptable. But far too often, you may simply be sold the mixed set of goods.

For example, when Mr. D. of Torrance, California, ordered a particular model Minolta camera from a New York mail-order firm, he was quoted the price of $174.90 for the camera and $10.90 for an "original Minolta case," as well as approximately $8 for shipping. A few days later he called to verify the price and this time was quoted $179 for the camera. And when he called several days later to cancel another order he found that the price of the case had risen to $13.60. Despite these price switches, Mr. D. eventually ordered the Minolta but received with it a less expensive case (not the Minolta), a cheaper-brand filter, and lesser-grade batteries than he had specified.

When computers are involved, this sort of bait and switch can be quite costly. In November 1985 Dr. K. from Glenview, Illinois, purchased a Compaq 286 Deskpro computer with a 59.8-megabyte hard-disk drive from a well-known New York mail-order firm. The Compaq is a 16-bit macroprocessing computer, and its hard disk needs a controlling board made by Compaq to "run" the hard disk as the computer was designed. Dr. K.'s nightmare began in July 1986, however, when his computer broke down, and he brought it to a local repair service. Here he discovered that the wrong controlling board was placed on the computer. He also learned from Compaq that the firm that had sold him the computer was not an authorized dealer and could not purchase the correct board directly. Even so, Dr. K. returned the failed hard disk and the controlling board to the firm, since he had bought the computer in good faith. All he got, however, was a runaround from the firm's customer-service and technical-support departments, with vague stories blaming

Federal Express for losing the part. Eventually Dr. K. had to purchase the board locally.

Walk-in Switching

In some of the smaller walk-in retailers today, you can see some of the more old-fashioned and blatant forms of bait and switch. For example, several times we've seen superstores advertising camcorders at ridiculously low prices in Boston-area papers. We call up and ask if a particular model is available. They say yes. And then when we've gone out of our way to visit the store, they tell us that it was "just" sold out. We've also found that even large superstores will assure a caller that a particular model is in stock and selling for a particular price, only to inform the poor soul once he or she has arrived an hour later that there must have been some mistake: the model is no longer in stock.

Sometimes you only hear about these practices after the fact. A salesperson from Lectra City, a major New England chain that went out of business in 1988, admitted to us that his employer would advertise one model four weeks in a row and never have more than one or two available. "I couldn't believe some of the stuff we got away with," he said. "On Sunday morning we were told to say that at twelve-thirty, we were sold out. The store opened at twelve. . . . Between twelve and twelve-thirty . . . we'd say the stock truck was late [even though we knew we weren't expecting another truck until Thursday]. . . . After twelve-thirty we just had to say they're out of stock, and we may have more later. If they persisted, we gave them a scrap of paper with a handwritten note that said 'Lectra City rain check for model XXXX.' "

He added that Lectra City would often run a sale ad for a VCR but have only one model in the store to sell. Or they'd have "one to show, and one to go. And, of course, we wouldn't sell the demo. . . . The philosophy at Lectra was. 'The more [people] you draw in, the more you can switch.' "

Major chains do occasionally get cited for bait and switch, of course. Bradlees and Sears, for example, have both been fined in past years for not carrying enough advertised merchandise in their stores.[6] Other stores still practice a variation on the out-of-stock theme, as well, by issuing "rain checks." The vice-president of marketing for a large consumer-electronics firm told us how this works: "There's lots of bait and switch going on, especially with popular brands like Panasonic and Sony. The store will advertise these brands at cost. Then they'll offer the consumer a substitution. Or they'll issue a rain check and just wait until the manufacturer's price comes down. The price on everything always comes down. Manufacturers and others always start at a high price—like real estate brokers—and then it comes down bit by bit. By the time the consumer gets the item, it costs less." In other words, you either get switched right away or you end up waiting months for your television set, by which time you're not getting such a great deal after all.

In the major electronics superstores and chains, however, this type of blatant bait and switch is practically nonexistent. The overwhelming feeling today among the big chains is that traditional bait and switch is bad business and that only the dumber retailers practice it. All store policies that we know of strenuously denounce the practice and threaten employees with dismissal if they disparage any of the merchandise on the floor. Instead, the major type of bait and switch today doesn't fit the textbooks.

The only difference between this practice and old-fashioned bait and switch is that the salespeople are more careful not to disparage advertised merchandise. They can do the dirty deed without outright lying: they simply won't sell it to you. For example, most retailers today have policies that practically force employees to engage in a variation of this new bait and switch (or what is more euphemistically called "stepping up the customer") if they are to earn a living. Almost all the major chains make employees earn the lion's share of their wages from commissions they make on selling merchandise. Thus, at one chain, salespeople earn a 1 percent commission on everything they sell, but earn the majority of their living from "spiffs" on particular items. A spiff is a bonus that a salesperson receives for selling selected merchandise; the most profitable items offer the most irresistible spiffs. For example, a $170 Sharp TV might net the salesperson a $1.70 commission, but a $300 Mitsubishi TV might net the salesperson a $3.00 commission plus a $12 spiff. If that salesperson sells many of the advertised Sharps, he or she is clearly not going to be able to support a family.

Superstores put stiff pressure on salespeople to sell specific merchandise by giving the biggest commissions and spiffs to them. A Fretter salesperson told us that he gets a $5.50 minimum wage for "things like a snowstorm when nobody comes in. But watch out if you don't at least make minimum wage in commissions for two weeks in a row. Watch out! The first week you get grief. The second week you get the ax." He added that at his store salespeople are expected to generate at least twenty-two points' margin for Fretter. Managers get reports twice daily on how much margin each salesperson is bringing in. In some stores, such as Sears Brand Central, moreover, sales staff are paid straight commission instead of a base salary.[7]

In the extreme, the commission system tempts individual salespeople to take the business of disparaging merchandise into their own hands. As one salesperson told us, "You can adjust the yoke on the back of the TV so that no matter what you adjust, it looks fuzzy." Other salespeople report using magnets behind a TV to distort the picture. A similar approach is to adjust, say, the picture controls on a TV—but not just any picture controls: only those that 99 percent of consumers wouldn't know to change. For example, on most Sony models today, there is a "picture" button that has a different shape and position than the more well known controls for contrast, brightness, and tint. A salesperson can turn this picture control all the way so that no matter how long customers twiddle the other controls, the picture will remain distorted. For the one in one hundred customers who know about this picture button (or to the store manager patrolling for this kind of practice), the crafty salesperson can always explain that a "previous customer must have fiddled with it."

Again, we don't know of any major store that officially encourages this type of bait and switch or that wouldn't fire an employee immediately who was caught practicing it, but we also know that the major stores put their employees under great pressure to "sell up" to the profitable merchandise that both the store and salespeople make their living on. It's a question of de jure versus de facto. Perhaps the most interesting thing about these commissions, in fact, is the complete secrecy with which stores and salespeople regard them. There is a deep feeling that if consumers knew how much salespeople and the store made on different items, this would put them at a competitive disadvantage—and also be very embarrassing. In fact, in our dozens of interviews with salespeople, the single most difficult thing for us to get them to tell us was their commission rates and so-called spiffs. Many salespeople would be amazingly open about just about any store policy, but when it came to commissions, they would immediately clam up. In general, we found that asking directly how one's commissions worked was like asking for the most intimate information about one's sex life. And even when we asked discreetly, the amount of outright lying or misleading innuendo was amazing. Often we got three or four different answers in the course of an interview, with the talk opening up as conversation went on. Only by making it clear that we already knew how the industry worked and that we knew many of the details of the chain at which the interviewee worked were we able to get even reasonably frank answers.

Switching people is easy once a low price draws them into the store. The advertised stuff often turns out to be such junk that no one would want to buy it anyway; there's no need to disparage it or claim it's out of stock. The consumer just has to look at it to know he or she doesn't want it. All the salesperson has to do is damn it with faint praise (e.g., "The energy rating on this air conditioner is awful, but it's cheap"), and the consumer, of his or her own volition, is switched off to other goods.

Sometimes all the salesperson has to do is *show* the item, and the customers make the switch on their own. For example, one store advertised a major-brand dishwasher that another salesperson called ". . . dogmeat. It has no insulation. It's being sold at cost. When you open the door, you see loose hinges. No woman would ever buy this." But of course, once a customer's in the store, chances are high that that's where the customer will make his or her purchase. Alternatively, a store may advertise a discontinued model or poor-quality brand (advertising a 19-inch TV by a "major brand," for example, without identifying the specific brand); only after going into the store will you find out what you can expect for your money. At absurdly low prices superstores advertise camcorders without playback, autofocus, or zoom; they advertise refrigerators without crispers and that come only in white and have a few cheap, wire shelves; they advertise washer-dryers with poor energy efficiencies and no delicate cycles, temperature controls, water-level controls, or lint filters.

"We advertise a 13-inch green TV by A-Mark," the Fretter salesperson told us. "It has no remote and it has a voractor tuner. And, of course, most people don't want a green TV. One reason we don't put a brand on the ad is so that if we ran out of the piece we can substitute another one that fits the same description. . . . We get a zero commission for selling this TV."

In retail lingo, the low-priced model used in the advertisement is called the "leader item," or "call-out item," because it leads to other models and calls customers into the stores. The model you get switched to is called the "step piece," because the salesperson tries to "step you up" to it. One superstore, for example, uses the Glenwood GAP22AA as the leader items and advertises it for $199.98. The store doesn't make any money by selling this piece, but it banks on stepping you up to the Hotpoint RB734, which sells for $329.98. One salesperson told us that the Sony KV1926 television is the biggest leader piece around. It costs a retailer $270 and it's advertised for only $279—clearly not enough profit to justify the sale. Again, the idea is to step customers up to a better-profit television once they're in the store.

Such practices are so widespread that even the highly reputable National Association of Retail Dealers of America (NARDA) encourages them in its educational materials for retailers. In NARDA's management aid on "price point merchandising," for example, Advisory Board member Dick Donaldson of Sid's Appliance in Tucson, Arizona, tells retailers: "You might want to position well-known (demand line) models at lower price points—and then use in-store selling skills to move the customers up to the more profitable models."

One salesperson explained to us how the store he had worked at, a well-known and highly reputable New England chain, would step up customers. "They wouldn't pay us a good commission on something advertised," he told us. "They want you to step up to items called 'Outstanding Value'—which they make better money on. These are actually called 'Outstanding Values" in the store. They're also sometimes called "unadvertised specials.' These are one of the salesperson's guideposts as to what to push. People like to think they're saving money, so they'll often buy one of these rather than whatever it was they saw advertised."

In the case of the green TV at Fretter, the step-up procedure would work as follows, explains a salesperson we interviewed: First the green TV would be advertised for $159.95. Then the escape piece is the Goldstar TV for $179. The step piece—the RCA TV for $200. Finally, the sell piece is the Hitachi TV for $250. What all these terms mean—*advertised piece, escape piece, step piece,* and *sell piece*—is that you just don't jump from a $159.95 TV to a $250 TV, but make sure that you have "bridge" pieces to guide customers along.[8]

Sometimes this switch can actually save consumers from their own ignorance. For example, retailers are almost forced to bait people with Sony models because many people *assume* Sony is always the highest quality. "We used the Sony KV1967 to draw people in, and we used the Toshiba CF917 as the step piece," the former salesperson for Lectra City told us. "In some cases we sold it at the same price. In some cases we charged $10 more for the Toshiba with the remote. We would tell people that since we ran out of the Sonys, we were selling the Toshibas for the same price even though they're a better value than the Sony. Toshiba had a one-year warranty, and the Sony had only ninety days, for example.

The Toshiba had a remote; the Sony didn't. Both have comparable prices. The Toshiba really was a better value."

He added that at Lectra City "learning to step was a way of life, not just a way of selling." Of course, sometimes, as in the case of the Sony above, both the salesperson and the customer profited, he said: the salesperson got a better commission by selling a Toshiba, and the customer got a better TV. Even so, the customer did not end up buying what he or she came in the store to buy.

"No salesperson is going to sell you something he's not going to make money on," a Highland salesperson told us. "Some people have the crazy idea that we're a public service. If you buy an ad piece and have a problem—good luck to you. You're not going to get any help. If the salesperson didn't make any money on you, he's not going to want to help you."

In the most extreme cases, a manufacturer may actually be paying a salesperson outright to push its particular merchandise. For example, IBM apparently was offering Businessland special incentives to sell its machines, such as larger margins on IBM computer sales. When Businessland started paying commissions on IBM computers four times higher than on Compaqs, Compaq dropped Businessland as a retailer.[9] Consider, too, the advice of an article on this practice that recently ran in *PC Week:* "Caveat Emptor. . . . The next time you go into your local computer store to buy a PC, the person behind the counter may not be as impartial as you think. . . . In fact, chances are, a major computer manufacturer is paying the salesperson's salary—or a portion of it."[10]

Salespeople have developed many simple ways to mysteriously "disappear" if they don't want to sell you something. A Chicago electronics dealer told us about a time he went into a major superstore, ad in tow, trying to purchase a VCR that he knew the store was selling at a loss. He figured he'd just buy up three or four of these VCRs at the below-dealer-cost price and then sell them at his own store for a small profit. However, no matter how many salespeople he tapped on the shoulder or how long he waited at the sales desk, no one would wait on him. The VCR might have been advertised to get people into the store, he said, but the superstore would be damned if anyone actually bought one of the things. And yet, no overt disparagement or claims of "out of stock" occurred.

The president of a Boston appliance chain told us a similar story. "I saw a GE TV advertised at Highland for $187," he said. "I knew my cost for this TV was $197, and I know that Nationwide, my buying group, can buy it as cheap as anyone. So I called the GE guy up just to make sure that this price was for real and he said, 'Yup, Highland is selling it for $10 below cost.' " At that point he went over to Highland to buy the TV. "The salesman wouldn't let me buy it for ten minutes," he continued. "He kept trying to sell me on a Sanyo. When I agreed, he tried to sell me the service contract. Only at that point did they finally let me buy the GE too."

As for walking in with a consumer magazine and demanding the specific model at the top of a ratings chart, forget it. "Don't walk into a store with *Consumer Reports*," one salesperson for a major superstore told us, and many others have confirmed his advice. "We won't wait on you. People who carry around these magazines are unlikely to buy at the time. They ask a lot of questions. They want to see model numbers that are discontinued. And they don't trust you when you try to sell them something else."

Again, the sad truth is that it's just plain uneconomical for a salesperson to try to waste his or her time to sell you some of the lower-margin merchandise. In fact, there are many rumors circulating (though none confirmed) that salespeople in certain establishments are fired for selling too many leader items. Therefore, the salesperson who was so eager to please when you first walked in might, for example, go to "see if it is in stock," once you ask for something that gives a low commission. After quickly finding another customer with better prospects, the salesperson may not reappear on your part of the sales floor for half an hour.

Another subtle way stores find to "switch" you to the higher-margin items is to identify the sales items poorly. You may think a good way to avoid being "sold up" is to go in and locate the sale merchandise on your own, then simply walk over to the cash register and buy it. Unfortunately, it's often nearly impossible to find a specific model without getting a salesperson's help. You can go wander about the 150 or so TVs in a superstore for fifteen minutes, for example, never actually locating the advertised items. While you're looking, there's a good chance some salesperson will latch onto you and sell you up to something else (conveniently forgetting about the sale item). And, of course, the pricetag on the floor piece may have nothing to do with the advertised price in the newspaper.

The president of a Boston-area electronics store told us that the reason it's so difficult to find many of the leader items is that "they're nail-down items." Retailers simply don't plan to let them leave the sales floor. He adds that another reason that it can be hard to locate advertised merchandise is because the store wants you to get a good look at the other merchandise (and at least ask the salesperson to locate the advertised model) before finding the advertised model and making the purchase.[11]

"Bundling" is yet another way to bait people into a store and get them to buy something they didn't intend to buy. Much like the stock splitting of mail-order firms, this in-store practice has retailers advertise a base item at a ridiculously low price, only to reveal at the cash register that to take advantage of this price you have to purchase some other much less well priced article. In the cellular-phone industry, for instance, retailers often offer low-priced phones that turn out to be available only when you buy a cellular contract with a specific company at a fixed price. In mid-1990 seven cellular-phone retailers were accused by the Michigan attorney general's office of using misleading advertisements in the sale of phone equipment, and law-enforcement agents and regulators in Illinois, Pennsylvania, Texas, Colorado, and California were looking into the practice.[12]

Another way retailers subtly switch consumers these days is through sins of omissions rather than commission. Basically, a salesperson compares two models and emphasizes the strong points of the one he or she wants to sell. Most consumers are so confused by these products that they are easily overwhelmed. How many people have the persistence, after all, to argue that there are only 250 lines of resolution on a TV when the salesperson shrugs and says that's impossible to believe from such a high-tech brand? Consumers are so confused that outright lying is often quite unnecessary.

Finally, walk-in retailers can also switch you to lesser-quality items in a similar fashion to mail-order firms. They might display a new model, for example, but then pull a refurbished version or resealed box (B-grade merchandise) out of the back room for you, say some salespeople we've interviewed. Worse still, you might see a new car stereo on the retail floor, only to have a B-grade unit installed by a technician. You may never know the difference, unless, of course, the stereo breaks down.[13]

MANUFACTURERS ENCOURAGE BAIT AND SWITCH TOO

You might wonder why manufacturers would allow their merchandise to be used for bait and switch. As a matter of fact, they don't—in the sense of the old-fashioned form: they constantly police the retailers for advertising their brand and then maligning it or claiming that it's out of stock. They may even sue a retailer who disparages their product.[14] Indeed, a major reason that the leading manufacturers engage in the price fixing we discussed in the last chapter is to counteract the endemic efforts by retailers to bait customers with competitive brands and switch them to uncompetitive ones. In this sense, there are checks and balances between retailers and manufacturers, and these checks and balances can sometimes work to the consumer's benefit.

The major manufacturers that have demand lines (brands such as Sony and Panasonic that attract people into stores) vigorously police retail dealers for bait and switch. They hate it when retailers use their brand names to draw people into the store and then switch them to another brand. And as long as vertical price-fixing laws remain relatively lax, manufacturers have even more power to limit bait and switch at the retail level; for all practical purposes, they now can control the minimum advertised selling price of their products, which stores formerly lowered ridiculously to "bait" customers. And indeed, that's just what they've done.[15]

However, manufacturers' dislike of bait and switch only goes so far. In fact, the new form of bait and switch is actually beneficial to them as well as retailers. As many salespeople have told us, the deal goes like this: The manufacturer says to the retailer, "Sure, I'll provide you with some low-quality product that we both know no one will want. I'll sell it for cost, and you can too. But the deal is that I'll expect you to also sell a reasonable amount of our step-up items, the stuff we both make money on."

Thus, although manufacturers may hate it when stores use bait and switch to switch customers to *other* brands, they seem to have no objections when stores use bait and switch to step the customer up to a pricier model of the *same* brand.

Sony even issues a sheet to retailers called "Suggested Profit Picture Guidelines." In this document, the company lists all its models along with a price called "ad pull." This is the price Sony recommends advertising to bring the customers into the store, or "bait 'em," as the president of a consumer-electronics firm told us. "Sony doesn't want their products baited for other brands, but they're happy to do it for their own products," he told us. An ad-pull item is basically the same as a leader item, although leaders tend to make a little money, whereas ad-pull items make virtually none. "You do sell ad-pull items," he told us, "but you just figure you'll make your money on the other stuff" (see Figure 4-1).

A Highland salesperson from Boston agrees. "It's the manufacturer who orchestrates the whole step-up strategy—for example, not putting fifty cents of insulation on a dishwasher just to scare off consumers. Virtually all manufacturers have a piece like this. But then they do it because the retailers want and need it."

Sometimes manufacturers engage in variants of bait and switch more directly. Some encourage retailers to advertise a model at its sales price less rebate, and then essentially force the consumer to spend extra money to get the rebate. For example, we recently saw some Energizer batteries advertised for $1.71. When we went to purchase them we noticed that the sticker price was $2.71 but that there was a $1 rebate. Now to get that $1 rebate, you first had to pay 5 percent Massachusetts sales tax on the larger amount. Next, you had to send in a hard-to-find rebate coupon. Moreover, you were obliged to pay for the envelope and postage. We figured 5 cents for extra sales tax, twenty-nine cents for postage, six cents for a personalized envelope, six cents for processing the rebate check at our local bank, and one cent for lost interest on the dollar (it took more than ten weeks to get the rebate check). Thus, the net rebate to us was really $0.53, not $1.00, and that doesn't even include the value of our time to do all the necessary work to get that $0.53. This isn't traditionally thought of as bait and switch, but it shares all the classic ingredients.[16]

THE PROBLEM OF PROOF

Even given the retailer's strong financial incentives, how can a salesperson keep you from buying what you really want to buy? It's easy, actually. Given consumer ignorance about these products, it's simple enough to switch people to buy what you want them to buy if they don't know what they want in the first place. In old-fashioned bait and switch, a store would advertise a specific model and then have to persuade the customer to buy another one. Today, customers often don't even know what specific model they want, so the switch is less blatant. What good does a retailer get from advertising a specific model at a low price when no one recognizes that model to begin with? Stores, say the salespeople we've interviewed, now advertise attractive prices ("price points") rather than attractive models, which makes the lure only implicit. For example,

SUGGESTED PROFIT PICTURE GUIDELINES
*** DISPLAY PRODUCTS ***
EFFECTIVE JANUARY 1, 1988

MODEL	SUGGESTED RETAIL	PROFIT SELL	SUGGESTED ADV. RANGE		COMMENTS
KV1367	339.95	249.00		CLOSEOUT	AD PULL
KV1326R	399.95	299.00	279.00 -	299.00	AD PULL
KV1380R	479.95	479.95	399.00 -	479.95	STEP SELL
KV1967	459.95	329.00		CLOSEOUT	AD PULL
KV1926R	499.95	379.00		OPEN	AD PULL
KV1981R	649.95	469.00	429.00 -	469.00	AD PULL
KV2040R	549.95	449.00	399.00 -	449.00	LEADER
KV2071R	579.95	449.00	429.00 -	449.00	BRIDGE
KV2075R	599.95	469.00	449.00 -	469.00	BRIDGE
KV2080R	729.95	529.00	499.00 -	529.00	STEP SELL
KV2084R	829.95	OPEN	481.00 -	499.00	AD PULL
KV20HFR	999.95	799.00	749.00 -	799.00	STEP SELL
KV2726R	849.95	599.00	567.00 -	599.00	AD PULL
KV2775R	999.95	749.00	699.00 -	749.00	BRIDGE
KV2781R	1099.95	899.00	799.00 -	849.00	BRIDGE
KV2780R	1149.95	949.00	899.00 -	949.00	STEP SELL
KV27HFR	1249.95	1099.00	999.00 -	1099.00	STEP SELL
KV27DS2	999.95	949.00	899.00 -	949.00	STEP SELL
KV27DS1	1149.95	999.00	949.00 -	999.00	STEP SELL
KV2782R	1249.95	1099.00	999.00 -	1099.00	BRIDGE
KV2783R	1299.95	1149.00	1049.00 -	1149.00	STEP SELL
KV2785R	1599.95	1399.00	1299.00 -	1399.00	STEP SELL
KV2786R	1599.95	1599.95	1399.00 -	1599.95	STEP SELL
KV27AVR	2399.95	2299.95	1999.00 -	2299.95	STEP SELL
ACCESS202	2299.95	2199.00	1999.00 -	2199.00	SPECIALTY
KPR36XBR	2499.95	1999.00	1799.00 -	1999.00	LEADER
KPR4110	2499.95	2199.00	1999.00 -	2199.00	BRIDGE
KPR4620	3199.95	2699.00	2499.00 -	2699.00	STEP SELL
KPR41DS1	3099.95	2699.00	2499.00 -	2699.00	STEP SELL
FD10A	119.95	99.00	89.00	99.00	AD PULL
FD10A NFL	119.95	99.00	89.00	99.00	AD PULL
FD2A	159.95	149.00	139.00 -	149.00	BRIDGE
FD35A	169.95	159.00	149.00 -	159.00	BRIDGE
FD3A	189.95	179.00	179.00	189.95	STEP SELL
FD42A	159.95	149.00	129.00 -	149.00	AD PULL
FD45A	259.95	229.00	229.00 -	259.95	STEP SELL

revised: 01/15/88

FIG. 4–1. SONY'S PROFIT PICTURE GUIDELINES THAT WERE DISTRIBUTED TO AUTHORIZED DEALERS IN 1988. Note the bait-and-switch strategy of having a low-margin "ad pull" item leading to higher margin "bridge" and "step sell" items. Note, too, the discrepancy between the so-called "suggested retail" price and what Sony really suggests the dealer sell the item for under "profit sell." The "suggested advertising range" in effect told the dealer the lowest acceptable advertising price. The Sony dealer who provided us with the chart told us that he routinely bought the "ad pull" models for just a bit less than the "step sell" models, but by advertising both at the minimum advertised price he could make almost no margins on the former (e.g., 60 cents on a $278.40 TV) but huge margins on the latter (e.g., over $100 on a $296 TV).

they advertise the fact that they have a 19-inch color TV selling for $199—a price that seems low for that kind of equipment. They advertise that they're selling a full-sized refrigerator for only $250. That's about all consumers can handle. It's what gets them in the store. As one salesperson from a major superstore told us: "A good value on a specific model may not have as much advertising value. When a consumer sees such a TV for less than $200, though, he thinks, 'this place must have low prices.'" The customer is then ripe for being switched to a profitable item.

Besides being ignorant, most consumers also are extremely insecure about their knowledge of complex electronics and appliances in the face of a supposedly savvy salesperson. You may go in there, ad and *Consumer Reports* in hand, sure that you want a particular Fisher rack system. But suddenly standing there, talking to a slick salesman who tells you that *Consumer Reports* writers are inept when it comes to audio and that only acoustic Neanderthals buy rack systems, you may feel compelled to "save face" by looking at the high-priced components the salesperson shows you. Similarly, if you're standing in front of two pairs of speakers and hear the salesperson, who supposedly lives and breathes stereo systems, proclaim how much "clearer" one of the pairs is, you may feel embarrassed to say that, frankly, they both sound identical to you.

This new kind of bait and switch is so subtle that most people don't even know it's happening. If a mail-order firm calls to switch a price on you, you're most likely to assume that in this particular instance it really had to do so. If a retailer doesn't rave about the model you're after, you're most likely to assume that the retailer knows more than you do, and you probably were going after an inferior brand. If a salesperson tells you that you have to pay for a case for the camcorder, you're most likely to assume that the camera doesn't normally include the case. Very few people will know enough about their purchases—or have enough confidence in their knowledge—to fight back against such tactics. After all, whom else do they have to consult? It's either the salesperson or no one. Fighting the system will just make you miserable.

Even if you do suspect the new tactics of bait and switch, moreover, they're almost impossible to prove. Because these tactics are so subtle, any individual case can be easily explained away. Reading consumer complaints and store actions makes this quite clear. Someone complains, for example, that a mail-order firm called back to raise the price of a camcorder *after* the order had been made. After three or four detailed letters of complaint to the attorney general and bureau of consumer affairs, the firm finally replies that this event was an isolated incident; although the company tries to keep its prices low, the shifting yen-to-dollar ratio occasionally forces the company to change prices at a moment's notice. Similarly, someone complains that a salesperson refused to sell her the specific Panasonic camcorder she was after and sells her a JVC instead, but, again, after vigorous complaints about bait and switch, the store replies that there must have been some misunderstanding, that of course the store will be happy to refund the customer's money or sell her the Panasonic. Retailers also correctly observe that there are lots of cranks out there who will complain about anything; a few stories don't prove anything at all.

Although we agreed that people make mistakes and that some complaints are unjustified, there is no doubt that these subtle forms of bait and switch happen frequently. First of all, the many salespeople we interviewed have told us so. Second, there are far too many letters of complaint about these sorts of occurrences to let us believe the events are just random slipups. Third, if these practices were really just innocent mistakes or justifiable behaviors, then why do consumers have to go through the attorney general's office to get retailers to respond? And, finally, articles in the trade press acknowledge that major chains like Sears offer variable commissions based on a unit's profitability and pay salespeople more to step up customers to noncompetitive (e.g., Kenmore) merchandise.[17] Even more telling, the Texas attorney general won a lawsuit in late 1989 in which Highland agreed to pay the state $50,000 in fees and costs and not to engage in deceptive advertising. The attorney general alleged that the superstore used "bait and switch" tactics on consumers "by advertising cheap merchandise (baiting) to get customers into Highland stores and having no intention of selling the cheap merchandise, but rather to switch customers to more expensive merchandise.[18]

On a somewhat brighter side, we can expect—at least for the time being—a continuing decline in the more hard-core forms of the practice. Not only will old-fashioned bait and switch remain pointless as long as consumers remain largely ignorant of complex electronics and appliances, but as long as price-fixing is rampant, guaranteeing meaningless "lowest prices" or having constant but meaningless "sales" are better tactics than bait and switch: after all, hard-core bait and switch presupposes that a merchant can advertise a model at a lower price than a competitor who carries the same model, and with price-fixing rampant, there simply isn't much merchandise that can be advertised at prices low enough to bait customers. Of course, we can expect price-fixing eventually to let up and retailers to swing back to bait and switch or other merchandising tricks in keeping with laws and regulations currently enforced—as long as consumer ignorance is there to allow them to do so.

In the meantime, how can you avoid being taken by such practices? We've come up with one fairly simple strategy ourselves for determining whether firms act ethically: although we've found that the BBB's and attorneys general are practically worthless when it comes to giving blunt advice, we've found that retailers will say the worst things about their competitors, particularly those engaging in unethical practices. The key is to get them in a position where it's very strongly to their advantage to disparage their competitors' pricing strategy. Whenever you get a particularly good price from one firm, we recommend calling or visiting other firms with the same model at a higher price and asking them if they think it is possible that everything is aboveboard at the low-priced store. If phrased with due deference and humility—a retailer may hesitate at first to disparage competitors' practices—your question will often get a remarkably frank and insightful answer. The problem with this approach is that it can take quite a bit of time and effort. But until the large-scale and impartial sources of consumer information are allowed to speak out as we describe in the last part of this book, it may be the only choice.

1. See, for example, sec. 7, "Bait Advertising and Selling," in the *Code of Advertising* (Boston: Sanders Report by the Consumer Affairs Foundation in Boston, 1985), pp. 10–11.

2. The examples described in this chapter represent actual experiences as reported in letters of complaint by the consumers. Some of these cases were resolved to the consumer's satisfaction after several letters. The purpose of the description is to illustrate certain practices, not to imply guilt or illegal action in any particular case, and therefore, unless we relied on other sources as well, we omit names of specific retailers obtained from these complaints.

3. In 1990, however, the major superstore Best Buy paid $200,000 to settle charges by the Missouri General of, among other practices, advertising merchandise with the intention of switching them to other products by means of "product non-availability, product disparagement, and/or product location and tagging within the retail stores." State of Missouri, ex rel., William L. Webster, Attorney General of the State of Missouri, Plaintiff vs. Best Buy Co. Inc., a Minnesota Corporation. . . . Petition for Permanent Injunction, Civil Penalties, Restitution and Ancillary Relief, p. 7. Best Buy also promised to avoid prohibited practices in the future.

4. "Dealer Profits Are Growing Despite Sickly CPU Margins," *Computer Reseller News*, April 17, 1989, p. 3. See also Adam Greenberg, "As PC Margins Ebb, Mass Merchants Heed the Call of Profit-Rich Peripherals," *Home Furnishings Daily*, June 6, 1988, p. 183.

5. "Consumer Affairs Reaches Agreement with Grand Central Camera," New York City Department of Consumer Affairs press release, January 19, 1988.

6. "Bradlees and Sears Face Fines for Out-of-Stocks," *Discount Store News*, January 18, 1988, p. 3.

7. "Sears' Brand Central Units Opening in the Chicago Area," *Home Furnishings Daily*, May 15, 1989, p. 106.

8. See also Manning Greenberg, "Philips' Segmented Market Strategy Brings Sales Approaching $2 Billion," *Home Furnishings Daily*, June 26, 1989, p. 93.

9. G. Zachary and Andy Zipser, "Businessland Is Compaq's Land Yet Once Again," *Wall Street Journal*, March 8, 1990, sec. B, p. 1, and James Miller and Karen Blumenthal, "Compaq Computer Drops Businessland as Distributor," *Wall Street Journal*, February 22, 1989, sec. B, p. 1.

10. "PC Makers Pay Retail Personnel Salary," *PC Week*, November 21, 1988, p. 76. For other discussions of step-up tactics, see Andrew Gaffney, "*TWICE* Report: Outlook for Changing Retail Market," *TWICE*, July 31–August 4, 1989, p. 28, and Robert B. Cialdini, *Influence: The New Psychology of Modern Persuasion* (New York: Quill, 1984), pp. 102–103.

11. As long ago as 1967, Senator Warren Magnuson described some of these practices with coauthor Jean Carper. See their *Dark Side of the Marketplace: The Plight of the American Consumer*, 2nd ed. (Englewood Cliffs, N.J.: Prentice-Hall, 1972), pp. 16–17. See also Sophie Julia Zebrowski, "Deceptive Advertising Relating to Product Prices," in *Consumer Protection from Deceptive Advertising*, ser. 10, vol. 3, ed. Fredric Stuart (Hofstra University Yearbook of Business, 1974), p. 312.

12. Julie Lopez, "Marketers Spy and Entice to Get an Edge," *Wall Street Journal*, May 14, 1990, sec. B, p. 1.

13. The New York City Department of Consumer Affairs repeatedly finds electronics stores selling old and reconditioned merchandise as new merchandise. This is analogous to selling gray-market merchandise and not telling the consumer. For example, a February 2, 1989, press release states: "Approximately 90 stores citywide have been cited by Consumer Affairs since August 1987 for misrepresenting reconditioned items as new."

14. See, for example, "GE Appliances Broadens Program Regulating Prices Advertised by Dealers," *Home Furnishings Daily*, January 23, 1989, p. 148; "Zenith Features Video, Sets Pricing Policy," *Home Furnishings Daily*, June 20, 1988; and Manning Greenberg, "Electronics Giant Sees Big Growth for 'Smart House' Device in the 1990s," *Home Furnishings Daily*, June 6, 1988, p. 96.

15. See, for example, "Panasonic Charges Retailer with Rigging Demonstrations," *Home Furnishings Daily*, September 19, 1988, pp. 91–92; "Nix on the Fix," *TWICE*, August 28–September 1, 1989, p. 6; Ira Teinowitz, "TV Makers Zap Price-Cutters," *Advertising Age*, June 6, 1988, p. 2; and Bob Gerson, "Zenith Co-op Rules Tighten: Won't Pay for Low-Ball Promos," *TWICE*, June 6, 1988, p. 1.

16. Recognizing the unethical tactics involved here, some state consumer-protection bureaus, such as Connecticut's, now consider it illegal to advertise or display an item at its rebated cost. Consumers can find out about the bargain only at the point of purchase.

17. "Sears Banks on Brand Central in Superstore Move," *Home Furnishings Daily*, February 20, 1989, p. 107; Mark Harrington, "Sears Sees 120 Free-Standing Brand Central Units," *Home Furnishings Daily*, February 20, 1989, p. 112; David Jones and Gerry Beatty, "Retailers React to Shifts in Market Conditions," *Home Furnishings Daily*, November 13, 1989, p. 106; and Francine Schwadel, "At Sears, Unpopular Pay Policy Reflects Fuss in Retail Industry," *Wall Street Journal*, January 31, 1990, sec. B, p. 2.

18. Press release issued by the Texas attorney general's office, December 8, 1989.

Service Contracts:
The Challenge of Reading
the Fine Print

It may surprise you to learn that one of the hottest new items in the superstores today doesn't have a single wire, switch, or button. In fact, these items are merely pieces of paper known as "service contracts" or, inaccurately, "extended warranties." These little-known products represent a great new hope for retailers who are having trouble keeping their heads above water. A retailer may be selling some items below cost to keep up with lowest-price guarantees or attract customers from other superstores, but nobody's advertising that they have the "lowest priced" service contract. Basically, the strategy is simple: sell a TV or VCR or camcorder or refrigerator or washing machine or microwave oven for virtually no profit but make a killing on the service contract. Most buyers will never know what hit them.

What is a service contract? Basically, it's an insurance policy on your shiny new appliance.[1] The principle is quite simple. By spending a little money now you can avoid a catastrophic and debilitating loss later on. For example, by spending $500 a year you can buy a medical insurance policy that will give you up to $200,000 in medical payments if you develop cancer. This $200,000 is something you might very well not be able to afford if you had to pay it out of your own pocket. Similarly, by paying $150 for a five-year warranty on a $400 VCR, you can save yourself the risk of paying for repairs which are often prohibitively expensive even for minor problems.

Take the sheet that a Highland salesperson having difficulty selling a service contract would hand you, the reluctant prospect. From the figures there, the cost of repairs seems huge (just like the costs of being stricken with cancer or having your house burn down), and you're immediately attracted to the idea of insurance. Of course, you already have a warranty, but the pitch you'll get about these contracts is that they take over where the warranty gives out. First of all, they may cover certain parts explicitly excluded by the warranty. Secondly, they may cover a longer period of time than the warranty—so if, say, your warranty expires after ninety days, you may have another year or so left with the service contract. Contracts may be administered by an independent service contract company (sometimes under the name of the retailer), by the manufacturer of a particular brand, or by the retailers themselves.

In many ways, this concept makes sense, since labor in particular can be quite costly on expensive and complicated items like televisions and washing machines, and it's nice to know you've already paid your dues. Furthermore, there's no doubt that many of these items tend to break down fairly frequently. Some contracts even cover maintenance and, for example, allow you to get your VCR heads cleaned annually after you pay a minimal deductible. Prices for this "insurance" vary considerably from about $30 to over half the cost of the merchandise, depending on things like the merchandise involved, the length of service, whether you're getting at-home service, and the specific parts covered.

You may be familiar with similar arrangements in the automobile industry, where these sorts of insurance policies have been around for years.[2] But because they're so new in the electronics and appliance world, things work a little differently. Most significantly, *in most states today, service contracts remain a completely unregulated insurance industry.* As commonly happens in unregulated industries, there are numerous fly-by-night agencies waiting to take advantage of unsuspecting consumers (and retailers, for that matter). There are golden opportunities, too, for retailers to tailor contracts highly favorable to themselves. It's not surprising then that service contracts have become *the most profitable item in many superstores.*

While operating our shopping consultation service, we investigated service-contract policies extensively, and we were astonished by what's actually happening on the sales floor. We talked to executives and sales reps at a dozen or so of the largest national service-contract companies, interviewed salespeople, and examined the contracts themselves. As in many slightly shady areas, we found everyone accusing each other of various improprieties but actual proof extremely difficult to come by.

What became clear early on, however, was that consumers knew virtually nothing about these contracts. Such ignorance combined with high-profitability and virtual non-regulation makes for an explosive mix.

THE PRESSURE TO SELL

Before we give the details on service contracts, let's place them in a little perspective. It's a common phenomenon in retailing that the margins on accessories and peripherals are not only a lot larger than on the main sale piece; sometimes they're the only items on which a retailer can make a profit. Thus, familiar computer central processing units are frequently sold virtually at cost because this is what attracts you into the store, and the store makes its money selling you monitors, hard drives, modems, software, and other such peripherals. Similarly, cameras are often sold at cost because the low price on the camera gets you into the store, and then you buy film, the carrying case, extra lenses, and so on.

Service contracts merely represent the latest incarnation in this world of add-ons. And in some cases, such as TVs and washing machines, they may be the only extra the store has to push. Even more important, the service contract may be the only place the store can make any money and subsidize the basic merchandise that has been priced unprofitably. As one Circuit City salesperson told us: "When Circuit City sells a service contract, it makes 100 percent profit. The salesman gets a $7 commission and Circuit puts the rest in its back pocket. If [Circuit City] ever eliminated service contracts, [its] stock would crash thirty-five cents a share. Service contracts are where all the profits are."

Dick Donaldson of Sid's Appliance in Tucson, Arizona, speaking at a retailer conference in 1987, agreed: "Power retailers are made or broke selling service contracts."

According to a recent article in the trade press, an "extended warranty program," has become the main "accessory" for mass retailers and generates sixty to seventy-five percentage points in initial markups.[3] The promotional literature sent by service-contract administrators to super-stores bears this out. The National Electronics Warranty Corporation, for example, tells dealers that its extended-service-contract program can be "the most profitable program in your store," and can "as much as double bottom line profits." Guardian Guarantee claims that dealers can earn "profits of 50% to 100%," while ServicePlan says they can "realize

GROSS MARGINS of 50%, 60% . . . even 70%." Similarly, Warrantech typically suggests selling its plan for nearly 100 percent above dealer cost (even at reputedly bare-bones mail-order houses), Independent Dealer Service's for nearly 200 percent, and American Warranty Group, Inc., for between 200 percent and 250 percent above the dealer's cost.[4]

"Ordinarily, the moment a customer walks out of your store you've lost the opportunity to sell them," says one Video Aid brochure. "Once [the customer is] gone, you can no longer sell any of the high margin add-ons, including the Video Aid Purchase Protection Plan, that can make a sale so profitable."

"By selling Warrantech Plans," claims that company's sales training manual, "you are keeping pace with your competitors, as well as using a valuable closing tool to complete each sale." Transamerica Administrative Services notes that its Service Saver Extended Service Plan program "provides new profit opportunities that require NO investment and NO inventory expense or space." And the president of ServicePlan, Inc., adds in a brochure: "In today's competitive marketplace . . . [s]ervice contracts have literally become not only the key to prosperity, but the key to survival for major electronics and appliance retailers."

According to an analysis by administrators of Universal Protection Plan, Inc., retailers and their salespeople can expect to keep 70 percent of a service contract's cost for themselves. And a trade magazine predicted that sales of extended service contracts will account for about 8 percent of retailers' total sales in 1990, with Sears making 12 percent of its total volume in these contracts.[5] It's no surprise, therefore, that salespeople are under tremendous pressure to sell them. Tempted to push contracts with meaty commissions (often for their managers as well), salespeople have their own reasons for wanting to sell as many as possible. And if they don't want to, management makes sure they will: many stores require their salespeople to sell a contract with a certain quota of sales—often as many as 50 percent.[6] As one former Sears salesperson put it, "The incentive . . . to sell service contracts at Sears is your job."

A salesperson for Montgomery Ward's Electric Avenue told us: "Our management is really pushy on service contracts. They don't even care if we lie in selling them." Explaining that salespeople who don't sell their 50 percent quota "get written up" and lose their jobs within twenty to thirty days, she added that "they don't care about the $1,000 computer sale; they just care about the service contract. When I come in in the morning, my boss doesn't even say, 'Hi, how are you?' He says 'Hi, how are your service contracts?' "

THE PERILS OF CONSUMER IGNORANCE

What is most unsettling, however, is not that stores want to push service contracts but that this whole system is almost completely unknown to the buying public. " 'Last year in the U.S. there was over $800 million worth of consumer electronics warranties sold,' " Robert Minnick, president of ComponentGuard, was quoted as saying in a trade magazine. " 'I would have to say that for 785 million of those dollars, the customers had no idea what they brought.' "[7]

Salespeople typically bring up the idea of buying a service contract only after the customer has decided to purchase a particular item, usually as a casual afterthought. Most frequently, the salesperson will mention that although the manufacturer's warranty is "only ninety days," the store can arrange things so that all parts and labor on repairs will be covered for the next three to five years. Then the salesperson will drop the subject until he or she is actually writing up the bill. At that point, the salesperson will mention the service contract again, which can be arranged for a mere "$150, a great deal considering that it will cost you nearly that much in labor for just one repair." The customer, who's about to shell out $400 anyway for the VCR, figures another $150 is no big deal, especially considering repair costs. The $400 VCR that brings the store $40 in margin is now sold with a $150 service contract that brings the store $100 in margin. The customer, meanwhile, who has nitpicked off about $10 on his VCR, who has scoured the newspaper for local ads, read the video magazines on the newsstands, and shopped competing stores—all in the name of saving a few dollars—this same customer now plunks down a 50 percent premium on the purchase with almost no thought at all.

Why? There are, of course, the irrational reasons. The customer has already made up his or her mind about the purchase. This was a distressing thing to do, and who wants to waver after all that work? At the same time, the customer didn't really know about service contracts and didn't shop around for them ahead of time. Moreover, he or she has a dim sense that even shopping around would have done no good. Stores don't advertise service contracts. Until you've actually decided to buy a piece of equipment, it's considered uncouth to ask for service-contract information. And even when you do seriously want to buy both equipment and a service contract, it is industry practice not to let you look at the actual contract until after you've purchased it. And then, even after you have, the print is so small and hard to read that most people never do.

But the most interesting reason people buy service contracts is that they're often actually good deals. The fact of the matter is that purchased items do occasionally break down, and when they do, it can be fantastically expensive and time-consuming to fix them. Moreover, consumers have a very deep and justified fear of being ripped off by service repair people.[8] Thus, having the peace of mind of a service contract, and a reasonable likelihood that it will save time and money on average, makes it a fairly good deal.

Of course, in a competitive market, the cost of a product would not be based on how much we value it, but on how much it costs us to produce. Thus, most of us would willingly pay $5 for a glass of water if there was no way for us to get it less expensively. But because water is plentiful and inexpensive to provide, most of us would consider it prohibitively expensive to be charged more than, say, 25 cents for a glass of water. But that is exactly what happens with service contracts. Because the system of selling them conspires against competition, we pay, so to speak, for the $5 glass of water rather than the 25-cent glass of water. Moreover, as we shall see, the $5 glass of water often doesn't have everything in it that we are led to believe.

Furthermore, although it makes a certain amount of sense to buy "insurance" for a complex piece of equipment, there are numerous things the customer doesn't consider, and that's just what the salesperson is counting on. First of all, do other stores sell service contracts? Do they sell them with better terms and costs on that particular model? For that matter, how often do VCRs actually break down? Do they tend to break down after the manufacturer's warranty has expired—in which case a service contract actually might be a good idea? How long is the manufacturer's warranty anyway—and what are its terms? Does the contract really cover the major causes of VCR breakdown—such as toddlers putting cherry licorice into the drive? Does the contract require a deductible—in which case its cost might add up to much more with a few calls? Can the insurer cancel the contract on the customer if it's used too frequently? Is there a limit to how much work can be done on the VCR? If the customer sells the VCR, can the contract be transferred? Can the contract be renewed? Is there a charge for transfer or renewal? And who will be fixing the VCR anyway—the wide range of authorized services allowable by the manufacturer's warranty or one guy in a shop thirty miles from the customer's house? Perhaps most importantly, what insurance company is backing this contract—an important thing to consider, just in case the contract company or retailer goes belly up.

Ah, but here's the catch: it's virtually impossible to get answers to any of these questions *before* purchasing the contract. Indeed, service contracts are one of the few instances left in modern American society in which *consumers are asked to enter into a contract without ever reading the terms*. And, unfortunately, these terms can vary enormously. Service can range from including complete in-home repair and the supply of a loaner product to requiring you to pay a deductible and ship your equipment to a service center. Companies can be well-intentioned and legitimate or they can be half-baked operations that take your money and run.

Without this information, it's also *impossible to comparison shop for the contract with the best terms*. And there are major differences. For example, Highland offers maintenance in its VCR contracts, which despite a deductible of $9.95 for each cleaning, allows the customer to get the heads cleaned "an unlimited number of times." In contrast, Lechmere's contract has no provision for maintenance of this type, although it also has no deductible. Again, certain consumers may prefer one type of arrangement to another, but since the contract is just tagged onto the sale and no one knows the terms anyway, there's no consumer choice involved.

You can be educated up to your ears with "facts to check" about service contracts, but you will not be able to dig these facts out of salespeople no matter how much you persevere. One technician even told us that the only way to become an educated consumer about service contracts was to actually work in the business. On the numerous occasions we have asked salespeople about the terms of their contracts, we got vague reassurances such as:

1. "I don't know anything about that. We just sell them."
2. "There are no terms. It's simple. You get all parts and labor for three years."
3. "I'm not sure. But you just have to call the store when you have a problem, and everything will be taken care of."

Only at one store we surveyed (which, interestingly, is unique in not compensating salespeople for selling service contracts) do salespeople routinely disparage the contracts. And only two or three times has a salesperson handed us any literature at all, and then it was a slick little brochure advertising the benefits of the contract and mentioning an exclusion or two at best. There was absolutely no way to find out the details before we decided to buy the contract—and sometimes not until we actually tried using it. Many contracts, in fact, consist merely of a few cheery promises printed on the back of a sales slip. The entire Lechmere contract, for example, is printed on the back of the receipt and says nothing about whether you can transfer the contract to another buyer, how the contract is backed, or whether you can cancel the contract if the purchase is stolen or returned. In the late 1980s, Highland documented its entire "Peace of Mind Extended Service Policy" on the back of its receipts, too, and in only two paragraphs:

> When purchased, this Extended Service Policy applies to merchandise on the opposite side of this form. The information shown under the extended service policy columns reflects the total months of service coverage including the manufacturer's warranty. The "Policy Deduct" column is the amount of per call charges after the expiration of the manufacturer's labor warranty.

> This Extended Service Policy gives you protection in addition to the manufacturer's warranty, if any, that comes with this product. Consult the manufacturer's product warranty to ascertain how long it lasts and what it covers.

Mr. S., a Bedford, Massachusetts, resident who purchased this 1988 contract (which cost $149.88 for a five-year term) had no idea what Highland would do about exclusions, transfer, renewal, insurance backing, or cancellation. It's highly unlikely, of course, that any contract would cover a machine that you demolished with a sledgehammer in a fit of rage, but the contract as it stands gives no details about where Highland plans to draw the line. When this $299 VCR breaks down, Mr. S. will presumably find out.

With little or no concrete information available, it's easy for a salesperson to misrepresent a contract's power. According to one store official, for example, salespeople frequently disparage compact disc players, claiming that the laser pickup wears out after two years, and that it's therefore desirable to buy a service contract for five years. What the salesperson fails to mention, the official adds, is that, "their extended warranty doesn't pay for parts that will wear out; it's for defective parts only." Conversely, salespeople may also emphasize the high cost of repairs but neglect to mention that most of the problems with these products occur during the lifetime of the manufacturer's warranty, so extending the warranty is often a bad investment.[9]

The legitimacy and terms of a contract can be hard to get out of retailers for several reasons. Perhaps most frequently, salespeople simply know none of the details.[10] Most retailers themselves have an enormously difficult time finding out the exact terms of the contracts they're selling, and often this ignorance is understandable, especially when a store is merely selling some independent company's contract. Stores spend their time educating salespeople about whatever they're selling—if they spend much time even there—and certainly not about the fine print of some other company's contract. Furthermore, these independent companies often send out the contract days or weeks after the purchase, so there's no physical contract in store to look at, even if a salesperson was willing. And, finally, it's simply not economical for salespeople to spend time educating consumers about warranties and service contracts; their business is to sell and sell fast. Many salespeople will say anything and everything, as long as they can make the sale, and telling you about possible exclusions of a service contract is definitely not in their best interest. Salespeople apparently believe that as long as you don't put things in writing, no one can hold anything against you legally. In the case of service contracts, this sort of "truth-stretching"—or outright lying—can persuade you to buy an unnecessary contract. Because so little concrete information is available about actual terms, it's particularly easy to promise just about anything.

It's even difficult to get the price of a contract, in fact, until you actually purchase a specific item. Thus, you can't directly compare the price of a Silo contract to that of a Circuit City contract on a $400 VCR without going through a complicated and possibly embarrassing charade. Instead, you take what you get: you may choose a model and the best price on that model, but you take whatever contract comes along for the ride. One Highland salesperson we interviewed explained that this hidden price list for service contracts is actually to the consumer's advantage. "The reason Highland doesn't give a service-contract price list," he explains, "is because they want to sell a five-year contract." The actual price list for a VCR selling for under $400 in 1988 gives the customer the following options: $149 for five years, $100 for three years, $70 for two years, or $40 for one year. But if all these options were displayed, many customers might be tempted to choose the one-year contract, even though they'd actually get a better per-year rate by choosing the five-year plan.

If you choose the one-year contract and renew it every year—which costs $59 and can only be done one year at a time—you'll lose even more money over five years.

The sales training manual for Warrantech Service Extension Plan offers another explanation for this close-mouthed strategy. "You should assume your customer wants and needs a Warrantech Service Extension Plan . . . and that he'll want the longest term plan available. . . . If he's reluctant, then suggest a shorter term plan, first a two-year, then a one-year. Remember, it's easier to come down in price than to go up," the manual tells salespeople. It then advises breaking the price down to a monthly or weekly figure. "Don't say a three-year contract is $120. Say a three-year contract is *only* $3.33 per month, or only 77¢ per week, or only 11¢ per day." Universal Protection Plan's sheet on "Successful Steps to Selling" offers similar advice, for similar reasons.

Advantageous terms or not, we believe that consumers should be able to make this choice for themselves after considering the alternatives. As things stand today, however, service contracts are sold based on their absolute value to consumers, not their relative value compared to other such contracts. Again, it's as if you were told to buy water at the price it would be worth to you if only one person controlled the water supply and could charge monopoly rates.

WARRANTY WARS

One particularly blatant form of "truth-stretching" involves the length of the manufacturer's warranty. Almost all service contracts available today run concurrently with the warranty, so that if you buy a three-year contract on a product with a two-year warranty, you're actually getting just one year of extra service. That's a big problem for retailers trying to sell you a contract. There is an obvious temptation to disparage a manufacturer's warranty—to say, for instance, that it's shorter than it is, or that it doesn't cover what it actually covers—to make a service contract seem more appealing. Since most consumers haven't memorized the warranty terms of every model on the market, this temptation becomes even greater.

We experienced this kind of misinformation firsthand when, on one investigation, we went into a major superstore to look at Fisher rack systems. We had already carefully examined the manufacturer's literature and knew exactly which model we wanted. We also knew that the manufacturer's warranty covered parts and labor for two years.

Well, the young man helping us was perfectly happy to show us the system and tell us about the great price we could have it for that day. But then we expressed concern about service. The salesperson explained to us that service was no problem, since for a slight fee we could buy a store service contract that would cover all parts and labor for the next three years. Great, we said, but what about the manufacturer's warranty? Wouldn't that cover things as well?

"Oh, no," said the earnest young man. "They only cover labor for ninety days. After that you're on your own. And labor can be very expensive, as I'm sure you know."

Well, we did know that labor could be very expensive. But we also knew that Fisher covered at least part of this system—parts and labor—for two years. So one of us replied, "That's strange. I believe I read somewhere that the warranty was for two years."

"No. It's only ninety days. But we can cover you for three years."

"No, no," we repeated. "We're quite sure of it. Can we look at the warranty?"

Here the salesperson hesitated. "Um, I don't think so. I mean, I'd have to open the box and everything."

We knew that the store had to conform to the Magnuson-Moss Warranty Act requiring merchants to have warranties available for customer inspection on all items. We told this to the salesperson, politely, of course.

"No, I've never heard that law before," he replied. "Although I know there's a law that you can see the warranty *after* you buy something."

With that reply, we knew something was terribly wrong. But after much persistence, the salesperson agreed to go ask the manager about the rack system's warranty. He returned ten minutes later, again insisting that labor was covered for only ninety days, but we might have been confused because there was some other system that had a longer warranty. No, we returned, we were quite sure that we had read about this particular system. Could we please see the warranty? At last, perhaps afraid of losing the sale, he retreated and somehow managed to dig up a copy of the warranty. And—lo and behold!—it turned out that we had been right after all. The warranty was for two years, parts and labor included, and buying a service contract would indeed tag on only one extra year of service. We left without buying either the service contract or the rack system.

We should stress, of course, that this salesperson wasn't necessarily "lying" to us. We really have no idea what was going on in his head. Possibly he just didn't know the warranty terms but knew he had to make something up to seem knowledgeable to customers. Possibly his manager had told him that all warranties were ninety days, so that although the manager might have been playing a game (to sell more contracts), the salesman was an innocent victim. Possibly the salesperson was simply confused; after all, there were at least four different warranties on different parts of the stereo system. And, of course, possibly the salesman was lying to us pure and simple. We simply can't prove anything. But what we do know for certain is that very few consumers would have the perseverance to uncover this sort of falsehood, whatever its source, nor should they have to.

Sins of omission are frequent as well. American Express, for example, offers a "Buyer's Assurance Plan," which allows consumers to double the manufacturer's warranty merely by using the American Express card and then sending in photocopies of the warranty and their receipt. Many banks offering Visa and MasterCard have similar programs, and major-appliance and consumer-electronics companies such as GE, RCA, Sony, and Whirlpool offer their own extended-warranty programs or service contracts, some of which you can obtain independently of the retailer. But a salesperson who has to sell a quota of his or her own store's contracts will rarely tell you about these options.

The result of all these shenanigans may even be making warranties an endangered species. Service contracts are so profitable and consumers so confused that some stores won't carry models with long warranties—and certainly won't tell consumers about them unless forced to. One Highland salesman told us that Highland won't carry the long-warranty Toshibas (which he calls "the best warranty in the business") because they want to sell service contracts. "Toshiba TV model numbers that begin with CF have a one-year warranty," he says. "Those that begin with CX have a 30-month warranty. At Highland, we only sell one CX model. That's because we can't sell an extended warranty on them."

The service-contract companies, primarily responsible for this state of affairs, milk it for all it's worth. "Labor costs . . . have soared to over $100 per hour for some items, and manufacturers have chosen to dramatically limit the terms of their factory warranties," says a brochure for National Electronic Warranty. "Many provide only 90 days coverage on both parts and labor." With such a short warranty, the famous claim that most breakdowns usually occur after the manufacturer's warranty has expired quite frequently comes true.

The Highland salesman adds that manufacturers have their own reasons, too, for shortening the length of the warranties. "Manufacturers today are not looking for repeat customers," he said. "there just isn't enough profit in something like a VCR. Thus, the manufacturers will try to do whatever they can to weasel out of any repairs. They look over claims real closely to see if there is any reason at all they can reject it." Together with service contracts, this attitude may soon make the standard manufacturer's warranty obsolete.

FLYING BY NIGHT

One of the worst nightmares of a service-contract owner has come true for far too many consumers. You buy a five-year TV service contract in good faith for, say, $150. Two years later, well after your manufacturer's warranty has expired, the retailer you purchased the contract from goes belly up (as many do in this very competitive business).

This is exactly what happened to many contract-holders when Pacific Stereo, a major California chain with more than fifty stores, folded in the early eighties. The same can be said for BrandsMart, an East Coast chain, and Kennedy & Cohen, a Florida chain with about twenty stores, both of which "went under and left their customers holding worthless service contracts," according to one retailer we talked to.[11]

Even more distressingly, one now-defunct Boston-area electronics chain used to keep all the money from the service contracts it sold rather than sending it along to the independent administrator. It originally purchased one thousand contracts from the underwriter but then sold five thousand contracts to consumers and kept every cent of the money. In short, the chain received money for five thousand contracts but paid the underwriter for only one thousand of them. Since they sent the physical contract out only when a consumer made a claim, they didn't have to worry about running out of their original one thousand.

"We never sent out the contracts until the customer called up three or four times to piss and moan," admitted a former salesperson for the firm, estimating that only five out of a hundred customers would call at all. "We were told as salespeople that it takes ninety days to receive a contract, and if they didn't receive it in that time there would be no problem as long as they had their receipt."

Now that this retailer is out of business, one wonders what will happen to all the service-contract holders whose purchases have not yet broken down but aren't officially registered with the administrator. Some of these people have filed complaints with the Massachusetts attorney general, but chances are high that not much can be done to wring money out of a bankrupt company. According to the president of a large New England service company, these people were simply left "holding the bag."

The key to protecting yourself against such a fiasco, of course, is to make sure that the contract you buy is backed by a reputable insurance company. But, again, the big catch is that since you can't comparison shop for a service contract, you actually have very little to say about whether or not you approve of the backing. As it turns out, many of the service contracts today are underinsured. David Cohen, the president of Tri-City Sales, went so far as to tell us that, "The backing is all make-believe on service contracts. The big guys are all underinsured. Yeah, there are companies backed by firms like Lloyd's of London. But the reserves aren't increasing with the service contracts' increasing sales."

Even some of the service-contract administrators themselves warn potential dealers to be wary of underinsured competitors. "While there are many legitimate administration companies, the apparent bankruptcy of yet another service-contract administrator has left an increasingly bad taste in the minds, not to mention the wallets of many retailers," the Video Aid Corporation (mixing its metaphors) tells dealers. Without proper backing, it continues, "then you, and only you, will bear the ultimate responsibility for servicing the contracts you have sold." What this warning doesn't mention is that if the dealer decides not to back the contract, the consumer is left with a worthless piece of paper.[12]

Many large dealers, such as Sears, Highland, Montgomery Ward, Silo, Circuit City, and Fretter, don't even bother with outside insurance and insure their contracts themselves. These companies seem to operate on a pay-as-you-go basis; that is, they set up no escrow account specifically to pay out claims, but instead, like the much-maligned social security system, simply use revenue from new contracts to pay for claims on old contracts.[13]

Referring to one of the major superstores, the president of a large electronics store in suburban Boston cautioned consumers to consider "How safe is a self-insured company losing money?" Of course, if you really want to spend a lot of time investigating insurance backing of a self-insured company, you can try to get hold of a retailer's annual report and examine any escrow account the retailer may have for service contracts. However, few people standing at a service counter about to purchase a new refrigerator have the time or inclination to do so.

Even if a service-contract administrator or self-insured retailer has remained alive in five years, you may not be able to get your equipment serviced. There simply may be no technicians around who know how to service a five-year-old machine—or have parts with which to service it. According to Cohen, "If service contracts *really* work—and I emphasize the *if they work*—they're the best thing the consumer can buy; it's also the best opportunity for the retailer to make a profit in his entire store. The problem is that I don't think the technical people are going to be there when the problems happen."

When we asked him to elaborate, he replied, "It was RCA two years ago, GE last year, and Thomson this year. Do you think technicians are going to keep obsolete parts around? Do you think Thomson is not going to try to rationalize its international operations? How about the stray VCR that RCA buys from a Samsung? Do you think they're going to stock parts for that? This is going to be one of the great fiascoes of our time."

One solution, said a Highland salesperson, is finding a contract that will allow technicians to replace an item they can't service. According to this salesperson, the Highland contract (or one of the three Highland contracts that we currently know of) says "that if we can't fix something, we'll replace it for $9.95. This is important, for example, if you buy a Samsung and find that it's impossible to get parts in five years." We agree, but again, it's nearly impossible to know whether you can do so or not, since despite numerous attempts, we can't seem to find any written policy from Highland which confirms this claim.

SERVICE

Several years ago Mrs. C., a Chicago attorney, bought a Sanyo compact disc player at a suburban Fretter and purchased a service contract as well. After three months of happy use, however, the player started jumping from track to track, and Mrs. C. called the store. She was instructed to take the machine into a local appliance shop for service, since at that time

Fretter had arranged for this shop to honor its service contracts. When Mrs. C. brought the compact disc player into this little shop, however, it turned out the shop wasn't authorized to service Sanyo compact disc players. The service people refused to honor the contract and told Mrs. C. to take her problems back to Fretter.

At first, the salespeople at Fretter were unhelpful. At that time they didn't offer in-store service (as most Fretters claim to do today). It was an unfortunate situation. A month or two went by and Mrs. C. still had a broken compact disc player and a wholly useless service contract. She wrote several letters to the Fretter manager and, later, to Fretter headquarters, and, eventually the store agreed to replace her purchase.

Although that story had a happy ending, Mrs. C. had to spend a lot of time and energy making it that way—and fortunately she had the clout as an attorney to pull it off. To avoid such problems, it's clearly desirable to find out exactly who's going to be servicing the product before purchasing a service contract. If the designated repair shop won't service your brand, as in Mrs. C.'s case, your contract will do you no good at all. Furthermore, if the designated repair shop is inconvenient or even of poor quality, you probably won't want the contract either.

In some cases, for example, buying a service contract may mean that you actually severely limit your choice of service technicians. When we finally bought our stereo rack system (the one with the two-year warranty), for example, we purchased a three-year service contract from Lechmere. This contract not only extended the two-year warranty by a year, but allowed us to have "in-home" service for all three years, something we wouldn't have had at all under the manufacturer's warranty. As luck would have it, the amplifier wouldn't function at all after day one. Now, if we had no service contract, we would have taken the system to any authorized Fisher technician. As it stood, however, to get the in-home service we had contracted for, we had to go through Lechmere, and Lechmere had subcontracted the service to a company that turned out to take between 8 and 12 weeks each time we needed repairs.

Of course, we had the warranty and still could have gone to any authorized Fisher dealer for the first two years. However, only the contract allowed us the luxury of having a technician come to our home. Besides, after the warranty had expired, we had no choice but to use the company Lechmere had designated for us and abide by its waiting periods. Furthermore, if we hadn't opted for in-home service, we would have been forced to drive to the one location (a half hour from our home) of this service, rather than choosing one of the several closer authorized Fisher service centers.

To their credit, many retailers have responded to these sorts of problems by offering their own "in-store service." Here, however, there's a perplexing riddle: is the service in the store or isn't it? Believe it or not, this is actually a tricky question, with lots of accusations about scams floating in the air. Because retailers seem to be constantly changing their policies to meet consumer perception, it extremely difficult to know exactly what is happening.

From what we can piece together, however, the scenario goes something like this: Originally the major superstores contracted out with local technicians to honor their service contracts (as in the case of Mrs. C. and Fretter). Little stores fought back, justifying their own higher prices by claiming that you could come back any time for "personalized service." In response, a few of the superstores started adding their own "in-house" service, although most small retailers we talked to still don't believe that these claims can be true or that the service can be very good. And, in fact, definition of "in-house" is tricky. It can mean a full-time service facility on each store premises equipped with technicians who actually work for the chain on a full-time basis. More frequently, however it means (a) a desk in a store where you can bring your equipment and from which the clerk will send your equipment to some centralized warehouse or outside technician; (b) a counter in the store labeled "Service Department," which is actually a front for the desk described in (a); (c) an actual service department staffed by subcontractors who show up a couple of days a week for a couple of hours; or (d) an actual service department that is equipped to service certain types of items sold in the store—or make a few simple repairs like cleaning VCR heads—but that send out everything else. In all these cases, however, the stores promise customers that they have "in-store" service.

In mid-August 1988, for example, Highland and Fretter were claiming that they offered "in-store" service. Several Highland salespeople we interviewed confirmed this claim, admitting however that Highland jobbed out appliances but planned soon to service them in-store as well. Nevertheless, despite these claims, the president of a service company that does a lot of work for the major New England superstores told us: "Fretter and Highland say they do service in the stores. But all they do is cleaning and fuse replacements. I should know, because one of my former employees works for Highland, and that's all he does. That's not my definition of a technician. . . . Anything else is done in Franklin [a Boston suburb]. And what they can't do in Franklin, they send to us."

A Fretter salesman from a Boston suburb admitted to us that as of September 1988 workers in the service department got $10 an hour. "They do head cleaning and free up the salesperson's time. Eighty percent of the problems they solve are operator errors—the stuff that happens when there's nothing wrong with the equipment, but the people just didn't read the manual or can't understand it."

Despite promises of in-store service, then, the Fretter service department remains minimal as of this writing. "We strictly use manufacturers to repair our stuff," explained the Fretter salesman. "We do blanket contracts with them. When we buy their stuff, we also expect them to repair it for reasonable rates. One problem with this approach is when we change vendors. For example, we used to sell Sharp but don't anymore. We had to call up a local service shop to get it repaired."

The good news is that the superstores do indeed appear to be enhancing their in-store service as time passes, perhaps because consumers eventually find out what's really going on in these cases and small retailers have so much to gain by exposing scams. But until there's enough exposure about both service and other aspects of service contracts, retailers who want to survive will no doubt continue to do as little as they can get away with.

1. Note, however, that to our knowledge, no retailer selling service contracts even uses the word *insurance*. They even grimace if you mention the term and warn that a service contract has nothing to do with insurance. We suspect that's because they're afraid if they use that loaded term they might become regulated by government. Nevertheless, when the salesperson describes what is being sold, he or she will use the same language that an insurance person would use.

2. Not that auto service contracts are immune to abuse. In May 1990, for example, New York's attorney general announced that price gouging by auto dealers on service contracts cost New York consumers over $25 million in excess charges in 1989 alone and that price gouging on these contracts nationwide cost an estimated two million customers about $300 million. See also "Insure Against Future Repairs?" *Consumer Reports*, April 1990, p. 227.

3. Adam Greenberg, "Report: Camcorder Add-on Buyers Prefer Mail," *Home Furnishing Daily*, July 25, 1988, p. 89. See also Frank Lovece, "The Protection Racket," *Video*, June 1986, pp. 72–75.

4. For example, see Murray Slovick, "Service Contracts: Extending Your Bottom Line," *Audio-Video International*, June 1987, pp. 112–113.

5. "Extended Service to Account for Bigger Piece of the Pie," *TWICE*, January 22–26, 1990, p. 15.

6. For example, See Slovick, pp. 112–113.

7. Greg Tarr, "Retailers Turn to Third Parties to Provide Extended Warranties," *Home Furnishings Daily*, November 20, 1989, p. 84.

8. For example, see John Phelan, *Regulation of the Television Repair Industry in Louisiana and California: A Case Study,* Staff Report to the Federal Trade Commission, Stock #1800-00166, November 1974.

9. For example, see "Service Contracts: Hype or Help?" *Changing Times,* August 1986, p. 72.

10. See, for example, "SCIC Approves Disclosure statement," *NARDA News,* June 1989, pp. 28–29.

11. See also Slovick, p. 112, and James Willcox, "Extended Service Industry Benefits from New Players," *TWICE,* June 4–8, 1990, pp. 28–29.

12. See also Ron Goldberg, "New Marketing Plans Bring Warranties to the Masses," *TWICE,* January 8–12, 1990, pp. 28–30.

13. For example, see Lovece, p. 75.

Shopping in the Dark: Consumer Adaptations to Ignorance

Consumers are human beings. We cannot fly from store to store at the speed of light. We cannot study the internal mechanics of merchandise with X-ray vision. We cannot remember the millions of products, features, and uses with the ease of a supercomputer. And these limitations are just as true of rocket scientists as of the ordinary person on the street.

The painful truth is that because we can't be smart shoppers anymore, we have become confused and "ignorant" shoppers. We may be brilliant, insightful, savvy people in other areas of our lives, but when it comes to knowing which insurance policy will provide the most comprehensive coverage or which personal computer will best meet our accounting and educational needs for the money, we are all kindergartners. This ignorance regarding our purchases profoundly affects just about every aspect of our lives as consumers.

Strangely enough, few of us even notice that there's a problem with the way we shop—partly because we've adopted ways to function in spite of the current confusion and partly because we (falsely) assume that this confusion is inevitable. People just don't get outraged if you tell them that they are buying the wrong products for the wrong reasons or that these wrong decisions ultimately cost them time, aggravation, and money; they simply reply that "that's the way things are."

Of course, such reactions are common to all problems that have no obvious solutions. No one objected for thousands of years that there were no electric lights. Even though people couldn't work at night, even though sitting inside a building was often a glum, depressing affair, even though overall efficiency was dramatically less than today, with no alternative, complaining not only would have been pointless, it would have been downright pathological. Nor did people for thousands of years object when they didn't have cars and telephones and indoor plumbing. From our perspective, their world might seem to have been much less efficient, diverse, and pleasant, but the people experiencing what we would consider to be problems were hardly if ever aware of them, and often regarded their lives as vast improvements on the miseries of even earlier eras. Similarly, since most people today see no better way to shop, they either disregard their ignorance about products or accept it as an unavoidable and generally minor frustration. Nevertheless, the effects of consumer ignorance, albeit obscure to the casual observer, extend far beyond a few bad purchases and an occasional annoyance.

THE EFFICIENCY EFFECT

To understand the influence of our ignorance, we first must consider some basic economic theory about efficient marketplaces. An efficient marketplace is simply one which produces the things people want most for the least cost. Now, economists generally contend that maximum efficiency and public welfare (at least in the short run) depend on a purely competitive marketplace; in contrast, a purely monopolistic marketplace— with no competition at all—produces inefficiency and social waste.

Of course, in the real world there is no such thing as either a purely competitive or purely monopolistic marketplace. Rather, all real economies lie somewhere on a gradient between two opposite poles— monopoly and competition—and can be categorized as having a certain degree of monopoly power. The more the competition, the less the monopoly power, and vice versa. In the real world, then, economists summarize the theory of perfect competition as follows: the less competitive a marketplace, the less efficient it is.

One tenet of this theory is that a perfectly competitive market requires perfectly informed consumers.[1] When consumers aren't so informed, a select group of companies gain monopoly power for themselves, thereby diminishing productivity. The result is a phenomenon we call the **Efficiency Effect: The more ignorant the consumer, the more inefficient the marketplace.**[2]

THE INNOVATION EFFECT

In our society there is a widespread and rather extraordinary belief that the key to innovation lies in the hard work and ingenuity of producers. Admittedly, we occasionally grant that the "system" can profoundly influence innovation, as we do when we more than happily acknowledge that communism greatly inhibits innovation. But when it comes to other "system-based" constraints on innovation, such as the high cost of educating consumers about purchases, we often draw blanks.

The fact remains, however, that no matter how clever the innovator or useful the item, only profitable innovations will be introduced—and certain systemic conditions govern profitability. Businesspeople are not technologists. Even in "technology-driven" businesses, the ultimate concern is not technological but market possibilities. In other words, the basic economic laws of supply and demand, as well as inventive genius, govern innovation.[3] Accordingly, it only stands to reason that innovations requiring vast resources to educate consumers about their merits (i.e., innovations with high "information costs") won't get developed—or at least will not be widely sold. This situation is becoming increasingly common with high-technology consumer equipment, where the expense of educating potential customers about features leads many firms to choose against introducing such items. The same can be said for items that require shoppers to spend hours of time searching them out or learning about them, as well as movies, books, video games, on-line information services—indeed, all the intellectual products coming to dominate our economy.[4] The result is what we call the **Innovation Effect: The more ignorant the consumer, the less innovation and genuine product diversity in the marketplace.** In contrast to the efficiency effect, which says that consumer confusion decreases the *value* (the price-to-performance ratio) of products already available, the innovation effect says that consumer confusion also reduces the number of types of products available to us in the first place.

Some sellers get around the innovation effect by selling products with hard-to-explain benefits to a very small group of targeted individuals—perhaps hoping that as these consumers become more familiar with the product and educate their friends and associates about it, the costs of informing consumers will come down. Most high-technology goods have been distributed along the lines of this strategy. Whether they be stereos,

VCRs, personal computers, or fax machines, they are first sold in specialty stores with high levels of service and therefore high information costs, but are eventually sold through mass retailers as consumers become familiar with the products.

Such a strategy assumes that after paying these high initial information costs, as well as higher costs from lack of economies of scale in production, companies don't have to charge so much that they price themselves out of a market altogether. This is not always the case. Take computer software, an industry characterized by high fixed costs, low variable costs, and significant consumer confusion. Many small firms have innovative ideas that they can't implement primarily because of the high cost of educating consumers about benefits. Computer software also has tremendous economies of scale—most of the costs are up-front development costs, not the costs of later reproducing the software for individual customers. Thus, when high information costs shrink the market for a particular piece of software to 1 percent or 2 percent of what it would otherwise be, the fixed product costs must be allocated over this smaller number of products sold, thus raising the price even further and ultimately shrinking or even eliminating the market. Software categories with few people willing to pay large informational and product premiums—for example, the relatively cash-poor home-education market as compared to the business market—thus tend to experience stifled program development. One way a few innovators have found to get around this problem is to rely on shareware networks and favorable reviews of independent computer societies and magazines—methods which, as we shall see, represent the wave of future consumer information.

THE MORALITY EFFECT

The price we pay for our ignorance, moreover, extends beyond the borders of economics and efficiency into the world of ethics. Here our framework comes from a field of economic analysis known as game theory, essentially a rigorous mathematical model of marketplace behavior. One model in this field, known as the asymmetric information games (AIG) theory (also referred to as noncooperative games of incomplete information), argues that if information is distributed unequally among rational people, a successfully working marketplace involving those people will generate a certain amount of deception. Anyone who doesn't deceive, in fact, will be driven out of the market; they will lose the game, so to speak, by going bankrupt.[5] This conclusion doesn't mean that everyone playing the game will profit by being deceptive but that certain players will founder if they are not—or can't risk being caught being— deceptive.

In a marketplace characterized by consumer ignorance, sellers stand to gain by exaggerating the functional value of their goods (since ignorant consumers can't differentiate truth from falsehood, and falsehood is cheaper). In other words, they have an incentive to cultivate an unrealistic appearance for their wares. We call this third phenomenon of consumer ignorance the **Morality Effect: The more ignorant the consumer, the more deception in the marketplace.** Although the term *morality* may imply otherwise, this effect holds regardless of intention. Many sellers legitimately argue that their deceptions were unconscious or "mistakes," and we can sympathize with both their regret and the difficulty of their situation. But this sympathy does not change the fact that whether mistake or not, whether fraud or incompetence, deceptive behavior misleads consumers.

Defining *deception* without reference to motivation—although previously rare among consumerists—is hardly unorthodox: in the study of animal behavior, for example, naturalists commonly speak of "deceptive behavior" while maintaining that they are not speaking of any conscious will or motivation on the part of the animal. Evolutionary biologists say that females of one species of firefly "deceive" males of another species by mimicking responses to their mating signals and then eating the males. They say that a certain species of snake "deceives" predators by splitting into two during a chase, the nonessential tail end wriggling off and attracting the attention of the predator, while the head and vital organs remain frozen, apparently dead.[6] Whatever is going on in the animal's mind is irrelevant: deceptive behavior is simply defined as any action which signals something other than what it appears to signal. Even plants are said to deceive: the *Stapelia lepida*, or carrion flower, has star-shaped petals which look and smell like the carrion on which the larvae of flies mature. These petals "trick" the female fly into laying her eggs on the flower, thereby pollinating the flower as she crawls out. The eggs subsequently die. Such a phenomenon involves deception, and yet it would sound rather ludicrous to accuse the carrion flower of conscious ill will. Similarly, from the standpoint of economic well-being, it makes no difference whether a seller's "deception" is the result of intentional lying or whether it is mere incompetence; either way, such behavior produces the same economic consequences.

In this chapter and the next, we'll try to illustrate the Efficiency,

Innovation, and Morality Effects, not by using abstruse economic equations and graphs, but by showing how ignorance works itself out in the consumer's, and then the seller's, day-to-day decision making. Only in this context will it make sense for us to propose the large-scale solution to the consumer information crisis that we outline in Part III of the book.

CUES TO QUALITY

Whatever our level of knowledge about quality, as consumers we decide all the time about which merchandise to choose; with varying degrees of frustration and anxiety, we somehow pick a brand of mayonnaise, a make of car, or a model of vacuum cleaner. We may not know in a scientifically sound sense which brand of juice truly has the best combination of taste, nutrition, and price, but after serving just a little time in the supermarket ranks, we feel fairly content choosing "Matt's" apple juice or "Walsh's" grape juice in lieu of fifteen or twenty equivalent choices. Similarly, even though we haven't personally tested the picture quality of three hundred available televisions and don't really know if we could get a better price for similar performance, some of us can bring ourselves to take out a credit card and charge up five hundred bucks for a Sony stereo TV.

Illogical as it may seem, we get most of the information we need to make these and even more complicated choices from the people selling the products themselves. As we saw earlier, we no longer live in a simple marketplace in which we can learn about purchases from our own experiences or from those of our close associates. While we may consult a consumer publication or call an expert friend now and then, for the vast majority of our purchases, we rely simply on what the manufacturer or retailer has to tell us. This reliance on sellers for information is the most fundamental adaptation to our ignorance. Of course, we usually don't rely on the sellers to the extent of buying exactly what they tell us to, but, rather, we rely on them without realizing it by applying certain "cues" or "rules of thumb" to their information. Whenever we cannot judge merit directly, we must rely on these "proxies" to stand in for our knowledge of quality. Rather than evaluating every wire in a stereo system, for example, we simply might rely on the brand name. Similarly, rather than running all over town comparing costs on cornflakes, we simply might rely on a certain grocer's reputation for low prices.

Let's now look more closely at these and other cues on which we rely, sometimes unconsciously, when we shop for goods and services. Unfortunately, such cues don't correspond a hundred percent with actual merit. As we shall see, the ultimate result of such decisions, multiplied billions of times a year, is a huge and unnecessary cost to us all.[7]

The Wealth Cue:

"If They Advertise a Lot, They've Got to Be Good"

Many people think that the most important part of an advertisement is the content—what the ad says. The fact of the matter, however, is that advertisers primarily aim to get us to recall the item's name when we are about to make a purchase. Why? We instinctively trust a familiar name more than an unfamiliar one. And so the goal of the advertiser is, essentially, to make the name of its offering as familiar as possible. For many marketers effective promotion simply requires getting their product before the public—period. The main purpose of advertising is not to convey any specific information about the product but rather to convey the mere fact that the company has enough money (and success) to advertise at all.[8]

Like the steam engine before the gas engine, moreover, this system works, at least in a rudimentary way: after all, with so much exposure, true danger or incompetence is bound to surface: we assume that a familiar name probably belongs to an established and successful company, and such companies are at least likely to have good, if not the best, products. Simply put, we assume that "success breeds success." In the case of lawyers, one proxy we use for competence is an opulent office. In the case of real estate brokers it can be a luxury car. In the case of corporations it can be advertising and the ceaseless repetition of a name.

When consumers use "wealth" as a cue to quality, however, they tempt companies to put significant resources into creating the appearance of wealth, without regard to actual merit. When promoting pain relievers, for example, the leading pharmaceutical companies routinely spend tens of millions of dollars proclaiming the uniqueness of their wares, when, in fact, each company is merely selling plain aspirin. The idea is to get consumers to think of a well-advertised brand name such as "Bayer" rather than just going in for any old bottle of "aspirin."[9]

Just as militaries tend to wage war with weapons, the "wealth" cue forces companies to wage war with information, producing an "information arms race" much like a military arms race. And just as militaries spend huge amounts on weapons systems just to cancel out another nation's potential combat advantage, companies spend huge amounts on promotion just to compensate for a competitor's information advantage.

The result is huge waste. In a world where—for good reason—credibility comes from screaming the loudest, great inefficiency results because much of the screaming tends to cancel other screaming out, leaving the net effect of advertising as zero.[10] The maxim of Stuart Chase, coauthor of the influential 1927 book *Your Money's Worth,* is still true today: "Advertising makes people stop buying Mogg's soap and start buying Bogg's soap. . . . Nine-tenths and more of advertising is largely competitive wrangling as to the relative merits of two undistinguished and often undistinguishable compounds. . . ."[11] Furthermore, the company that screams the most tends to get the business. And, by extension, the greater the confusion, the larger the percentage of information wasted on useless or outright false information.

The Price Cue:

"If It Costs More, It's Better"

A permutation of the "wealth" cue is the commonly held view that price reflects quality. Indeed, this "price" cue has statistical validity: more-expensive items do tend to be better than less-expensive ones, especially in a truly competitive marketplace, where consumers are well informed. We can be reasonably certain that a $500 bicycle will hold up better than a $50 one or that a $300 pair of shoes from a department store is made with better materials than a $10 pair from a dime store.

The problem with the price cue quite simply is that price is only an imperfect gauge of value. And when prices are relatively close, it may be very hard and not worth the time and money to tell which product is the better value. Real-world choices, for example, do not involve deciding whether a $500 bike is better than a $50 bike but rather deciding whether olive oil selling for $6.95 is really better than the olive oil selling for $4.50 or whether the washing machine selling for $650 is really better than the washing machine selling for $490.

Conscious that without other information, price will be a deciding factor, retailers, for example, often conduct "price lining," to simplify options of consumers who are known to judge quality by price. Retailers select a finite number of distinct prices and tag all merchandise at one distinct level or "price line": say, selling all belts at $6.50, $8.00, or $15.00 and selling all wrap skirts at $23.00, $32.00, or $41.00. Retailing texts contend that this practice helps consumers (and salesclerks!) who would otherwise be confused by small price differences. The price lines convey the clear message that the $41.00 skirt is "better" than the $23.00 skirt.[12]

The result is that the price no longer reflects relative value.[13] As one retailing text put it: "A promotional store may offer an assortment of sweaters for $19.99, created from the lines of four vendors. The unit cost of each may be $10 to $13, returning varied margins to the seller at the single $19.99 price point."[14] Thus, although the original unit cost may indeed have reflected quality (the $13 sweater may have been slightly better than the $10 sweater), the retail price ($19.99 for both of these sweaters) does not.

Of course, any shopper who knew the true quality of sweaters wouldn't be fooled by the $19.99 price tag and would be able to select the better value. But few of us have such keen eyes for sweaters, stereos, or many of the complex products we buy today. It's no surprise then, that the more ignorant we are and the more complex the things we buy, the more price and quality tend to be out of step.[15]

The price cue also keeps prices unnecessarily high, as when a store suggests with a lofty pricetag that chocolates, liqueurs, or even televisions are top quality.[16] We heard about one jewelry store, for example, that couldn't sell any of a certain unusual rock, which it had displayed for many months. The manager went away one day and left a message to his assistant to halve the price. The assistant misread the message and doubled the price instead. To everyone's surprise, every single gem was sold within a few days. People wanted to buy "high-quality" jewelry, and when the jewels were priced too low, didn't think of them as having sufficient quality.

Perhaps nowhere are these wasteful price hikes more graphic than in the case of private-label goods. Ike Lagano, research chief for the Associated Merchandising Corporation, cites studies showing that whatever the true cost, merchants should price private-label goods for 20 percent less than brand-name goods: "Less than that, the consumer will gravitate to the national brand," he says. "And, on the other hand, if it's a 30 to 35% differential, the consumer will think there's something wrong with the private brand."[17] Similarly, the *Wall Street Journal* noted that private-label detergents, identical in composition to the brand labels, must sell in supermarkets for no more than 20 to 25 percent less (even though they could easily charge 50 percent less) because consumers won't trust a private label if they think the price is too much lower than a name brand; they'll assume that some important ingredient must have been omitted.

Often retailers don't have to overtly manipulate prices to profit from the price cue: our own psychology trips us up. Many stores, for example, create a "reference price," which we use to decide whether any given item is too expensive. The first price most of us see tends to become the price associated with quality, whether or not that association has any basis in fact. Say one store has four TVs by a certain manufacturer that you like, selling for $200, $250, $300, and $500, respectively. If the salesperson shows you the $200 TV first, you tend to keep that figure in your head as a reference price, a price at which you know you can get a decent set. When he next shows you the more expensive sets, you are likely to think the prices rather steep. Most retailers contend that you probably end up buying the $200 TV, or, perhaps the $250 TV if it has a few extra features. On the other hand, if the salesperson starts by showing you the $500 set, and then shows you the other three models after $500 becomes your reference price, you are much more likely to end up buying a more expensive model.[18] By establishing a high reference price for quality, then, retailers often get us to pay more than we otherwise would.

In his book *Industrial Organization and Public Policy,* economist Douglas Greer cites a study that used *Consumer Reports* data to show only a weak correlation between price and quality.[19] We did a similar but less rigorous survey using data in *PC Digest,* a major personal-computer ratings service which accepts no advertising, and found remarkably little correlation between ranking and price. In one month, the top-rated computer was the least expensive of the ten rated, even though ratings were purely based on functionality, not price.[20]

The Brand Cue:

"If I Know the Brand, I Know the Quality"

In today's mass economy, brand names make a lot of sense as cues to merit. By marketing a name, sellers can convey a vast amount of information with one simple symbol. Without the efficiency of brand names, in fact, consumers would be crushed by the proliferation of choices and would have to spend an intolerable amount of time making each of them.[21]

You don't need cues like brands names when you're dealing with simple commodities such as apples or lettuce. Eighteenth-century Americans didn't need them either in their simple country stores; except for patent medicines, there would be virtually no brand names on anything. People would simply ask for flour, not a particular brand of flour. But as we find it more and more difficult to immediately grasp a commodity's intrinsic value, we increasingly must rely on brand names. We may assume that if we buy one Stouffer's frozen dinner, a dozen others will be of similar quality and value. Or we may assume that if our friends are happy with their Toyota Camry automobile, then we'll be happy with a Toyota Corolla.

With the spiraling rise in the number of high-tech goods in the electronic age, brand names are becoming less useful. As products become increasingly complex and targeted to more specialized needs, the information contained in the brand name becomes too simplistic. A brand name, for example, won't reveal what specific computer configuration best fits your needs. Thus, more and more customized and expensive information must either be added to the costs or left out altogether.

As products and companies continue changing rapidly, moreover, last year's superior brand often becomes today's inferior brand. For example, one year Okidata made the best computer printer, another year Epson, another year Qume, and another year IBM. Because no one can keep up with these brand changes, you often hear people insisting on buying a Magnavox television or a GE refrigerator because "that's what we've always had, and we've been happy with it," unaware that they have many equivalent or better choices.

With the proliferation of brands today, moreover, most people just can't keep track of them all. Few of us have time to test which of ten different brands of spaghetti sauce tastes best—much less remember it so that we can encourage that manufacturer by buying the brand again. Few of us can remember, either, a reliable brand of tires when we have a flat. Since it's impractical to test all the different brands, we end up picking one that seems adequate and sticking with it. The result is that we reduce any company's incentive to make a truly superior product.

As companies attach the same brand names to a wider and wider range of offerings, the proxy value diminishes even further. Today's major consumer companies sometimes slap the same brand name on dozens of very different items. Some of the major Japanese and Korean conglomerates actually put the same brand name on thousands of different goods ranging from cars to computers to consumer electronics to major appliances to ships to high-rise buildings.

This diffuse branding results in what can be called a *carry-over cue:* we falsely assume that what was true in the past will be true in the present and that what is true of one model will be true of others. We assume, for example, that if Brand A connotes quality in one type of merchandise, that quality carries over to all its other goods. And yet, as any service technician will tell you, the same company can make great dishwashers and lousy washing machines. The carry-over cue holds even within one type of good, moreover: if we know several people who have adored Brand X's top-of-the-line television set, we assume that we'll be getting that same quality when we buy one of the same brand's more moderately featured models.

Indeed, manufacturers and retailers are often forced to carry high-end merchandise and promote it aggressively—not because they want or intend to sell it, but just because people think the quality rubs off to the lower-quality items. That's how running shoes, for example, are often marketed. A company like Nike gets top athletes to use one of its special high-end shoes. The shoe we see in a typical suburban shoe store is completely different, but we know only the impressive brand name and buy accordingly, ignoring equal- or better-quality shoes for the same price.

The More-Is-Better Cue:

"The More Lights and Buttons, the Better"

The more-is-better cue, named after the deep-seated American conviction, is almost self-explanatory. If we see two VCRs in a similar price range, we decide to buy the one that can do more "tricks." If we're comparing two stereos, we decide to buy the one with bigger numbers on its list of "specs," even if we're not really sure what these numbers mean. And sometimes all we care about is that our purchases *look* big or feature-packed.[22]

Not recognizing that "more" can mean absolutely nothing in terms of function, we often force sellers to up extravagantly the number of gizmos that represent about as much as the emperor's new clothes. Take the number of events on a VCR. The fact is, 99 percent of people who buy a VCR will never program more than two events or two weeks into the future. And yet for a long time one of the biggest-selling VCRs was a machine that could be programmed to record multiple events for up to a year in advance. With the possible exception of the Time's Square gala on New Year's Eve, it's hard to imagine anyone thinking of something to program a whole year ahead of schedule, much less needing to do so.

The same argument can be made for the number of video heads. Salespeople have told us repeatedly that almost every VCR purchaser thinks this is one of the most important features to consider. But our own informal surveys indicate that more than 90 percent of consumers don't know why. They'll either admit this ignorance straight out or refer to their "techie" friend. The fact remains, however, that four heads helps only with slow motion. And other than a tiny minority of consumers who do high-quality editing on their VCR (in which case they'll probably want digitally enhanced slow motion anyway) the only two real uses for slow motion are for scrutinizing porno flicks and sports events. We don't know a soul who has ever once used slow motion on a mainstream movie. Even sports fans almost never use this feature, if only because much of the excitement of watching a sports event is watching it live, and you can only use slow motion on a prerecorded video.

Or take the megahertz rating of PC processors. Most people think that the higher the speed of the processor, the faster and better the computer. But among other things, they probably don't know about wait states, bus architecture, RAM cache, and a dozen other features that might make a computer with a faster processor run slower than one with a slower processor. What happens is that a lot of people buy unnecessarily expensive computers with faster processors than needed.[23]

More frequently, however, we're just plain confused by technical matters, especially by complicated electronic equipment. Often this confusion prompts us to assume that anything with more lights and buttons must be better. Moreover, we assume that anything with roughly equal numbers of lights and buttons must be equivalent, and so we comparison shop accordingly. The problem is that often the components of these systems can be absolutely awful. The manufacturer, using the more-is-better cue, has put all its money into the front display screen. But we don't know this and don't want to spend the energy finding out.

Supposedly, for example, the higher the oversampling rate on a CD player, the less distorted the sound. Up to about "four times," oversampling rate indeed makes a detectable difference. After that point, however, there really isn't anything that 99 percent of consumers can appreciate. Even so, manufacturers keep coming out with CD players with higher oversampling rates, and consumers keep thinking that if a player has a higher rate it must necessarily be better. Even the audio magazines that decry such practices keep printing these meaningless specs.

The Hype Cue:

"If the Box Says It's Better, I'll Take It"

It often makes sense to believe what manufacturers tell you about products. If a manufacturer stakes its prestige on the line, promoting its chocolate as the "richest" chocolate or its blender as the "most powerful" blender, then you can be fairly sure that if the item isn't the richest or most powerful, it must be fairly close. Such claims are called *hype* or *puffery,* and unless deemed deceptive they are completely legal. They also are often quite useful, even though they are unverifiable or exaggerated.

Sometimes the hype we rely on to judge purchases is less overt but no less persuasive: instead of telling us directly why an item is right for us, sellers associate it with certain qualities, such as affluence, glamour, or sexiness. The ads either show people very similar to us using the article (and by association we think it must also be appropriate for ourselves) or it shows people that we would like to emulate using it (and by association we think that it will help us be like them). We may want to buy a certain perfume, for example, largely because we like to think of ourselves as akin to the gorgeous young actress who promotes it on television. We may want to buy a certain car largely because we feel that people of our position and status in life tend to drive such models. Of course, few people would openly admit buying for these reasons alone, but clearly they do to a very large extent or we wouldn't see so many ads associating a brand of cigarettes with a rugged cowboy or associating a brand of whiskey with trendy young professionals.

Given the dearth of alternative information, this hype (or puffery) cue makes a lot of sense; if the ad didn't tell us that the stereo was "state-of-the-art," we might not realize that it was comparable to the higher-priced Sony. Furthermore, even if the car isn't truly "luxurious," the very fact that our neighbors will perceive it as such may well be worth the price.

Relying on such hype ultimately costs us plenty, however, because most of it is extremely vague and usually involves trivial assertions of comparative merit, especially when there aren't really that many real differences between products. Thus, we hear all sorts of heroic but unevidenced claims.[24] Sometimes it even seems that just about every article on the shelf, whether it be soap or toothpaste, televisions or software, is "new," "improved," or "revolutionary."

The fact that we buy according to such meaningless statements only perpetuates them. When we choose using these kind of cues, we escalate the information arms race: just as we force companies to establish their relative wealth through advertising (the wealth cue), we also force them to create excess hype about the quality or image of their products (the hype cue). And although this hype works for a while, over time people become impervious to it and force inflated terminology: good becomes better, better becomes best, and best becomes revolutionary.

And why should the manufacturer or salesperson object? If customers demand these more-expensive features, why not appease rather than lose them? And if the consumers pay lots of attention to these features, why not advertise them prominently as if they mattered? And so on it goes in a vicious circle. Some powerful manufacturer promotes a new, improved feature, we become convinced that this feature must matter, and we even start demanding it. Soon, to satisfy that demand, manufacturers engage in an escalating war of exaggeration.

Buying on the basis of the hype cue costs us, because it costs money to plant these images in our minds, money that would better be spent on improving the products. *The Nader Report on the Federal Trade Commission* observed "new" laundry detergents with "enzymatic magic" had substantially the same ability to clean clothes as did more "ordinary" detergents. Nonetheless, the report continues (with language perhaps a little too extreme for our tastes, but nonetheless telling),

> this does not prevent Colgate or Proctor & Gamble from spending millions to advertise a product that then costs double the already inflated price of other detergents. . . . It is also becoming apparent to many that all the consumer is purchasing from Proctor & Gamble, Colgate, and Lever Brothers are the lies he is told about the product. There is little doubt that toothpastes, mouthwashes, deodorants, cleansers, soaps, detergents, and so on are priced between five and twenty times their cost of production. The American people must eventually grow tired of paying $1 for a tube of toothpaste that costs no more than 15 cents to make. It is these purchases that rob the American people of billions of dollars every year. . . . The advertising does not concern truly new advances in technology or enhanced qualities of the given product. It employs the invention of empathy mechanisms and contrived distinctions among products that are in reality identical. This is what Americans are paying billions every year for—to be told that there are distinctions where there are none, to be told that products are new when they are not new.[25]

As our inability to distinguish hype from merit leads to cynicism, furthermore, the genuinely innovative idea suffers. Go into a software store, for example, and read the boxes of the different programs. They all tend to sound the same. Such words as "revolutionary," "innovative," "easy-to-use," "powerful," and "instantaneous" cover the boxes. How is a consumer expected to decide from among the different claims? Software companies that recognize that they can't scream the loudest tend not to try at all. It's like the boy who cried wolf: when just about everyone is already claiming to be new and revolutionary, are we really going to pay any attention to the genius who really does come out with something novel, especially if that genius doesn't yet have the money to tell us in a voice as loud as the others?[26]

Hype also means that products that take an extremely long time to learn about and locate (i.e., those with high "search costs") tend not to get introduced. We suspect that's because consumers often refuse to buy items that they can't evaluate economically, partly because such items tend to be so hyped. As a rule, for example, the companies that sell computer software vastly puff its range and depth of use, making consumers cynical of all such claims in future purchases and thereby holding back the whole industry. Some people hold off buying for many months after a product comes out, waiting to see what the reviewers say and if reality matches hype. Similarly, many people postpone or never buy stereo systems or computers because they never get around to spending all the time they feel they need to research a good system.[27]

The Merchant-Reputation Cue:

"Once a Good Deal, Always a Good Deal"

One very common way that we narrow our field of choices is to restrict shopping to one or two trustworthy stores. This practice reflects a version of the *carry-over cue:* we assume that if we have seen good-quality merchandise at good prices, then the remaining unfamiliar merchandise will have similar characteristics. Again, like all the cues, this adaptation makes some sense: since few of us have the time to compare exhaustively every bottle of shampoo out there, it's immensely comforting to know that if we go to the U-Save Discount Drug Store, we'll be getting a proven brand at a reasonable price.

But there are grave problems with this reputation approach as well. First of all, stores are in the selling, not the product-evaluation, business. They often stock tens of thousands of items, which are not only becoming more complex than ever but are changing with increasing frequency. At the same time, few stores have in-depth product-evaluation departments. Their primary concern is simply to stock items that sell, and in this they basically want to purchase brand-name merchandise at the least cost with the least competition and the highest potential for markup.

The way stores stock and sell their merchandise reflects this bias. High-margin items tend to be in the most visible and most frequented parts of the store. And stores offer salespeople tempting commissions for pushing high-margin items. Such a situation is hardly conducive to consumers' getting the highest-quality merchandise.

The truth of the matter, moreover, is that when we decide that a store has good prices or high quality, we almost always do so on the basis of a few high-visibility items. Witness the pervasive use of loss leaders throughout the retailing system—whether in supermarkets, consumer-electronics dealerships, or department stores; retailers know that a few conspicuous bargains will induce people to come into the stores and buy everything else for highly profitable prices. Similarly, many consumer-electronics retailers, even the so-called "discount" mail-order houses, will often discount well-known brands of camcorders but sell all the lesser-known brands, as well as accessories, for premium prices. Many people who have bought a camcorder at a superb price will then proceed to order a service contract or vast quantities of tapes, batteries, and adapters (and perhaps a relatively obscure brand of answering machine or VCR as well) from the same company, all the time assuming that they are getting a great deal and all the time penalizing stores which truly do sell these items at bargain prices. Consequently, retail prices become increasingly divorced from retail cost, minimizing the efficient allocation of resources throughout the entire economy.

Product-Specific Cues:
"I Know a Good Tomato When I See One"

The list of cues above is hardly exhaustive, of course. There are hundreds of more specific cues that each of us has picked up over the years to make otherwise impossible choices between nearly identical merchandise. For example, people determine hosiery's quality using scent, a detergent's cleaning strength using suds level and aroma, a soap's mildness using color, a syrup's thickness using darkness, and the "pickup" of cars using tension in the accelerator pad.[28]

Again, though, the problem is that all too often these cues don't correspond to real quality and consequently cost us money. "Tomatoes may look good but taste bad. A shirt may be carefully sewn, but the dye may run. Virtually any food may contain harmful additives," observe economists Dennis Smallwood and John Conlisk. "In fact, it is difficult to think of products which have the property that a brief inspection will completely reveal quality."[29] Nevertheless, because we use these superficial cues, we force retailers to try to trick us into buying what would otherwise be unsalable (though sometimes perfectly adequate) merchandise. Here it's worth considering a passage from Paul Blumberg's *The Predatory Society*, in which he quotes one of his students describing his experiences as a stock boy:

> The most general rule my product manager taught me was that I shouldn't make any packages which were all good. In other words, I was told to put a rotten apple in every bunch. Specifically, when I was bagging potatoes, I was told to put some old green potatoes in every bag. I was also told to *put the not-so-good-looking fruit on the bottom of the trays, the good-looking ones on top.* This practice was especially common with strawberries—putting the soft ones on the bottom. Another general rule I learned was that I should *put the bad side of any fruit down.* This included items such as tomatoes, pears, or any item which had one side which looked better than the other. . . . Apples, oranges, tomatoes, and other fruits and vegetables were regularly sprayed with ethylene gas to improve their appearance. [Italics ours.]

Admittedly, this description indicates that the merchant often tried to disguise completely undesirable goods through these techniques, but the need to spray fruit and hide unattractive skins would be unnecessary if consumers could judge an apple by something other than a shiny red and unblemished skin.

Finally, the sheer number of simplifying cues itself generates excessive and inefficient product differentiation and makes the consumer that much more confused. The reason here is quite simple: Different consumers use different cues to judge merit. One consumer emphasizes price, another name recognition of the brand, and another the number of bells and whistles on the package. Thus, where one product of the appropriate quality would have sufficed for the informed buyer, three products exist for the relatively uninformed buyer. Indeed, economists have observed that expert buyers—for example, those purchasing for large companies—tolerate much less product differentiation in staple goods than everyday consumers.[30]

THE   HIGH   COST   OF   IGNORANCE

We may not cherish the thought of ourselves as ignorant consumers, but we also may not care all that much if the end result is just losing a few bucks on a TV set or buying a washing machine that doesn't quite get our clothes as clean as we had hoped. At most, we may feel outraged at the kind of deceptions and personal foolishness that our ignorance encourages, but even if we do, such outrage almost certainly will evaporate when we contrast it with what we consider to be larger problems. The truth, however, is that consumer ignorance is one of the costliest failures of our economy, ranking up there with such widely appreciated problems as unemployment and inflation.

Before we get into estimates—which may, at first glance, seem shockingly high—we must warn that no one before has ever satisfactorily studied the cost of consumer ignorance. And we have to include this chapter in that warning: although based on numerous scholarly publications and government statistics, many of our cost estimates are merely ballpark figures. We don't pretend to be either thorough in our results or thoroughly scholarly in our methods. To do so, assuming it could even be done, would require at least a book in itself. The data on consumer ignorance is spotty, at best, and problems of undercounting, double counting, and questionable assumptions are endemic to the available data. Partly because these costs are difficult to measure, but mainly because until now nobody has thought we could do anything about them, economists and social activists have paid very little attention to them. Nevertheless, the estimates here shed much light on a subject often overlooked, and where we have generated numbers, we are confident they reflect accurately the magnitude of the problems we are addressing.[31] We believe that even these estimates can (1) provide a preliminary estimate of what consumer ignorance is costing us, and (2) describe the subtle and often unrecognized ways we pay for this ignorance.

Moreover, in the process of trying to itemize these expenses, we are confident that we have shown that many expenses never before thought of as product-information expenses do indeed exist only as a result of consumer ignorance. The result is an incomplete number, but also a number far greater than has ever been imagined before. Furthermore, it's important to remember that many costs of ignorance are intrinsically unquantifiable and relate to issues of quality of life.

What we estimate is that Americans pay somewhere between $500 billion and $1.0 trillion a year—approximately 15 percent of the GNP—just to get information about our purchases.[32] The average American family, too, may spend as much as 950 hours per year gathering product information (about 9 percent of its nonworking, nonschool, nonsleeping time; or four hours for every $100 spent).[33] In other words, we spend more for product information than we do for all producers' equipment ($307 billion),[34] more than for all privately funded research and development ($66 billion),[35] and even more than on all research and development and manufacturing equipment combined. In fact, less than half of a product's prices may go for the production itself, with the balance going to physical distribution and information costs.[36] We also spend more on product information than we do for food ($562 billion), clothing ($221 billion), housing ($468 billion), household operation ($362 billion), medical care ($403 billion), transportation ($379 billion), and recreation ($223 billion). And these estimates don't even begin to encompass the costs in money, time, and energy that arise because we *lack* information.

How on earth, you may be wondering, could subscriptions to *Consumer Reports* and sales of a few buying guides add up to this kind of money? The answer lies in realizing that the vast majority of information is not directly paid for or sought. Just think about the eight minutes of commercials that take up every thirty-minute TV segment; the bulk of newspapers and magazines with editorial matter tucked between advertisements; the junk mail filling mailboxes every day; and the billboards that jump out along major thoroughfares. Think, too, about the hours we spend comparison shopping, driving from store to store, and talking to salespeople. Then think about the cost of advertising and promotion, all in the name of letting consumers know about the existence and relative merits of products. Think about the salaries and support of people such as travel agents, real estate agents, bank loan officers, manufacturer representatives or retail salespeople, whose job it is to sell for companies— because a certain portion of this job involves the exchange of product information. Think, too, about the costs of maintaining purchasing departments which seek out information in the course of buying basic goods and services. Think about all the research and development (R&D), manufacturing, and packaging costs that exist only because of consumer ignorance, that help support the "cues" that we use to evaluate merchandise. Consider the inflated real estate costs behind highly visible or prestigious locations. Add to that the more than $4 billion that local government spends each year simply picking up garbage, a large percentage of which is attributable to product information.[37] Add the cost to businesses and individuals of complying with consumer-protection laws—laws that would be unnecessary if consumers were better informed. And add all the less intuitive and harder to quantify "packaging" expenses such as salaries for movie stars and TV anchorpersons that have high name recognition and therefore strong marketing clout; or the cost of clothes, uniforms, and dry cleaning in various service businesses such as law, in which practitioners rely on presenting a pleasing and impressive "package" to clients—and clients judge them accordingly. You even have to add all the little marketing costs like the folding of toilet paper in hotel rooms. As Theodore Levitt describes how hotels communicate their competence in his *Marketing Imagination:* "The drinking glasses are wrapped in fresh bags or film, the toilet seat has a 'sanitized' paper band, the end piece of the toilet tissue is neatly shaped into a fresh-looking arrowhead. All these say with silent affirmative clarity that 'the room has been specially cleaned for your use and comfort.' "[38] Such costs represent only a very partial list of the costs of consumer information.

Despite this high cost, of course, consumers still lack good information, and this lack probably costs even more than all this product information put together. Here we can start by thinking about all the costs in dollars, time, and energy we incur for making the wrong purchasing decisions. Presumably, if we had optimal information, we'd also make optimal purchases. But clearly we don't. We can all think of extra repairs we had to pay for because we bought the wrong toaster or the wrong car. We can all think of a purchase that turned out to be a bad decision, a chair that we thought looked stylish but split in two, a shirt we thought was a good bargain but ripped at the seams, a VCR we thought was high-tech but turned out to be too complicated to program. Everything we pay to repair or replace these purchases is a cost of the lack of information. So too is the frustration of missing out on a favorite TV show because we were too confused to program the VCR, and so is the exasperation, time, and expense of losing valuable data to a computer program filled with bugs.

But these costs extend beyond buying the wrong toaster; they extend to just about every major life decision. Many of the highest costs here are unmeasurable: the cost, for example, to your happiness, not to mention your wallet, of choosing the wrong politician, school, career, home, or even spouse. Choosing the wrong career can mean poor performance, loss of self-esteem, boredom, bitterness, or depression—even alcohol-ism, child abuse, or suicide. Choosing the wrong doctor can mean years of extra pain, expensive tests and medications, time-consuming and humiliating lawsuits, and endless frustration and hostility; it can even mean your life. As long as product information remains so hard to get, we're going to have to live with a lot of this grief.

Just to give a flavor of the kind of costs we're talking about—and, remember, this is in addition to the $500 billion to $1 trillion estimate above—consider that a large portion of government waste, perhaps hundreds of billions of dollars of the $1.6 trillion that government spends, can be attributed to the fact that voters must choose candidates on the basis of the most pitiful information.[39] Consider that the federal govern-ment alone spends approximately $3 billion per year on consumer protection, all ultimately derived from our taxes, and all necessary because consumers lack the information to protect themselves.[40] Such costs pale before the considerable money that we shell out each year for excess and unnecessary repairs, as well as medical care and lost salary, all because we bought defective or misrepresented products.[41]

For some industries, too, there are figures available to show just how much we are paying for fraudulent or just plain unnecessary repairs—figures showing how our ignorance about evaluating repair shops perpetuates our ignorance displayed in making the initial purchase. Americans waste almost $21 billion a year on unnecessary or fraudulent auto repairs, for example.[42] Earlier, too, we showed how consumer confusion produces monopoly, and monopoly results in an inefficient economy, characterized by such things as overpaid and undermotivated employees, unutilized facilities, and inferior technology.[43] This problem is pervasive among service providers, including doctors, lawyers, plumb-ers, electricians, morticians, carpenters, and jewelers, who typically deal with very confused consumers and can use the monopoly power thus generated to support inefficient operations. The result is that the price most service professions charge is bloated by as much as 20 percent.

Another cost of lacking information involves product choice. As we saw in the discussion of the innovation effect, if consumers were already perfectly knowledgeable about goods and services before they even began to shop, the marketplace would offer much more genuine diversity and innovation. Choice costs are rather intangible, but they're the pervasive costs to all society of having relatively few products to choose from because of the difficulty of educating consumers about products' existence and benefits.

*   *   *

Just as the Founding Fathers of our country recognized the fundamental importance of an educated populace to a functioning democracy, so we must recognize the fundamental importance of educated consumers to a functioning market system. The increased complexity of society and its products makes good information more vital than ever. And yet, despite all the talk today about the coming "information age" or "knowledge society," the fact remains that the information available to consumers is characterized by relatively primitive conditions, not much different than those that exist today in Third World countries or the preindustrial West.

Unless we can fundamentally change the way consumers receive product information, all we can expect are more efforts devoted to fine-honing today's clearly inadequate consumer-information systems. These efforts result in the type of "information" we get from the life insurance salesman who spends all his time trying to get you to like him rather than clearly explaining the policy. As we shall see in the next chapter, consumer ignorance means that the likability of the salesperson or the superficial aspects of the product, rather than any concrete information about quality, is increasingly becoming the key ingredient to marketing success.

1. For example, Douglas Greer, *Industrial Organization and Public Policy*, 2nd ed. (London: Macmillan, 1984), p. 54; Richard Lipsey, Peter Steiner, and Douglas Purvis, *Economics*, 8th ed. (New York: Harper and Row, 1987), p. 263; and Paul Samuelson, *Economics*, 10th ed. (New York: McGraw-Hill, 1976), p. 485. Note, however, that in 1942 the world-famous economist Joseph Schumpeter published *Capitalism, Socialism, and Democracy* (New York: Harper and Bros., 1947), in which he argued that while competition may lead to maximum short-term efficiency and incremental innovation, monopoly profits are necessary to finance the technological breakthroughs underlying quantum leaps in efficiency and the introduction of fundamentally new products. There is thus a plausible economic argument that can be made that it is good to have ignorant or deceived consumers because this lets companies earn the monopoly profits necessary for major technological breakthroughs. This is a little bit like arguing, however, that you must kill the patient in order to save him. It may be argued that we need new safeguards to protect corporate monopoly power, but it's hard to imagine people arguing that the best way to create this monopoly power is through fostering ignorance and deception. More likely, companies will argue for such things as "industrial policy" (government sponsorship of megaprojects such as developing multibillion-dollar supercomputers) and strengthened intellectual property laws (patents and copyrights).

2. See Phillip Nelson, "Information and Consumer Behavior." *Journal of Political Economy*, March-April 1970, p. 311; Michael Riordan, "Monopolistic Competition with Experience Goods," *Quarterly Journal of Economics*, May 1986, pp. 264–265; Carl Shapiro, "Consumer Information, Product Quality, and Seller Reputation," *Bell Journal of Economics*, Spring 1982, p. 20; Richard Schmalensee, "A Model of Advertising and Product Quality," *Journal of Political Economy*, June 1978, p. 486; and William Comanor and Thomas Wilson, *Advertising and Market Power* (Boston: Harvard University Press, 1974), p. 43.

3. Jacob Schmookler, *Invention and Economic Growth* (Cambridge: Harvard University Press, 1966) and Neil Borden, *Advertising in Our Economy* (Chicago: Richard D. Irwin, 1942), pp. 226, 271.

4. E.g., see Comanor and Wilson, p. 245; Samuelson, p. 487; George Stigler, "The Economics of Information," *Journal of Political Economy,* June 1961, p. 223; and *Wall Street Journal,* February 24, 1989, sec. B, p. 34.

5. For example, see Eric Rasmusen, *Games and Information: An Introduction to Game Theory* (New York: Basil Blackwell, 1989); Andrew Schotter, "On the Economic Virtues of Incompetency and Dishonesty," *Research Report for the Office of Naval Research* (New York: C. V. Starr Center for Applied Economics, New York University, 1986); and Paul Milgrom and John Roberts, "Informational Asymmetries, Strategic Behavior, and Industrial Organization," *American Economic Review,* May 1987, pp. 184–193.

6. For example, see Robert W. Mitchell and Nicholas S. Thompson, eds., *Deception: Perspectives on Human and Nonhuman Deceit* (Albany: State University of New York Press, 1986).

7. Riordan, pp. 266, 278.

8. William Tyler, "Is Competitive Advertising Really Bad in Advertising? Reform with Care," *Advertising Age* 37 (March 14, 1966):61, as quoted in Comanor and Wilson, p. 2. See also Comanor and Wilson, pp. 24–25; Phillip Nelson, "Advertising as Information," *Journal of Political Economy,* July-August 1974, p. 745; Alfred Marshall, *Industry and Trade* (London: Macmillan, 1923), p. 306; Phillip Nelson, "The Economic Value of Advertising" in ed. Yale Brozen, *Advertising and Society* (New York: New York University Press, 1974), pp. 49–51; and Stuart Ewen, *All Consuming Images: The Politics of Style in Contemporary Culture* (New York: Basic Books, 1988), p. 247.

9. Charles Mann and Mark Plummer, "The Big Headache," *Atlantic Monthly,* October 1986, pp. 39–57, and Edward Cox, Robert Fellmeth, and John Schulz, *The Nader Report on the Federal Trade Commission* (New York: Richard W. Baron, 1969), pp. 23–24.

10. Daniel Boorstin, "Advertising and American Civilization," in Brozen, p. 16; Lawrence Friedman, "Game-Theory Models in the Allocation of Advertising Expenditures, *Operations Research,* September-October 1958; Joe Bain, *Industrial Organization* (New York: John Wiley, 1959), p. 389; Nicholas Kaldor, "The Economic Aspects of Advertising," *Review of Economic Studies* 18 (1950–1951):13; Arthur C. Pigou, *The Economics of Welfare,* 3rd ed. (London: Macmillan, 1929), p. 200; Edward Mazze, "Advertising and Market Power," in John S. Wright and John E. Mertes, eds. *Advertising's Role in Society* (Boston: West Publishing, 1974), p. 59; Marshall, p. 306; F. M. Scherer, *Industrial Market Structure and Economic Performance* (Boston: Houghton Mifflin, 1980), p. 389; and Comanor and Wilson, p. 245.

11. Stuart Chase, quoted in David Ogilvy's *Confessions of an Advertising Man* (New York: Atheneum, 1963), p. 152.

12. Delbart Duncan, Stanley Hollander, and Ronald Savitt, *Modern Retailing Management: Basic Concepts and Practices* (Chicago: Richard D. Irwin, 1983), p. 395.

13. Tibor Scitovszky, "Some Consequences of the Habit of Judging Quality by Price," *The Review of Economic Studies,* 1944–1945, pp. 100–105.

14. William Davidson, Daniel Sweeney, and Ronald Stampfl, *Retail Management* (New York: John Wiley, 1988), p. 409.

15. Comanor and Wilson, p. 23. See also, Riordan, p. 270; Scitovszky, pp. 100 ff.; W. Bradford Cornell, "Price as a Quality Signal: Some Additional Experimental Results," *Economic Inquiry,* April 1978, p. 303.

16. Thomas Nagle, *The Strategy and Tactics of Pricing* (Englewood Cliffs, N.J.: Prentice-Hall, 1986), pp. 195–196.

17. As quoted in Isadore Barmash, "Private Label: Flux," *Stores,* April 1987, p. 19.

18. Nagle, p. 250.

19. Greer, p. 59.

20. *PC Digest,* March 1988, p. 1.

21. Kenneth Clarkson and Roger Miller, *Industrial Organization* (New York: McGraw-Hill, 1982), p. 236. See also Borden, pp. 24–27, and Scott Cunningham, "Perceived Risk and Brand Loyalty," in Donald F. Cox, ed., *Risk Taking and Information Handling in Consumer Behavior* (Boston: Harvard Business School, 1967), pp. 507–523.

22. For example, see Vance Packard, *The Hidden Persuaders* (New York: Pocket Books, 1957), pp. 119–120.

23. For example, see *PC Digest,* April 1987, p. 3.

24. John Kottman, "Truth and the Image of Advertising," in Wright, p. 292; Boorstin, p. 16; and *Your Money's Worth,* p. 2.

25. *The Nader Report on the Federal Trade Commission,* pp. 20–21.

26. For example, John Tirole, *The Theory of Industrial Organization* (Cambridge: MIT Press, 1988), p. 295; Dave Methvin, "Press Releases Should Describe the Real Product," *PC Week,* May 14, 1990, p. 26; and Deidre A. Depke et al., "The Software Market Is Downright Mushy," *Business Week,* October 2, 1989, p. 98.

27. See, for example, Deidre A. Depke, "Home Computers: Will They Sell This Time? IBM, Tandy, and Others Say Yes," *Business Week,* September 10, 1990, pp. 64–74.

28. Greer, p. 55.

29. Dennis Smallwood and John Conlisk, "Product Quality in Markets Where Consumers Are Imperfectly Informed," *Quarterly Journal of Economics,* February 1979, p. 2.

30. E.g., Comanor and Wilson, pp. 114–143.

31. Specifically, we have tried to be as conservative as possible in our estimates by leaving out numbers where there were no reasonable bases to make an estimate. But we are confident that our numbers are accurate to within only ±50 percent.

32. We have developed these calculations at length in an unpublished paper too detailed and abstruse for a book of this nature. The major components of this figure are (1) total promotion and advertising expense, approximately $200 billion a year—see *Marketing & Media Decisions* (July issue, annually), *Marketing Communications* (August issue, annually), and *Advertising Age* (September issue, annually); (2) personal selling and purchasing expense (including personnel), approximately 9.5 percent of the workforce, or more than $300 billion a year—see *1986 Occupational Employment: Establishment Data,* "Employment by Industry and Occupation, 1986 and Projected 2000 Alternatives," U.S. Bureau of Labor Statistics, Department of Labor, and *1988 Occupational Employment: Household Data,* U.S. Department of Commerce, Bureau of the Census; (3) R&D, manufacturing, packaging, and overhead expense (including prime real estate) associated with presenting and disposing of product information—this figure is probably at least 2 percent of GNP, or $100 billion. Please note that these product-information costs are probably dwarfed by the opportunity costs associated with the poor product information we currently get. For example, the monopoly efficiency which is born of consumer ignorance and is endemic to our economy, particularly in the service sector, may represent as much as 10

percent of GNP. Similarly, much of the $1 trillion plus spent on repair and replacement of products would be unnecessary if consumers bought optimal products to begin with.

33. To get a quick feel for these numbers, remember that entertainment time as well as shopping time is characterized by the gathering of product information. For example, approximately 25 percent of TV time is devoted to advertisements. For an authoritative though incomplete compendium of time spent watching advertising see *1988 TV Dimensions* (New York: Media Dynamics, Inc., 1989), p. 284–288.

34. U.S. Department of Commerce, Bureau of Economic Analysis, *Survey of Current Business,* (Washington, D.C.: Government Printing Office, July 1988), p. 40.

35. In 1988 private industry funded $66.2 billion in R&D expenditures, while government spent $33.2 billion. See *Research and Development in Industry* (Washington, D.C.: National Science Foundation, 1989).

36. Unfortunately, there have been no major recent studies estimating the total cost of distribution and marketing as a percentage of sales. For earlier studies see Paul Stewart and J. Frederic Dewhurst, *Does Distribution Cost Too Much?* (New York: Twentieth Century Fund, 1939), pp. 117–118 and Reavis Cox, *Distribution in a High-Level Economy* (Englewood Cliffs, N.J.: Prentice-Hall, 1965), pp. 144–147.

37. Stuart Ewen, *All Consuming Images: The Politics of Style in Contemporary Culture* (New York: Basic Books, 1988), p. 234. See also U.S. Congress, Office of Technology Assessment, *Facing America's Trash: What's Next for Municipal Solid Waste,* OTA-0-424, GPO #052-003-01168-9 (Washington, D.C.: Government Printing Office, October 1989).

38. Theodore Levitt, *The Marketing Imagination* (New York: Free Press, 1986), p. 108.

39. Government expenditures were $1,574 billion in 1987, according to the Department of Commerce's *Survey of Current Business,* p. 57.

40. *Lying, Stealing, & Cheating in America,* special program aired on the ABC television network June 2, 1989.

41. U.S. Consumer Product Safety Commissions, *1987 Annual Report* (Washington, D.C.:n.p., 1987), p. 1.

42. Paul Blumberg, *The Predatory Society: Deception in the American Marketplace* (New York: Oxford University Press, 1989), p. 66. His figures are from Robert Sikorsky, "Highway Robbery: The Scandal of Auto Repair in America," *Reader's Digest,* May 1987, pp. 91–99. See also Randall and Arthur P. Glickman, p. 3, and U.S. Department of Transportation, National Highway Traffic Safety Administration, *Auto Repair and Maintenance,* NHTSA Report No. DOT MS 803 355, NTIS No. PB 282 896 (Washington, D.C.: Government Printing Office, May 1978); Sikorsky, pp. 92–93, 96, 99; and John Phelan, *Regulation of the Television Repair Industry in Louisiana and California: A Case Study,* staff report to the Federal Trade Commission, Stock Number 1800-00166 (Washington, D.C.: Government Printing Office, November 1974), pp. 31, 46. In late 1989, moreover, the New York City Department of Consumer Affairs reported that twenty-three of the forty-two transmission- and muffler-repair shops visited (nearly 55 percent) wanted to do unnecessary work or sell unneeded products or services.

43. See Greer, pp. 419–427.

The Promotional Society

If relying on others for information is the shoppers' most fundamental adaptation to consumer ignorance, sellers' providing information about their own products—or *self-promotion*—is the seller's most fundamental adaptation. Such promotion now pervades just about every aspect of our lives and has come to characterize our economy and society at large. Indeed, one of the defining marks of our ignorance is that we now live in a "promotional society."

Given current technological and market conditions, such a society is absolutely necessary and therefore justifiable. And yet, there are obvious problems with a society and economy pervaded by self-promotion. Most notably, we can't expect sellers to provide complete, unbiased information about their own products when their only reason for providing this information is to entice purchasers. Even if sellers did provide all the information customers wanted, they couldn't afford for long to do so in a competitive environment. For example, retailers often complain that they are forced to cut back service because customers just go into the store with the best information, "steal it" by taking up a lot of the salesperson's time, and then buy for a lower price down the street. However necessary it might be at present, asking sellers to provide shopping information is an inherently flawed concept.

UNCOUPLING THE CUES: HOW PROMOTION HINDERS COMPARISON SHOPPING

As we have seen, if cues such as price, brand, reputation, and the like always corresponded to value, we'd all be in great shape—whatever the cost and whatever the source. We wouldn't have to worry about understanding the inner workings of a computer or differentiating one washing machine from the next because we could rely on these simple cues to signal high-quality merchandise. The problem, however, is that the ignorance that makes these cues so useful is the very same ignorance that eventually makes them misleading. Part of the problem, as we have just seen, is that ignorant consumers force sellers to emphasize a given cue if they want to sell the product, and along the way this cue itself becomes the selling point. Value becomes irrelevant. In a world where appearance and reality are so hard to differentiate, a tremendous premium is placed on promotional skills. Eventually, the appearance starts to replace the reality.

Sellers are hardly innocent victims in this process. The pursuit of profit combined with consumer ignorance forces them to take advantage of the cues, which starts the process off. Then, as social psychologist Robert B. Cialdini explains in his book *Influence: The New Psychology of Modern Persuasion,* a few unscrupulous sellers disconnect the cue from the value that it supposedly signals. Eventually other sellers have to follow suit to survive, until the cue becomes nothing other than a promotional tactic, an expression of nothing outside itself. Wealth no longer means anything but a large advertising budget, and high price nothing but high price.

Separating the cue from the value is the easiest way to differentiate yourself from competitors. And, for sellers, differentiation is the key to maximizing profits.[1] While consumers prefer to have as many genuine choices as possible (competition), sellers feel otherwise: the more unique-seeming their product (the more their monopoly power), the better. Sellers want to differentiate their products, if only in appearance, to obstruct genuine price comparisons. Whether this differentiation is based on fact or fiction, knowledge or ignorance, is not an issue affecting profitability and competitive standing. The issue is only how to get consumers to buy from you, and at the highest-possible price.

Of course, in a truly competitive environment, one characterized by knowledgeable buyers, misleading differentiation poses no problem: consumers will refuse to pay for that which has no value. Consumer ignorance, however, allows sellers to artificially differentiate their commodities. In fact, when consumers don't know very much about products, only the unsophisticated seller has to resort to outright distortion. Rather, sellers can selectively play on the cues to hint that their products are superior to all others—without actually improving their product—and know that consumers will fall for such hints. No overt lie has occurred, but the message has been sent.

Here it's important to remember that what is best for the seller is not necessarily best for the economy. From the seller's point of view, promotion serves to boost sales, not to inform buyers of a product's relative merits. This discrepancy of goals creates a hugely inefficient product-information system, one characteristic of which is that the more consumers are confused by products, the less useful information is given out about them while the more money is spent promoting them.[2]

No wonder, then, that sellers have a vested interest in keeping us from genuinely comparing one product to the next: meaningful comparisons would reveal that what we thought was unique and well-priced is really no better, and perhaps worse, than twenty similar articles on the market. Throughout this century many laws have been passed to promote standards in various industries, which, in turn, serve to facilitate quality and price comparisons.[3] Companies, however, especially those with well-known brands, often don't want to facilitate this kind of comparison shopping because it tends to reduce their profits.[4] Sellers often succeed here, too, because few of us have the time, resources, or ability to eliminate the roadblocks to meaningful comparisons. How many of us realize, for example, that sellers often choose their own standards by which to judge their products? To measure a camcorder's ability to record at low levels of light ("lux" rating), one manufacturer may measure the capacity to pick up *color* at these levels, while another may measure the capacity to pick up *black and white*. Similarly, one manufacturer may measure the average brightness across the entire screen of a projection TV, while a competitor measures brightness at the very center of the set's picture tube. Still, both manufacturers call this measurement "brightness." Such multiple standards, each applied selectively, add up to no standards, and allow many camcorders to "have the best lux rating" and many projection TVs to have "superior brightness."

Sellers also commonly add meaningless pseudofeatures—such as new styles or model numbers—and pawn them off as reflections of true uniqueness. These pseudofeatures are in some ways pseudostandards, because they put each item into an incomparable category all its own. In fact, we estimate that in the consumer-electronics business alone, more than 50 percent of the models and brands on the market have nothing to do with genuine differences in performance but merely serve to reduce competition and increase prices for retailers and manufacturers.

Often pseudofeatures appear in the form of incomprehensible but authoritative jargon that makes a product sound special and unique. One ad for Tera televisions, for example, reads as follows: "The Tera ran way ahead of the field . . . thanks to Non-Linear Compression, Dynamic Aperture, and Double Differential Contour Correction." Although we suspect that very few people scanning *Video* magazine and looking for a television would truly understand this language or know if "double differential contour correction" was something that they really wanted to pay for, they would definitely get the impression that the Tera must be a state-of-the-art, quality set while actually understanding nothing about it and not being able to compare it to anything else on the market.

Perhaps the best testimony to this practice comes from the relatively small number of manufacturers responsible for producing virtually the same appliance under dozens of different model numbers and brand names. Many manufacturers issue dozens of virtually identical rack systems or televisions, for example, but sell them all under different model numbers and promise to distribute them selectively: this practice allows retailers and manufacturers to minimize price competition on any given model, since if you can only find any given model in one store, you aren't going to be able to comparison shop for it.

Matsushita, for instance, sells virtually identical camcorders under its own Panasonic and Quasar labels, but it also sells those camcorders to other companies which sell them under the Magnavox, Philco, Sylvania, GE, NEC, Olympus, Sears, and J. C. Penney labels.[5] Despite the equivalence of these camcorders, each brand name implies a different quality. Similarly, dishwashers manufactured by White Consolidated Industries are sold under *fifteen* different brand names: Admiral, Brown Stove Works, Caloric, Crosley, Gaffers & Sattler, Glenwood, Magic Chef, Montgomery Ward, Modern Maid, Panasonic, Peerless-Premier, Roper, Sears, Sunray, and Whirlpool.[6]

Manufacturers also artificially differentiate products by changing some insignificant feature and slapping on a new number. This new model allows salespeople to explain why the model you saw in Store A cost less than the apparently identical model in front of you: "Oh, they're selling last year's model," they say (last year's model had a brown rather than a black nameplate), "That model has inferior wiring" (without explaining why), or "That model doesn't use Xygloo shielding of the capacitator" (without explaining what that means or whether it makes the least bit of difference). With groceries and other items that can't be given a different number, a related tactic is to sell different sizes, thus obscuring direct comparisons. For example, warehouse clubs sell cereal in different box sizes than do supermarkets.

The highly promoted secret ingredient—whether it be in toothpaste or aspirin or the preparation of wine—can only be ascribed to a variation on this pseudofeature theme. How can you possibly decide the difference between toothpastes, for example, if all the ingredients are identical except for this "secret ingredient"? Or how to compare a brand-name shampoo to a store brand if all the brand name gives you is a reference to a "secret formula"? The same can be said for the prevalent coinage of terms uninterpretable to the uninitiated (and sometimes to everyone but the person who coined the term) such as "micro-black" picture tube (for televisions) and "micro-enzyme action" (for laundry detergents).

Consider, too, the ambiguous ingredient—such as the name of a designer on a private-label line of clothes in a department store—which implies superior clothes. Similarly, companies may give a fancy name to a standard part, as Toshiba did by calling the defrost function on its microwave oven a "Jet Defrost" with a trademark registration beside it—implying that Toshiba ovens did something different than all other microwave ovens.

As Chase and Schlink pointed out years ago, the lack of objective standards lays the groundwork for more blatant forms of puffery and distortion.[7] If you can't make your product sound good using such objective standards as product-specific cues, you have little choice but to rely on other cues, such as hype. Because sellers want consumers to know only their strong points, they selectively emphasize features that make them stand out from the crowd—and they can get away with it, too, knowing that consumers are too confused to pick up this kind of distortion and that no standards exist to prove true strength. Persuasion becomes the dominant force in determining what you choose to buy.

Economist Frederick Scherer describes this pervasive practice of "persuasion through partial disclosure and innuendo":

The consumer is told, for instance, that Anacin contains 23 percent more pain reliever than other leading headache remedies, but not that the pain reliever is plain aspirin. Or a savings and loan bank proclaims that no other bank offers higher savings account interest rates without mentioning that virtually all of its rivals pay the same ceiling rates. When the regulators move in on such practices, advertisers invent new and more subtle ways of "puffing" their products' merits.

Although Scherer acknowledges that most consumers have been made sufficiently cynical to avoid being taken in by such half-truths, he points out that "some must be gulled, however, for advertisers would not try to mislead if they thought they were convincing no one."[8]

Advertising provides the most obvious example of this artificial differentiation through puffery.[9] Perhaps the most damning testament to the poor quality of most advertising comes from the profession itself, which proclaims a catechism of "K.I.S.S.", for "keep it simple and stupid." Most advertisers operate on the principle that all their appeal must come from a simple proposition or image that the consumer can grasp within seconds. This principle leaves no room for subtlety and certainly not for any concrete information. In fact, paradoxically, the more complex a product is, the less advertisers tend to describe it and the more they tend to rely on vague images. Any fair description would violate the K.I.S.S. principle, these ads imply, so why even try?

THE MORAL DIMENSION OF IGNORANCE AND PROMOTION

You're probably not aware of too much deception when you go shopping. Why should you be? By definition, effective deception goes undetected. In fact, if it could be detected, especially among companies that rely on reputation, no one would bother to do it. In other words, you probably notice very little of this deception in your day-to-day shopping, because if you went around convinced that specific sellers were trying to cheat you, you wouldn't buy from them, and the deception would have failed. The more common response is to think that deception probably takes place in general but that we personally can outsmart the system, or at least avoid major injury.

Perhaps the only deception that we as consumers sense at all is the deception of advertisements. Even a representative of the Advertising

Association acknowledges the prevalence of critics. He quotes an eminent British journalist as saying:

> The prejudice against the adman is ancient, classless, suprapolitical and quite impervious to the evidence. One thing on which left wing Members of Parliament and Tory Knights of the Shire usually agree is that advertising is a dubious, antisocial and almost criminal activity.[10]

Stephen Fox, in his authoritative book on the history of advertising, talks at length about "the continued public suspicion of advertising and a willingness to believe the most ridiculous charges against it."[11] In 1981 a *Newsweek* poll asked Americans to rate the honesty and ethical standards in eleven fields of work. Advertising came in dead last.[12]

In fact, respectable opinion in our society has never been very fond of this business. In the nineteenth century, when modern advertising and salesmanship got their first toehold, only marginal businesses, such as those producing unorthodox medical concoctions, advertised. Codes of ethics for professions such as law and medicine strictly forbade advertising.

Slowly but surely, of course, advertising has forced its way into virtually every nook and cranny of our economy—but not without a lot of kicking and screaming. Until the end of the last century, for example, most magazines accepted no advertising, and when they did, relegated it to the back of the book. It was only sheer economic necessity that forced most of them to welcome advertisers actively. Similarly, as radio stations in their early days began to consider carrying ads, many complaints arose. Thus, in the early 1920s, Secretary of Commerce Herbert Hoover called it "inconceivable that we should allow so great a possibility for service to be drowned in advertiser chatter."[13] Even today, we witness this begrudging acceptance as law and medicine give in to wholesale advertising, while almost everyone who is interviewed on the subject seems to regret it—even if they think it's necessary.

Government policy also reflects our ambivalence about this activity. On the one hand, it recognizes advertising's vital role in our economy. On the other hand, it has empowered dozens of agencies to regulate selling practices to promote efficiency and limit advertising's power. The FTC alone has regulations that restrict literally thousands of advertising and selling practices ranging from using words such as "premium," "free," and "wholesale" to labeling merchandise such as furs, gasoline, and credit cards. The FDA, too, requires pharmaceutical companies to prove that all drugs are both safe and effective before allowing them to enter the U.S. market and specifies very strict labeling requirements about appropriate uses and precautions. Furthermore, the USDA requires meat packagers to grade all beef according to preestablished standards before marketing it, thus obviating false claims of quality. Such requirements also aim to allow consumers to buy confidently without earning master's degrees in rump roasts. The government, then, seems focused on trying to encourage the competitive and informational aspects of advertising, but whenever practical, curbing its often inefficient and misleading aspects. Nevertheless, the sense that advertisements are somehow deceptive persists.

Advertising is hardly the only area of selling in which deception is so pervasive. In fact, deception may be even more rampant in less obvious areas where it is the only way many sellers can survive in today's market. As one writer has noted about the causes of the recent scandals on Wall Street: "Granted, individuals can destroy the integrity of the markets, but the markets can also destroy the integrity of the individuals. In short the very structure of the securities industry works to destroy ethical conduct."[14] Here the author is speaking only of deception in financial markets, but the principle is universal. In his recent book *The Predatory Society,* sociologist Paul Blumberg concurs:

> A businessman who starts out with the very best of intentions frequently finds his integrity worn down by the inexorable temptations of the system. . . . A moral order whose central credo is "Take care of number one" is not going to be a restraining force on the pressures for deception built into the system. Moreover, what all this deception reveals is not that human nature is evil or greedy innately, but merely that people behave rationally and logically in response to the imperatives of a system. In a different game with different rules, behavior changes, and what is often assumed to be innate greed may become innate altruism. . . . The culprit, then, is not innate human corruption or even self-interest, but simply the rules of the market system, which often reward people for acting indecently and punish them for acting decently.[15]

Rather than Blumberg's rather vague "rules of the marketplace," however, we think that the real culprit here is consumer ignorance. Just as natural selection favors "individuals who successfully manipulate the behavior of other individuals, whether or not this is to the advantage of the manipulated individuals," so a marketplace characterized by ignorance favors sellers who successfully manipulate or deceive consumers.[16] According to economists Michael Darby and Edi Karni, the only way a company faced with ignorant consumers can survive in a competitive economy is to engage in a certain amount of fraud (or systematic incompetence).[17]

Furthermore, we reward this fraud or incompetence by buying the products so promoted. Quality and virtue get punished and annihilated in a world of ignorance and dishonesty.[18] Economist Eli Cox explains that when consumers can't accurately evaluate a large proportion of products on the market, promoters can make false claims with impunity—and "all competitors who expect to stay in business are likely to have to resort to similar practices."

Of course, our society has certain restraints on false claims, but as we shall see in the second section of this book, society's powers and resources are limited and leave incentives to stretch the law in the pursuit of profit.[19] As economist George Akerlof argues, for instance, in the used-car business, consumers often have a hard time telling a good car from a lemon. Dishonest sellers exploit this ignorance by offering inferior cars and increasing their profits, ultimately driving the more honest sellers out of business. As consumers start to figure that all used cars are bad, notes Arkerlof, they create a self-fulfilling prophesy: even a truly good used car will decline in value to a small fraction of the purchase price just one day after purchase. After a while even if you want to sell (or buy) a high-quality used car, you can't. Thus, concludes Akerlof, "the cost of dishonesty . . . lies not only in the amount by which the purchaser is cheated; the cost also must include the loss incurred from driving legitimate business out of existence."[20]

Again, our intention here is not to assert that sellers and advertisers purposefully cheat consumers, but rather to say that those who don't do so, in effect if not in intention, aren't likely to prosper in an environment of ignorance. Perhaps that is why Adam Smith said: "I have never known much good done by those who affected to trade for the public good. It is an affection, indeed, not very common among merchants, and very few words need be employed in dissuading them from it."[21]

There is a widespread view that if enough people engage in a certain practice, and if no one is taking steps to police it, then it becomes acceptable, especially if it's impossible to survive without practicing it. We concur: rather than chastising "evil" retailers or manufacturers, we're more inclined to believe that economic necessity has forced them to engage in deceptive practices. Furthermore, we believe that if most sellers could make a living upholding their highest ideals, they would certainly like to and would encourage those structural changes that would make this possible.[22] Much of the spirit behind industry self-regulation has in fact reflected the desire to set up structures that encourage ethical behavior.

On the other hand, such sympathy rapidly dissipates when stores and manufacturers not only engage in these practices to survive, but applaud them. Rather than acknowledge the unfortunate necessity for deception, companies will often refer to these activities as "creativity," as did the airline industry in reference to its practice of advertising discounts that were good only on round-trip purchases while displaying the one-way fares.[23] Even more disturbing are trade-journal articles like the one which essentially recommended legal bait and switch tactics. Entitled "SELL UP—Everyone's Doing It!" it featured the following summary:

> Selling-up off advertised bargains is the name of the game. If you're a retailer, you better learn how to do it successfully, properly and consistently. . . . One business after another has come to recognize the need to sell up to better product in order to survive.[24]

It's also hard to sypathize with entire industries such as candymakers or cigarette manufacturers who try to survive by persuading the public that their offerings are harmless or even healthy.[25]

Furthermore, we believe that when consumer-protection agencies condemn or fine a few specific companies engaging in these widespread practices, they themselves are behaving unethically. When the National Advertising Review Board recently forced Montgomery Ward to drop its "lowest-price" guarantee, for instance, there was no mention of dealing similarly with Montgomery Ward's competitors who made equally if not more misleading guarantees. Similarly, we can understand the fury attributed to Sears, Roebuck and Company when New York's Attorney General accused them of bait and switch. It's unreasonable and unfair to single out one conspicuous vendor when the entire industry needs an overhaul.[26]

D O   E T H I C S   P A Y ?

Such arguments, of course, fly in the face of the common sentiment that ethics pay. The belief underlies the official policy of self-regulating trade associations such as the Better Business Bureau and the Direct Marketing Association, and it's also the party line of leading business schools. In fact, in the late 1980s John S. R. Shad contributed $30 million to the Harvard Business School to teach the students that ethics pays. The belief that ethics can be taught usually translates into the argument that ethics pay. While one of us (J. S.) was studying at the Harvard Business School, this belief was supposed to be self-evident and not a matter for discussion: unethical behavior was only for the foolish or the uncouth.

Why do so many people think that ethics pay? Numerous trade magazines answer this question explicitly, especially regarding advertising. Consider this typical comment from *Computer & Software News:* "Resellers have realized that it is best to advertise ethically because of the long-term payoff of a satisfied customer."[27]

The leap from "ethics should pay" to "ethics do pay" has been made easily. Study after study shows that although they regard ads as somewhat deceptive, most consumers deny being influenced at all by them. Thus, the deception is benign. Meanwhile, leaders in the advertising industry argue that although advertising once was rife with deception, it now has cleaned up its act.[28]

How can such sentiments be reconciled with the Efficiency Effect and Morality Effect, which contend that ignorant consumers foster an inefficient marketplace and deception by sellers? How can they be reconciled with a 1985 New York Times/CBS poll showing that 59 percent of Americans believed that business crime was very common, while another 34 percent believed that it occurred occasionally? Blumberg, in citing this poll, observes that "most Americans believe that business crime is widespread and increasing, that the majority of corporate executives are dishonest, and that most white-collar criminals either get away with their crime or are inadequately punished."[29]

What has happened is that what once outraged us has become a harmless fact of life: promotion may be deceptive, we tell ourselves, but it's no big deal because we don't pay attention to it anyway. Forty-five years ago, when most forms of modern promotion—TV and radio—were very new, people were acutely concerned about its propensity to distort. Nearly half a century later, we assume that promotion—and advertising in particular—has become absolutely essential to the health of a modern economy. The tendency to distort is still there, but we have tended to overlook this peccadillo because, from a practical standpoint, there's almost nothing we can do about it.

This situation leads us to say, "Why should any of this disturb me?—I know it's all a lot of lies anyway." And it leads the promoter to justify deceptive behavior by saying, "Since the consumer knows this is a lot of bunk anyway, there's really nothing immoral about it." Unfortunately, what's missing in this line of reasoning by both consumers and business is that all this bunk—whether immoral in content or not—leads, not surprisingly, to tremendous inefficiency and waste.

The truth is that when business leaders and trade journals proclaim to their audiences that "ethics pay," they simply mean that the *appearance* of ethics pays. This is where courses on moral precepts or so-called ethical upbringing can help: they can teach people what ethical behavior looks like and teach them that it's important to *seem* ethical. They cannot, however, give people any economic incentive for *behaving* ethically. Only when real ethics start to pay will we start substituting them for their mere appearance. And real ethics will start to pay only when buyers and sellers are fully informed of their alternatives.

THE RISE OF THE PROMOTIONAL PERSONALITY

The widespread belief that ethics pay also suggests that anything that doesn't pay must be unethical. Indeed, this suggestion represents a sad underside to the pervasive belief. As John Maynard Keynes said, "We must pretend to ourselves and to every one that fair is foul and foul is fair; for foul is useful and fair is not."[30] Today, there is a very strong attitude in our country that admires the deceiver and detests the sucker. It is not one of those openly acknowledged beliefs but a hidden value that can only be inferred from behavior. We call arrogant and manipulative people "confident and shrewd" if these people are achievers. We call humble and trusting people "unassertive and stupid" if these people are failures.

Thus, consumer ignorance has led us to value the promotional company, the company that benefits by exaggerating its success and uniqueness. Paralleling this promotional company, moreover, we have also come to value certain character traits among the individual personalities that work in it. Despite our superficial praise of such values as honesty and sincerity, talent and hard work, the ultimate adaptation to our igonorance has been the emergence of something we might call the "promotional personality," which, like the promotional company, feigns skill in the race to succeed and has become the de facto ideal of the admirable human being.

The heart of the promotional personality is the emphasis on appearance over substance. The basic tricks of the trade are simple: confidence, friendliness, and good grooming. With these simple qualities you will have the "people skills" necessary to sell yourself, and, ultimately, to sell your product, whether or not it is the best value. After all, if we can't judge a product on its true merits, and especially when the cues to quality have become the tools of promoters, it's only natural that most of us will choose to buy the product of the most appealing seller.

Thorstein Veblen developed the basic framework for this promotional personality in his *Theory of the Leisure Class*. In that 1899 book he argued that people were tempted, at the cost of great waste to society, to engage in conspicuous consumption and conspicuous leisure in order to prove their success and wealth.[31] We might adapt Veblen's basic theory and say that the promotional personality is characterized by two basic attributes: conspicuous achievement and conspicuous friendliness (or altruism). Conspicuous achievement involves surrounding yourself with material objects that suggest financial success or intellectual ability, as well as displaying conspicuous confidence. The wisdom of such strategies for living may be summed up in the phrase "nothing succeeds like success." People, lacking real knowledge of merit, presume that if you surround yourself with objects of merit, then you must be valuable. And they also assume, along the same lines as the wealth cue, that if you act with very visible confidence, then that confidence must reflect some genuine merit. A particularly vivid illustration of these principles comes from John Molloy's *Dress for Success* books, which contend that proper dress can strongly improve your chance for success in the business world. Clothes should make you look successful, competent, and confident. Lack of time and energy and money invested in appearances will likely result in failure.

Conspicuous friendliness (or altruism) is another aspect of the promotional personality. The basic reasoning here is that it is not enough to have something somebody else wants (as exhibited through conspicuous achievement), it is also necessary to tell the rest of the world that you always have their, not your own, best interests at heart. Dale Carnegie's *How to Win Friends and Influence People* is the archetypical expression of this personality structure: the pervasive smile, the willingness to rapidly make (and presumably break) friendships, the phrasing of all propositions in terms of what will please others rather than yourself, and the promise that if these maxims are mastered with complete sincerity, great financial and social success will follow.

Many books emphasize these strategies under various denominations. In the "psychology" section of one chain bookstore on Manhattan's Fifth Avenue, we found at least twenty-five different titles all promising to give the reader the secret to success, the secret to selling, the secret to happiness, and all these secrets involved cultivating this promotional personality. Of course, the granddaddy of all these books is Dale Carnegie's, which has sold more than 15 million copies since it was first published and may be considered the bible of the promotional personality.

In appealing language Carnegie gives readers simple tips that are bound to bring them success in today's world: "I find that smiles are bringing me dollars, many dollars every day." "A man without a smiling face must not open a shop. Your smile is a messenger of your good will." "Talk in terms of the other person's interests." "If you would win a man to your cause, first convince him that you are his sincere friend. Therein is a drop of honey that catches his heart; which, say what you will, is the great high road to his reason."[32]

What Carnegie says is true. But that's not the point. Although traits such as confidence, friendliness, and good grooming sound admirable, they also can cover up incompetence and greed. In such cases, the traits become nothing other than euphemisms for smugness, flattery, and exploitation. Consider, for example, the language of a critic of this kind of behavior:

> There is a group of people who know very well where the weapons of automatic influence lie and who employ them regularly and expertly to get what they want. . . . The secret of their effectiveness lies in the way they structure their requests, the way they arm themselves with one or another of the weapons of influence that exist within the social environment. . . . All that is required is to trigger the great stores of influence that already exist in the situation and direct them toward the intended target. . . . This last feature of the

process allows the exploiters an enormous additional benefit—the ability to manipulate without the appearance of manipulation.[33]

Of course, we're not arguing here that promotional personalities are in any way consciously deceptive. For one thing, there is no hard-and-fast line between appearances and reality, and given our ignorance, it can always be said that attention to appearances is the only way to convey true merit. On the other hand, Europeans have traditionally despised the casual friendliness of the Americans, their tendency to both quickly make and drop friends, seeing it as deceitful and manipulative. Many Americans would disagree, calling the Europeans arrogant snobs in return. But, again, motivation is irrelevant. Because there is always a temptation and a payoff for bringing appearance out of line with reality, whether or not people know they have passed that borderline is not important. People can't be expected to indict themselves or reflect on motives vital for their success.

However you judge it, though, the promotional personality is an inevitable feature of our current consumer-information system and has been affecting our lives for years. In the 1950s it led Vance Packard to observe that "in sales jobs the more successful men tend to be those who are more imposing-looking; those who have a striking manner and command instant attention." It led Les Giblin to write: "It is a sad but true fact that many men of mediocre ability get further than others who have outstanding talents, merely because they know how to *act confidently*." And it led the Carnegie Institute of Technology to find that "85 percent of success is due to personality factors, to the ability to deal with people successfully."[34] Over thirty years later it led Stuart Ewen to observe that "the primacy of style over substance has become the normative consciousness."[35]

1. For example, see Joe Bain, "Product Differentiation Advantages," *Barriers to New Competition: Their Character and Consequences in Manufacturing Industries* (Cambridge, Mass.: Harvard University Press, pp. 114-115, 121-125); Michael Spence, "Product Differentiation and Welfare," *American Economic Review,* May 1976, p. 407.

2. Douglas Greer, *Industrial Organization and Public Policy,* 2nd ed. (London: Macmillan, 1984), p. 65; F. M. Scherer, *Industrial Market Structure and Economic Performance* (Boston: Houghton Mifflin, 1980), pp. 381–383.

3. For an in-depth discussion of these principles see Greer, p. 84. See also John K. Galbraith, *The Affluent Society* (New York: New American Library, 1958), p. 201.

4. Greer, p. 91. Similar stories about seller opposition to universal standards appear in Doris Faber's *Enough: The Revolt of the American Consumer* (New York: Dell, 1972).

5. Cliff Roth, "The OEM Connection: Who Makes What?" *VideoMaker*, April-May 1987, p. 33.

6. "The Private Brand Picture." *Appliance*, September 1987, p. 61.

7. Stuart Chase and F. J. Schlink, *Your Money's Worth: A Study in the Waste of the Consumer's Dollar* (New York: Macmillan, 1927), pp. 181–182.

8. Scherer, p. 380. See also "Maligned Safety Rules Turned into Promotion," *Wall Street Journal*, November 7, 1989, sec. B, p. 1.

9. Robert E. McAuliffe, *Advertising, Competition, and Public Policy: Theories and New Evidence* (Lexington, Mass.: Lexington Books, 1987), p. 7, and Michael Schudson, *Advertising, the Uneasy Persuasion: Its Dubious Impact on American Society* (New York: Basic Books, 1984).

10. M. J. Waterson, *Advertising, Brands, and Markets* (London: Advertising Association, 1984), p. 3.

11. Stephen Fox, *The Mirror Makers* (New York: Vintage Books, 1984), p. 319. See also Faber, p. 152.

12. *Newsweek*, May 4, 1981, p. 51.

13. Herbert Hoover, quoted by Roger Draper in "The Faithless Shepherd," *New York Review of Books*, June 26, 1986, p. 15.

14. Tim Stone, *New York Times*, March 19, 1989, sec. F, p. 3.

15. Paul Blumberg, *The Predatory Society: Deception in the American Marketplace* (New York: Oxford University Press, 1989), pp. 173–175.

16. J. R Krebs, J. R. Davies, and N. B. Davies, *Behavioral Ecology: An Evolutionary Approach* (London: Blackwell Scientific, n.d.), p. 309.

17. Michael Darby and Edi Karni, "Free Competition and the Optimal Amount of Fraud," *Journal of Law and Economics*, April 1973, p. 67.

18. Edward Cox, Robert Fellmeth, and John Schulz, *The Nader Report on the Federal Trade Commission* (New York: Richard W. Baron, 1969), p. 38.

19. Eli Cox, "Costs of Puffery," in eds. John S. Wright and John E. Mertes, *Advertising's Role in Society* (St. Paul: West Publishing, 1974), pp. 295–296. See also *The Nader Report*, p. 15, 64; and Arthur C. Pigou, *The Economics of Welfare* (London: Macmillan, 1924), pp. 179, 181.

20. George Akerlof, "The Market for 'Lemons': Quality Uncertainty and the Market Mechanism," *Quarterly Journal of Economics*, August 1970, p. 495.

21. Adam Smith, *The Wealth of Nations* (New York: Modern Library, 1937). See also Amitai Etzioni, "Good Ethics is Good Business—Really," *New York Times*, February 12, 1989, Business Section, p. 2.

22. E.g., see Michael Pertschuk, *FTC Review: 1977–84*, Committee on Energy and Commerce, U.S. House of Representatives, 98th Congress, 2d Session, Committee Print 98-CC (Washington, D.C.: Government Printing Office, September 1984), pp. 5–6, which confirms this statement in the words of a manufacturer.

23. Jennifer Lawrence, "State Ad Rules Face Showdown," *Advertising Age*, November 28, 1988, pp. 4, 66.

24. Robert O'Neil, "SELL UP—Everyone's Doing It!" *Dealerscope Merchandising,* January 1988, p. 34.

25. Vance Packard, *The Hidden Persuaders* (New York: Pocket Books, 1957), p. 58.

26. It is often argued that such highly visible cases can serve as a deterrent to other potential violators. But while this may be true of prosecutions of tax violators and other white-collar criminals, it is much less so of consumer-protection-law violators. That is because first offenders get off lightly. They are primarily told just to cease and desist. The premium is placed on stopping the deception rather than penalizing the offender. It is only repeat violators that face significant penalties. The result is that until a deceptive advertiser is actually cited, there is very little incentive to adjust one's advertising practices.

27. Alice Bredin, "Deception in Ads Can Prove Costly in the Long Run," *Computer & Software News,* February 27, 1989, p. 37. See also "Corporate Ethics: A Prime Business Asset," *Business Roundtable,* February 1988, p. 4, and Kenneth Blanchard and Norman Vincent Peale, *The Power of Ethical Management: Integrity Pays! You Don't Have to Cheat to Win* (New York: William Morrow, 1988).

28. Stanley Cohen, "The Responsibilities of Power," *Advertising Age,* November 9, 1988, p. 132.

29. Blumberg, p. 206. See also Raymond A. Bauer and Stephen A. Greyser, *Advertising in America: The Consumer View* (Boston: Harvard Business School, 1968), pp. 344–345, and Don Yeager, "Survey: Appliance Ads Aren't Trusted," *Home Furnishings Daily,* February 26, 1990, p. 113.

30. As quoted in Paul Samuelson, *Economics,* 10th ed. (New York: McGraw-Hill, 1976) p. 817.

31. Thorstein Veblen, *The Theory of the Leisure Class* (New York: Mentor Books, 1962), pp. 70–71.

32. Dale Carnegie, *How to Win Friends and Influence People* (New York: Simon & Schuster, 1981), pp. 99, 102, 128, 173.

33. Robert B. Cialdini, *Influence: The New Psychology of Modern Persuasion* (New York: Quill, 1984), pp. 23–24.

34. Vance Packard, *The Pyramid Climbers* (New York: McGraw-Hill, 1962), p. 93 and Les Giblin, *How to Have Confidence and Power in Dealing with People* (Englewood Cliffs, N.J.: Prentice-Hall, 1956), pp. 4, 40–41. Giblin cited the Carnegie Institute of Technology study which analyzed the records of 10,000 persons.

35. Stuart Ewen, *All Consuming Images: The Politics of Style in Contemporary Culture* (New York: Basic Books, 1988), p. 2.

PART II

PSEUDOSOLUTIONS: THE OLD CONSUMERISM

CHAPTER 8

The Consumer-Protection Agencies

Surely someone out there somewhere is doing something to help consumers survive the complicated and confusing marketplace. Indeed, the United States in the latter half of the twentieth century is hardly an underregulated society: in the past century, and particularly in the past three decades, we've set up a wealth of regulatory agencies, both public and private, to promote fair competition and protect the consumer's interest. At the national level alone, regulatory commissions with some influence over the consumer's life include the Federal Trade Commission, the Interstate Commerce Commission, the Civil Aeronautics Board and the Federal Aviation Administration, the Federal Power Commission, the Securities and Exchange Commission, the Drug Enforcement Agency, the Environmental Protection Agency, the Department of Agriculture, the Food and Drug Administration, and the Federal Communications Commission. There are also hundreds of state and local consumer agencies, including bureaus of consumer affairs, insurance commissions, and offices of weights and measures. In addition, there are private or semiprivate groups with consumer-protection functions, including more than a thousand occupational licensing and certifying boards, more than a hundred Better Business Bureaus, and more than a dozen arbitration boards set up by various industries. All of these organizations claim to have truth, accuracy, and consumer education at heart.

Unfortunately, for various structural reasons, no existing consumer organization—whether government or private—will ever be able to provide the kind of consumer education that will maximize either social or economic welfare. It's even doubtful whether these organizations will ever be able or willing to enforce their own legal and ethical standards.

A   WEALTH   OF   CHOICES

For thousands of years people have recognized that consumers need basic protections. Perhaps the earliest form of such protection appeared during the Roman Empire with the regulation of weights and measures. The idea here is simple: standards allow people to make decisions efficiently. Imagine if every time you bought chicken you had to take along a little scale to make sure the weight was exactly as stated. If you couldn't trust the weight marked by the grocer, life would be incredibly inefficient for everyone: the consumer, the grocer, the butcher, and the economy as a whole. Consumers would have to spend much more time choosing which grocers to trust and then periodically test them to make sure this trust was justified; grocers would need more shelves and space to make money on such slow consumers; and because many consumers wouldn't want to bother with this hassle of personal testing, butchers would have to advertise extensively to create increased brand (or breed) trust. Fortunately (thanks to government regulation), we can trust the grocer's scale. Similarly, we must have a certain level of trust in statements made by sellers to make appropriate and efficient buying decisions.

Today's consumer-protection agencies were all founded on the principle that consumers need a certain minimal level of protection for the good of society and the free market as a whole.[1] Before the late nineteenth century, however, government controls were minimal at best. In early America, a localized, rural economy meant that the slogan "caveat emptor" still reigned as the leading consumer-protection device; and there was little need for government to step in when choices were limited and members of the community would quickly discover anyone selling shoddy merchandise.

As any marketplace becomes more complex and the products less readily understandable to individual consumers, however, the need for consumer protection increases. Confusing products tempt sellers to take advantage of this seemingly inevitable buyer ignorance; in turn, government and industry watchdogs begin initiating regulations. Therefore, as the United States urbanized, as the populace grew larger and transportation more accessible, as merchants began mass-producing goods and shipping them by train to strangers in distant towns, the self-policing system began breaking down. Of particular concern were the adulterated and misbranded foods and drugs, which were not only deceptively labeled but dangerous to boot. As early as the late 1870s, a handful of people began pushing for national legislation to control these substances, but the real breakthrough came in 1906 with the publication of Upton Sinclair's *The Jungle,* which revealed the shocking practices in the meat-packing industry. The result was the 1906 passage of the Wiley Pure Food and Drug Act.[2]

Ever since, there have been many steps taken towards improving consumer protection and education, particularly during waves of consumerism (roughly, 1906–1914, the 1930s, and the late 1950s–early 1970s) that usually followed some crisis. One of the most important federal moves began in 1914 with the establishment of the Federal Trade Commission (FTC), which remains the foremost national agency concerned with consumer protection. At the same time, forward-looking businessmen decided that they'd better step in to protect themselves before the government got to them. Many local advertising clubs, which had previously been calling for more ethical standards of advertising, began setting up "vigilance committees" devoted to eliminating abuses and creating advertising codes and standards through voluntary efforts of advertisers.[3] Many of these committees even began hiring full-time professionals after 1914, the same year that the FTC was established, to conduct their widespread activity.

In 1912, George W. Coleman, a Boston advertising executive, extended the self-regulatory effort nationally by forming a National Vigilance Committee, which in 1921 changed its name to the National Better Business Bureau of the Associated Advertising Clubs of the World and in 1926 became a fully independent corporation. As early as 1912, the organization began setting standards for the patent-medicine industry and later added standards for others, including the battery, hosiery, shirt, and insulation-material industries. It also set ethical guidelines for selling and advertising. In 1946 the organization was renamed the Association of Better Business Bureaus, Inc., headquartered in New York City, and it served as a full-time organization with an executive staff.

Meanwhile, surrounding the year (1936) that saw the formation of Consumers Union, new standards were set to control deceptive advertising. For example, in 1937 the National Association of Broadcasters adopted the first industrywide code, which set rigorous ethical standards for both advertising and programming. By the early 1950s, however, the original enthusiasm was fading, and "puffery and one-upmanship" became the "rules for success" in the glamorous advertising industry.[4] This laxity, combined with increased complexity and choice of products, ushered in a wave of consumerism in which government took further steps to protect shoppers. Consumer advocates bandied about phrases such as the "consumer right to know" and "consumer protection"; Vance Packard's 1957 book *The Hidden Persuaders* and John Kenneth Galbraith's 1958 book *The Affluent Society* explored some of advertising's questionable practices; President Kennedy outlined his "Consumer Bill of Rights" to Congress in 1962; Rachel Carson's 1962 book *Silent Spring* exposed the dangers of pesticides and chemicals; President Johnson created the Office of Special Assistant to the President for Consumer Affairs in 1964; and Ralph Nader so heavily indicted the auto industry in his 1965 book *Unsafe at Any Speed* that at least eight major federal consumer-protection laws followed, including the Highway Safety Act in 1966. For the next decade, moreover, Congress passed numerous laws to strengthen federal consumer-protection laws and regulate trusts.[5] In fact, between 1966 and 1973 alone, Congress passed more than twenty-five pieces of consumer, environmental, and regulatory legislation,[6] and many states, counties, and cities set up consumer-protection agencies of their own, often under the auspices of the state attorney general.

Just as in earlier years, as government agencies built up their regulatory powers, so self-regulation increased. In 1970, for instance, the Association of Better Business Bureaus, Inc., reorganized by merging with the Association of Better Business Bureaus International into the Council of Better Business Bureaus, Inc. The same year saw the formation of trade organizations such as the Major Appliances Consumer Action Panel (MACAP), which handles individual consumer complaints against major-appliance manufacturers. Today the council's New York City office monitors and investigates complaints against national advertising, while its Virginia office produces educational materials and ethical guidelines. Meanwhile, 160 local Better Business Bureaus nationwide offer consumers business-performance reports, informational brochures, and reports on charitable organizations, and many mediate consumer complaints, issue informational pamphlets, generate press releases, and offer speakers to various groups.

GOVERNMENT PROTECTION

Because of government regulation, consumers today are definitely in better shape than those a hundred years ago. Agencies at both federal and state levels do indeed monitor the most overt fraud and the most marginal companies. No longer can a huckster blithely expect to sell you a patent medicine loaded with morphine to calm your baby. No longer can a con artist expect to advertise a full-featured brand-name dishwasher for $50 and then try to persuade you that the machine destroys silverware and that you ought to buy a no-name dishwasher for five hundred bucks instead. There are penalties for these sorts of practices, fines to be imposed by the government, licenses to be revoked, and reporters to be notified, all of which means that we can be pretty sure today that when we buy a television in the mainstream marketplace, we'll be getting something with a picture and sound and a channel changer and not a box likely to blow up in our living room. But whether under today's consumer-information system we can be sure of protection from anything but this kind of unsophisticated deception and gross waste is highly debatable.

Federal Protection

The most important agency devoted to consumer protection from deceptive retailing at the federal level has a telling name: the Federal Trade Commission (FTC). This agency consists of a Bureau of Consumer Protection, a Bureau of Competition, and a Bureau of Economics, and today is headed by five commissioners, all presidential appointees, one of whom is appointed to serve as chairman. In addition to FTC headquarters in Washington, D.C., there are ten regional offices, each of which has numerous attorneys who conduct investigations and litigations, recommend cases, and provide local outreach services to consumers, business-people, and officials. At least in theory, the FTC is charged with protecting both competition and consumers in virtually every American industry except those specifically regulated by other federal agencies.

Besides studying various industries, issuing reports, and recommending legislation to Congress, the FTC can investigate and litigate complaints, imposing fines of up to $10,000 per day and requiring firms to advertise that previous claims were false or misleading. In years past, for example, it has forced Warner-Lambert to advertise that its mouthwash Listerine did not prevent colds and forced ITT Continental Baking company to advertise that its Profile bread had "fewer calories" simply because they sliced it thinner than ordinary bread![7]

Despite these and other achievements, however, the FTC has certain inherent limitations that will prevent it from ever playing a major role in protecting consumers, a task to which it devotes about 70 percent of its budget.[8] By nature the FTC is slow, arbitrary, and unable to enforce or extend its rulings, partly due to the time-consuming, intricate procedure required to investigate and litigate a complaint.[9] In 1972 Phillip Schrag, an attorney previously with the New York City Department of Consumer Affairs, estimated that the FTC took an average of 4.37 years from the initiation of the investigation phase (which might begin several months after a complaint is received) to the issuance of a cease-and-desist order; if appeals are included, cases have been known to take over twenty years to complete.[10] There's little indication that anything has been done since 1972 to speed up matters.

The few cases that make it through the elaborate procedure also tend to be limited and arbitrary. Although FTC attorneys do look through advertisements in newspapers and trade publications every day, says Boston regional office staff attorney Bill McDonough, they tend to concentrate on fraud in certain narrow industries. And sometimes these industries are chosen just because an FTC attorney personally happened to have a bad experience with one. In the late 1980s, for example, FTC attorneys in Boston were putting concerted effort into the rare-coin industry. "For the dollars that we have (and we just had another freeze) our priority is to try to get restitution for consumers who suffer total or almost 100 percent loss," said McDonough at the time. "About four people (three attorneys) are currently working on the rare-coin case."

A limited case selection would be more acceptable, of course, if the rulings set precedents for other businesses and these precedents were enforced. Unfortunately, given the broad mandate of the FTC, such power would be inordinately expensive. Consider the FTC's case against Sears, Roebuck and Company back in 1976. In July 1974 the FTC's Chicago branch issued a complaint against the retailer, alleging bait and switch in the sale of higher-priced household appliances. The FTC claimed that Sears promoted appliances worth over $50 and then tried to switch customers to more expensive items which brought salespeople higher commissions. For example, when customers came in to buy a sewing machine advertised at $58, salespeople described it as "noisy, unable to sew buttonholes, and not available for half a year" in order to sell a more expensive model.[11] In October 1976 the FTC approved an order barring Sears from using bait and switch tactics in the sale of major appliances.

All that was well and good, but nothing in the ruling established any way to monitor Sears's practices in the future—nor did it establish any way to bar other retailers from bait and switch or its variations. Sears, and everyone else, already knew that bait and switch was illegal. The ruling simply made one retailer stop a specific instance of it.

Even more fundamentally, American consumers will never be able to rely on the FTC as their protector, since the commission is subject to the ebb and flow of politics. In the past decade the commission has been scarred by incredibly petty and embarrassing infighting among commissioners with different theories of government protection.[12]

Above all, it's simply uneconomical for the federal government to provide the kind of consumer protection necessary to eradicate all but the most blatantly illegal promotional practices. As current leaders of the FTC are well aware, every form of protection has a pricetag, and not every offense is worth the taxpayer's money. In its ad-substantiation program, for example, the FTC generally permits misleading ads, as long as they don't seriously harm a substantial number of people.[13] Chairman James C. Miller III elaborated this view, noting that consumers can protect themselves from quite a few abuses without the interference of any agency at all: "Consumers are better judges of products and services than many people in Washington give them credit for [sic] and there's no free lunch. The preparation of these reasonable basis reports results in costs being added to those very products consumers are purchasing."[14]

This attitude carries over to other areas of consumer protection as well. Again, a "few" distortions here and there by electronics stores, for example, are simply not worth getting excited over in the eyes of the economists guarding the Washington pocketbook. "Getting electronics stores to tone down their ads is just not something tax dollars ought to be spent on," explains McDonough. He gives the example of something advertised for $14 with the claim that the usual price is $25, when, in actuality, it always has sold for $14. "If we [the FTC] decide that the $14 is a fair value, given the current market, then we don't see this as a problem. The consumer is still getting a good buy. . . . Our view is that we can't remedy the selling situation by passing a bunch of laws: these will just restrict innovation and competition."

The agency's funding and staff, as well as statutory authority, were seriously undermined during the Reagan administration, and even today the agency retains a tendency to favor sellers over consumers. But, again, even if the FTC were to regain its former vigor under a more consumer-oriented administration, its inherent limitations would prevent it from ever playing more than a minor role in consumer protection and education. To understand why, just consider the frequent criticisms leveled at the FTC even before the tight reins of the 1980s—in the heyday of consumerism, in fact. In the late 1960s, for example, a group of graduate students dubbed "Nader's Raiders" criticized the FTC for its ineffectiveness and for focusing on trivial cases. This report led the Nixon administration to begin its own study through the American Bar Association. The conclusions by these and other contemporary critics were the same: the FTC was unsystematic, arbitrary, disorganized, and ineffective.[15]

Reforms followed on the heels of this report, and the commission in the early 1970s gained significantly greater clout (much of it lost in the 1980s) to tackle both consumer problems and antitrust cases. Nevertheless, even *while* the FTC was at the height of its power, basic flaws remained. In 1974, for example, Robert Sabatino not only showed that the FTC failed to establish priorities for action, but argued that it missed remedying most deceptive and fraudulent practices: "action is usually not begun until a complaint is filed; complaints occur only after injury to consumers has taken place; and many consumers do not recognize deceptions, and do not know how to complain when they do."[16] In 1977, consumer writer Kenneth Eisenberger accused federal consumer-protection agencies, including the FTC, of being "inefficient in their problem-solving methods." He also cited a federally authorized 1975 study by a private company of fifteen federal agencies that revealed five major shortcomings: (1) inadequate policies for handling telephone complaints; (2) poor record-keeping; (3) lack of formal policies assigning responsibilities; (4) inconsistent consumer-response policies; and (5) inconsistent classification of complaints.[17]

"Some people also think that the FTC stuffs complaints about misleading advertisements into a file drawer and does nothing at all unless it receives many complaints about a particular firm," wrote John Dorfman, at the time a consultant to Consumers Union and the New York State Consumer Protection Board and author of *Consumer Survival Kit* and *Consumer Tactics Manual,* just before the Reagan administration's cutbacks. "That happens to be, in my opinion, true."[18] Nor were educational efforts at the federal level any more effective: a 1979 report by the advertising and government panel of the American Academy of Advertising claimed that "so far we have a fair amount of documentation that consumer information programs are almost totally without impact."[19]

State and Local Regulation

Apologists for ineffectual federal agencies often argue that the proper place for business regulation/consumer protection is at the state and local level. In fact, there's been lots of publicity recently about how state attorneys general have stepped in to fill the gap left by the federal retreat from consumer protection.[20] Indeed, both state and local bureaus do have certain advantages, as well as a list of impressive accomplishments. On the other hand, these bureaus have as many inherent limitations as the FTC.

Many states can trace their consumer-protection function back to the late nineteenth century, although formal consumer-protection bureaus weren't established until the 1960s or 1970s, the last great wave of consumerism.[21] These bureaus vary considerably in organization and duties, although as far as consumer protection goes, most of them enforce essentially the same laws—modeled on the FTC act. Some state and city departments also license professionals and businesses and may even regulate charities as well. In many states, the bureaus are divisions of the attorney general's office (which is responsible for many other matters besides consumer protection). Such bureaus may be named things like the department of consumer protection or the department of business regulation. Other states protect consumers through both the attorney general's office and a separate consumer-protection bureau. In a few states the department of agriculture takes major responsibility for consumer protection.

Some states specifically divide responsibility among these bureaus, with some branches of the network handling individual mediation, others handling investigation and litigation, and either or both responsible for "education." Often the attorney general's office prosecutes offending businesses, for example, while a separate office of consumer protection mediates individual complaints and generates educational material. In other states, particularly those with powerful city bureaus, the division of responsibility is more obscure, or apparently divided according to the personal interests of the reigning bureau chiefs.

Specific functions vary considerably between states as well.[22] So does the interpretation of "consumer education": while some bureaus offer pre-recorded messages on a toll-free hotline and/or issue educational pamphlets and/or give public lectures, others have no specific educational programs.[23] In one way or another, however, all of these agencies primarily are designed to resolve complaints against state and local businesses. They can be particularly effective if they receive many complaints against a particular company or investigate a deceptive practice with a wide-ranging impact.[24] Complaints can involve just about any type of business, although most relate to "automobiles, housing and landlords, appliances, home improvements, credit, mail orders, advertising, utilities, food, and clothing."[25]

There's no question that state and local bureaus handle many complaints and issue numerous pieces of educational literature. Some states have undeniably impressive achievements as well, a few even in the field of consumer electronics and major appliances. For example, in the late 1980s Missouri's attorney general's office devoted a substantial percentage of its consumer-protection resources to combating deceptive advertising (including alleged bait and switch, double tagging, and fraudulent reference pricing) by the consumer-electronics superstore Best Buy. And at about the same time, New York's attorney general Robert Abrams charged the Panasonic Company with fixing the retail prices of sixteen Panasonic- and Technics-brand electronics in stores including Best Buy, Circuit City, Fretter, Highland, K-Mart, Lechmere, Montgomery Ward, Polk Brothers, Silo, Target, and Venture. Such actions talk in dollars, too: many state agencies report settling thousands of complaints each year and saving consumers hundreds of thousands—sometimes millions—of dollars each year.

Behind these impressive numbers, however, lie some serious problems. Most obviously is the incredibly broad mandate assigned to just about every state and local agency in the country, essentially equivalent to the entire regional economy. Doing so in more than a superficial way is tough—especially given limited staff and funding. And even in the most consumerist states, staff and funding simply are inadequate for this herculean task. At best, state and local agencies have to operate like the IRS and try to monitor a tiny percentage of the offenders, publicize convictions, and thereby hope to dissuade others from engaging in illegal practices. Thus, the impressive figures above show only that the attorneys general do an admirable job weeding out the grossest violations, or as some have acknowledged, that a great deal of the money recovered comes from a few big cases.[26]

One agency simply cannot regulate a state's entire economy, and the ambitious and idealistic souls who hope to do so are quickly disillusioned. Consider one attorney's words, as he departed from the New York City Department of Consumer Affairs:

"My departure from the Department of Consumer Affairs was not a resignation of protest but one of disappointment. Although the Commissioner and the City had given the Law Enforcement Division all the political, financial and legal support that could reasonably be asked . . . , we were having little discernible impact on the level of consumer fraud in New York. . . . At one time during the drafting of the Consumer Protection Law, I had actually imagined that a good law, properly administered, could wipe out misleading sales practices altogether. Our experiments shed little light on whether enough law enforcement could ever do the job, but they do suggest that given our toleration of the way in which adversary and judicial systems now operate, the amount of resources constituting 'enough' would be more than any government should devote to the problem."[27]

Susan Grant, director of Consumer Fraud Protection at the Massachusetts Northwest District Attorney's Office, expressed similar sentiments when she noted the difficulty and expense of enforcing retailing laws regarding matters such as displayed prices. "It's an extremely time- and labor-consuming type of enforcement. For example, you must look at ads over time, and you must get in-store records."

A broad mandate isn't the only reason for enforcement problems. Even more fundamental are the largely draconian consumer-protection laws that look good in elections but that mean nothing to the retailers because they're never enforced. "It's a lot easier to pass a law than to spend money," noted Scott Harshbarger, now Massachusetts attorney general. "You have so many regulations that few are enforced. It makes it harder to distinguish between the egregious and [the] minor offender." In 1990, for example, the federal government's General Accounting Office found that over 9 percent of gasoline sampled was mislabeled by over half a point below the posted octane rating, costing American consumers an estimated $150 million for octane they didn't receive.[28] Of course there are laws that the amount of octane posted at the gas pump is supposed to correspond to the amount you get. But nobody's going to bother checking each individual gas station, and clearly what happens in reality and what happens on the books have little to do with each other. Interestingly, the level of cynicism about meaningless laws is so high that when we mentioned this 9 percent figure to Harshbarger, he expressed relief that the figure was so low!

Similarly, when one state reformulated its retailing laws in 1990, ostensibly to protect consumers from such practices as meaningless lowest-price claims, phony "regular" prices, and inaccessible model numbers and prices, the changes benefited retailers more than consumers. All the top-ranking officials in consumer protection that we questioned expressed extreme frustration at this four-year process of revision, largely because it was dominated by retailer interests and because it produced regulations that even the officials themselves couldn't understand, much less enforce or convey to retailers.

"These regulations are an example of convoluted legalese that's hard for people to understand," said one official, who happens to be an attorney herself. "Take a look at the comparison-prices section. Your eyes will cross and brain overheat." Even the chairman of a large local department store observed that simply enforcing the standing regulations (last revised in 1977) would have greater benefit than establishing new regulations "so incomprehensible to most advertisers that . . . [the regulations] will either be misunderstood or ignored." If every state had as many pages of regulations, national retailers would have to check through over one thousand pages of extremely complex and confusing state retail rules before advertising nationally. And this doesn't even include national-level regulations such as those of the FTC or citywide regulations such as those by the New York City Department of Consumer Affairs.

As many observers have noted, politicians have a tendency to sponsor convoluted regulations, primarily because they are too difficult for average voters to assess but readily understandable to special interests with the resources and motivations to scrutinize them. "It was all PR," said another top-ranking consumer-protection official (who asked to remain unnamed) of the glowing newspaper write-ups of the new state retailing regulations. He added that although his bureau's original intentions were pro-consumer, the results were undeniably pro–special interest retailer. "What looks positive in the press release might not be positive in reality," he said. The heart of the problem can be understood by considering a simple truth: whereas the consumer has thirty stores, a hundred brands, and a thousand products to worry about, the businessperson only has one. A seller therefore can devote the same amount of time to protecting his or her interests on this one product as a consumer might divide between a thousand. Moreover, although promoting the product, brand, or store means the businessperson's livelihood, most consumers don't have the resources—whether time, money, or ability—to do anything about a problem which is only of secondary interest.[29]

Given this basic consumer apathy toward any particular product or retailer, it's easy to understand why even government agencies set up to represent consumers are never particularly motivated to pursue any specific issue; instead, they focus on making impressive-sounding pronouncements about business ethics and pursuing well-publicized issues. Even politicians elected by consumers tend to issue appealing abstractions but cave in to special interests when it comes to specifics. It's an open question whether the four years, thousands of hours, and hundreds of thousands of dollars spent revising the state regulations mentioned above might not have been better spent enforcing the existing regulations. But it's also probably true that the politically oriented officials involved found rewriting regulations more exciting work than enforcing them and anticipated that the voter appeal of writing a new law supposedly benefiting consumers would be greater than enforcing existing laws.

Of course, some laws do get enforced. But the political interest of any state attorney general often means picking on weak or highly visible, unpopular opponents. Government officials often act as though they're thinking: "What good will it do to protect the public interest if I'm not re-elected? Better to compromise and stay in power so that I can do good in the future." As Harshbarger told us: "Nobody will appreciate it if I go after a retail store. The total [cost to consumers] may be millions or billions, but for the individual consumer it's probably only cents. The poor elderly person who loses an isolated $1,000 on some scam is a much more appealing target." Given these constraints, and the broad mandate from which to choose, it's always better to go not for errant electronic superstores but for sexier issues such as drugs, crime, or the environment which will captivate the press and the public.[30] " 'Attorneys General are primarily motivated by politics, personal publicity, election-year rhetoric and action based on polls and headlines,' " Harshbarger said in the *Boston Globe*.[31]

For similar reasons, these agencies also tend to target rather arbitrary areas—such as polluters, or a car model already in the news as unsafe—that pique a particular official or that will generate favorable publicity. For example, Audi first managed to get itself on the "Okay-to-Kick List" because of allegations (later discredited) of a sudden-acceleration problem on its series 5000 cars, a problem which ostensibly caused a number of deaths. Audi was later found to be offering a massive discount on these models, but only having 5,500 in stock compared to an expected demand of 24,000. The FTC and a half-dozen state attorneys general launched a highly visible investigation of the company's alleged bait and switch practices. The allegations were given further credence by an additional Audi program to give salespeople an extra $250 bonus for selling two other slow-selling Audi lines, the Audi 80 and Audi 90, and presumably switching customers from the Audi 5000 series to these two models. Despite the crackdown, these alleged bait and switch tactics were extremely mild compared to standard but less visible practices in the computer, consumer-electronics, and major-appliance industries.[32]

The same political motivations extend to educating consumers, which is only a minor goal next to protecting them. This problem is compounded by the broad number of subjects covered by the agencies' well-intentioned pamphlets—as well as the space and time limitations—

and leaves all the educational efforts by state and local agencies universally vague. Thus, educational efforts tend toward generalities (such as "Watch out for bait and switch" or "Check the reputation of a mail-order firm") or occasional materials targeting blatantly dangerous or fraudulent merchandise (such as get-rich-quick schemes or unsafe toys). Consumers are told to "learn something" about service contracts before they buy one but not told that it's nearly impossible to get this information from salespeople. They are told to check the quality of a model before buying it but not which specific models are really good. Overall, the message is that if you want to be a smart shopper, caveat emptor. Consumers perpetuate this system because they have even less time and inclination to check up on the rhetoric of consumer-protection agencies than they do the promotional rhetoric surrounding the products they buy.

Then, too, there are many important functions that these agencies can't fill at all—either because they aren't worth tax dollars or because they require stepping on too many toes. Neither public nor private agencies can litigate individual complaints or act as private attorneys; they cannot recommend specific firms, services, brands, or products; and, because of stringent procedural and evidentiary requirements, they will never be able to act quickly or efficiently. For the most part, too, they can't monitor sales and advertising claims unless they are looking into a particular case of misrepresentation, fraud, or deception.

Besides severely restricting the types of cases these bureaus can prosecute and regulate, a limited budget and political orientation also restricts staff and may force the agencies to hire poorly motivated workers. Job security has always made government employees notorious for their lack of motivation. We experienced this apathy ourselves while we were running our consumer-information service. Like any consumer, we were entitled to copies of consumer complaints about various companies under the Freedom of Information Act (with names of complainants removed, of course). The trouble was, we didn't just want one or two copies about one store, which was the kind of request the office was used to receiving: we wanted every complaint about all the superstores and discounters in the Boston area for the past three years.

Now, when you think about it, our request was perfectly reasonable, even if we were running a business. After all, if you were about to spend upwards of $1,200 on a camcorder, wouldn't you want to make sure that the store you were buying it from was reputable? And wouldn't a good way to find out about that reputability be to call up the local consumer complaint office and find out what types of complaints had come in about the stores you were considering? That's certainly what most consumer-education materials issued by these very same offices tell you to do. What we were trying to do was to put this advice into practice for our customers (since our business was to do the research work *for* the busy shopper). But we were met with obstacles on all sides. When we first called we were transferred from person to person. Finally, we talked to someone who said we'd have to write an official letter requesting access. We did so, and no one replied. We wrote again and then called to see what was happening. The woman we talked to complained that it would be a tremendous burden to search out all those complaints, not to mention photocopying all of them. Still, we insisted that we were entitled, and she said she'd be back in touch in the next few days. Another month later, we got a letter, telling us that there would be a charge of $6 per hour plus 20 cents a copy, and we could not have the materials until we prepaid the cost. So, we wrote again, asking for the total fee. They took a month to reply, so we called, got the figure a few days later, and immediately sent the check. Another month went by, and when we called we were told that they'd never received our check. So, we sent yet another check and then, to force a deadline, arranged to come in on a specific date to look at the complaints.

At this point almost half a year had gone by since our initial request. And even when we did come into the office, we were handed a pile of photocopied papers, many of the originals of which had been written in blue pen or pencil, which meant their copies were completely illegible. Nobody in the office made any attempt to help us read them—or even sympathize with our task. In fact, we got the distinct sense that we were considered utter nuisances because we were trying to put this information into a usable form for consumers—something the agency should have been trying to do itself.

The fact is that going out into the real world and carefully checking policies and claims requires great motivation. So does vigilantly monitoring the ever-changing nature of abuses in the marketplace. But most of the people we've talked to in consumer agencies (other than some of the idealistic chiefs who don't do the day-to-day work) find it unpleasant even to do just a little photocopying. Most consumers find that calling such a bureau means (1) a busy signal, (2) transfer from person to person, (3) suggestions to talk to the company first, and/or (4) writing a complaint, which is simply skimmed over unless it relates to a big case. Contrary to popular belief, describing your grim experience to a state or local agency will not generate embarrassing newspaper headlines or punitive measures: either the store or the manufacturer will offer you compensation or some plausible excuse, and you will simply be told to take the matter to small claims court if you still have a problem. Then your complaint will be stuffed into a drawer and forgotten, and life will go on as usual, everybody content except future customers of the store or the manufacturer.

Getting a bureau staff to tackle an investigation can be equally difficult. Even in the Missouri case against Best Buy, says Henry Herschel, chief counsel for the trade offenses division of the attorney general's office there, it took over three years to persuade the agency to take on the problem. Part of this reluctance is related to the limited budget, which forces most state and local agencies to practice antiquated gathering, storage, and analysis techniques for data. Although many agencies claim to scan newspaper ads regularly for deceptive advertising practices, for example, few, if any, have the staffs to patrol regularly the thousands of stores they're responsible for and see what's actually happening out on the sales floor. The data that they do gather is often kept on neglected file cards.

Even bureaus that boast computerized databanks or have resources similar to those of federal agencies rarely if ever make much use of their data. Often the information is entered too late or analyzed at too superficial and general a level to be meaningful. For example, the Massachusetts attorney general's office does generate records of types of consumer complaints, but the people who are supposed to use them don't even know what they mean or why one complaint comes under one heading versus another. Not only are these records six months out of date and essentially unreadable (a three-inch stack of printouts filled with tightly packed abbreviated computer codes), but according to Paul Schlaver, head of the Cambridge consumer-protection office, they are never used but simply put into categories and counted, presumably to show the voting public how well its elected attorney general has done that year.

To some extent a state bureau's strength depends on the legislature's current appropriations, as well as the philosophy of its attorney general (and presumably that of the public who elected—and may reelect—him or her).[33] Former Texas attorney general Jim Mattox and New York's current attorney general Robert Abrams, for example, both strongly favor state regulation of advertising. In contrast, New Mexico's attorney general, Hal Stratton, contends that government regulation of advertising of any sort harms consumers more than helps them—by raising prices.[34]

Stratton inadvertently brings up another major problem with the entire state and local system: there are just too many companies operating on a national basis, and many states and localities feel unequipped or unauthorized to deal with them. According to Stratton: " 'State Attorneys General should stick to enforcing the various fraud and consumer protection statutes passed by their respective legislatures, and save involvement in national regulations for when they're elected to Congress.' " In other words, for a nationally operating company, the FTC, as we saw earlier, is saying "let the states take care of it," and the states are saying "let the FTC take care of it."[35]

Admittedly, the eighty-year-old National Association of Attorneys General (NAAG) and the increasingly common multistate task forces may be able to help this situation to a certain extent, since they propose to organize attorneys general from many states and unite their efforts. Over the last few years, NAAG has issued tough antitrust enforcement guidelines, and, indeed, it shows signs of clamping down on many of the deceptive and fraudulent pricing practices, particularly in regard to sale items. As this book went to press, NAAG was organizing an effort to regulate reference pricing, particularly among bedding, furniture, blinds, electronics, and appliance retailers. Clay Freedman, assistant attorney general in Missouri, was organizing twenty-three states to share information and draft new standards about constant sales, bait and switch, lowest-price guarantees, and other deceptive pricing information. By sharing resources and strategies, states will be able to pursue many more of these cases, publicize them more effectively, and consequently magnify fines.[36] The National Association of Consumer Agency Administrators (NACAA) also has the potential to enhance the efficiency and efficacy of state agencies. By publishing newsletters, this organization provides a way to share ideas.

Even so, the actual achievements of NAAG and NACAA, like the achievements of the more powerful state and local agencies, reflect the conspicuous taking on of a few biggies rather than tackling large-scale fraud and deception. Both organizations share the same massive subject load as the state agencies—only magnified to include just about every business in every state of the nation. In fact, as nationally minded groups, they have the same limitations as the FTC as far as concentration on all but the most pressing matters. Furthermore, because they are run by elected officials, the chosen issues by both NAAG and the state and local agencies tend to be just as politically motivated as those of their constituent agencies.

OCCUPATIONAL LICENSING

Consumer information involves not only tangible goods, of course. Consumers must make equally complex judgments about the quality of service professionals—whether they be doctors, lawyers, barbers, morticians, plumbers, accountants, electricians, beauticians, or psychologists. And here consumers have yet other groups ostensibly protecting their interests. In the United States today more than eight hundred occupations are regulated by states, not to mention those subject to federal or local regulation.[37] Government-sanctioned licensing boards, a sort of cross between state consumer-protection agencies and totally private regulators, purportedly exist to assure an otherwise ignorant consumer of a minimal level of competency among these professionals and technicians.[38]

An extensive body of literature, however, strongly suggests that these boards exist more to enhance the prestige of and protect licensees than to protect the public. As Benjamin Shimberg, a senior researcher at the Educational Testing Service, has repeatedly and eloquently argued, "The mythology of licensure holds that licensing laws are passed because an outraged public demands them. Nonsense! Virtually all licensing laws have been passed at the behest of the occupational groups to get certain benefits for their members and incidentally to help the public."[39]

Thus, there are stringent testing requirements to keep newcomers from entering the profession, but weak retesting requirements to ensure that those already in it are still competent. According to Shimberg,

Once licensed, practitioners are usually licensed for life. In most professions, they may renew their licenses indefinitely, even when they are no longer in active practice, by simply paying a fee. Their skills may deteriorate; their knowledge may become outdated; their health and physical coordination may become impaired. Yet as long as they do not run afoul of their boards by being convicted of felonies, causing serious injuries that attract wide attention, or violating regulations that have an economic impact on professional colleagues, it is unlikely that their right to practice will be challenged.[40]

Most people will give you knee-jerk defenses of this whole system: for example, "Can you imagine a bunch of self-proclaimed doctors walking around?" or "We can't just have every Tom, Dick, and Harry walking into the house and fooling with the electricity." But just for a moment, take the naive perspective that there could indeed be a better way—and that our current system just may be crawling with vested interests and illogical aberrations. Consider that right now all the professions require their students to take a constant battery of tests to weed out the unqualified, which seems sensible enough. And yet if testing made sense, then why is it that once we have left school, all testing comes to a virtual standstill for the rest of one's working life? How has this situation come about? Is it good?

The basic situation is this: Licensing laws, despite their connection to testing, really have more to do with power. All groups with power steadfastly resist being held accountable by having their performance tested. The various major occupations in the United States all are powerful special-interest groups that can avert any proposals of lifelong testing and dissemination of test results. At the same time, to minimize competition, all occupational groups restrict entry into their fields, primarily by encouraging tests and licensing procedures to weed out as many potential competitors as possible. Thus, a situation develops where there is likely to be far too much testing of the young and weak and far too little testing of the old and established.

Given these motivations, it's hardly surprising that licensing laws vary widely from state to state, often with no apparent relationship to value. For example, while New York State requires future barbers to have only 1,000 hours of training, Michigan requires 2,000 hours plus a two-year apprenticeship.[41] Nor should we be surprised that the requirements for entry are often unnecessarily stringent—Illinois requires licensed barbers to spend 1,872 hours in a barber college and pass a test before beginning a twenty-seven month apprenticeship.[42]

SELF-REGULATION

More consumers (82 percent) recognize the Better Business Bureau (BBB) as the place to turn for assistance than any other agency, according to a 1986 poll by the advertising agency Ogilvie and Mather. Ninety-nine percent of consumers polled had heard of the BBB, and most viewed its members as having higher business standards than nonmembers.[43] Even government agencies often recommend going to the BBB and other self-regulatory agencies first. As James Shannon, the Massachusetts attorney general at that time, put it in an introduction to the consumer guide produced by self-regulatory agencies (which he was "pleased to note" was "produced and distributed at no cost to the taxpayers"): "While my office won't hesitate to take action against anyone or any business that attempts to defraud consumers, we have found that a well-informed consumer can often detect a scam, and, therefore, avoid problems. . . . If, however, you are dissatisfied with the quality of a product or service, and cannot obtain satisfaction from the business, contact your local Better Business Bureau (BBB) or consumer program."[44] In other words, it seems that most American consumers and their representatives trust self-regulatory agencies to fill gaps left by government agencies.[45]

Admittedly, too, self-regulation has some tremendous things going for it. Principally, it's not as limited by restrictive budgetary and political concerns as are government agencies. Some of the 160 local BBBs nationwide have been quite effective at getting members to help consumers retrieve money and repair and/or replace merchandise (through mediation and/or arbitration); at persuading offending businesses to drop deceptive advertising claims; and at keeping files on less than honorable establishments.[46] For example, the Better Business Bureau of Metropolitan New York, Inc., issues well-documented file reports on specific firms that include background information, advertising review, and specific law-enforcement action taken. They also issue periodic subject reports, such as one about buying photographic and electronic equipment by mail.

The Council of Better Business Bureaus (CBBB) also regulates advertising through its National Advertising Division (NAD) and through its joint sponsorship with the American Association of Advertising Agencies (AAAA), the American Advertising Federation (AAF), the Association of National Advertisers (ANA) of the National Advertising Review Council (NARC) and its National Advertising Review Board (NARB), which consists of fifty members representing national advertisers, advertising agencies, and the public sector. The NAD may investigate a practice in response to its own observations or to complaints from local BBBs, individual consumers, competitors, or groups outside the self-regulatory system, and if the NAD fails to resolve the matter, it can be appealed to a five-member panel of the NARB. Both groups claim to work for "truth and accuracy in national advertising" through business self-regulation. Each month the NAD releases a public report of closed cases, detailing the advertiser, advertising agency and the product involved, the bases for questioning the advertising, the advertiser's response, and the NAD's decision. Action by the NARB forced Montgomery Ward to curtail its deceptive "lowest-price" guarantees in the ads for its Electric Avenue division.

But self-regulation also has serious problems. Roy Ahmen, in his report to the American Academy of Advertising, sums up the dismal situation faced by consumers when he notes that "most of the [government] regulation under which advertising now operates is due in part or in whole to the failure of earlier self-regulatory efforts."[47] The most fundamental problem with self-regulatory agencies, however, is that they have no incentive to protect consumers except to prevent the government from doing the protection; in fact, the formation and strength of self-regulatory groups invariably can be traced to times when government regulation threatened to intensify.[48] Admittedly, this threat can be a strong incentive, and most self-regulatory groups began with great enthusiasm and promise. Unfortunately, this zeal waxes and wanes according to the political climate, and consumers cannot count on the BBB or any other self-regulatory agency to be there for them in times when attention switches away from issues of public protection. And contrary to the desires of the Reagan and Bush economists, as the threat of government regulation falls off, so does self-regulation.

Even at the heyday of both government and self-regulation, in the early 1970s, economist John McTighe complained that over the past sixty years

> high ideals and concern for the public's well-being on the part of advertising leaders have been generally ineffective in bringing about enforceable self-controls. Real efforts at self-regulation have been made only when outside controls and economic factors forced advertisers to regulate themselves. Apparently, the advertising industry will accept self-control when it is the most profitable thing to do.[49]

Advertising historian Otis A. Pease adds that anyone who has closely examined the advertising industry's search for ethical standards "would find it hard not to conclude that it arose not really from a desire to benefit the public or to safeguard the consumer . . . but rather from a desire to preserve the effectiveness of advertising." Simply put, unethical advertisers may lead the public to mistrust all advertisers.[50]

Not surprisingly, then, different political and economic climates in each region mean that effectiveness of self-regulatory agencies varies considerably from bureau to bureau.[51] As Eisenberger observed (again, even back in the "good old days"):

> Although Better Business Bureaus provide some good services to consumers, the overall effectiveness of their programs should be questioned and kept in perspective. . . . Many bureaus are grossly understaffed, and files are often outdated. There may be no new entries in a company record over a period of several years simply because no one has gone over the bulk of the latest complaints.[52]

Our more recent observations of the Boston Better Business Bureau indicate that this observation continues to be true. Not only are some major firms completely absent from the database (because it's not "efficient" to enter them unless someone inquires about them), but bureau members almost never investigate an ad unless a consumer brings it to their attention. Even then, "investigation" usually means a form letter to the retailer and the medium that carried the ad, asking for an explanation. And perhaps there is eventually a reprimand.

Furthermore, at many local bureaus, obtaining a BBB report turns out to be a complete waste of time. To begin with, it can be nearly impossible to get through on the phone. We tried calling the Boston bureau and found that trying the regular number more than ten times a day spread out over morning, midday, and late afternoon for three weeks yielded nothing but a busy signal. Frustrated, one of us wrote the same bureau a letter which began: "For several weeks now I have been trying to reach you by phone with no success: the line seems perpetually busy, and the operator tells me that other people have complained about this as well but nothing can be done." The letter was returned to us a few weeks later with the following reply scribbled at the bottom from Information Central Manager Ellen Keaney: "As a non-profit organization serving 4 N.E. states, and inquiries from across the N.E., we are very busy. Writing is a quick solution to the busy phone."[53] Even if you do get through, it can take weeks or even months to get the reports—and writing a request letter just prolongs the process. If you're waiting to find out where to buy a new refrigerator, you probably don't have weeks of months. Incidentally, the CBBB's NAD has an even worse record, averaging at least six months to process a complaint about deceptive advertising, according to consumer reporter John Dorfman.[54]

Perhaps the worst frustration of all, however, is that even after all that time and effort, many BBB reports about particular firms turn out to be so vague that they're essentially meaningless. Eisenberger reports that on a form sent to consumers by the Los Angeles Better Business Bureau, one of the answers that may be checked reads: "This company has a satisfactory record. Bureau files show we have received only infrequent reports of customer dissatisfaction. These matters have been given proper consideration when brought to the company's attention by the bureau." But as Eisenberger rightly asks, what is a "satisfactory" record? What does "infrequent" mean? What constitutes "proper consideration"? The bureau does not define these terms adequately. "You can be sure," quips Eisenberger, "that many consumers would furnish definitions quite different from the people evaluating bureau files."[55]

Reports issued by the Boston Better Business Bureau show similar problems. The Boston office's one-page "profiles" of member businesses simply list the year in which the company was incorporated, the number of employees, the location of the branches, and the names of the managers, and then make a generalization about the firm's complaint record such as: "Our files show that this firm has responded to all matters brought to its attention and has maintained a satisfactory business performance record. This is neither an endorsement nor a guarantee of satisfaction." Bureau members continually boast about this disclaimer, in fact, reminding us that they don't "make judgments."

Gary Duncan, supervisor of the Boston bureau's complaint division, explained that despite its computerized operation, the Boston Better Business Bureau doesn't even collect—much less release to consumers—information about the nature of complaints. For example, it doesn't know how many times a specific firm has been accused of bait and switch or how many times a firm falsely guaranteed a lowest price. The database simply lists how many complaints were made in a given year and how many of these were resolved, partially resolved, disputed, or unsubstantiated. And even this extremely limited detail is off-limits to consumers (and journalists).

Part of this reluctance to specify the nature of complaints or indict member firms is that all BBBs have an inherent conflict of interest. Dues from retailers represent the major source of their funding, after all, so the bureaus all have a definite interest in keeping them happy except in cases of gross misconduct. BBB leaders also frequently are affiliated with major companies.[56] At the very least, this relationship and fear of lawsuits precludes any BBB from endorsing or recommending a particular company, good, or service—functions left unfilled by the government agencies as well. And at the other extreme, cynics have quipped, self-regulation may be akin to asking the Hell's Angels to guard a rock concert.

Admittedly, some steps are taken to diminish bias. For example, the CBBB disqualifies panelists from advertising reviews if their employing company manufactures, sells, or advertises a good or service which directly competes with those sold by the advertiser involved in the proceeding—or if the panelists believe they cannot reach an unbiased decision.[57] But even such controls do not change the self-regulatory agency's fundamentally pro-member orientation.

In fact, conflicts of interest may lead BBBs to actions that exceed reluctance. For example, Eisenberger reports that one ex-employee of the Los Angeles Better Business Bureau claimed that she was fired for giving out too much information about companies. He adds that bureau reports about a company can

> sometimes be grossly misleading. An inquirer may be told that a firm has a satisfactory record, with no mention of serious charges filed against it. A consumer contacting his or her local bureau on a Monday night may be told that the company deals fairly with customers. Another consumer, who calls on Tuesday, may be told that the firm has been convicted of false advertising and gone out of business. Misleading reporting is sometimes unavoidable, but the nature of the reporting itself can cover up serious, negative aspects of a company's operation that may even be known by the bureau.[58]

Even when the bureaus have the consumer's best interests in mind, they have no enforcement power to penalize advertisers—and most of the companies they supposedly regulate know this. These agencies must rely entirely on persuasion and the potential embarrassment that public exposure could bring to a company—a power which has only limited efficacy and depends on the tenacity of a local BBB. Furthermore, any complaint that suggests fraud or other illegal activity must be referred to a government agency from the beginning. Some people have argued that the threat of government intervention is enough to curb many companies, but this argument loses much persuasiveness once you consider the ineffectiveness of government agencies.[59]

The fact that MACAP actually boasts about "satisfactorily" resolving "more than half" of "justified" complaints against appliance manufacturers (when over half of the total complaints submitted were judged unjustified to begin with) gives a taste of the low expectations of these organizations.[60] Other consumer arbitration boards, such as the National Futures Association (for commodity traders), state bar associations (for lawyers), and the National Association of Security Dealers (for stock brokers), have similar problems.[61] The truth is that the goals of any self-regulatory agency just aren't very ambitious—the focus being to prevent fraud rather than to educate consumers. The BBB's official, written goal may be to eradicate dishonesty from the marketplace. But lack of incentive, conflicts of interest, and lack of power all mean that its practical goal amounts to eliminating just the grossest, most outrageous forms of dishonesty. Consequently, the more subtle distortions of fact—namely, the constant sales and other practices we've charted in this book—are left totally unchallenged.

Of course, the BBB emphasizes that its primary function is not gathering information or hounding businesses. Rather, it primarily serves to educate consumers before they buy. The Boston Better Business Bureau claims that 85 percent of its activities involve giving information to consumers about businesses and buying *before* any transaction occurs. But paradoxically, if the BBBs put so little effort into information gathering and analysis, then the quality of this prepurchase information must necessarily be poor.

The BBB may have one very useful function: relieving a consumer's stress. Instead of feeling absolutely helpless, the very existence of the famed bureau makes consumers think that they can do something about fraud, deception, and misrepresentation. We suspect, however, that consumers who have had any specific dealings with a BBB, never getting through on the phone and receiving meaningless reports, will soon lose even this comforting delusion.

THE NEED FOR OPINION

As the marketplace grows increasingly complex, the need for consumer protection will grow proportionately. Expanding the role of the current government and self-regulatory consumer agencies to fill this need, however, would be like tripling the workload of an employee who already has trouble finishing projects. No matter how impressive their objectives, inherent limitations will prevent all existing consumer agencies from ever doing more than eliminating the most blatant abuses. These agencies focus only on the symptoms of the real problem, and none has the power or inclination to dig out the root—consumer confusion.

Part of the problem in eliminating consumer confusion has arisen because consumer education as opposed to consumer protection plays only a minor role for even the best of the existing consumer organizations. But more fundamental is the fact that no matter how much money an organization has and no matter how much goodwill towards the consumer, unless it can *rate* and express *opinions* about specific companies, sellers will continue to take advantage of ignorant consumers lost in a complex marketplace. Unfortunately, political, economic, and legal forces, such as fear of lawsuits, pressure from powerful special-interest groups or dues-paying members, and limited budgets, often prevent agencies from airing their knowledge in public forums or giving consumers concrete recommendations. Of course, most of us would just as soon not have government—nor trade groups with their inherent conflicts of interest—take on such a role, so the inflated claims, limited goals, and poor execution may actually be desirable. They give us hope that virtue is rewarded and deception punished but don't force us to confront the fact that it is often more expensive and difficult to confront corruption and minor everyday deception than it's worth.

1. See E. Scott Maynes's "Consumer Protection: The Issues," *Journal of Consumer Policy* 3 (1979): 98 and his "Consumer Protection: Corrective Measures," *Journal of Consumer Policy* 3 (1979): 191.

2. See, for example, *"Who's Minding the Store": 100 Years of Consumer Protection in Connecticut"* (n.p.: State of Connecticut, 1986), pp. 5–6.

3. B. Charles Wansley, *History and Traditions,* rev. ed. (n.p.: Council of Better Business Bureaus, Inc., 1983), p. 3; John A. McTighe, "Self-Regulation Efforts of Advertisers, Their Agents and the Media," in *Consumer Protection from Deceptive Advertising,* ed. Fredric Stuart, ser. 10, vol. 3 (n.p.: Hofstra University Yearbook of Business, 1974), p. 84.

4. McTighe, p. 95.

5. The consumerism phenomenon has been discussed many times. See, for example, Joe L. Welch, *Marketing Law* (Tulsa: PPC Books, 1980), p.14 and *Who's Minding the Store.*

6. *Who's Minding the Store,* p. 17.

7. U.S. Congress, House of Representatives, Committee on Energy and Commerce, *FTC Review: 1977–84* by Michael Pertschuk, 98th Congress, 2d Session, Committee Print 98-CC (Washington, D.C.: Government Printing Office, September 1984), p. 12. See also John Dorfman, *Consumer Tactics Manual* (New York: Atheneum, 1980).

8. Budgetary estimate from interview with Bill McDonough, staff attorney at the Boston regional FTC office.

9. Welch, pp. 10–11. Also see Kenneth Eisenberger: *The Expert Consumer* (Englewood Cliffs, N.J.: Prentice-Hall, 1977), p. 216.

10. William Brun, "The Role of State and Local Consumer Protection Agencies in Advertising Regulation," in *Consumer Protection from Deceptive Advertising*, pp. 8, 26–55, quoting Phillip Schrag, *Counsel for the Deceived* (New York: Pantheon Books, 1972), p. 184.

11. Eisenberger, p. 218.

12. For example, see *FTC Review: 1977–84* and Richard J. Leighton, "Miller, Pertschuk Battles Give FTC a Bad Name," *Legal Times*, August 20, 1984, p. 8.

13. Roy Ahmen et al., *Advertising and Government Regulation*, Report No. 79-106 (n.p.: Advertising and Government Panel of the American of Advertising, 1979), pp. 7, 11.

14. Pertschuk, p. 15.

15. *"Who's Minding the Store"*; *FTC Review: 1977–87*, p. 12. See also John T. Lucas and Richard Gurman, *Truth in Advertising: An AMA Research Report* (n.p.: American Management Association, 1972); *Report of the ABA Commission to Study the Federal Trade Commission* (Chicago: American Bar Association, 1969); and *Report of the American Bar Association, Section of Antitrust Law, Special Committee to Study the Role of the Federal Trade Commission* (Chicago: American Bar Association, 1989). For other views of the FTC's ineffectiveness during this period, see Warren Magnuson and Jean Carper, *The Dark Side of the Marketplace: The Plight of the American Consumer*, 2nd ed. (Englewood Cliffs, N.J.: Prentice-Hall, 1972), p. 33.

16. Robert Sabatino, "Federal Government Agency Activities" in *Consumer Protection from Deceptive Advertising*, p. 15.

17. Eisenberger, p. 255.

18. Dorfman, p. 5.

19. Ahmen et al., p. 39.

20. For example, Bruce Silverglade, "Regulation Didn't Die—It Moved," *Houston Post*, August 30, 1988, p. 3E, and Stephen Labaton, "States March into the Breach," *New York Times*, December 18, 1988, sec. 3, pp. 1, 26.

21. For more information, see Brun, p. 27.

22. Eisenberger, p. 253.

23. Dorfman, p. 7.

24. Eisenberger, pp. 253–255.

25. Ibid., p. 236.

26. Unpublished July 21, 1988, letter from David A. Talbot, Jr., special assistant attorney general for consumer affairs, to Tom Curtis of *Texas Monthly Magazine*. See also Eisenberger, p. 253.

27. Brun, p. 49, quoting Schrag, p. 184.

28. *Gasoline Marketing: Consumers Have Limited Assurance That Octane Ratings Are Accurate*, #RCED-90-50 (Washington, D.C.: General Accounting Office, 1990), p. 3.

29. F. M. Scherer, *Industrial Market Structure and Economic Performance* (Boston: Houghton Mifflin, 1980), p. 482.; Mancur Olson, *The Logic of Collective Action* (Cambridge, Mass.: Harvard University Press, 1965), p. 165; Paul J. Quirk, *Industry Influence in Federal Regulatory Agencies* (Princeton, N.J.: Princeton University Press, 1981), pp. 13, 16; James Gwartney and Richard Wagner, *Public Choice and Constitutional Economics* (Greenwich, Conn.: Jai Press, 1988), pp. 19–20; and Maynes, "Consumer Protection: The Issues," p. 107.

30. For example, see Frank Phillips, "Attorney General's Race Finds New Life as Lead Tightens," *Boston Globe*, May 20, 1990, p. 25; David Nyhan, "Shannon Shoots from the Hip, *Boston Globe*, March 19, 1989, sec. A, p. 29.

31. Frank Phillips, "Shannon Scores Big over DA Harshbarger for Attorney General," *Boston Globe*, June 3, 1990, p. 41.

32. Bradley Stertz, "U.S. Study Blames Drivers for Sudden Acceleration," *Wall Street Journal*, February 2, 1989, sec. B, p. 1, and "Audi Rebate Program on 5000 Model Has the Look of Bait and Switch," *Wall Street Journal*, June 21, 1988, p. 41.

33. See Dorfman, p. 187.

34. James Mattox and Hal Stratton, "Should States Regulate Ads?," *Advertising Age*, August 8, 1988, p. 18, 20.

35. Ibid.

36. New York Attorney General's *Annual Report*, (n.p.: n.p., 1987), p. 68.

37. K. Greene and R. Gay, *Occupational Regulation in the United States* (Washington, D.C.: U.S. Department of Labor, Employment and Training Administration, 1980).

38. Simon Rottenberg, ed., *Occupational Licensure and Regulation* (Washington, D.C.: American Enterprise Institute for Public Policy Research, 1980).

39. Benjamin Shimberg, "Regulation in the Public Interest: Myth or Reality?" address delivered at the annual meeting of the Clearinghouse on Licensure, Enforcement, and Regulation (CLEAR), September 8, 1989, p. 1; Idem, "What's the Future of Licensing," address before the American Occupational Therapy Association Conference "1990 and Beyond: The National Agenda for State Regulation of Occupational Therapy," October 14, 1989, pp. 6, 21–22; Benjamin Shimberg, Barbara Esser, and Daniel Kruger, *Occupational Licensing: Practices and Policies* (Washington, D.C.: Public Affairs Press, 1973), p. 210; and Milton Friedman, *Capitalism and Freedom* (Chicago: University of Chicago Press, 1982), pp. 137–160.

40. Benjamin Shimberg, *Occupational Licensing: A Public Perspective* (Princeton, N.J.: Center for Occupational and Professional Assessment, Educational Testing Service, 1982), p. 122. See also Shimberg, Esser, and Kruger, pp. 193, 237.

41. Shimberg, Esser, and Kruger, p. 137.

42. Shimberg, *Occupational Licensing: A Public Perspective*, p. 39.

43. As printed in the *1989 Massachusetts Consumer Resource Guide* (Boston: Consumer Affairs Foundation, 1988), p. 287.

44. Ibid., n.p.

45. Consumers also have recourse to several other major self-regulatory groups, such as MACAP and the Direct Marketing Association, as well as the advertising code set by the National

Association of Broadcasters. But we concentrate on the BBB, since it's by far the most important and powerful of these organizations. Furthermore, the limitations of the BBB almost always apply to these and other smaller self-regulatory organizations.

46. Dorfman, pp. 6–7 and 156–157; "Who's Minding the Store"; Eisenberger, p. 230.

47. Ahmen et al., p. 56.

48. McTighe, pp. 83–121; Eisenberger, pp. 266–267; William H. Ewen, *The National Advertising Review Board: 1971–1975: A Four Year Review and Perspective on Advertising Industry Self-Regulation* (n.p.: NARB, 1975), p. 1.

49. McTighe, p. 115.

50. Otis A. Pease, "Advertising Ethics," in eds. John S. Wright and John E. Mertes, *Advertising's Role in Society* (St. Paul: West Publishing, 1974), p. 274.

51. E.g., Eisenberger, p. 261.

52. Ibid., p. 264. See also Maynes, "Consumer Protection: Corrective Measures," pp. 197–195.

53. See also Doris Faber, *Enough: The Revolt of the American Consumer* (New York: Dell, 1972), pp. 110–111 and "Ask the Globe," *Boston Globe*, December 19, 1989, p. 66.

54. Dorfman, p. 6.

55. Eisenberger, p. 265.

56. Ibid., p. 264, and William H. Ewen.

57. William H. Ewen. Similarly, all MACAP's panelists are totally independent of the appliance industry, mostly consisting of people involved in consumer research or education. Furthermore, the only compensation they receive for their work are travel funds to attend about ten meetings a year.

58. Eisenberger, p. 265.

59. Ibid., p 263; Dorfman.

60. Statistics from Eisenberger, p. 267, who seems to agree with MACAP that this is an admirable achievement.

61. Jeff Bailey, "Commodities Abuses Have Long Continued Despite NFA Scrutiny," *Wall Street Journal*, October 16, 1990, sec. A, pp. 1, 12; Martha Brannigan, "Critics Argue That Legal-Fee Arbitrators Tend to Side with Their Fellow Lawyers," *Wall Street Journal*, October 16, 1990, sec. B, pp. 1, 9; Michael Siconolfi, "Stock Investors Win More Punitive Awards in Arbitration Cases," *Wall Street Journal*, June 11, 1990, sec. A, pp. 1, 6.

CHAPTER 9

The Mass Media

Serving in part to alleviate consumer confusion, the growth of modern mass media has been one of the great achievements of the twentieth century. Nevertheless, many observers have wondered why the media cover specific consumer products so rarely and so poorly when many people would be extremely interested in this kind of news.[1] Why do you hardly ever see a market-basket comparison showing which supermarket in town has the best prices, for example? Why do you so rarely see an article exposing the bait-and-switch tactics of local department stores? Why do you so rarely see newspapers rating the quality of service among local appliance stores?

Our first blatant experience with this phenomenon came one Christmas when a major local television station in Boston interviewed us as personal shopping consultants for consumer electronics merchandise. Pleased at this opportunity to warn consumers that "sales" weren't always sales, we told the producer beforehand about how we had data documenting meaningless "sales" constantly run by specific local stores. The producer insisted, however, that we not mention any specific stores on camera. His remarkably frank explanation was that he didn't want to do anything that might alienate advertisers.

About the same time, we also offered a leading Boston newspaper summary statistical information on specific area retailers, illustrating relative prices, competitiveness, and significance of price claims. The editor refused us without expressing the least glimmer of interest. Of course, we had no specific evidence, but we couldn't help wondering if this paper's heavy reliance on advertising revenues from the very stores we named tipped the decision to deny information which was clearly of great and immediate interest to readers.

Following both of these experiences, we decided to dig a little deeper into the literature to see if there was any basis for our suspicions—suspicions that the media, classically considered society's watchdog, had serious conflicts of interest and other limitations that might prevent it from ever solving the problems of consumer confusion.

NOT BITING THE HAND THAT FEEDS YOU

Few people today maintain that the press simply mirrors reality. Almost every serious student of the media acknowledges that, given limited space, time, and budget, choices have to be made about which of the many events in the world are going to rate as "news." Even if that bias isn't harmful or malicious, there's bias built into every editorial judgment. When an editor decides that it's news when the mailman bites your dog but not news when your dog bites the mailman, that's bias. Compounded, it shapes the image of the world portrayed.

The deeper question, however, involves the nature of this bias. There is a vast literature on the subject, and, interestingly, much of it is contradictory. While many authors contend the press consists of middle- and upper-class conservatives, for example, others insist that it is a hotbed of "East Coast" liberals. Another group of authors takes a different tack, attributing bias not to the political or economic status of the journalists themselves but rather to the underlying structure of the press; for example, they claim that the division of labor in the modern newsroom or the economics of a newspaper greatly influences the type of coverage that the media can offer. Still other critics argue that outside forces such as technology or subscribers shape the news. Marxist scholars argue that the media is a mere puppet of powerful capitalists, for example, while "maligned" businesspeople argue that the media is a mere puppet of leftist radicals.[2]

Undoubtedly, all of these approaches have some degree of merit. In fact, as Columbia University sociologist Herbert J. Gans argues in his book *Deciding What's News,* the actual bias of the press is almost certainly determined by a "tug of war" between these powers.[3] The question remains, however: is any one power strong enough to produce a systematic bias? The answer, we believe, is often yes, and the power that most consistently biases the media belongs to the people who finance it, principally the advertisers.

Sins of Omission

Overwhelming evidence suggests that the media avoid exploring whole realms of information of great public interest because of inherent conflicts of interest. This bias exerts itself most profoundly not in acts of commission, but acts of omission, not in what the media choose to cover, but in what they choose not to cover.

The explanation lies almost purely in economics. Television networks and local stations, for example, get nearly 100 percent of their revenue from advertisers, who buy minutes of time to promote goods and services. As one author put it: "Networks are essentially in the business of selling a national audience to advertisers."[4] Newspapers and magazines rely less overtly on advertisers than do television and radio stations, but selling advertisements still constitutes a major, if not *the* major, source of income. Currently, newspapers make 75 percent of their revenues from ads and devote about 65 percent of their daily space to them (as opposed to 22 percent of TV time devoted to ads). Magazines make roughly half their money selling advertisements.[5] It may even be said that many magazines charge readers only for the sake of showing advertisers that potential purchasers are really going to read the magazines and the advertisements within it. Television advertisers, in contrast, can be confident that if they know the audience size of the station on which they advertise, they also know that their advertisement will be seen.

Whatever their other goals, then, newspapers, magazines, television stations, and radio stations are first and foremost profit-making enterprises, and even if their news reporters strive to remain "objective," their effort as a whole has got to make money. The problem arises when this pursuit of profit conflicts with the pursuit of truth.[6]

As for-profit businesses, the media enterprises clearly can't afford to ignore advertisers when choosing editorial content. Nor can the smaller, self-supporting publications who can afford to do so expect to have any significant impact. Without the power that comes from the advertiser's pocket, no radical or alternative paper has a chance to compete.[7] The catch-22 here is that if you want clout, you can't have it: If you have enough money for clout, through advertising revenue, you're under the advertiser's thumb. If you're under no one's thumb, you don't have enough readership to make any difference anyway.

As media ownership in this country becomes more concentrated, moreover, advertisers may gain even more power over content.[8] For example, because many large magazines are involved in several publishing industries—other magazines, books, and so forth—they can't afford to alienate an advertiser in one medium at the risk of ad withdrawal in another. A newspaper which carries very little drug advertising may not be able to run a story unfavorable to the pharmaceutical industry because its parent company also happens to own medical journals which rely on the drug houses for their livelihood. Similarly, publishers may refuse books because they happen to be owned by a corporation that doesn't like the book's image of specific corporations or of corporate practices.

In theory, of course, all respectable publications keep a steel door bolted between the editorial and business offices. It's also true that many journalists feel antipathy towards advertisers and resent their interference. "Many [journalists] are also unhappy about advertising *sui generis*," notes Gans, "because advertisements take up time or space that could otherwise be devoted to news, and because they fear that the lack of credibility of advertising will damage their own credibility."[9] Newspapers boast their "independence" and "objectivity," and reporters insist that overt pressure by the business office is a relic of the past.[10] As Ben Bagdikian of the University of California's School of Journalism writes:

> Modern media, it is said, are immunized by professional ethics from letting advertising influence editorial content. . . . [Newspapers and magazines] generally insist that their advertising departments never shape the articles, stories, and columns produced by professional editors and writers. Radio and television, the most pervasive media in American life, have varied nonadvertising content like game shows, situation comedies, cops-and-robbers serials, news, talk shows, documentaries, and musical recordings. These, broadcasters usually insist, are independent of the thirty-second and sixty-second commercials dropped into normal programming. In short, nineteenth-century money changers of advertising have been chased out of the twentieth-century temple of editorial purity. It's a pretty picture.[11]

Unfortunately, Bagdikian goes on to say, the picture is deceptive. And indeed, if the business and editorial offices were truly independent, then magazines like *Consumer Reports* wouldn't feel compelled to refuse all advertising to retain credibility. Almost every working journalist knows an unofficial story of someone who lost a job or received an extreme threat by writing a story that embarrassed a big advertiser. "In almost every news organization," writes Bagdikian, "there has been, at some time, an editor who permitted publication of a legitimate story that unexpectedly brought retribution from the owner. A reporter or editor is fired, demoted, or otherwise reprimanded. That lesson is observed by everyone in the news organization."[12]

Newspapers and magazines also devote enormous energy to attracting advertisers. Publications sponsor complex marketing studies so that they can slant editorial content to the right group of readers—readers who will purchase products that advertisers want to sell.[13] They also take out ads in trade publications, noting the promotional value to potential advertisers. For example, in late 1988 the *Boston Globe Magazine* took out a full-page ad in *Advertising Age* promising potential advertisers that "if you want Bostonians to notice your car, park it in the new full-bleed format *Boston Globe Magazine*. It's the biggest, brightest and best way to reach the sixth largest automotive market in the U.S."[14]

Certain sections of magazines and newspapers are specifically designed to attract revenue from advertisers. Fashions, food, and real estate, for example, were originally designed as "advertising bait." While some of these sections are now genuinely useful, others are mixtures of "light syndicated features and corporate press releases," while a few have been handed over completely to the advertising departments to fill with whatever material will best sell ads.[15]

Meanwhile, cutthroat competition for ads aimed at the "upscale consumer" who will buy expensive items is forcing magazines and newspapers to create "added value": advertising packages loaded with options such as free research or free vacations "much the way a car dealer throws in air conditioning or a rebate to close a sale." Magazines, competing for the same national-advertising dollars as other national publications and television, are even more pressed to offer added value than newspapers, which often control an entire region.[16]

Another source of revenue from advertisers comes from "product placement," a common practice in television, movies, and print media in which advertisers pay big bucks to have their wares mentioned favorably. According to the *New York Times*, in 1989 it cost advertisers an average of $50,000 for each brand-name mention in a movie. Meanwhile, marketers are paying media to display commercials disguised as news segments for TV and "advertorials" disguised as news articles for print media.[17]

It's hardly surprising, then, that advertisers influence media content. Most overtly, advertisers may withdraw patronage, but letters or phone calls from irate advertising agents or corporate executives "asking for reply time or threatening retaliation" can also keep the media in line.[18] Not only can and do corporations take out what they call "counteradvertising" in major publications, but some even have their own in-house production facilities, allowing them to create high-quality and highly influential responses. Advertisers have the clout to sit down with network executives to demand rebuttal time or to point out where the shows went wrong.[19] "Given the eagerness with which newspapers protect major advertisers," notes Bagdikian, "it is understandable that by now advertisers expect that when the interests of readers are in competition with the interests of advertisers, the newspapers will protect the advertisers."[20] Observes *Newsweek* reporter Steve Waldman, "consumer [TV] reporters have begun quietly but severely censoring themselves. Reporters . . . now weigh news value against potential revenue loss and career damage."[21]

Admittedly, advertisers don't always retain the upper hand, and major corporations routinely complain about "hatchet jobs" and "trial by television."[22] What's more, advertiser control is much less overt than it was forty years ago, when no mainstream newspaper would accept ads from Consumers Union because its magazine, *Consumer Reports,* tested and reported, sometimes negatively, name brands advertised in newspapers."[23] For the most part advertisers today don't have to lift a finger to dominate content: the message is subtly present in all decisions, leading to an almost unconscious avoidance. Most censorship is therefore self-censorship by the editorial staffs themselves, brought on by the anticipation that superiors might disapprove of a story because it would alienate advertisers and other powers. This process occurs "so naturally," note Professors Edward S. Herman and Noam Chomsky, "that media news people, frequently operating with complete integrity and goodwill, are able to convince themselves that they choose and interpret the news 'objectively' and on the basis of professional news values."[24]

Even if this control by advertisers is largely unconscious and unarticulated on the part of network decision-makers, it still has a palpable effect on editorial choices. Reader and viewer likes and dislikes matter, of course, since no one will see an ad if no one is reading the paper or watching the show, but there's little difficulty in choosing the subset of shows or articles that please advertisers as well as audiences. In other words, pleasing the audience is a necessary but not sufficient condition for running a story. What's essential is that the story not offend advertisers. One media commentator notes that even if most of the public would enjoy watching "The Adventures of Ralph Nader," for example, it would be hard to sell to advertisers.

Given the incredible effort devoted to delivering the right audience to advertisers, it's logical to assume that editors and producers also would try not to alienate any advertisers that they already have. Thus, the final arbiter of the content of what gets printed or aired is not what the audience wants, but what advertisers are willing to pay for. Winning readers or viewers is more often than not seen merely as a way of winning more advertisers. Sometimes this orientation means avoiding content of interest to readers—such as price-comparison charts—that would also irritate advertisers, creating what Bagdikian calls a "no man's land" of subject matter that few reporters dare enter.[25] Says Herb Denenberg, a consumer reporter for Philadelphia's WCAU-TV, " 'Everyone loves it if you're chopping up the city of Philadelphia, but if you're chopping up car dealers or department stores, [many stations] don't want to touch it.' "[26] Even magazines, which rely less than any other medium on the advertising dollar, rarely tackle these taboo subjects, if only because magazines today tend to restrict themselves to very specialized subject matter such as fishing or fashion. The result is that media coverage of practices such as the marketing of unsafe consumer products usually just "scratches the surface of these problems" while it wholly ignores the "systemic features that produce such abuses and the regularity with which they occur."[27]

Bias on the Air

Television, with its nearly complete dependence on the advertising dollar, presents the extreme example. Advertisers have a tremendous influence over programming choices, and even indirect decisions involving which brand of cigarette villains should smoke can lead to heated debate.[28] If such subtle use of a product generates so much tension, imagine the pressure programmers must feel to avoid shows which directly implicate a major advertiser or its products.

In fact, there's no shortage of examples documenting the way network executives avoid negative revelations about corporate America that will cast doubt on their advertisers or even disrupt the "buying mood."[29] Thus, we read in the *Wall Street Journal* that ABC and CBS declined to run certain commercials for a film satirizing the advertising business, *Crazy People*, that went so far as to mention brand names. The article quotes Matthew Marto, CBS's vice-president of program practices, as explaining, "[I]n a couple of instances, the clients of this network are portrayed in a way that might be troubling to them." Meanwhile, we read in the *Boston Globe* that when a major TV station tried promoting an investigative series condemning a product that radio stations had been hyping, eight of the eleven stations approached refused to run it.[30]

Of course, any specific incident could have mitigating influences— perhaps, for example, the radio series was simply of poor quality. Furthermore, blatant ad-yanking may be relatively rare among the corporations who do business with the major networks, since the nationwide exposure is too valuable to squander. Still, most media critics and even some media executives agree with Bagdikian that "no network produces a program without considering whether sponsors will like it. Prospective shows usually are discussed with major advertisers, who look at plans or tentative scenes and reject, approve or suggest changes."[31] Networks expend vast energy measuring their audience and which programs they watch, primarily so they can match ads with the right viewers. The high cost of producing news documentaries, furthermore, often forces networks to avoid controversial topics that might offend potential sponsors. In fact, as Todd Gitlin, a sociologist at the University of California at Berkeley, wrote in the *Nation,* "To advertisers, programs amount to packaging for commercials."[32]

Even educational and public television fall under the sway of adver- tisers. Although these stations do not air any commercials, they credit the corporation sponsoring each broadcast at the beginning of every show. The control these sponsors exert can be seen in the shake-up at public-television station WNET in 1985 when one of its documentaries contained material criticizing "multinational corporate activities in the Third World." According to Herman and Chomsky, sponsor Gulf & Western followed by withdrawing its corporate funding to the station, its CEO complaining that the program was "virulently anti-business if not anti-American," and that the station's carrying the program was not the behavior "of a friend" of the corporation. The London *Economist* observed that "'most people believe that WNET would not make the same mistake again.'"[33] Not surprisingly, most of public stations concentrate on cultural and artistic programming, rather than issue- oriented exposés.[34]

Local stations are particularly vulnerable to advertisers because they need advertisers more than advertisers need them. If a local advertiser doesn't like the way a local news channel is treating his company, for example, he can decide to transfer his advertising budget over to one of many other local channels or even to the local newspaper or radio station. Thus, station executives have a particularly strong incentive to keep advertisers happy, often at the expense of content. One author even described how the auto dealers of Oklahoma City blocked TV station KWTV from airing a consumer story that would have shown how auto dealers in that city were adding a controversial surcharge to their repair bills to cover "shop costs that aren't normally totalled in a customer's bill." It's important to note, too, that networks are vulnerable to local pressure from their local affiliates.[35]

Bias on the Page

Despite the alternative sources of revenue available to magazines and newspapers, advertisers dominate their content almost as much as they do that of television. Media critic Michael Parenti, for example, describes several reporters who were told by editors to write only positive pieces about local businesses and cites a veteran reporter for a local "independent" paper in Ohio, who recalled that the advertising manager cum editor there once warned him to be especially careful when he wrote about the local brewery, since it was the paper's best advertiser.[36]

Or consider the case at the *Beaumont Enterprise and Journal* as described by Curtis D. MacDougall. Apparently an editor was fired at this paper because he ran a comparative grocery shopping list in the paper's family-living section. The paper's publisher called the piece "the most irresponsible story that had ever been run in the paper." It could, he explained, "conceivably have had a rather severe economic impact upon the business. It could have affected our ad lineage."[37]

Such overt acts of commission are relatively rare, but perhaps not as rare as most of us would hope. When the Credit Union National Association unveiled a program to protect consumers against high-pressure car salespeople, for example, and announced it in a Tallahassee, Florida, paper, several local dealers pulled their ads. Similarly, when the *Toronto Star* ran some hard-hitting travel articles, Canada's thirteen largest tour operaters boycotted the paper and withdrew several million dollars of advertising.[38]

Papers are most likely to expose a business if they are not under direct advertising pressure from that business, consumer advocate Ralph Nader has observed. "The only way to tackle press reform," he reasons, is to determine what a newspaper does and doesn't do in its own circulation area. For example the *Washington Post* will fearlessly cover issues dealing with the Pentagon, Standard Oil, and General Motors, but when it comes to its local area, it is not as active in investigating price-fixing in supermarkets or the fire hazards in Washington restaurants, which are very bad. The reason for this is advertising pressure. GM or Standard Oil doesn't support the *Washington Post*. The local drug chains, the department stores, and the restaurants pay the paper millions of dollars in advertising revenues. There isn't a memo posted in newsrooms saying not to cover some local problem, but there is a lack of sensitivity, an inbred lack of interest, in doing so.[39]

Many stories of subtle and not-so-subtle omissions are hard to come by, however, because no one wants to acknowledge them. Several government officials we interviewed while doing this book, for example, told us about newspaper reporters they knew who futilely tried to do stories about local electronics firms or appliance stores, all of which were heavy advertisers in the papers. We've even talked to television consumer reporters who tried to do stories about these futile attempts and the advertising bias involved, only to be refused by their own stations. One official predicted that however many press releases he issued about electronics stores, he'd have to go to each paper and "stand on his head" even to get a little blurb printed on a back page. But despite the prevalence of such second-hand gossip and unattributable anecdote, no one is willing to put his or her name or position behind them—perhaps for obvious reasons.

Still, the evidence is there in the studies done by serious students of the media. In fact, both Bagdikian and R. C. Smith have documented what is probably the most notable suppression on these lines, which occurred in the tobacco industry. Despite the strong evidence linking tobacco to disease and to death, most media for years either ignored the evidence entirely or portrayed it as controversial. This neglect contrasted with the diligent reporting of many other less serious or widespread medical conditions.[40] Clearly, if magazines and newspapers refused to run articles about the dangers of tobacco—a habit with extremely serious health and social consequences for the American public, a habit believed to have caused 300,000 deaths per year—how much easier it must be to refuse negative articles about retail stores—practices which only result in monetary loss and aggravation, and which also supply far more advertising than cigarette advertising ever did.

Evidence is only circumstantial, of course, but it's hard not to wonder if this isn't what happened in 1976 when the Federal Trade Commission tried the world's largest retailer, Sears, Roebuck and Company for bait and switch. The *Chicago Tribune* at the time was receiving $5 million annually in advertising revenue from Sears. Although the hearings involved eighteen former Sears employees from thirteen states and twenty-five consumer witnesses from eleven states, this paper printed not a single word about the case for its eleven-day duration. The only notice it gave to Chicago readers about this event was a four-paragraph condensed report a week later, taken from a *Wall Street Journal* bureau file.[41] (Fifteen years later, the FTC is unable to find any record of the outcome of the case.)

The *New York Times,* which received about 18 percent of its advertising revenues from the auto industry in 1973 and 1974, found itself in a similar dilemma when in those years that industry was pressuring Congress to repeal the seat-belt and air-bag regulations thought to save between 5,000 and 10,000 lives a year. According to Parenti, the paper

> ran stories that were, as one *Times* staff person admitted, "more or less put together by the advertisers." *Times* publisher Arthur Ochs Sulzberger openly admitted that he urged his editors to present the industry position in coverage of safety and auto pollution because, he said, it "would affect the advertising."[42]

Of course, none of this means that journalists don't occasionally devote themselves to serious probing or that the press never steps on powerful toes. In fact, for years journalists have had reputations as reformist muckrakers, whether or not they would label themselves as such. "Contemporary journalists do not, for the most part, see themselves as reformers," observes Gans, "but the ones I studied were proud whenever a story resulted in official investigations and in legislative or administrative reform."[43] The American press, in fact, is known for its investigative reporting, resulting in exposés that reveal legal or moral misbehavior such as the Watergate affair in the 1970s.[44] Gans likens the values of modern American journalists to those of the Progressive movement of the early twentieth century, notably the "advocacy of honest, meritocratic, and anti-bureaucratic government." On the other hand, when it comes to investigating business, journalists seem to have much less zeal.[45] In fact, whereas the *New York Times* has more than a half-dozen investigative political and law-enforcement reporters, it doesn't have a single full-time investigative consumer reporter. And of 1,110 members in the organization of Investigative Reporters and Editors in the 1980s, only 6 had corporate life as their beat.[46]

Ralph Nader observed early in his career that the only way to get the press to cover a muckraking type of consumer issue was to turn the issue into the kind of news that no self-respecting publication could neglect. Editors in general won't accept articles disparaging a retailer or manufacturer, but they'll carry one that has been "forced" on them by a major institution or government agency such as the local attorney general's office or the National Highway Traffic Safety Association. As Nader put it: "In a really controversial issue, especially one dealing with big business, the press will cover the story much more readily if the issues are paraded and discussed than go out on its own and investigate."[47]

When Nader was trying to get newspapers to name automobiles by make and model, for example, he learned that one of the best approaches was to bring the issue before a Congressional hearing. Then he knew the press would cover the issue and could claim to advertisers that they were just doing their jobs—not crusading. "I learned a long time ago you just don't take auto news to the automotive editor," he continued. This editor

thinks his only job is to write a column praising the new car models which will be run alongside an auto industry ad in the back of the paper. If the automotive editor isn't doing that, he is interviewing auto industry executives about car production or probing for gossip about who will get what job in the Detroit executive suites.[48]

Usually only when public opinion leads government agencies to ferret out corruption will the media report it. At such times reporters may even favor consumer groups over businesses. But because these stories are generated by outside groups rather than the journalists themselves, they tend to be somewhat arbitrary and sporadic.[49]

Bias in the "Consumer" Magazines

Browse through a well-stocked newsstand, and you'll quickly see that guides to the perplexed consumer hardly are lacking. If you're buying an automobile there's *Car and Driver, Road and Track,* and *Motor Trend;*

if you're buying a stereo there's *Stereo Review, Audio,* and *Digital Audio and Compact Disc Review;* if you're buying a TV there's *Video, High Fidelity,* and *Video Review;* if you're buying a computer there's *PC Magazine, Byte, Family Computing, Compute!, InfoWorld, Macuser, MacWeek, Software Digest, MacWorld, Personal Computing, PC Digest, PC Week,* and *Computer Buyer's Guide and Handbook;* and if you're buying just about anything, there's *Consumer Reports, Consumer Digest, The Washington Consumers Checkbook, Changing Times,* and *Consumer Guide.*

All of these publications—and others published by various groups or "unions" of consumers—may make the above arguments seem moot. After all, even if the majority of media largely ignores consumer needs, these magazines distinctly claim to give the kind of background and sometimes even specific recommendations that will help the confused consumer wade through a vast array of choices. And unquestionably, they give a sense of the options available. In a world where salespersons are harried and can only spend a few minutes with a given shopper, this function is valuable. Nevertheless, with the very notable exception of *Consumer Reports,* these magazines almost universally fall prey to advertisers as do other media.[50]

PC Magazine, which bills itself as "The *Independent* [italics added] Guide To IBM-Standard Personal Computing," is also the biggest trade publication of any type in terms of advertising revenue, reporting an intake of $100.6 million in 1988.[51] This situation hints at a fundamental dilemma faced by most consumer magazines: to get readers to look at them, they must proclaim their absolute objectivity and concern for the consumer's interest, but to finance themselves, they must get the money from the companies they rate. The result often is a bias favoring goods from large advertisers, despite frequent claims about objectivity. Consumer magazines tend to be very upbeat no matter what is reviewed, and while it's acceptable to damn with faint praise, it's never acceptable to criticize directly.[52] The whole situation is akin to paying a judge at the discretion of the defendants that the judge evaluates. The only reason that we tolerate such unfairness in evaluation is that we haven't come up with a more practical alternative.

The influence of this bias works itself out subtly. The most visible evidence comes in the refusal of these magazines to make direct, hard-hitting comparisons such as "Branch X tends to be unreliable and overpriced compared to Brand Z." You'll also rarely if ever see a statement such as "Branch Y loads its CD players with expensive extras that make no audible difference but which look good on paper." What the magazines do instead is make either overly general or overly specific statements. For example, a magazine will run a three-page article on a specific model filled with hundreds of detailed facts about it. But the article will neglect what most people really want: how that model compares to other models on the market.[53]

These magazines tend to operate on the hieroglyphics principle. They want you to read into a very complicated code of etiquette, which only they know how to decipher. They want you to know that unless they're screaming wildly in favor of a product, they're probably just damning it with faint praise. And they want you to approach their reviews like a jigsaw puzzle. Each product has something positive said about it. They want you to put together all the positive things said about the different products (often in the context of many back issues), and then, having put all the pieces of a high-quality product together, go back to each review to figure out, from what *hasn't* been said, what each product must be missing.

These magazines test products as a public relations device more than as a helpful guide to consumers. Testing one item at a time in great depth precludes comparing results with other tests. Furthermore, articles usually don't even attempt to define what the test results mean or which results, for all practical purposes, are useless. This practice gives the magazines a spurious objectivity and can often hide the fact that no serious thinking has gone into figuring out what features are really useful (it is always easier to read the results of an oscilloscope than to judge what those results mean). Or even worse, it can be an attempt to hide the fact that on the next page appears an advertisement for that very product. In this case, presumably, the magazine merely uses the tests to shield the fact that conflicts of interest prevent it from giving truly objective evaluations.

On the other extreme are articles containing frank but also quite general comments about what to look for and avoid. For example, a discussion might counsel readers to watch out for manufacturers that tend to inflate their lines of resolution figure on TV monitors, but won't mention specific brands. Readers then have to go into stores and try to see if they can tell whether a TV that claims to have 440 lines really only has 420—a humanly impossible task, even with the best of eyes!

"Unquestionably [these magazines] have a policy to be positive," notes Peter Mitchell, a writer for various consumer magazines including *Stereo Review* and *High Fidelity*. "Their reviews will go from moderately favorable to wildly enthusiastic. I believe it's actually a written policy not to have negative reviews. Negative reviews will be thrown in the wastebasket and the equipment sent back to the manufacturer." He adds that part of this policy undoubtedly comes from advertising pressure: "Manufacturers are very willing to cancel contracts with magazines that give them negative reviews."

Adding to the bias is the fact that some reviewers earn their basic income as consultants to specific manufacturers and view consumer electronics as "an exciting industry where just about everything is good to excellent," says Mitchell.

Sometimes these magazines will criticize certain features or models, but only after they cease to be relevant. For example, when Toshiba first came out with its noninterlaced TV, consumer magazines hailed it with great fanfare as offering a vastly improved picture. But only two years later, when a new and much improved noninterlaced scanning system came out, did one of the major video magazines note that the earlier system really made virtually no improvement over standard TV sets?

People shopping for specific electronic or computer equipment often complain that these magazines are biased and useless. "Magazines like *Video Review, Video, High Fidelity,* and *Audio* don't regard themselves as consumer-guidance magazines," explains Mitchell. "Their target reader is the hobbyist. This reader knows he's very interested in the subject matter and wants to get heavily involved. They're not aimed at random newsstand buyers but [at] subscribers who read every issue."

Consequently, many of these magazines throw a lot of facts at savvy aficionados who truly enjoy making their own decisions about which speaker or receiver to buy. But for the first-time buyer who wants a specific recommendation and some perspective, these magazines offer nothing but information overload. Consider, for example, this representative sentence from *Stereo Review:* "Naturally, there was no detectable wow & flutter; the digital process itself precludes that."[54] This kind of writing assumes an awful lot from readers, and, as a salesperson trainer for the stereo chain Tweeter, etc., pointed out, the average person looking at the spec sheets in *Stereo Review* responds with a "huh?"

Jack Reggio, a former salesman at numerous consumer-electronics companies, agrees. "[These magazines] don't care if you understand," he says. "They're just platforms for advertising. The great majority of salespeople can't even understand the audio specs. . . . People are looking for an opinion. They look at me and say: 'Tell me. Make up my mind.' "

The trainer at Tweeter adds that these consumer magazines just can't tell shoppers how a piece of equipment "hits them on a gut level. That's really how people buy. They simply want to know what's really important when you buy something like this. And that's what the magazines don't say."

THE MEDIUM IS THE MESSAGE

Despite these constraints, of course, the media have been known to offer valuable consumer-education materials. Market-basket studies do appear now and then. Papers like the *Wall Street Journal* occasionally analyze retailing practices. And, of course, it's even possible for a book like this one to appear. But the problem with all these materials—and the way they differ from the high-tech consumer-information system we propose in Part III—is that their information is too little, too late. No matter how good any individual study, article, or book, it becomes outdated almost as soon as it appears and has limited impact. For example, although the *Wall Street Journal* ran a story on the ridiculousness of price-matching polices, the story didn't run until mid-March 1989, too late for the consumers who had been misled by such claims for years. Furthermore, the article reached only a limited and select audience, only superficially described how such claims can succeed, and told the sellers' side of the story more than the shoppers'.[55]

The basic problem inherent in all existing media, whether print or broadcast, is that they are not conducive to getting readers the right information at the right time in the right place. For example, an article about how to buy a baby crib buried on page 20 of a newspaper is not going to attract much attention. Readers probably won't ever notice it. Even if they do, at the particular time the article is printed they're not likely to be in the market for a baby crib. And given the small audience for the article, the newspaper would never be able to provide more than a tiny amount of space for it. In fact, given the above considerations, such an article probably would never be written, even though over the span of several years, a huge number of people would have been interested in it.

Above all, the nature of today's media itself, even without advertising pressures, means that sporadic articles and books cannot possibly keep up with the constantly changing products and selling practices in any sort of systematic fashion. In 1964 Marshall McLuhan wrote a book called *Understanding Media,* in which he argued that "the medium is the message." The form in which information is delivered, he explained, has a profound impact on its content. Just as the structural requirements of a haiku poem or a sonnet prevent the detailed development of a love story, so too do the structural requirements of today's media result in the impossibility of high-grade and useful consumer information. Combined with the severe restrictions imposed by advertising, the consumer has little chance to get current and reliable shopping information from the media. As we shall see, today's technology is reaching a point at which we can avoid these limitations, if we choose to do so.

Of course, the most obvious example of the medium shaping the message comes from the advertising bias just discussed.[56] But even if the existing media weren't subject to the tastes of the advertisers that employ them, other inherent limitations would keep the media from ever adequately educating consumers. For example, time and space limitations force networks to appeal broadly to viewers of all educational levels and political stances by featuring quick visual images and simplified issues. Thus, one key reason that television cannot do product reviews has nothing to do with advertising and everything to do with the fact that it is a mass medium that risks losing its audience (and gaining a lawsuit) if it narrows its focus too far.

To avoid controversy, for example, networks tend to choose correspondents who will stay away from advocacy of any sort. The goal is to create a "balanced" news story, ideally following a "point-counterpoint" format with correspondents providing some sort of neutral synthesis. In fact, network policies expressly forbid correspondents from taking sides or advocating any controversial cause. "In these circumstances," notes one author, "there is little incentive for correspondents to form deep or systematic opinions about the world they report."[57] As one article in the *Columbia Journalism Review* put it, "The appetite these days is for fairly safe, less controversial, sociological investigative stories. . . . If you look across the country, you see papers doing a great job of covering prisons and juvenile crime and child abuse. But you don't see people asking how Exxon got to be bigger than five or six countries in the world."[58]

Even Virtue Has Its Limitations

One of the most revealing ways to see the structural limitations—as opposed to the bias—of the media is to look at the limitations of a publication that accepts no advertising revenue at all. The most striking example here, of course, is the scrupulous consumer magazine *Consumer Reports,* the largest and most respected consumer publication in the United States, which for its fifty-year history has stringently shunned the slightest association with retailers or manufacturers and indisputedly offers valuable shopping tips and other information to consumers about product features and industry trends and scams. These merits notwithstanding, *Consumer Reports* inevitably plays a relatively small role in the mix of product information we receive. Consider the figures. Of the approximately $5,000 each American household spends on product information per year ($50 billion—minimum—divided by 90 million households), less than 60 cents will go to *Consumer Reports.*[59] And of that 60 cents, only about 11 cents will go towards gathering product information. Let's look at *Consumer Reports'* budget:[60]

1986 Revenue[61] $45,806,000
1986 Product Information Gathering Expense[62] . . . . $ 8,482,000
1986 Marketing, Fulfillment, and Miscellaneous Expense . . . $31,234,000

Now let's compare this budget to other "product-information expenditures" for specific brands. And please note that *total* expenditures are probably three to four times higher, since the numbers below represent advertising expenditures alone—not packaging, sales help, and other promotional tactics:[63, 64]

Airwick . . . . $ 8,216,000
Raid $13,025,000
Lysol $11,833,000
Uncle Ben's Rice $27,416,000
Kool-Aid $29,785,000
Hershey's Candy Bars $30,650,000

Assuming that the number of dollars spent at least somewhat reflects the quality and quantity of information, we need to ask how this imbalance has arisen. We believe that the answer lies in the nature of the medium with which *Consumer Reports* has been forced to work. The fact is that while this well-intentioned publication definitely names names, makes very explicit recommendations, and doesn't hesitate to pan particular products that it considers overpriced, deceptive, or unsafe, the nature of the print medium too often produces information that is far too impractical, dated, incomplete, inconvenient, and noncustomized for the average consumer.

National Orientation

One of the most serious flaws in any consumer magazine is that a national print format precludes practical information about actual purchasing—particularly information about localized service, availability, and pricing. It makes no sense for a national magazine like *Consumer Reports* to keep close track of what's going on in local stores around the country, but as a result the articles can't distinguish between a model that is sold to 100 stores in the United States and one sold to 5,000 stores. It also makes no sense for *Consumer Reports* to consider models or brands only available in limited regions of the country or to keep track of whether a model is actually yet on store shelves or whether it has been discontinued. Including such information would produce long and tiresome lists, most of which would be irrelevant to any given reader. Nevertheless, without such information, people often stand in their local retailer with an issue of the magazine in hand, frustrated because not a single TV in an article's list is actually in the store. In short, there's no concrete information about where to go to get the best deal, nor a way to learn, and no information regarding which low-priced suppliers, such as mail-order firms, are reliable.

Wall Street Journal reporter William Matheson reported a vivid example of the availability problem in one of his columns.[65] He described a University of California economist who one spring wanted to give his friend "the best" VCR on the market as an anniversary gift. The most recent issue of *Consumer Reports* rating VCRs had appeared the preceding March, and the economist used this issue to find that the highest-rated model was the RCA VPT391. He proceeded to call several local dealers, all of whom told him that the model didn't exist and then either hung up or tried to switch him to a Japanese branch on special. Eventually the economist called RCA's parent company, Thomson Consumer Electronics, only to be told that the VPT391 had been a limited-production model and that he should now look for the nearly identical VPT390. The Thomson spokesman also noted that the VPT390 and three related models, including the highly rated VPT391, all had been eight months old when *Consumer Reports* published its ratings.

Although Matheson quoted a spokesperson for *Consumer Reports* as regretting "having tested an aging, limited-edition model," and claiming that the publication usually flushes out such problems before going to press, this kind of situation occurs quite frequently. Salespeople find it particularly infuriating, since potential buyers come in demanding items that no longer exist.

"Last year *Consumer Reports* rated Panasonic air conditioners number 1," noted a Fretter salesman. "They didn't tell consumers that the machine was merely an experiment. No one had the machine to sell. From what I know, there wasn't one available in New England." He then described a GE microwave oven that the magazine rated "just as GE stopped making it." A Lechmere salesperson from a Boston suburb agreed. "People can find only about 30 percent of the models in a *Consumer Reports* rating in our store."

A national orientation also limits the value of the prices given in *Consumer Reports*, despite the fact that the value of any product or feature to a consumer is critically dependent on price. In fact, almost all consumer publications still rely on list price as provided by manufacturers in calculating "value for their money," but, as we've seen earlier, list price often has very little relation to prices in local stores.

"Admittedly, *Consumer Reports,* like certain other consumer publications, lists "best price" as well as "list price." The basic problem with this "best price," however, is that it's usually just the lowest price the reporter has seen the model selling for at a handful of discount stores or mail-order firms. If the reporter didn't happen to see it on sale, this so-called best price might not be a best price at all. As the vice-president of one electronics firm commented, "I like *Consumer Reports'* best price because we're usually $50 to $100 less than it."

Occasionally, the "best price" may indeed be the lowest price around. But too often in such cases the publication obtained the price from some obscure mail-order firm, from which it may be unreasonable to expect the average person to buy—or even know about. Furthermore, because prices vary significantly by region, it's impractical for any magazine to include this variation by adding extra space and complexity—even if the magazine could afford to gather it in the first place.

Lack of contact with the actual merchandise on the sales floor, moreover, sometimes results in more serious inaccuracies. The television ratings in the May 1988 issue, for example, not only ignored reliability but neglected all brands less than several years old, even though many of these new brands were available in stores. Note that such errors are often unintentional: nobody can question this publication's impartiality. In a world where many proclaim such objectivity but haven't taken steps to ensure it, *Consumer Reports* deserves its special reputation.

Problems of Time and Space

Complicating the lack of relevant availability and pricing information is the relatively long time it takes to publish a magazine article. Printing and distribution alone usually take six weeks. The same topics are not covered every issue, and so consumers must often wait months to get the information they're looking for. *Consumer Reports* takes six months from article concept to completion—four months for testing and writing the report, and then six weeks for printing and distribution. What this means is that if you're looking for a VCR in September, you may have to use the same March *Consumer Reports* as did the University of California economist above, which was based on research done the previous September—a full year earlier. The general buying advice given in the accompanying article may still be useful even if several brand-new features are missing, but you won't be able to find any specific models rated.

This time lag is part of the reason that so many salespeople told us that they avoided any customer carrying a *Consumer Reports* into the store: they knew full well that the shopper would only want to buy one of the models on the list, but they also knew that the models on the list had been discontinued months earlier. "When people come in with *Consumer Reports* we walk away," said one former Fretter salesperson. "The concept is good, but the magazine doesn't come out fast enough." A Highland salesperson agreed: "*Consumer Reports* is so far out of date [with respect to consumer electronics products and major appliances] that [its specific model recommendations are] worthless to the average consumer."

The magazine format also precludes both specific (e.g., *Stereo Review*) and general (e.g., *Consumer Reports*) magazines from covering anything more than a tiny percentage of all the products in the marketplace. *Consumer Reports* attempts to cover a diverse assortment of major consumer products in the United States, including televisions, life insurance, insecticides, motels, cereals, banks, blazers, fast-food chains, automobiles, major appliances, toothpastes, movies, and lipsticks. It has eleven issues a year (the twelfth is the annual buying guide), and each issue has about eleven articles, only about half of which are in-depth articles about a particular product. On average, each in-depth article tests about twenty models or varieties. This means that the publication covers a total of about fifty product categories a year and tests about a thousand total items. But there are probably more than a million different consumer products in the United States (which means that a given item is likely to be reviewed on average approximately once in a thousand years!). And that means that even *Consumer Reports,* the best of the consumer publications, covers maybe one-tenth of 1 percent of those products—and that excludes such localized services as taxis, doctors, and retailers.

Even if it were economical to provide information on all these products, we would be talking about a magazine 100,000 pages in length every month. And it is probably not humanly possible—let alone practical—for an individual to cope with such a bombardment of information. Even within the categories that are covered—such as TVs—consumer magazines judge less than 5 percent of the extant merchandise (twenty out of five hundred–plus TVs), and that 5 percent may not even be representative. Not surprisingly, new consumer buying guides are constantly citing the superficiality and lack of perspective of their competitors.[66]

Admittedly, *Consumer Reports'* broad coverage does have an advantage over the specialized magazines. The latter publications, which cover one product type in depth, suffer from a different type of completeness problem. They tend to keep writing the same story again and again in slightly different words. A magazine on video goods, for example, must include in each of its twelve annual issues at least one article related to VCRs, rather than running one complete and authoritative article in a single issue.

A Lack of Customization

Even if *Consumer Reports* and other consumer magazines were 100 percent accurate, availability-oriented, comprehensive, and up-to-date, they'd still have limited value, particularly in regard to rating charts. Although on the surface these ratings seem to meet a shopper's need to be told specifically what to buy, they all have a fatal flaw: assuming the "average" person's needs rather than customizing recommendations. When *Consumer Reports* rates VCRs, for example, it fails to emphasize that features appropriate for one person might be inappropriate for others. Admittedly, the articles accompanying the charts often allude to different needs—but, as any salesperson will tell you, when it comes to making a purchase, the vast majority of readers simply look for the model or brand at the top of the chart. As we shall see in the chapters that follow, the advanced technology of the information age may be the only solution to the built-in inadequacy of the magazine format. Indeed, although the magazine *Consumer Reports* still doesn't use such new technology to customize its information, its publisher, Consumers Union, already offers a primitive version of the kind of interactive consumer help we foresee by providing an on-line version of the magazine via information services such as CompuServe and Prodigy.

Published ratings made a lot of sense when most products were as simple as insecticide, tires, soap, or old-fashioned TVs. But as more complex products have arrived, and as old products have become increasingly differentiated to meet varying needs, this primitive type of rating system becomes less valuable. For example, *Consumer Reports* rates approximately twenty VCRs once a year, but it doesn't distinguish between recommendations for different types of people. What happens if you care a lot about sound quality and want "Hi Fi"? What happens if you already have five remote controls cluttering up your coffee table and want a VCR with a universal remote control? What happens if you don't already have picture-in-picture special effects on your TV and so want to have them on your VCR? Computers, with their extraordinary number of options, provide an even better example of differential needs. Do you want a computer with a slow, medium-fast, or very fast processor? Do you want 256 kilobytes of random access memory, 640 kilobytes, 1 megabyte, 2 megabytes, 4 megabytes, or 8 megabytes? The old-fashioned rating systems simply can't provide a very useful service to consumers facing this level of complexity.

Reading the rating charts is a little like going into an electronics store that has one hundred TVs and being told that they can be ranked hierarchically for every customer who walks in the store. Everyone knows that different features on TVs are better and worse for different types of people. But these unilinear rating systems targeted to the "average" consumer necessarily overlook that fact.

Treating consumers as a homogeneous whole not only ignores consumer needs, but also runs against the whole grain of commerce. Much of business involves trying to figure out peoples' very different needs and then providing products to suit them. In fact, the whole history of retailing and marketing in the last two hundred years involves catering to increasingly complex and individualized consumer needs.[67] And yet the fact is that a single magazine, written by a handful of writers and testers, cannot be all things to all people.[68] Articles simply have to aim at the average person, and certain "experts" or aficionados out in the world are bound to be disgruntled. Numerous audio experts we talked to—whether salespeople, technicians, consultants, or writers—emphasized the shallowness of the magazine's recommendations in this area. Video experts noted that rating TVs hierarchically based on "picture quality" is an outdated concept, given the many factors that can alter broadcast quality. Or as one Fretter salesperson asked, "How can *Consumer Reports* compare dishwashers with mechanical controls to those with electrical ones? They're apples and oranges. You just can't compare them on the same chart." Other people complain that the publication forgets mundane but crucial (to them) details such as "How can I get this large refrigerator through my front door?" or "Will a service contract cover an icemaker bought separately from a refrigerator?"

Despite the admirable intentions of the most outstanding consumer-interest magazines, the very nature of the print medium imposes unavoidable limitations on their utility. For instance, *Consumer Reports'* noncustomized print format means that readers inevitably pay for information on product categories that are not of immediate interest to them. This phenomenon becomes extreme in the popular computer magazines, which every month print more than two thousand pages of information cumulatively. How do you find the time to wade through all that mess to get to what you want? Moreover, even with that two thousand pages, it's very likely that an article won't be written on the hardware or software in which you're interested. The result is that you'll probably have to wade through a lot of back issues or wait a couple of months until your topic is next covered. Furthermore, it's expensive getting all those magazines in the first place. So, chances are you'll probably not get a number of the major information sources that might be available to you.

The fact is, there are somewhere around forty-five thousand computer-related articles written per year in approximately 120 U.S. computer-related publications. And at least ten times that number of computer-related ads appear simultaneously. If we assume that the average publication results in a stack of material one foot high per year, then we are talking about a pile of material the size of a twelve-story building.[69] From a practical standpoint, a huge amount of useful information slips by people because it's just not worth the time and expense to locate it when it's distributed in a magazine format.

1. For example, see Lester Telser, "Advertising and the Consumer," in ed. Yale Brozen, *Advertising and Society* (New York: New York University Press, 1974), p. 120 and Nicholas Kaldor, "The Economic Aspects of Advertising," *Review of Economic Studies* 18 (1950–1951):5.

2. For a thoughtful analysis of these different approaches to media analysis, see Herbert J. Gans, *Deciding What's News: A Study of CBS Evening News, NBC Nightly News, Newsweek and Time* (New York: Vintage Books, 1980), pp. 78–79. For examples of different approaches, see David S. Broder, *Behind the Front Page* (New York: Simon & Schuster, 1987), pp. 322–323; Michael Parenti, *Inventing Reality: The Politics of the Mass Media* (New York: St. Martin's Press, 1986), pp. 6, 109; Howard Simons and Joseph A. Califano, eds., *The Media and Business* (New York: Vintgage Books 1979); Edith Efron, "The Media and the Omniscient Class," in ed. Craig E. Aronoff, *Business and the Media* (Santa Monica, Ca.: Goodyear, 1979), pp. 31–32; and "The Business Campaign Against 'Trial by TV,'" *Business Week*, June 2, 1980, pp. 78–79.

3. Gans, p. 81.

4. Edward Jay Epstein, *News from Nowhere* (New York: Vintage Books, 1973), pp. 79–80. See also Marshall B. Clinard and Peter C. Yeager, *Corporate Crime* (New York: Macmillan, 1980), pp. 221–221.

5. Ben H. Bagdikian, *The Media Monopoly,* 2nd ed. (Boston: Beacon Press, 1987), p. 153, and Parenti, p. 62.

6. Parenti, p. 28; Mark Green, "How Business Sways the Media," in Aronoff; and Jon G. Udell, "Economics and Freedom of the Press," in Aronoff, pp. 212, 55–72.

7. Edward S. Herman and Noam Chomsky, *Manufacturing Consent: The Political Economy of the Mass Media* (New York: Pantheon Books, 1988) pp. 4, 14–15.

8. Bagdikian, p. 9.

9. Gans, p. 255.

10. For example, Broder, pp. 325–326 and Muriel Fox, "Business/Media Influence: Who Does What to Whom?" in Aronoff, pp. 152–169.

11. Bagdikian, p. 153.

12. Ibid., p. 255. See also Steward Brand, *The Media Lab* (New York: Penguin, 1988), p. 210.

13. See Bagdikian's book.

14. *Advertising Age,* October 24, 1988.

15. Bagdikian, p. 136.

16. Cynthia Crossen, "Magazines Offer 'Extras' in Battle for Ads: They Provide Lavish Parties, Free Research," *Wall Street Journal,* January 4, 1989, sec. B, p. 1.

17. Randall Rothenberg, "Messages from Sponsors Become Harder to Detect," *New York Times,* November 9, 1989, sec. E, p. 5. See also Claudia Deutsch, "The Brouhaha over Drug Ads," *New York Times,* May 14, 1989, sec. F, p. 8, and Joseph Pereira, "Kids' Advertisers Play

Hide-and-Seek, Concealing Commercials in Every Cranny," *Wall Street Journal*, April 30, 1990, sec. B, p. 1.

18. Herman and Chomsky, pp. 26ff.

19. William H. Miller, "Fighting TV Hatchet Jobs," *Industry Week*, January 12, 1981, pp. 61–64 and Gans, p. 260.

20. Bagdikian, pp. 166–167.

21. Steven Waldman, "Consumer News Blues: Are Advertisers Shifling Local TV Reporting?" *Newsweek*, May 20, 1991, p. 48.

22. E.g., see Miller pp. 61–64; Herman and Chomsky; and Bagdikian, p. 132.

23. Bagdikian, p. 42.

24. Herman and Chomsky, pp. xii, 2. See also Gans, p. 276, and Parenti, p. 36.

25. Bagdikian, p. 137, 167, which also discusses how the media and advertisers have become co-dependents. See also Norman E. Isaacs, *Untended Gates: The Mismanaged Press* (New York: Columbia University Press, 1986), pp. 163–164, and Gans, pp. 20, 46–48, 255.

26. Steven Waldman, "Consumer News Blues: Are Advertisers Stifling Local TV Reporting?" *Newsweek*, May 20, 1991, p. 48.

27. Parenti, pp. 109–110.

28. See Erik Barnouw, *The Sponsor: Notes on a Modern Potentate* (New York: Oxford University Press, 1978).

29. For example, Herman and Chomsky, pp. 16–17, and Barnouw, p. 112.

30. Laura Landro, "Film Satirizing Ad Industry Plays to a Touchy Audience," *Wall Street Journal*, April 3, 1990, sec. B, p. 1, and Susan Bickelhaupt, "Stations Nix Channel 5's Radio Promo of Diet Story," *Boston Globe*, May 2, 1989, p. 65.

31. Bagdikian, p. 156. See also Parenti, p. 48; Todd Gitlin, "When the Right Talks, TV Listens," *Nation*, October 15, 1983, p. 335; and Isaacs, p. 8.

32. Epstein, p. 83; Barnouw, pp. 68–73; and Gans, p. 256.

33. Herman and Chomsky, p. 17.

34. Barnouw, pp. 60, 67–68.

35. Scott Cutlip, "The Media and the Corporation: A Matter of Perception and Performance," in Aronoff, p. 148. See also Gans, pp. 253, 257, 259.

36. Parenti; pp. 49–50.

37. Curtis D. MacDougall, "Business's Friend, the Media," in Aronoff, pp. 44–54.

38. "Toronto Paper Feels Travel Industry's Fury," *Wall Street Journal*, July 25, 1989, sec. B, p. 1, and "Car Makers and Credit Unions Encourage Honesty," *New York Times*, October 22, 1989, sec. F, p. 15. See also Mary Ellen Schoonmaker, "The Real Estate Story: Hard News or Soft Sell?" *Columbia Journalism Review*, January-February 1987, pp. 25–30.

39. Robert F. Buckhorn, *Nader: The People's Lawyer* (Englewood Cliffs, N.J: Prentice-Hall, 1972), pp. 69–70.

40. Bagdikian, p. 170, and R. C. Smithy, "The Magazines' Smoking Habit," *Columbia Journalism Review*, January-February 1978, pp. 29–31.

41. Isaacs, p. 163, and "The Media's Conflicts of Interest," *The Center*, November-December 1976, p. 20.

42. Parenti, p. 48.

43. Gans, p. 205.

44. Ibid., p. 56.

45. Ibid, pp. 68–69, 156.

46. Bagdikian, p. 56.

47. Buckhorn, p. 65.

48. Ibid., p. 68.

49. MacDougall, pp. 50–52; Gans, p. 121; and Harold E. Davis, "Conflict, Consensus, and the Propaganda of the Deed; Or One Sure Way to Manipulate the Media," in Aronoff, pp. 33–43.

50. See, for example, Joseph B. White, "Comfy Ride: Car Magazine Writers Sometimes Moonlight for Firms They Review," *Wall Street Journal*, May 15, 1990, sec. A, pp. 1, 6.

51. William M. Bulkeley, "Battle of the Computer-Magazine Titans," *Wall Street Journal*, February 24, 1989, sec. B, p. 1.

52. Gail Pool and Michael Comendul express similar sentiments in their "The Computer Magazines' Puffery Problem," *Columbia Journalism Review*, September-October, 1985, pp. 49–51.

53. For example, Michael W. Miller, "Computer Magazines' Electronic Spinoffs Give Readers a Quick Way to Talk Back," *Wall Street Journal*, October 19, 1988, sec. B, p. 1.

54. *Stereo Review*, June 1988, p. 58.

55. Francine Schwadel, "Who Wins with Price-Matching Plans? Not Shoppers, For Few Bother Ever to Collect," *Wall Street Journal*, March 16, 1989, sec. B, p. 1.

56. The obvious exception here is *Consumer Reports*. However, although this non-profit organization is largely supported through its circulation, it also relies on significant postal discounts and tax-free status. Thus, the question remains as to whether it could survive economically without government subsidies.

57. Epstein, pp. 137, 168–170.

58. Doug Underwood, "When MBAs Rule the Newsroom," *Columbia Journalism Review*, March-April, 1988, p. 30. See also Robert Goldberg, "Offended? Don't Watch!" *Wall Street Journal*, July 31, 1989, sec. A, p. 8.

59. To derive this figure, we divided *Consumer Reports'* 1986 annual revenue by the approximate number of American households in 1986. For a similar type of estimate, see E. Scott Maynes's "Consumer Protection: The Issues," *Journal of Consumer Policy* 3 (1979):104.

60. Figures from the 1986 annual report of Consumer Union, the non-profit organization that runs *Consumer Reports*.

61. Figures do not include revenue and expenses for the other publications put out by Consumers Union, such as *Zillions* magazine and numerous books.

62. This figure includes expenses for testing/technical ($5,555,000), editorial ($1,569,000), library ($432,000); survey research ($404,000), and annual questionnaire ($522,000). The major items it excludes are marketing ($17,712,000), paper, printing and mailing ($10,383,000), and fulfillment ($2,085,000).

63. According to Donnelley Marketing's *11th Annual Survey of Promotional Practices* (Oak Brook Terrace, Ill.: Donnelley Marketing, 1989), p. 3, media expenditures for consumer-products companies usually run about one-third of total promotion expenditures, excluding the cost of personal selling and in-house marketing personnel.

64. "Ad $ Summary," in *Class/Brand Year-to-Date*, Vol. 14 (New York: Broadcast Advertising Reports, Inc./Leading National Advertisers, Inc., 1986), pp. 4–21.

65. William Matheson, "How Good Is the VCR? Man It's Outta Sight," *Wall Street Journal*, May 26, 1988, sec. 2, p. 29.

66. "C&SN: Same Face, New Publication," *Computer & Software News*, November 14, 1988, p. 10.

67. Theodore Levitt, *The Marketing Imagination* (New York: Free Press, 1986), pp. 128, 217.

68. E.g., see Peter H. Lewis, "How Useful Are Product Reviews?" *New York Times*, September 10, 1989, sec. F, p. 12.

69. The figures 45,000 and 120 come from a promotional piece for a CD-ROM publication called *Computer Library*.

PART III

REAL SOLUTIONS: THE NEW CONSUMERISM

The Manifesto of Consumer Empowerment

It is not from the benevolence of the butcher, the brewer, or the baker, that we expect our dinner, but from their regard to their own interest. We address ourselves, not to their humanity but to their self-love, and never talk to them of our necessities but of their advantages.

—*Adam Smith*

In this book we've described some problems of today's product-information system. We've noted the huge sums spent, the lack of good information, the loss of efficiency and innovation, and the propensity of today's sellers to distort and even deceive while promoting their wares. In this book we've also critiqued the "checks and balances" to the monopoly power born of consumer ignorance: the consumer media that are intrinsically incapable of providing perspective and the ineffectual government and non-profit information sources.

But our real target is not particular practices or institutions, which are merely consequences of a faulty model—or theory—of how to protect and educate consumers. Our critique is of the consumer education and protection system itself. We accept that the current incarnation of the market economy, including the consumer-oriented philosophy that underlies it, is a magnificent achievement. Nevertheless, as our market economy's technological, institutional, and economic foundations become obsolete, a new consumerism is emerging based on new information technology, new information institutions, and new information economics. This new model, inspired by the necessary compromises of the present model, will profoundly transform not only the marketplace but the social relations and mores that depend on it.

LAISSEZ-FAIRE, COMPETITION, AND CONSUMERISM

In 1776 economist Adam Smith argued in *The Wealth of Nations* that the marketplace didn't need direction from the government. The selfish and unregulated interests of individuals would collectively act as an "invisible hand" which would produce the greatest wealth for society. For example, under the self-regulating effects of competition, if a businessman got too greedy and charged uncompetitively high prices for a product, someone else would surely come along and offer the product more cheaply, thus bringing the first businessman's self-interest in line with society's welfare.

The concept that a so-called laissez-faire (literally, "let do," that is, let people do as they wish) marketplace could produce the greatest benefit to society was a remarkably new and extraordinary powerful idea. And it has been an idea responsible for much of the wealth and progress of the modern world. Assuming that a free market left to its own devices inevitably leads to a competitive market was a reasonable assumption in Adam Smith's day, when products were simple and sellers were small and numerous.

As we have seen, however, with the onset of the Industrial Revolution, the laissez-faire market became plagued by increasing confusion and monopoly imperfections. To minimize these imperfections (as well as to ensure "fairness" and "ethical behavior"), many government agencies have been set up in the past hundred years to regulate the economy, and it became accepted that consumerism—the promotion of the consumer's interest—required increased government control. This link between consumer welfare and government control led to much debate. Adam Smith had placed the welfare of the consumer at the centerpiece of his free-enterprise system and had claimed that competition was the way to achieve that welfare. Now, with the advent of regulatory agencies, it became clear that the laissez-faire approach did not guarantee a competitive market.

The notion that consumer interests could best be served through increased government control developed over the decades, fostered by such "consumer activists" as Upton Sinclair and, later, Ralph Nader. These activists weren't necessarily motivated by formal economic theories, but they were acutely aware of the inefficiency and abuse in the modern marketplace. They observed that the complexity and impersonality of the modern world made it impractical to expect people to be adequately informed about all the products they might purchase. Consequently, advocates of consumer interests reasoned that government must step in to protect consumers and promote a more efficient economy.

It is only because of a short-term historical anomaly, roughly the time between the Industrial Revolution (beginning in the late eighteenth century in England) and what is often called the Information Revolution (which is beginning in the last quarter of the twentieth century), that consumerism and government regulation have been so closely linked. Once the technological and institutional capacity to provide information about products catches up with the corresponding capacity to produce them, this close association should break down. Government will, as always, remain the foundation of peaceful, honest, and efficient commerce, but as we shall see, consumer welfare will no longer depend on elaborate consumer-protection laws and regulations. Given the right information technology, consumers and true competition can once again thrive within the free-enterprise system, just as Adam Smith once argued in the context of a much simpler economy. Ironically, businesspeople, facing the overwhelming competition characteristic of the new laissez-faire marketplace, will probably redouble their efforts to use government to preserve and maximize their monopoly power.

NEW ECONOMICS AND NEW INFORMATION PROVIDERS

Before the Industrial Revolution, producers and consumers were one and the same. Most people grew their own food, wove their own clothes, and built their own houses. When producers and consumers first separated, products were simple and familiar, and consumers needed little information about them. With industrialization and the proliferation of new and more complex products, however, consumers had to rely increasingly on external sources for information—first, trusted neighbors and friends and, later, sellers of the products themselves. Today, this seller-financed information system has reached its economic apotheosis through the efficient and diverse economy brought about by modern mass advertising and personalized electronic shopping.

In this chapter we argue that powerful new information technology can change the economics of product information to such an extent that producers will have to give up their information-providing role. In other words, a promotional economic system (where producers finance the dissemination of information about their own products) can persist only in a society with low-grade information technology. In the new market of the future, however, people who produce products will operate separately from people who produce information about these products—just as consumers once separated from producers—and leave the economy with two types of companies: those that sell products (i.e., affect supply) and those that sell information about those products (i.e., affect demand). We call the latter organization *independent consumer-information companies (I.C.I.C.s)*, privately run companies which sell information about products without selling the products themselves and without having any ties to the companies that make and sell the products. Given the right information infrastructure, these companies will become the low-cost, high-quality way to deliver reliable product information to the marketplace. The existence of I.C.I.C.s means that people in the business of supplying products will no longer be in the business of creating demand for them. Therefore, these new companies will have fulfilled the economist's dream of the perfectly competitive market with its separation of demand and supply.[1] For the time being, you can think of an I.C.I.C. (pronounced "I see, I see!") as sort of a computerized and customized *Consumer Reports* or as a car brokerage service without ties to car dealerships. Each I.C.I.C. is a personalized consultant for consumers analogous to the organizations that businesses now use for buying advice. Already hundreds of technology-based I.C.I.C.s have emerged to sell ostensibly bias-free information on doctors, childcare, restaurants, films, mortgage rates, and even potential spouses. Such services have become economical only with new information technologies such as "900" numbers, which allow customers to obtain customized information over the phone while billing the call to their telephone number.

Rather than throwing more facts at consumers, I.C.I.C.s will use new technologies to help sift out better information and then synthesize and customize recommendations. As many people before us have observed, the novelty of the Information Revolution lies not only in the ability to generate or even send information but to process it, to transform massive and unfiltered information into a usable form. "We need understanding businesses devoted to making information accessible and comprehensible," writes Richard Saul Wurman in *Information Anxiety*. "We need new ways of interpreting the data that increasingly directs our lives and new models for making it usable and understandable, for transforming it into information."[2]

Given the right information infrastructure and corresponding information economics, such information companies will emerge spontaneously. They already exist, albeit in very primitive form. But they will grow and thrive as never before. New information technologies such as 900 telephone service, on-line computer networks, and microcomputers with high-capacity storage (for example, CD-ROMs) have already led to the growth of a whole new generation of still-primitive yet forward-looking I.C.I.C.s which will sell recommendations about such choices as colleges, restaurants, computers, home-mortgage rates, and tourist haunts.

Such independent consumer-information companies will bring consumers real perspective, that is, useful and customized evaluations of goods and services. They will save the individual from drowning in a sea of facts. Akin to what information industry gurus call expert knowledge "agents" (or, sometimes, assistants, guides, navigators, or "infobots"), these consumer "agents" will be able to use new technologies to navigate through oceans of otherwise meaningless data and to tailor information to individual needs. An I.C.I.C., whether an actual person (like a real estate agent) or a "smart" computer program, would offer specific recommendations about what to buy, where to buy it, and at what price, depending on a consumer's specific needs.

In contrast to these I.C.I.C.s, today's more traditional consumer media, which purport to present the "objective" facts—specifications, tests, descriptions, and opposing but equally plausible viewpoints—ultimately obscure insight. Ironically, in fact, it is the current media's obsession with "objectivity" that precludes any hope of perspective. Indeed, if "modernism" has taught us anything, it is that even so-called facts are biased. Objectivity defined as the presentation of complete facts and competing viewpoints might have made sense in the nineteenth century, when political and consumer issues were relatively simple. Today, however, this form of objectivity translates into facts so overwhelming in number that they become uninterpretable. We easily can spend hours listening to two talented debaters presenting opposite sides of a consumer issue and know nothing afterwards. Few of us want to read through hundreds of pages of Congressional documents or study the long labels filled with obscure terms of all the drugs in the local pharmacy. Ideally, we'd prefer reliable and concise evaluations of available data. When the authors of this book were running our consumer-information business, for example, we quickly learned that people looking for VCRs had little interest in a well-researched and easy-to-read forty-page essay delineating all the pros and cons of every available feature. People simply wanted to know "Which one should I buy? What is your opinion?" Similarly, when top business executives want an action memo from a subordinate, they want a one-page summary recommending what to do and very briefly why. They don't want a hundred additional pages of detailed justifications. These executives figure that they hired this employee in the first place because he or she was competent, and if the recommendation turns out to be wrong, the employee can always be fired.

Here, then, is how I.C.I.C.s might save you from having to be an expert on every consumer decision you make. *Want to buy a VCR for your summer home? You contact your favorite I.C.I.C., which happens to be accessible via your home computer (the "Omnimedia machine" described in the next chapter), and state that you'd like a VCR with a cable-ready tuner, at least two video inputs, and a built-in Super VHS adapter. The I.C.I.C. promptly recommends a high-quality model, pointing out that cable-ready is a meaningless feature, and then tells you where to get it for the best price. It may also ask you if you want to see a simulated version of the VCR conjured up on your high-resolution flat-screen monitor or whether you'd like to try out a few of the features. Want to find out which of five health-insurance options best meets the needs of your family? Another I.C.I.C. might ask you about your family size, income, savings, and predicted medical expenses, and then, using a sophisticated database, choose the most cost-effective plan for you. Want to know which cardiac surgeons in town have the best records for bypass surgery? A third I.C.I.C. accessible via your personal computer will immediately tap into an up-to-date database, compiled from requisitioned hospital records from around the nation, and recommend a physician, as well as noting whether the physician's prices are in line with his or her track record. You could even prop your flat-screen computer on top of your grocery cart and ask (by speaking or writing) an I.C.I.C. to recommend a breakfast cereal with the highest fiber and lowest sugar content at the best price. You'll pay for all this advice—the I.C.I.C.s are all private companies—but you'll more than get your money back by purchasing the right product and saving all the time and energy you might otherwise have spent in purchasing the wrong one.*

MULTIMEDIA: THE CONVERGING OF THE MEDIA

The success of the independent information companies depends on certain new technologies through which the media used by sellers to provide product information will gradually become one and the same as the media used by third-party information providers (the I.C.I.C.s). This process is part of the general and widely noted move towards "multimedia," a term widely used today to signify the convergence of TV, radio, print, telephone, computer, and all other means of communication into a single medium.

The trend towards multimedia means a whole new way of functioning for information providers and users. Nicholas Negroponte, director of the Media Lab at the Massachusetts Institute of Technology (MIT), depicts this historical trend as the merging of the broadcasting, publishing, and computer industries.[3] Stewart Brand, in his book on MIT's Media Lab, describes the situation this way:

> Telephones, radio, TV, and recorded music began their lives as analog media—every note the listener heard was a smooth direct transformation of the music in the studio—but each of them is now gradually, sometimes wrenchingly, in the process of becoming digitalized, which means becoming computerized. . . . With digitalization all of the media become translatable into each other— computer bits migrate merrily—and they escape from their traditional means of transmission. A movie, phone call, letter, or magazine article may be sent digitally via phone line, coaxial cable, fiberoptic cable, microwave, satellite, the broadcast air, or a physical storage medium such as tape or disk. If that's not revolution enough, with digitalization the content becomes totally plastic—any message, sound, or image may be edited from anything into anything else.[4]

The move towards multimedia can be traced specifically to four emerging and already feasible technologies. All of these technologies exist in prototype form, but for various reasons, including high price, lack of standards, and inadequate software, they have not yet become widely available:

1. *High-quality TV*—Within about five years, high-definition television (HDTV) sets should be commercially available in the United States. These sets will have at least 35-mm (movie quality) images and compact-disk quality sound, and will be able to transmit much better text and graphics than today's sets. At the same time, flat-screen technology should develop, so that these TVs could lie flat on the wall like a painting or be carried about like a pad of paper.

2. *High-capacity memory devices*—By the mid-1990s, most computers should have enough memory to store significant amounts of sound and images, as opposed to just text and simple graphics. New optical media, such as CD-ROM (compact disk, read-only memory), CDI (compact-disk interactive), and DVI (digital-video interactive), already can store hundreds of thousands of pages of information (or alternatively, dozens of hours of voice-quality audio and more than an hour of TV-quality video) on a portable, compact-disk-shaped information-storage device. Within a few years these machines will be as affordable to use as VCRs are today.

3. *High-speed telecommunications networks*—The telephone system today transfers information over its network using wavelike analog signals. By the early twenty-first century, sending digital rather than analog information over current copper phone networks will allow us to transmit data into the home more than fifty times faster than the rate that is commonly used today and allow us to transmit simultaneously voice, text, high-quality graphics, and at least primitive video images.

But it is the switch from analog to digital technologies, *combined with* the replacement of copper-wire networks with optical-fiber networks, that will not only make possible video on demand, but video on demand with images far better than anything we currently have on our TV or movie screens—images, for example, as good as those we are accustomed to see on the magazine page. Optical fiber is not only becoming relatively affordable, decreasing in cost at a rate of roughly 30 percent per year, but both local phone companies and long-distance carriers have already laid more than a million route-miles of fiber in the past decade;[5] most intercity and regional telephone wiring is already fiber; many international calls also have shifted to fiber; and company spokespersons themselves are talking about how this new technology will allow them to bring consumers "videophones, push-button home shopping, news reports tailored to your interests, movies whenever you want to see them, and even high-definition television" as conveniently as the telephone companies now bring phone service.[6]

Once optical fibers reach the home, moreover, they could be connected to a wireless local-area network within a single dwelling. This would provide consumers with even more convenient access to the world's information resources. Many business offices already use such high-speed wireless networks to access information, and it's only a matter of time before such networks become affordable to consumers.

4. *New input devices*—Today, most people "communicate" with their computers either by typing on a keyboard or by sliding a device known as a mouse along a desktop to direct the cursor on the screen. In the future, people will also be able to speak directly to their computers and to hand-print messages to them. Both speaker-dependent speech recognition (where a computer is trained to recognize only a particular voice) and handwriting recognition (where characters must be clearly written) are already quite powerful. Although both types of systems need lots of high-speed and expensive processing power and memory, by the year 2000 the cost of such power should fall precipitously, thus making them affordable to the average consumer.

There has been no shortage of forecasts about these new information technologies. One particularly noteworthy forecaster is Apple's John Sculley, whose company is actively working to make its "Knowledge Navigator" a reality by the early twenty-first century. Sculley predicts that this "future generation Macintosh" computer will use artificial intelligence to become

a discoverer of worlds, a tool as galvanizing as the printing press. Individuals could use it to drive through libraries, museums, databases, or institutional archives. This tool wouldn't just take you to the doorstep of these great resources as sophisticated computers do now; it would invite you deep inside its secrets, interpreting and explaining—converting vast quantities of information into personalized and understandable knowledge.[7]

Sculley goes on to describe this Knowledge Navigator as having two navigational joysticks on each side, "like a pilot's controls, allowing you to steer through various windows and menus opening galleries, stacks and more. You might even be set free from the keyboard, entering commands by speaking to the Navigator." Although you'll have the option of a computer small enough to be sewn into your shirt pocket or embedded in the walls of your home, you might also have a screen large enough to display full-color pages of high-definition, television-quality text, graphics, and computer-generated animation. Whatever the size and shape, moreover, the Navigator should be able to produce high-fidelity sound and synthesized speech. Over time, this intelligent "agent" will learn your particular tastes and turn information into knowledge customized to you. Says Sculley, this "software'agent'" is

> your opinion surrogate, the ultimate objective observer. It will wander around throughout dozens of databases, pulling together whatever it thinks you, the user, are interested in. You won't have to search through the stacks of libraries—the world's largest library will exist on your desktop or your lap. . . . By customizing knowledge so each of us—individually—can learn or work at our own pace, this new personal computing device will be a tool that is fun and comfortable to use. Just as a car takes you wherever you want to go without your worrying over how the ignition key works the engine, so the Knowledge Navigator will drive you anywhere through the available store of knowledge.[8]

Sculley is hardly alone in these predictions. *Fortune* magazine described this technological future in similar terms:

> Computers that don't look and act like computers will surround you—shirt-pocket and notebooklike devices that respond to handwritten and spoken queries and commands, maybe even gestures. . . .
> In the view of many scientists, the computer is being transformed from a number cruncher into a machine for insight and discovery. . . .
> Converging with these new insights and new computing power is the rapid emergence of telecommunications networks. It is as if—for a change—high-powered cars and sleek highways to accommodate them were arriving at the same time. Telecommunications experts see nothing less than a world linked by great computerized networks that process voice, data, and video with equal ease.[9]

It is in this coming world, a world where everyone who has something to communicate will be using the same multimedia, that independent consumer-information companies will be able to flourish as never dreamed.

WHY I.C.I.C.S MUST ULTIMATELY TRIUMPH

The Rise of Electronic Shopping

Leading retailing magazines are fond of running articles about how electronic shopping is the wave of the future. The theory is that electronic retailing almost certainly will triumph over more traditional practices because it can cope more effectively with increasing product confusion, decreasing available shopping time, increasing information relative to product costs, and a general competitive need to reduce selling costs. As one of the top retailing magazines put it:

> *C3PO and R2D2, retailers of the year, 1995. . . .* Not as far-fetched as it may sound. Artificial Intelligence Expert Systems are coming to retailing and will have the capability to interact with customers and suppliers. They'll be able to sell specific products based on *customer* wants. . . . The emerging systems will be high tech–high touch. . . . Given the future labor shortage, merchants will have to turn to the C3POs and R2D2s of the future.[10]

Much of this electronic shopping should take place right inside your own home, since in-home shopping can offer lower prices, a broader selection of merchandise, reduced shopping time, and better product information. Going to a store and searching through tens of thousands of goods, for example, potentially takes much more valuable leisure time than sitting at home and doing the same things with only a few verbal commands to an in-home shopping center. Eliminating the need for retail selling space, retail personnel, and retail inventory, moreover, potentially lets in-home retailers offer consumers substantially lower prices on many types of goods. Furthermore, in contrast to in-store retailing, which can only provide products for which there is a significant local market, in-home retailing is only concerned with the total national or even worldwide market, regardless of local demand.

Admittedly, if you shop at home you can't examine the product or have it demonstrated the way you could while standing in a store. But you'll soon be able to scrutinize merchandise so well on your computer screen that this difference may seem trivial for most purchases (even clothing, which many people insist must be tried on and touched, is already one of the most successful mail-order products; you can always return it if the fit or fabric is wrong). Moreover, only a small percentage of the relevant information about products now comes from inspection. The rest comes from advertising, packaging, and personal advice—all areas in which in-home retailing will probably excel. In short, you should be able to get as much or as little information as you want without leaving home: rather than relying on the increasingly hard-to-find and increasingly under-trained salespeople that populate retail stores today, you'll be able to consult a well-informed electronic sales consultant.

The technology for electronic in-home shopping is still quite primitive, thus relegating it to a relatively minor role in the total retailing mix. Still, its importance should grow as technology improves, which it almost inevitably will. In-home shopping is already quite popular in the form of mail order, and some truly innovative electronic-shopping ventures have already arrived. Almost everyone, for example, is familiar with the home-shopping networks now available on cable television. In these passive setups, you sit in front of your set and watch a stream of merchandise. When you want to order something, you just dial a toll-free order number. Past customers even have membership IDs and can enter orders using a touch-tone phone. Information and orders from repeat customers are handled electronically.

More sophisticated cable-based home-shopping systems allow customers to interact with their television sets. GTE's Main Street, for example, allows you to pick which merchandise you want displayed. It works by finding requested information and then sending it down an information pipeline (usually the cable) in a discrete electronic "packet." You share this pipeline and the packets of information on it with hundreds of other subscribers, but your TV picks up just the images you want as you enter them into your telephone keypad. You also use your keypad for ordering.

In one of Main Street's test locations, too, GTE is using optical fiber rather than cable networks. One of the great appeals of optical fiber is that it will make the cable system function like the telephone system. Specifically, rather than sharing channels with other households, every household can choose to watch a different program.

Consumers with home computers today can also participate in interactive home shopping via services like Comp-U-Card or Prodigy. Comp-U-Card (the "warehouse club of electronic shopping") lets subscribers buy thousands of items for significantly less than many retailers charge, merely by paying an annual $30 membership fee plus on-line charges.[11] You see the item, its features, and its price described on your computer screen, and then you charge it to a credit card account, either by entering information into your computer or by calling a toll-free phone number.

We believe that such a service foreshadows the decline of retailer-controlled electronic shopping and the emergence of manufacturer-controlled electronic shopping. In fact, Comp-U-Card advertises itself as "low-cost because we bypass the retailer." The truth, however, is that Comp-U-Card functions as a retailer itself and provides little information about the brand-name products it sells, undoubtedly forcing many customers to go to stores for major information before using the service.

Prodigy, a computerized vehicle on which retailers advertise and sell, adds color and graphic images to the home-shopping experience and includes grocery shopping and expert advice. All information about products and orders is handled electronically. Because Prodigy utilizes the relatively narrow information capacity of the telephone network, it can transmit only text and relatively simple graphics, in contrast to a cable-based interactive service such as GTE's Main Street. On the other hand, TV monitors do not have the same clarity as most computer monitors, so at least until the advent of high-definition TV, a computer-monitor-based system such as Prodigy will be better for displaying text.

Of course, for all the promised convenience and economy inherent to in-home shopping, in-store retailing is not going to disappear. Still, it's going to improve the way it conveys product information to consumers, in keeping with changing information technology. Stores must compete over the quality of information they provide just as they must compete over everything else; consumers are much less likely to buy products with unknown or misunderstood benefits. Stores that provide the best information at the lowest cost will succeed here, but to do so they will need to turn to the new information technology.

More salespeople will not be a viable option. The increasing discrepancy between labor costs and product costs—brought on by ever-improving automation in production—will leave stores no choice but to continue decreasing the quantity and quality of salespeople. Moreover, improved information available from fledgling electronic information devices will make it more difficult for salespeople to compete. Nor will more printed information be viable. We're already inundated with information about stores and their merchandise. What we need is not more but better information. We need to be able to come into a store, say we have a runny nose, and immediately locate a drug for it.

Retailers have already begun to tackle such problems by providing do-it-yourself video displays for their customers.[12] Home centers, for example, let you press a button to activate a tape describing various window treatments that are sold elsewhere in the store. Although these passive videos seem to be successful as vehicles for training salespeople, they have limited value for customers, who rarely want to wait through a long presentation to find a specific bit of information.

A slightly better approach used to provide consumer information involves interactive information kiosks, which are immobile structures provided and maintained by the retailer. By pushing a few buttons in response to questions printed on a screen, these kiosks direct you to a specific product or dispense coupons in response to your requests. In certain shoe stores, for example, kiosks note styles of shoes available and even allow you to order them in sizes and colors that the company can't afford to stock locally. In certain supermarkets, kiosks recommend recipes and then tell where in the store you can find each ingredient.

There are also other versions of in-store interactive devices. For example, in certain beauty parlors, you can use a computerized makeup machine to see how a hairstyle or touch of eyeshadow will alter your overall appearance. And many computer software and hardware stores today have machines with demo disks on them, which allow unassisted customers to explore the features of a computer or piece of software.

Despite the obvious savings of the salesperson's time and the more uniform information in kiosks, kiosks don't represent the future of electronic retailing. They waste precious store space—especially if they're intended to be used by many people, most of whom may have to wait in line to use them. Customers may also have to walk back and forth between kiosk and merchandise, and they can't expect a store's kiosk to memorize their personal preferences. After spending a day jumping from one kiosk to the next in a future world full of such devices, we suspect that many customers will opt to stay home with their in-home shopping centers.

A better approach, and the one that we think will be critical to the long-term success of in-store electronic information, are "kiosks" that are portable, wireless, and book-sized. One innovative approach along these lines is called the "videocart," already used by some large discounters and supermarkets. On your shopping cart is a flat-panel display that changes as you move around. Wherever you're standing, it tells you about nearby specials and other information that might prove useful. Videocarts give shoppers convenient information while allowing stores to save the space needed for freestanding kiosks.

An even better source of information for shoppers might involve an electronic salesperson running on the customer's own portable computer (rather than the store's). Customers could carry around their own pocket computers. When they walk into a store, they could then tap into the store's information services—but use their own information equipment. We know of no retailer currently marketing such a system, but many of them already have the information services in place to implement this approach. For example, Sears, K-Mart, and J.C. Penney sell at least a percentage of their merchandise on Prodigy. They also use Prodigy to provide basic information on their products. With the development of cellular telephones and laptop computers, it's now conceivable that a customer could walk into a store and use his or her own computer to find out about the store's products.

Electronic Shopping Without Promotion

Picture yourself in an electronics superstore asking the store's computer about the best buys—or picture yourself at home sitting at the kitchen table and getting the same kind of information—and add one little twist: instead of getting the information about merchandise from the store, you now can choose an independent consultant to describe it. Or imagine that the yellow pages are available electronically, as they soon will be. You have a choice to wade through these yellow pages listings on your personal computer, sorting through incompatible and relatively low-quality sales spiels, or you can obtain one or two trustworthy opinions from an independent consultant (an I.C.I.C.). Which would you do, assuming the cost were the same for either option?

Such choices show clearly why the forces propelling retailers to expand their electronic-shopping offerings ultimately will reduce their overall power. Electronically provided information eliminates the once striking differences between seller-provided information and I.C.I.C./media-provided information. Today, going into a store to learn about a product differs considerably from picking up a magazine to get the same

217

information. But in another decade or two, both experiences will almost certainly be electronic; both experiences will almost certainly provide information to the consumer in identical ways. As we've seen, the cost of human labor is forcing retailers and manufacturers to rely increasingly on electronic/automated consumer education. Almost every major U.S. retailer and manufacturer has already put together research teams to automate its consumer education. When Best Buy, one of the largest consumer-electronics chains in the country, started replacing its car-stereo sales help with a touch-screen information kiosk, Greg Maanum, the audio merchandising manager there, described the move to self-selling as follows: "This format is absolutely the lowest price for a product a consumer can get. It is our goal to be the lowest priced in the market."[13] By the end of 1989 there were 15,000 interactive shopping terminals in stores of all sorts. By 1995 the number is forecast to rise to 100,000. Such electronic education is the exact method on which the independent consumer-information companies will also be relying. Instead of giving consumers a choice between an impersonal magazine and a live demonstration, these future techniques will give them the choice between one computerized demonstration and another computerized demonstration.

The key to the triumph of the independent consumer-information company lies in this fact: ultimately, the way you get information from an independent consumer-information company should be very similar to the way you get information from a highly developed electronic retailer—except that the I.C.I.C. will lack the retailer's bias and so provide superior information. Today's promotional tactics by their very nature provide only partial information, thus requiring that we go to many sources to get the full picture. Many products have become so complex, too, that no amount of partial explanations will ever lead to a complete understanding. Using the I.C.I.C., in contrast, will save consumers both time and money. Instead of listening to five different sellers and trying to make sense of their incompatible and biased claims, the consumer will only have to rely on the one trusted I.C.I.C. he or she has chosen. This not only saves considerable time, but also greatly enhances the chances of making a superior purchase. The business community well understands this principle. When institutional investors want to invest in a particular industry, they don't go to each relevant company and ask for the facts. They hire a prestigious research analyst from an investment house whose livelihood depends on studying the particular industry and making recommendations to outside investors. For similar reasons, once the medium of information becomes identical, I.C.I.C.s will become the dominant consumer-education vehicle.

I.C.I.C.s will gather even more steam, given synergistic effects with certain compatible forms of retailing. Since buyers already paying to get better information from I.C.I.C.s will refuse to pay an additional 20 percent premium to get superfluous information from sellers, sellers will reduce their information role to reduce costs to a competitive level. Retailers with the lowest built-in information costs will be the ones to prosper.

Based on current trends, then, what we foresee is that electronic retailing in the form of computer shopping, information kiosks, and so forth will initially have the edge over I.C.I.C.s (in fact, it already does) because it requires less retraining of consumers: most of us carry around a deeply ingrained notion that anyone who wants to sell us anything is supposed to provide "free" information about his or her wares. Retailers are also much wealthier than existing independent information providers. And if present experience is any indicator, retailers are also much more innovative—if only because of their greater wealth. But as both sellers and third-party information providers start providing consumer information through the exact same medium, we see this advantage gradually dissipating. Although the 1990s and the first decade of the twenty-first century will still belong to the electronic retailers, thereafter I.C.I.C.s should become the dominant product-information delivery mechanism.

This sequence has already begun, as a few companies at the fringes of our economic system have begun to gradually squeeze information costs out of their products. Warehouse clubs, for example, have grown over the last five years and constitute one of the most important innovations in retailing in the last quarter century. These no-frills stores operate on profit margins of 8 percent to 12 percent as opposed to the 20 percent to 30 percent margins of discount stores and the over 30 percent margins of department stores. One of the major sacrifices consumers make at these warehouses is sales help. Shoppers have to know what they want before they go into the club or at best learn by merely looking at the merchandise. An I.C.I.C., designed to provide good product information at low cost, would work hand-in-hand with customers needing service but unwilling to pay the traditional price for it.

Warehouse clubs are only a first step towards wiping out unnecessary information costs, of course. The prices at these clubs are still higher than they have to be, because these clubs carry name brands (backed by large ad budgets, i.e., by high information costs) and special derivative models that are noncompetitive. These clubs also perpetuate consumer ignorance because they operate in a vacuum of information and don't even attempt to explain to consumers new and complex features and products. Nevertheless, the warehouses, as well as discounters and superstores, do give us a taste of the retailing world to come by emphasizing price and selection over service. As consumers become less and less willing to pay for service—often shopping at the high-service stores but buying at the discounters—service will probably be reduced even more. And as I.C.I.C.s step in to provide this service, and do a much better job providing it than any retailer or manufacturer ever before, product information may disappear from stores completely.

Other indications of the future are the manufacturers who bypass both wholesalers and retailers and sell directly to the customer, as happens now in the computer industry. Thanks to widely read product reviews in computer magazines, companies with superior products but no retail distribution can now sell directly to the public. In 1991, for example, the three largest PC manufacturers that sold directly to the public—Dell Computer, CompuAdd, and Northgate—did more than $1 billion in business.

"GOOD" INFORMATION VERSUS THE "IRRATIONAL" CONSUMER

Many people we've queried about the concept of the I.C.I.C. immediately say that such unbiased, customized sources of recommendations will never flourish because consumers are "too irrational" to keep them in business. We quiz these critics about what they mean by "irrational," and they respond with observations such as "people buy on impulse," "they don't read labels," "they don't want to read or listen to objective opinions," "they buy things that they feel will make them happy; shopping is emotionally driven." They argue that new information technology serves only an elite, well-educated, and affluent group and ignores the vast majority of humanity, which impulsively purchases merchandise and is swayed in its decisions by all sorts of information that doesn't appear to have any relevance to the product itself. Moreover, skeptics argue, when most people are confronted with information about the merits of particular products, they ignore it.[14]

Professors of marketing add to this skepticism by pointing out the impossibility of a rational marketplace. Consumers, they argue, buy not only product functionality but also psychological satisfaction. In other words, the cost of a bottle of perfume covers not only the materials and the pleasing aroma but also the prestige and sex appeal of having the bottle on your bureau and the scent on your pulse point. No I.C.I.C.s pronouncement that Brand X perfume is identical to "Eau de Paris" is going to take away that psychological value.[15]

As many economists have argued, however, much of this seemingly irrational emphasis on intangible value is actually quite rational and can be ascribed to the difficulty in getting good, direct information. It's not irrational to pay extra for a prestigiously labeled gin of identical quality to a no-name brand if your peers truly accord you more prestige for doing so because they don't know any better. It's not irrational either to sell your stock in a quality company if everyone else's misinformed beliefs about the company cause the value to drop and panic to ensue. If other people are largely ignorant, it actually makes a lot of sense to buy what will make you look savvy or affluent or sophisticated or sexy in their eyes.

Today, moreover, anyone who didn't continually act on impulse and the barest of clues would have to spend his whole life shopping and even then he would only be able to allow himself to shop for a very narrow selection of merchandise. Consider one economist's definition of what in theory would be a rational consumer: "He first lists all conceivable courses of action and their consequences; he then ranks the consequences and chooses the best; finally, he sticks to his choice in a consistent manner."[18] Of course, this "rational" behavior is utterly impractical today. Consumers must rely on instinct and primitive rules of thumb to guide purchasing behavior. In fact, as the same economist goes on to argue, "If businessmen were to consider every item of information they receive—every piece of news, letter, or telephone call—as giving rise to a problem which needs to be studied and analyzed, they would have no time to conduct their business." Thus, to simplify otherwise agonizing decisions, we may stick tenaciously to one particular brand, even one virtually identical to several others.[17]

People note that consumers purchase a tremendous amount of merchandise on impulse. But it's questionable whether long deliberations would actually be much more practical. Since most thoroughly impulsive purchases are relatively inexpensive, how much would people gain by using their time and energy to plan whether or not they wanted a particular chocolate bar, a particular can of soup, or a very specific and appealing artifact for their coffee table? The best strategy indeed might be to put themselves in situations where they can make as many quick, impulsive decisions as possible—especially given the fact that extensive research probably won't provide much better information anyway.[18]

It's also noted that consumers are irrationally loyal to many brands, preferring more expensive premium products to other less expensive but functionally identical products. As we saw in the first part of this book, name recognition alone is one of the primary purposes of advertising and is what the consumer often goes by in making his or her purchasing decisions. Thus, consumers are hardly foolish to rely on well-recognized names. A familiar advertised brand is more likely to have a consistent product and to have at least a fairly high quality.[19] Much of the consumer's so-called irrational behavior, then, can be traced to astute judgment.

Practical people of the marketplace commonly observe that consumers are quite happy to be ignorant.[20] According to this view, it's acceptable to feed buyers the most ridiculously simplistic pablum about products because this is all they will tolerate. But we must wonder if these practical people are mistaking cause for effect. For it seems to us that no one has yet invented a way of providing high-quality consumer information in an affordable, entertaining way. And that given the present difficulty of gathering this information, practical consumers have no choice but to accept the pablum.

The real question is this: if, wherever you were, you had an infinitely knowledgeable and trustworthy friend—one, moreover, who gave advice for free—would you still behave so "irrationally"? The answer for most people would almost certainly be no. Of course, the conditions set up here are certainly utopian, and the question therefore becomes whether you still would value good, objective information if it were possible to access it relatively conveniently, entertainingly, and affordably. Our whole point is that as consumers can have access for the first time to objective information that actually meets their needs, they will no longer feel forced to rely on as many of the "irrational" factors that have guided them in the past.

Having said all this, we don't mean to imply that it will be easy to change the consumer's buying habits. Nor are we arguing that good consumer information will stop people from buying for prestige or status. What will happen, however, is that as I.C.I.C.s provide expert and impartial opinions about quality, prestige will tend to merge with concrete attributes such as functionality, safety, production costs, or ecological effects of use. Today many consumers choose to buy a Mercedes over a no-name comparable competitor largely because they know their friends and business associates will immediately recognize the name Mercedes. In the future, people with better information will still want to impress their friends and business associates, but when I.C.I.C.s recommend brands of cars with the highest quality and value, lower-rated cars will lose their prestige despite their large advertising budgets and their former reputations. It's hard to believe, of course, that even impartial product ratings could stop people from buying items such as overpriced bottles of perfume to impress their lovers with their devotion or to impress their friends with their wealth. And yet it is conceivable that if enough I.C.I.C.s decry the excess and hype associated with particular brands of perfume, these brands will tend to lose their prestige value. The price of a gift will still be very important, but lovers and friends will be more impressed with purchases (such as a gold watch or a diamond) whose high price reflects underlying value. As Cornell economist E. Scott Maynes has observed: "If complete information replaced imperfect information and everyone knew and accepted . . . that gin is gin, regardless of price of container—then price variation would be drastically reduced and these Veblenesque [status-oriented] messages robbed of most of their content and relevance."[21]

A more serious obstacle to the relatively rational system we have envisioned is that most of us have an ingrained belief that information should be free. In fact, many consumers are outraged at the idea of paying anything at all for "information,"[22] partly because they have been taught so for decades by the media, the companies that finance the media, and the government, and, more generally, because product information costs have always been bundled and (whenever possible) hidden in the cost of a product. To get consumers to realize that there is "no free lunch," after all years of pretending otherwise, is not going to be easy. Moreover, perhaps because information is so easy to copy and because most of us feel we shouldn't have to pay for it, consumers seem to have virtually no compunction about "stealing" it—say, by taking advice from a high-priced retailer and then buying from a discounter. Consequently, retailers that try to charge for information—through higher prices—soon lose all control over the information they give out. A successful national network of independent consumer-information companies will depend upon an American public that has learned to recognize the value of good information and has learned to pay for it.

* * *

The brief economic reign of the seller-financed product information system, the promotional system, has so far lasted about one century. And it will probably be a potent force in the marketplace for another fifty years. But ultimately, seller-financed information represents a transitional mechanism, in place only until we have better information technology.

It took close to a hundred million years for the small, shrewlike, and sharp-eyed mammals to win out over the reptiles. But just as the large and successful dinosaurs who ruled the earth eventually died out, so will the keep-it-simple-and-stupid promoters who rule the business world today. This time, however, it will not take one hundred million years for these new dinosaurs to become extinct. It will take only decades. And in the place of the old dinosaurs will be the I.C.I.C.s and the product- and quality-oriented companies they nurture.

1. Economists assert that there can be no advertising in a perfectly competitive marketplace, where the functions of creating demand and supply are necessarily separate. What we do here is merely suggest a historical mechanism by which this state will be achieved. See, for example, Jules Blackman, *Advertising and Competition* (New York: New York University Press, 1967), pp. 34, 39 and F. M. Scherer, "Product Differentiation, Market Structure, and Competition," a chapter in *Industrial Market Structure and Economic Performance* (Boston: Houghton Mifflin, forthcoming).

2. Richard Saul Wurman, *Information Anxiety* (New York: Doubleday, 1989), p. 50. See also Wurman's quotation of Carlos Fuentes on p. 194; Anthony Smith, *Goodbye Gutenberg: The Newspaper Revolution of the 1980's* (New York: Oxford University Press, 1980), p. 326; John Naisbitt, *Megatrends* (New York: Warner, 1982), p. 17; Stewart Brand, *The Media Lab: Inventing the Future at MIT* (New York: Penguin Books, 1987), p. 258; William Bulkeley, "Fighting Back Against Data Overload," *Wall Street Journal*, October 20, 1989, sec. B, p. 1; and Andrew Pollack, "An Avalanche of Information Is Coming to Video Screens." *New York Times*, July 23, 1989, p. 7.

3. Brand, p. 19. See also Ithiel de Sola Pool, *Technologies of Freedom: On Free Speech in an Electronic Age* (Cambridge, Mass.: Harvard University Press, 1983), p. 212, and M. Sirbu, F. Ferrante, D. Reed, *An Engineering and Policy Analysis of Fiber Introduction into the Residential Subscriber Loop* (Pittsburgh: Carnegie Mellon University, May 1988), p. 24.

4. Brand, p. 18.

5. Paul Shumate, Jr., "Optical Fibers Reach into Homes," *IEEE Spectrum*, February 1989, p. 43; U.S. Congress, Office of Technology Assessment, *Critical Connections: Communication for the Future*, OTA–CIT–407 (Washington, D.C.: Government Printing Office, January 1990), p. 48.

6. Joel Dreyfuss, "The Coming Battle over Your TV Set," *Fortune*, February 13, 1989, pp. 104–105, and Gary Slutsker, "Good-bye Cable TV, Hello Fiber Optics," *Forbes*, September 19, 1988, p. 176.

7. John Sculley with John A. Byrne, *Odyssey* (New York: Harper & Row, 1987), p. 403.

8. Ibid., p. 408.

9. "Technology in the Year 2000," *Fortune*, July 18, 1988, pp. 92–93.

10. "A Decade of Change: 1978–1987," *Chain Store Age Executive*, November 1988, p. 63.

11. Low-cost retailers are often not as inexpensive as they might seem. That's because they tend to sell highly visible name-brand merchandise, just the type of stock that regular stores are likely to use as loss leaders or try to switch customers away from.

12. *Discount Store News*, June 18, 1990, p. 4.

13. Mark Harrington, "Best Buy Expands Concept," *Home Furnishings Daily*, June 18, 1990, p. 104.

14. For example, see Nicholas Kaldor, "The Economic Aspects of Advertising," *Review of Economic Studies* 18 (1950–1951):5.

15. E.g., see Raymond A. Bauer and Stephen A. Greyser, "The Dialog That Never Happens," *Harvard Business Review*, November-December 1967.

16. George Katona, *The Powerful Consumer* (New York: McGraw-Hill, 1960), p. 138.

17. Ibid., p.141.

18. For a highly developed theory of "rational ignorance" applied to voting rather than consumer decisions, see Part III of Anthony Downs's *An Economic Theory of Democracy* (New York: Harper & Brothers, 1956).

19. For extended versions of these arguments, see George Stigler, "The Economics of Information," *Journal of Political Economy*, June 1961, p. 223; William Comanor and Thomas Wilson, *Advertising and Market Power* (Cambridge, Mass.: Harvard University Press, 1974), pp. 14, 23; George Stigler and Gary Becker, "De Gustibus Non Est Disputandum," *American Economic Review*, March 1977, p. 82; and Douglas Greer, *Industrial Organization and Public Policy*, 2nd ed. (London: Macmillan, 1984), p. 68.

20. Also, see Phillip Nelson, "The Economic Value of Advertising" in ed. Yale Brozen, *Advertising and Society* (New York: New York University Press, 1974), pp. 49–51, for benign effects of misleading advertising.

21. E. Scott Maynes and Terje Assum, "Informationally Imperfect Consumer Markets: Empirical Findings and Policy Implications, *Journal of Consumer Affairs* (Summer 1982):77.

22. On the other hand, if you call the data a "consultation" rather than "information," people are more than happy to pay significant amounts of money for it.

The Multimedia Ideal: Omnimedia

At various times in U.S. history we've discovered that our continued prosperity and vigor depended on building new technological and institutional foundations. Such times are brought on by technological innovation. Thus, the postal, railroad, electric utility, telephone, and highway systems were all created in response to new technological developments—inexpensively printed newspapers, the steam engine, the electric light bulb, the telephone, and the automobile, respectively.[1] Many of these foundations (which economists often refer to as "infra-structures") underlie today's private institutions. Banks couldn't exist without the monetary system, broadcast TV couldn't exist without government administration of certain frequencies in the electromagnetic spectrum, electric appliances couldn't exist without electric utilities and their rights of way, mail-order companies couldn't exist without universal telephone and postal service, business contracts couldn't exist without a legal system to back them up, and suburban shopping malls couldn't exist without a transportation system. Today, the time is ripe for building another new infrastructure, an information infrastructure unlike anything we have ever seen before.

A flourishing consumer-information industry assumes just such an underlying foundation or infrastructure. Although this infrastructure is developing spontaneously as new technologies arise, certain political forces are impeding the process, forces based on ingrained attitudes, public apathy, and the power of special-interest groups. We can counter these forces only by rethinking the use of our nation's information infrastructure. Most people studying this area today concentrate on reducing producers' costs. But we now need to recast our infrastructure by considering consumer costs, particularly the huge cost to consumers of gathering even inadequate information about products.

A THREE-PART PLAN FOR THE NEW INFORMATION INFRASTRUCTURE

In this chapter and the two that follow, we propose three such sets of policy recommendations. This chapter explores the converging of media into the purest and highest form of multimedia, which we have termed "Omnimedia." As we saw in chapter 10, various new technologies—including high-quality TV, high-capacity memory devices, high-speed telecommunications networks, and new input devices—are moving us toward a single, all-purpose medium. In this chapter, we propose ways of rethinking government policies in order to facilitate and optimize this move. In Chapter 12 we will propose a system for certifying the objectivity of information provided by I.C.I.C.s. Finally, in Chapter 13 we propose a new government-sanctioned institution—the National Institutes of Product Information (NIPI)—that would use new product-tracking technology to provide a central source of information about prices and quality, a one-stop information source that I.C.I.C.s would use to gather objective data such as model numbers, features, and retail prices. Just as we can't efficiently gather certain types of factual information such as gross national product (GNP) and census data without a centralized authority sanctioned by the government, so too with these types of product information.

Of these three components of a new information infrastructure—Omnimedia, certified I.C.I.C.s, and NIPI—Omnimedia is the most fundamental in that the other two components must use it as a foundation. Only an Omnimedia-based telecommunications system will allow I.C.I.C.s to provide perspective to consumers while still making a profit. And only an Omnimedia system, together with profitable I.C.I.C.s, will allow the National Institutes of Product Information to break even in its efforts to collect facts from the marketplace and then sell them to I.C.I.C.s.

The structural and historical relationship between these three components—Omnimedia, I.C.I.C.s, and NIPI—is analogous to the three components of the monetary system—money, private banks, and a central bank (known in the United States as the Federal Reserve). The

Federal Reserve (like NIPI) is a semipublic bank, which requires the existence of privately run member banks (like privately run I.C.I.C.s), and these banks in turn require the efficient transaction technology of money (like I.C.I.C.s require the transaction technology of Omnimedia). Money, banks, and central banks all evolved spontaneously to a certain extent. But their efficiency was also improved by sound government policies. As we shall see, we can expect the same for Omnimedia, certified I.C.I.C.s and NIPI. Furthermore, the policies set up to strengthen the monetary system involved intricate components that seemed arbitrary, totalitarian, and impractical to cynics of earlier eras, although today most of us take these complexities for granted.[2] At first glance our ideas for a new information system may also seem arbitrary and overly ambitious. But we believe that beneath their surface complexity lies a deep elegance and compelling logic. Simple solutions won't work.

With or without any specific legislation, consumer empowerment will grow. And there's also little question that many of our specific ideas for encouraging it can be replaced with more practical and efficacious steps. Technology undoubtedly will change in ways we can't foresee, as will the political climate. Rather than setting out an all-or-nothing scheme, then, what we are trying to do is encourage a certain way of thinking, a mindset about consumerism that must filter into the American consciousness if we want to have the best possible future.

OMNIMEDIA VERSUS MULTIMEDIA

The first and most fundamental part of the new information infrastructure we are proposing involves a new telecommunications infrastructure, one based on the ideal of Omnimedia. Whereas multimedia refers to the world as it is, Omnimedia refers to a never quite achievable ideal—and therefore requires a term of its own. Omnimedia as an ideal for world communication signifies a communications system that can send and receive all forms of information—audio, video, text, and graphic. It signifies media with perfect resolution—audio quality that matches the capacity of the human ear and imaging quality that matches the capacity of the human eye. Lastly, it means media available and easily accessible anywhere on the face of the earth—whether in a car, a store, a home, a boat, or an airplane. Omnimedia means media that can do everything that all other media combined can do and more. It would supersede the incompatible babble of today's telephones, stereo systems, newspapers, TVs, pagers, magazines, cellular telephones, books, and computers.

OMNIMEDIA VERSUS MASS MEDIA

The gradual converging of all today's discrepant media—TV, radio, print, computers, etc.—into a unified Omnimedia is indeed the single most important trend for U.S. communications policy. It will create new battlefields between industries. Today the media are characterized by independent fiefdoms with substantial monopoly power—one cable company per town, one or two major newspapers per city, one telephone company per region, and three national broadcasting TV networks. Incipient Omnimedia technologies have already begun to challenge these independent and very powerful groups, and the consequence has been a clash of private interests that are trying to protect and expand their turf at the expense of the public interest.[3] As various industry participants— cable, broadcast, newspaper, and telephone—make accusations about each other's motives, the leading media trade journals have started resembling supermarket tabloids.

The telephone companies, for instance, would like to provide electronic yellow pages, which would allow you to sit at your computer terminal and contact everyone who that very day is trying to sell a product or hire a worker. But the newspapers strenuously oppose this idea for fear that they would lose a significant part of their classified and general advertising revenue.[4] The phone companies also want to provide interactive video services, but both broadcast and especially cable companies vigorously oppose this competition. The cable companies, in turn, would like to provide more interactive phonelike services, but the phone companies fear that the cable companies will just siphon off the highly profitable business and ignore the traditional public policy mandate to provide universal service. Meanwhile, the broadcast companies insist that local cable companies not only be forced to carry their programs but that they place them in a priority position on the cable.

Our present-day media providers do all agree that the trend toward a universal means of telecommunication (called "Omnimedia" in this book) threatens each of them economically. Once consumers have access to interactive information, all media financed by advertising—radio, TV, newspapers, magazines—will become technologically obsolete. Remarkably, although advertising has existed for less than 1 percent of human history, today no one questions its economic necessity; few people can even conceive of a world in which certain means of communication might be financed without it. And indeed, there has yet to be an economical way either to identify or to charge individuals for picking up TV or radio programs over the airwaves.[5] Even so, advertiser-financed media is based on an anachronistic principle: to provide people purchasing information, you must use what people do want to learn to force them to learn about what they don't want to learn. If consumers had more control of both their media and their promotional messages, the two could no longer coexist.

This is exactly what is happening today. As new information technology brings about Omnimedia—media that are interactive and give users complete control over what they see and hear—we can expect consumers to exploit this power and filter out of their experience whatever is not of direct use. Instead of the publisher putting together the package of editorial and advertising matter, consumers will do so according to their individual needs.[6] Over time, in fact, almost all information costs will be incurred directly and voluntarily by the people who buy goods and services. As the American Newspaper Publishers Association cautioned its members in a December 1988 report, "the new telephone technologies make it possible for advertisers to reach buyers directly, bypassing newspapers and other traditional media."[7]

Omnimedia might allow the following scenario: *Newspapers, magazines, and yellow pages are available electronically. If you want to buy a bicycle, you'll go to your electronic yellow pages and find out about all the bicycle dealers in your area and any specials they might be running. You might even get an interactive tour of the store, including detailed information about any particular models that strike your fancy. This will be much faster and more comprehensive than any search you could do in your local newspaper for relevant ads. Similarly, if you're reading about bicycles on your on-line database, you probably won't want to view car ads on the same page. The car ads will just have to wait until you're going to buy your next car, and when that time comes, you won't be interested in wading through bicycle articles to get to them.*

Already we can see evidence of this consumer sovereignty. A growing number of consumers videotape TV programs and later skip over the ads when they play them back.[8] One company even sells a device that allows the VCR to detect and filter out the ads automatically.[9] Similarly, with the new picture-in-picture (PIP) feature available on TVs, you can jump to another channel (say, music television or one of fifty-plus other cable channels) while an ad runs on the main channel and then instantly switch back when the ad is over. Because PIP keeps a little picture of the original channel in a corner of the screen, you don't risk missing the original program, as you do when you switch channels during ads with a remote control.[10]

To some degree, it's possible that the media will be able to get around these apparent technological hurdles. The videotex service Prodigy places ads on the bottom of every screen over which the viewer has no control. Even so, it's hard to imagine that future readers and viewers will ever let these ads get as intrusive as a TV commercial or a full-page magazine ad. It's also easy to imagine viewers purchasing inexpensive utility programs to block out advertising. As MIT's Nicholas Negroponte has forecast, "the advertising you want can reach you in greater depth than ever, while the advertising you don't want will be screened out more easily and actively than ever."[11]

Such newfound technologies, of course, do not mean that advertising will disappear. After all, one of the major reasons people buy newspapers and magazines is for the advertisements. One in five television viewers claims to enjoy watching commercials.[12] But interactive media means that if advertising is going to survive, it will have to survive on its own—because consumers ask for it. Advertisers will no longer be able to coerce consumers into viewing ads by squeezing them between television programs or magazine articles. You'll go to the advertiser, probably on a toll-free basis, bypassing the media (the "middleman") entirely. From the advertiser's perspective, this will simply be one more step in a long progression from mass marketing to micromarketing, from targeting huge masses of people to targeting the specific individual. Interestingly, most observers of advertising cite this move as the wave of the future, accounting for the proliferation of speciality magazines and other techniques that target specific audiences. The unforeseen conclusion, however, may be that micromarketing will ultimately destroy advertising's financing of media altogether.

THE ROAD TO OMNIMEDIA

The only hope we have of achieving true Omnimedia in this country is to develop a telecommunications infrastructure that can support it. The three main strategies involve: (1) wired transmission, (2) wireless transmission, and (3) Omnimedia machines.

Wired Omnimedia Transmission

Right now we get our telecommunications in one of two basic ways: over-the-air or over-the-wires. Unless we have cable TV, we pick up over-the-air television or satellite signals with an antenna or a satellite dish. If we use a cellular telephone in our car, we pick up over-the-air signals. If we watch cable TV or talk on the telephone, however, we use a signal passed through a cable or a wire that has been hooked up to a media machine in our home. Until recently the two main wired-transmission technologies in the United States were "twisted pair" and "coaxial cable." Twisted pair is what the local phone company uses to connect to your telephone. Coaxial cable is what your local cable-TV company uses to connect your TV.

To transmit high-quality images and sound, on the other hand, Omnimedia will have to rely on an even better kind of "wire" to transmit signals: switched optical fiber ("switched broadband network"), which, as we've seen, is well on its way to becoming affordable, and which is already being selectively installed. In technical terms, "switched" refers to the ability to have two-way information on demand (just as we now have on the telephone—in contrast to a television or cable system) and "broadband" refers to the relatively high capacity of optical fiber to transmit information. What's holding back the installation of this network in the United States is the assumption that optical fiber won't generate valuable new services for the American public. This assumption leads public-utility commissioners to argue that the only economical justification for installing optical fiber is to replace worn-out copper wiring. And such an approach means that it will take a minimum of fifty years, beginning in the mid-1990s, to finish installing optical fiber, because the twisted-pair wiring already in our homes needs replacement only at the rate of 1 percent to 2 percent per year. In other words, most Americans won't benefit from optical-fiber networks until well into the twenty-first century.[13]

But if we factor into our calculations the additional services and revenue that a nationwide system of optical fiber would make possible, if we assume that optical fiber will bring to American homes services worth three to five times what plain old telephone service brings, then instead of taking fifty years to implement, we could justify rewiring most of America within just one decade—that is, not long after the year 2000. The Japanese already seem to understand optical fiber: according to FCC chairman Alfred Sikes, "Nippon Telegraph and Telephone Corp. plans to have fiber optics running into every household in Tokyo with children by the mid-1990s, along with family computer terminals to take advantage of the new information services."[14]

In the United States, though, this is the juncture where politics comes to the fore. The possibility of the phone companies providing an Omnimedia conduit (i.e., a "switched fiber-optic network" or "integrated broadband network") and stealing away business frightens today's reigning media and public-utility commissions. Notes Robert Pepper of the FCC's Office of Plans and Policies:

> In the long-term, integrated broadband network development prob-
> ably implies the fundamental restructuring of the domestic U.S.
> telecommunications and mass media industries. Institutional rela-
> tionships and arrangements will be under pressure, historical alli-
> ances may change, and new regulatory structures will have to
> evolve. This is an unstable environment in which no existing player
> is guaranteed an outcome. Therefore, the tendency is to protect the
> past, rather than look forward. If policymakers permit this backward
> view to prevail, a significant opportunity to advance our telecom-
> munications infrastructure and industries may be lost."[15]

The cable industry would be most immediately and devastatingly affected by such competition. As a result of continued cable-industry lobbying, the law presently forbids phone companies from providing any services that might compete with cable. Cable companies know that competition from phone companies means not only the end of their monopoly profits on the provision of video services (and at least a two-thirds drop in the value of their assets) but a threat to their very survival.[16] Although cable companies could try competing with the phone companies in wiring America's homes with optical fiber, the latter are in a better position to do so: cable companies are in a worse position than telephone companies to provide truly interactive ("switched") information flow. With your telephone, for example, you can already dial to connect to any other telephone on the face of the earth. With your cable TV, however, you can at most choose from a hundred or so channels available in your community. Nor can we expect the telephone company and cable company both to provide wired telecommunications services, since past experience with such networks suggests they are natural monopolies. A town may start out with two phone companies or two cable companies, but if the marketplace is allowed to work freely, the town ends up with one phone company and one cable company. Once wired service provided by the phone companies provides both audio and video services, there will no reason for the cable companies to provide wired services at all.

The advent of an Omnimedia network also threatens broadcasters. Today, the physical limits of the radio spectrum prevent more than at most a half-dozen TV stations from broadcasting in many areas of the United States. This gives existing stations tremendous monopoly power and resale value. A switched fiber network, giving the public access to literally an infinite number of channels, would undermine this value.

Over-the-air broadcasters, however, don't oppose the phone companies as fervently as do cable companies, because these broadcasters recognize that all TV is going to become wired TV anyway. For the broadcasters the immediate question is whether they are better off allying with the cable-TV companies or the phone companies. At the moment, they seem to be playing the two against each other. Cable, meanwhile, seems willing to appease broadcasters by promising to carry their signals gratis ("must carry") in exchange for support in opposing the phone companies. Broadcasters seem to enjoy this courtship and haven't yet made a decision to back either group, but it seems pretty obvious that eventually they will align themselves with cable, possibly because so many broadcasters today currently own cable franchises.[17]

Ultimately, despite all opposition, a switched fiber-optic network will inevitably be installed in America. As one observer put it, "modern technology, combined with consumer needs, has made the ultimate adoption of switched, high bandwidth services [i.e., optical-fiber services] to the home inevitable, unless some major catastrophe, such as nuclear war or melting of the popular icecaps, upsets the economy."[18] Even so, we shouldn't be blinded to the fact that cable and other interests have tremendous power to postpone this day of reckoning. To investors, even a few years can mean a lifetime.

The argument we are making about wired Omnimedia is nicely summed up by Opt in America, a non-profit organization which subtitles itself "The Public Interest Organization for the Information Age" and which is "dedicated to removing the barriers that hold back development of a nationwide telecommunications infrastructure for the Information

Age." The group's philosophy states: "Nothing prevents universal deployment of switched fiber optic cable to every home in America. Nothing except the lack of a visionary national policy." We agree that the time is ripe to install a switched optical-fiber network, and that what is holding us back is not technology or economics but the limited vision of our politicians.

Wireless Omnimedia Transmission

Most of us are hardly aware that information is all the time flying through the air around and through us. When we turn on a car radio or our portable TV, we may sometimes think about this ever-present information, but the electromagnetic spectrum—nature's capacity to transmit over-the-air information such as TV, radio, and cellular-telephone signals—is not something that makes front-page news.

The electromagnetic spectrum, however, will never provide as much information transmission capacity as optical fiber. You can always add more information capacity with more fiber, but the universe was created with only a limited number of electromagnetic frequencies through which you can transmit information. For this limited, invisible resource to be used efficiently, it must be managed wisely. And we need to use this resource efficiently if we want convenient and cost-effective access to consumer information. We'll need to rely on remote (i.e., nonwired) devices if we want to sit in an easy chair and read an Omnimedia "magazine" or consult an I.C.I.C. without having to plug into the optical-fiber connector on the kitchen wall. We'll also want portable computers that let us tap into shopping information services while we're strolling the aisles of a retail store.

Unfortunately, the use of the airwaves is a government-controlled monopoly dominated by special-interest groups. For more than seventy years the government (most visibly the Federal Communications Commission) has been developing electromagnetic-spectrum policy as a patchwork quilt of laws guided more by political realities than market forces or concern for the public interest.[19] The fact that some 430 different services (such as taxicabs and motion-picture companies) have each been assigned a separate portion of the spectrum is just one example of today's piecemeal and inefficient system. Today, it's impossible to find a reputable scholar who has much praise for the way we manage the electromagnetic spectrum. In contrast, those who have benefited from the free use of this spectrum have fought fiercely to protect their privileges. The laws governing use of the electromagnetic spectrum have become a Byzantine nightmare. The public doesn't understand them. Congress doesn't understand them. And all the groups who have licenses to use the airwaves understand is that they want to preserve their privileges.[20]

The value of spectrum to special interests can be understood with one simple fact: spectrum is rapidly becoming the most valuable natural resource in the United States. Already, conservative estimates place the aggregate value of spectrum rights above $100 billion. By the year 2010 this amount could easily exceed $1 trillion.[21]

The key to wireless communications policy is to let the free market play a greater role in determining how airwave rights should be used. We don't need government, for example, to tell broadcasters that they can no longer have their huge (and free) chunks of spectrum, as some have proposed. We just need to offer the broadcasters' portions of the electromagnetic spectrum to the highest bidder. The eventual winners of such transactions wouldn't be broadcasters but the Omnimedia services of the future. (Just consider that cellular-telephone companies already pay ten times as much for spectrum as do broadcasters.)[22]

The goal of our spectrum policy should be simple: to foster an Omnimedia infrastructure to benefit consumers. With our current policy, the so-called information age simply won't arrive. There'll never be enough spectrum for inexpensive portable Omnimedia machines. And, as a consequence, there'll also never be enough spectrum for independent consumer-information companies to provide the high-quality and convenient services that the public will eventually demand.

The kind of spectrum we'll need for efficient Omnimedia transmission will need to have three key attributes: it will need to be *interactive, digital,* and *cellular.* Interactivity is crucial if we want to ask questions and demand specific information. Today's cellular telephones already provide interactive spectrum, but the information passed back and forth consists of voice alone. Today's higher-quality information sources (that is, those consisting of both sound and picture) so far remain one-way: we can't yet talk back to our TV sets or ask them questions. Efficient Omnimedia transmissions will also need to be digital if we expect to use a single information conduit—whether it be twisted pair, coaxial cable, optical fiber, or an electromagnetic wave—to send audio, video, and text together. Digitalization will also allow us to compress a lot of information into a smaller amount of space than is now possible.

Finally, "cellular spectrum usage" will allow us to access Omnimedia transmissions conveniently in each of our homes. What the term "cellular" refers to is the reusable properties of the otherwise limited electromagnetic spectrum. The same portions of the spectrum can be used again and again in different geographical regions, and therefore the same frequencies can be used by broadcasters living in different areas. Local TV stations throughout the entire country thus share the same band of spectrum. Channel 2 in Boston, Channel 2 in New York, Channel 2 in Chicago, and Channel 2 in Los Angeles all run different programs using radio waves of the same frequency. Similarly, instead of having only twelve VHF channels in this country (a maximum of seven of which are usable in any one locale due to the interference they cause each other), we have thousands. The same principle works on an even finer scale with cellular telephones. A given area is divided up into "cells," each with its own transmitting and receiving equipment. Thus, within a large metropolitan area, the same frequencies can simultaneously be used by many different people as long as they're located in different parts of the city. On a yet smaller scale we can say the same for portable telephones, garage-door openers, and TV remote controls.

We have to take full advantage of this "reusability" of electromagnetic frequencies if we want convenient information, information accessible anywhere at any time, without messy wires. Optical fiber will form the backbone of the Omnimedia system, but anything that needs to be hooked up to a wire won't be conveniently accessible at all times and all places. Thus, in addition to optical fiber, we'll want wireless Omnimedia to make the final link to all the portable Omnimedia machines whether on the road, in a store, or in the home. We'll want to pick up Omnimedia as easily as we pick up a book, a magazine, or a cellular phone. And to do so we'll have to divide the spectrum into as many small cells as possible, just as we've already begun to do with cellular telephones.

One technology to divide spectrum into much smaller cells is called personal communication networks (PCNs). Instead of cells being more than a mile in size, as they are with cellular telephones, PCN cells are no bigger than a few square city blocks. Numerous companies have already applied to the Federal Communications Commission for an allocation of spectrum to set up such networks. Cable companies, in particular, are enamored of this technology. They already have wires running into neighborhoods, and they could use PCNs to introduce interactive services and eventually challenge the telephone company monopoly on local service.

Each home ultimately will need to have its own personal communications cell. Already all of our homes have some personal spectrum allocated for such things as baby monitors, cordless telephones, wireless alarm systems, wireless camcorder microphones, garage-door openers, and TV remote controls. But this amount of spectrum—less than 2 megahertz (2MHz)—cannot satisfy the needs of the future. Indeed, we believe that each home would require at least 30 MHz of spectrum allocated for personal use to carry the high-quality pictures and sound brought into each house by optical fiber. This 30 MHz is equivalent to the spectrum used by five TV channels or more than all of the allocated FM radio channels combined, and given today's way of thinking, it's an unheard-of sum, amounting to nearly 3 percent of the prime spectrum available on earth. Ironically, when the electromagnetic spectrum was first discovered, politicians wondered if they had the right to allocate the spectrum on people's property to third parties such as TV broadcasters.[23] Today, in contrast, most people have no sense that the electromagnetic waves over their property might legitimately be considered theirs (nor can we expect politicians to risk their necks by fighting special interests to give consumers something they don't even know they want). But such a mindset is exactly what we'll need if people are going to be able to take maximum advantage of the information age: it ought to be considered a natural right that all Americans have access to at least 30 MHz of the spectrum that passes over their residence.[24]

As the number of in-home devices using wireless technology increases, we also must recognize the inefficiency and absurdity of having government make decisions about the way we use electromagnetic spectrum within our own homes. Today, every time a new in-home wireless technology—such as home security or baby monitoring—comes along, the FCC must go through a long and complicated process of deciding whether the new product has a right to claim a portion of the spectrum and whose share of the spectrum may be diminished thereby. Moreover, once allocated to a specific purpose, such spectrum remains idle most of the time. Most Americans, after all, still don't have wireless security or baby monitors. Fortunately, the contorted bureaucratic procedures used to allocate specific frequencies are no longer necessary. Utilities could instead employ the new technology that allows hundreds of different wireless devices to share the same frequencies without canceling each other out. In 1991 Apple Computer requested 40 MHz of spectrum to set up just such a wireless network within the home.

An efficient, wireless Omnimedia system will make obsolete much of today's spectrum equipment, such as cellular telephones, radios, TVs, garage-door openers, and wireless alarm equipment. Thus, new spectrum policies can be phased in only over a matter of decades. As a practical matter, an Omnimedia wired network will probably develop at least a decade before a similarly flexible Omnimedia wireless (that is, remote) network.

Omnimedia Machines and HDTV

Whether information comes via optical fiber or the electromagnetic spectrum, we're going to receive it using "Omnimedia machines." Whatever we call them (telephones, computers, televisions, or something else) and whatever they look like, these machines will serve the same function: receiving and transmitting many kinds of data. In America, Japan, and Europe, companies are already developing such machines.

An ideal Omnimedia machine must be able to display images and play sound identical to what we perceive in the real world. Some machines must come with screen sizes as large as living room walls and others with screens as small as watches, as thin as paintings, and as portable as magazines. Whatever the size or form, Omnimedia equipment must have sufficient intelligence to interpret all kinds of information, from that in a human's voice, to the data embedded in radio and TV waves, to the information transmitted via the telephone company's optical fiber.

Most politicians who regulate our communication machines profess to support the coming information age while at the same time opposing the specific steps necessary to bring it about. To date, it is the future of TV that has received the most political attention. As of 1990 the United States was thought to be many years behind the Japanese and Europeans in developing the next generation of TV technology, so-called high-definition TV or HDTV.[25] This has led many industry groups—most notably TV media and electronics manufacturers—to see our lag in HDTV development as a threat to America's economic survival. The successful protestations of these industries, in turn, have convinced many of those in government that foreign-led HDTV technology ultimately could not only cripple the U.S. economy but also seriously weaken our national defense and our cultural influence, as well as diminish the esteem with which other nations regard us. Accordingly, political interest in HDTV focuses almost completely on negative reasons—factors such as the technology's potential to undermine America's competitive standing in the world should others be the proprietors of HDTV know-how.[26]

Specifically, the tens of thousands of pages of government reports and testimony on HDTV have ignored almost completely any discussion about what use we'll have for it. This can only be because almost everybody thinks the answer is obvious: it'll be used for more of the same—just prettier TV and movie images.[27] The debate has focused on who makes and controls the components that go into an HDTV. This orientation is understandable, given the industry groups that have so far set the terms of the debate. But the importance of HDTV has more to do with the minds and human capital of society. What's been missing almost completely from the arguments in favor of a national HDTV policy is HDTV's capacity to finally bring the information age into American homes.

High-definition television is a long-delayed improvement on our fifty-year-old TV technology. Such machines have the sound quality, image quality, and screen proportions of a typical movie. By law any high-definition television produced in the United States must be able to receive signals sent using both the old standards and the new HDTV standards. However, even HDTV is still a primitive technology that will almost certainly become obsolete in the next decade or two.[28] Today the best proposed HDTV systems have only about a tenth the picture resolution of high-quality magazine print.[29] This new technology simply is not going to provide anything close to the image quality of the proposed Omnimedia machine. Thus, it makes sense to at least try to build an HDTV system with some capacity to evolve.

Such a system would be a "smart" TV, also known as an open-architecture receiver or extensible TV. Unlike today's "dumb" TVs, smart TVs will be able to read, interpret, and act upon many different types of signals. Even more important, they can "grow" and "evolve," learning to use signals that haven't been invented yet. If you have a smart TV that is picking up today's broadcast signals, and someone decides to change the signals so that they can send even more information (as will happen when optical fiber becomes widely available in homes), you will not be obliged to discard your existing set.[30] Already computers can serve as high-quality smart TVs, easily adaptable to present and future forms of transmission, and that fact should give hope to the American computer industry, which knows that smart TVs would probably be sold by American computer companies rather than Japanese consumer-electronics companies.[31]

Despite HDTV's advantages, certain interest groups would like to make sure that these powerful sets never come into being, mainly because different existing media have different potentials to provide Omnimedia services, depending on the amount of information capacity available to them. Of the special-interest groups opposing smart TV, perhaps the most influential is the television broadcasters.[32] As Ernest Hollings, chairman of the U.S. Senate Commerce, Science, and Transportation Committee, put it: "Our broadcaster friends are the most powerful I know. . . . They can change votes right and left, and that is quite understandable. We live and breathe by TV, and that is our reelection. If the local broadcaster calls, you are going to do him a favor."[33]

"I am worried that what we are seeing on this panel are three very large, very powerful dinosaurs [the three major TV networks] who are protecting their feeding grounds," observed Representative Jim Cooper in the 1988 hearings on HDTV before the House Subcommittee on Telecommunications and Finance, one of the few politicians who directly challenged the broadcasters' arguments. "It worries me very much that due to your vested interests and a very narrow channel bandwidth [information capacity] you are willing and interested to do virtually everything within your considerable power to slow the access of the American consumer to this magnificent new technology including downplaying its attractiveness to the average consumer."

Cooper added that despite glorious past achievements, terrestrial broadcasters, with their limited information capacity, have a "very large vested interest" in a perhaps obsolete technology. To broadcast with a quality that compares to the Omnimedia standards, they will need a larger share of the electromagnetic spectrum than they currently have. Furthermore, national broadcasters will have to fight for that precious spectrum against many other private and public radio services, especially the cellular Omnimedia companies, which will want to use the same airwaves.[34] "It worries me very much," he said, "that some of you gentlemen may have invested in the horse and buggy business and Henry Ford's out there cranking out new models."[35] George Gilder, in his book *Microcosm*, agreed: "[P]oliticians around the world are propping up this obsolete system in the name of progress."[36]

Even the FCC grudgingly recognizes the obsolescence of terrestrial broadcasting, which it has so long defended against all opposition. As one senior official there admitted: "Ultimately, everything below a gigahertz will be mobile in nature [i.e., all the airwaves will be taken over by personal communications]. We can't tell the broadcasters about this; they would be furious. It's like telling an employee who's been working for you for thirty years and making lots of money that he's out of a job.

Sure, he's going to get mad. But everybody at the FCC thinks it will eventually happen."[37]

Admittedly, right now terrestrial broadcasters still have the upper hand, and it's highly unlikely that the FCC will deprive broadcasters of their precious spectrum. In 1989, the FCC Advisory Committee on Advanced Television (HDTV) Service didn't even consider the idea of not giving broadcasters a greater share of the existing radio and TV frequencies for HDTV, let alone phasing in a procedure to force them to give up what they already have. In Congressional subcommittee hearings, some broadcasters even broached the subject of taking spectrum away from other users.[38]

Despite the FCC's claim to objectivity, this organization is in fact beholden to the broadcaster interests. Public interest attorney Henry Geller has pinpointed the problem. "The [FCC] is regarded as a 'political plum'; with enough political influence anyone can be appointed to the FCC. That is not true of the Federal Reserve Board or the SEC," he observes. "As long as the selection of [people] for key administrative posts is based upon political reward rather than competency, little else that is done will really matter." He adds that through "regulatory capture," agency members often identify with the industry they supposedly regulate. These industry members often wield more control over FCC appointments—and reappointments—than the president or Congress. Some FCC members even plan to work for broadcasters upon leaving the agency.[39]

An Omnimedia machine would have a much better chance to develop if politicians spent less time obsessed with foreign threats to our competitive strength and more time stopping the threat posed by special-interest groups within our own society—in particular, the broadcast and cable industries. We must recognize that these industries—and the politicians that support them—are doing more to hold back America's information industry than any foreign country. Of course, picking on foreigners isn't going to cost any votes, so it's almost always a popular strategy. That's why throughout the world, the politicians with the worst domestic problems are often the ones that spend the most time claiming the acts of foreign countries are the source of their own countries' problems.

OMNIMEDIA   AND   FREE   SPEECH

Like all powerful technologies, Omnimedia holds out the prospect of both great benefits and great dangers. It offers the prospect of a whole new paradigm of publishing, one that would eliminate today's media monopolies and thus expand free speech by making it economical and practical for just about anyone with talent and something to say to communicate ideas to the rest of the world.[40] Without proper safeguards, however, Omnimedia could be used to threaten free speech and bolster media monopolies.

Because most vital information is likely to be conveyed by just a few networks, we must aim to distinguish between the monopolistic and competitive aspects of Omnimedia. This means separating control of the conduit (optical fiber and airwaves) from control of the information itself. We already make such a distinction in the regulations that govern the post office and telephone companies. These institutions have been designated as "common carriers" and are not allowed to have any control of the information that they distribute. In contrast, today's broadcast, newspaper, and cable-TV companies can parlay control of an information conduit into control of the messages they transmit.

Perhaps no one has argued for common carriers more eloquently than the late Ithiel de Sola Pool of MIT, who noted that "where monopoly exists by public favor, public access is a reasonable condition."[41] Pool wrote that our traditional notion of a free press "rests on the assumption that paper, ink, and presses are in sufficient abundance that, if government simply keeps hands off, people will be able to express themselves freely. The law of common carriage rests on the opposite assumption that, in the absence of regulation, the carrier will have enough monopoly power to deny citizens the right to communicate."[42] Clearly this has already happened in the case of television and cable service: ordinary citizens don't even think that they might have a right to broadcast a television program on demand. We just don't think that such license is part of our "freedom of speech." It simply hasn't been practical to make the inherently monopolistic newspapers, cable services, and broadcasters into common carriers.[43]

If we want to use Omnimedia to increase freedom of speech, then, we must not permit whichever companies control the conduit—specifically, the wired and wireless Omnimedia networks—to diverge from their primary mission: providing a low-cost, high-quality interactive information pipeline to every home. These companies should profit from leasing use of their conduit, not from providing the information that goes over it, nor the equipment used at either end.

Following this model, it would make sense to allow the Bell operating companies to carry video services through their (high-capacity) optical-fiber networks. We'd gain not only higher-quality visual and audio data, but also many new kinds of services. Undoubtedly such a development could cripple existing cable and broadcast companies, whose power in the marketplace comes less from high-quality content than from controlling a limited number of channels. Even so, this weakening could be a worthwhile sacrifice if we consider that it will allow us to choose from all the video programming in existence in lieu of the forty programs now showing on our local cable system. And, again, this type of selection would lead to all sorts of new video programs—including interactive consumer-education materials.

Not that certain reigning powers won't object to paying the phone companies—or anyone else—for conduits such as spectrum that they now get for nothing. For example, if television broadcasters had to compete with the many other potential users of spectrum and pay for their huge chunk of prime electromagnetic frequencies, they would probably be seriously weakened and forced to revise their programming significantly.[44] Similarly, if the government had to pay for spectrum usage just as it now has to pay for aircraft bombers and national highways, it undoubtedly would cut back either on its spectrum utilization (which isn't very efficient) or expenditures on other programs. Government agencies, which now have free use of nearly 40 percent of the spectrum, are not going to sit idly by while their budgets effectively are cut.

Unfortunately, the local phone companies, the most logical providers of optical fiber, would also like to control the data transmitted over their networks. And powerful political forces—many of the nation's leading politicians and regulatory commissions—are bent on letting them have their way.[45] The arguments put forth by the Bell companies primarily fall into two categories: (1) they believe they can set up a Chinese wall—enforced by regulators—between their competitive and monopolistic businesses, and (2) they believe that the most efficient way to provide consumer information services is to allow phone utilities to own the information going over their wires and to let these companies sell the equipment that will enable consumers to use that information.

Unfortunately, there's relatively little evidence that it's possible to separate competitive from monopolistic businesses, except with huge and highly motivated regulatory agencies—a highly unlikely state of affairs.[46] The world doesn't need "competitive help" from telephone companies. It doesn't need them using their monopoly profits to subsidize already very competitive and innovative equipment and information businesses.[47] It certainly doesn't need them to become our sole sources of information.[48] Nor does the world need the telephone companies to provide equipment. Let them install a high-quality information infrastructure and leave competitive industries alone. New information services provided by other concerns could easily quadruple present demand for telephone services. Thus, even without freedom to enter competitive businesses, phone companies would still be left with plenty of options to increase their profits and contribute to America's well-being.

THE NEED FOR VISION

A period of tremendous conflict between government-regulated communications media is imminent. The danger is that each of these powerful media will engage in a turf war (fought out in the battlefield of Congress and the FCC rather than the marketplace), with the American public being the loser. Existing media will do everything in their power to suppress the new Omnimedia. In fact, from this perspective, the greatest short-term enemy of the new consumerism in this country are neither retailers nor manufacturers but the existing corporations that control the distribution of information. As one Washington observer has noted, "Washington's media lobby—broadcasters, publishers, and their trade associations—has the distinction of being perhaps the most formidable and invisible lobby around. And . . . it usually gets what it wants."[49] Of course, we can't blame firms in the information business for pursuing their self-interest. Nor can we blame them for suppressing views that might harm their bottom line. As consumers and citizens, however, we don't share the media's self-interests, and we are under no such strictures. The framers of the Constitution did not believe they could wipe out sin or the pursuit of self-interest. Their goal was simply to set up laws and a system of checks and balances to prevent the pursuit of self-interest from conflicting with the public interest. Likewise, our goal should simply be to make sure that the entrenched media cannot get away with abusing their powers. If voters can comprehend the media's hidden agenda and can vote out of office those politicians who are beholden to the media's interests, there is nothing to fear.

Many of the decisions necessary to improve our telecommunications infrastructure require a long-term perspective. Unfortunately, we have a long-standing tradition in this country of consuming rather than investing, of putting money and political emphasis on projects with a short-term payoff. Endless turf battles can be averted only with a large over-reaching policy consensus, a positive vision of where we want to be.[50] The sole principle guiding us thus far has been deregulation, which has become an end in itself rather than a means to an end. Yet just as the widespread development of the electric power and telephone communications infrastructure in the 1890s laid the foundation for the industrial expansion of the twentieth century, so a commercialized Omnimedia infrastructure in the 1990s will be vital for the economic and cultural development of the twenty-first century.

1. U.S. Congress, House, *Public Policy Implications of Advanced Television Systems*, Committee Print 101-E (Washington, D.C.: Government Printing Office, 1989), p. 572. See also U.S. Department of Commerce, National Telecommunications and Information Administration, *Telecom 2000: Charting the Course for a New Century*, NTIA Special Publication 88-21 (Washington, D.C.: Government Printing Office, 1988), pp. 165–166.

2. The author of the Declaration of Independence, Thomas Jefferson, for example, opposed the formation of a centralized banking system on the grounds that it was undemocratic. And not till the twentieth century was the idea of fiat money (money not backed by gold) widely accepted as well as the need for federally insured bank deposits.

3. E.g., see David Jefferson, "Enterpreneurs Bump Heads with Powerful Newspaper," *Wall Street Journal*, January 2, 1990, sec. B, p. 1.

4. For an excellent discussion of the newspaper industry's political efforts opposing the telephone companies from providing Omnimedia-like technologies, see Phillip D. Mink, *Newspaper Publishers and Freedom of Speech* (Washington, D.C.: Citizens for a Sound Economy Foundation, 1989).

5. Daniel Boorstin, *The Americans: The Democratic Experience* (New York: Random House, 1973), p. 154.

6. See Anthony Smith, *Goodbye Gutenberg: The Newspaper Revolution of the 1980's* (Oxford: Oxford University Press, 1980), p. 313.

7. Mink, p. 50.

8. "VCR Threat to Ads Is Expected to Grow," *Wall Street Journal*, November 30, 1988, sec. B, p. 1. See also Joan S. Lublin, "VCR Advances May Increase Zapping," *Wall Street Journal*, January 4, 1991, sec. B, pp. 1, 3.

9. George Gilder, "The Ad Killers," *Forbes*, February 20, 1989, p. 76.

10. In the future it may even be possible to intercept ads before they arrive on your TV. See "Clairvoyant Computer Would Even Zap TV Ads," *Wall Street Journal*, August 15, 1989, sec. B, p. 1.

11. Stewart Brand, *The Media Lab: Inventing the Future at MIT* (New York: Penguin Books, 1987), p. 208.

12. "How Much Commercial Appeal?" *Channels*, September 1988, p. 68.

13. For general discussions of the cost to install fiber optics under different scenarios see U.S. Federal Communications Commission, Office of Plans and Policies, *Through the Looking Glass: Integrated Broadband Networks, Regulatory Policy and Institutional Change*, by Robert Pepper (Washington, D.C.: Government Printing Office, 1988); M. Sirbu, F. Ferrante, and D. Reed, *An Engineering and Policy Analysis of Fiber Introduction into the Residential Subscriber Loop* (Pittsburgh: Carnegie Mellon University, May 1988); Bruce Egan and Lester Taylor, *Capitol Budgeting for Technology Adoption in Telecommunications: The Case of Fiber* (New York: Center for Telecommunications and Information Studies, Columbia University, 1989); Paul Shumate, Jr., "Timeframes for Fiber to the Home" in *The 1989 Telephone Industry Directory* (Morristown, N.J.: Bellcore, 1989), pp. 259–262; and Lois Therrien, "Fiber Optics: Getting Cheap Enough to Start Rewiring America," *Business Week*, July 31, 1989, p. 86.

14. Charles Mason, "Sikes: FCC Must Help Innovation," *Telephony*, September 18, 1989, p. 9. According to NTT's own estimates, 30 percent of Japanese households will be connected to optical fiber by 2005, with the balance connected by 2015. See *Realization of VI & P: A Service Vision for the 21st Century* (n.p.: NTT, March 1990), p. 15.

15. Pepper, pp. 105–106. See also "Bell Atlantic's Ray Smith," *Telephony*, January 1, 1990, pp. 18, 22; and Dawn Bushaus and Deborah Pfeiffer, "Fiber to the Home: A Family Affair," *Telephony Transmission Special*, November 1989, p. 27.

16. Harry Shooshan and Charles Jackson, *Opening the Broadband Gateway: The Need for Telephone Company Entry into the Video Services Marketplace; Rebuttal to Reply Comments of Tele-Communications, Inc.*, paper submitted to the Federal Communications Commission (Washington D.C.: National Economic Research Associates, Inc., January 20, 1988). These authors estimate that cable companies sell for approximately three times what they would in a competitive marketplace. The Consumer Federation of America has estimated that cable companies earned approximately $6 billion a year in monopoly profits in 1988. See also Ithiel de Sola Pool, *Technologies of Freedom: On Free Speech in an Electronic Age* (Cambridge, Mass.: Harvard University Press, 1983), p. 52; "Mooney Reassures Wall Street: Cable Will Weather Telco Threat," *Broadcasting*, February 1989, p. 34; "Glimmer of Carriage Compromise Between Telcos, Broadcasters," *Broadcasting*, February 6, 1989, p. 27; Gary Slutsker, "Good-bye Cable TV, Hello Fiber Optics," *Forbes*, September 19, 1988, p. 178; "NCTA Votes 15% Dues Surcharge to Fund Telco Fight," *Broadcasting*, October 3, 1988, p. 29; and Tom Kerver, "Titanic Struggle Pending?" *Cable Television Business*, January 1, 1989, p. 11.

17. For other reasons that broadcasters might want to join the cable ranks, see "Malone Envisions Synergies in Cable-Broadcasting Future," *Broadcasting*, May 8, 1989, p. 31; Krista Van Lewen, "NCTA's New Friend, Old Foe," *Cable Television Business*, February 1, 1989, p. 11; "The Grace Under Pressure of Jim Mooney," *Broadcasting*, May 22, 1989, p. 36; and "NBC's Wright Takes Anti-Telco Stand," *Broadcasting*, April 17, 1989, p. 33.

18. Harry Shooshan and Charles Jackson, *The Inevitability of Switched Broadband Transmission to the Home*, unpublished report (Washington D.C.: National Economic Research Associates, Inc., 1987), p. 1.

19. *Telecom 2000*, pp. 175, 177.

20. U.S. Federal Communications Commission, Office of Plans and Policies, *Spectrum Management Policy in the United States: An Historical Account, Appendix B,* by John Robinson, NTIS document PB85-204550 (Washington, D.C.: Government Printing Office, 1985), pp. 3–4, 45–46, 52, 79–81; Douglas Webbink, "Spectrum Deregulation and Market Forces," paper delivered at a conference sponsored by the Center for Telecommunications and Information Studies, Columbia University, October 14, 1988, pp. 43–45, 259; U.S. Congress, House Committee on Energy and Commerce, *High Definition Television, Hearings before the Subcommittee on Telecommunications and Finance* [hereinafter referred to as *High Definition Television Hearings*], 100th Cong., June 23, 1988, Serial No. 100-188, 1989, p. 321; Charles Jackson, "Use and Management of the Spectrum Resource," in ed. Paula R. Newberg, *New Directions in Telecommunications Policy,* vol. 1 (Durham, N.C.: Duke University, 1989), pp. 259, 264, 267, 269; and Henry Geller, "Reforming the Federal Telecommunications Policy Process," in Newberg, ed., p. 318.

21. The value of the 50 MHz of spectrum used for cellular telephone is alone estimated to be worth between $46 billion and $97 billion. See U.S. Department of Commerce, National Telecommunications and Information Administration, *U.S. Spectrum Management Policy: Agenda for the Future,* NTIA Special Publication 91-23 (Washington, D.C.: Government Printing Office, February 1991), pp. 89–92, D1–6.

22. Numerous studies have come out recommending greater use of the free market to allocate spectrum. For a compendium, see *U.S. Spectrum Management Policy: Agenda for the Future.* This study also notes that the cellular spectrum on a per-megahertz basis has a 1991 market value worth at least ten times as much as that possessed by broadcasters. Specifically, the market value of the broadcasters' more than 200 megahertz of spectrum is estimated at $11.5 billion, whereas the market value of the cellular telephone companies' 50 megahertz of spectrum is estimated, as noted above, at more than $45 billion. The inefficient use of spectrum by broadcasters has been noted widely. See *U.S. Spectrum Management Policy: Agenda for the Future,* p. 156; testimony of Jeffrey Hart, professor of political science at Indiana University in U.S. Congress, House, Committee on Energy and Commerce, *High Definition Television, Hearings,* 100th Cong., March 8, 1989, n.p.; and Mark Lewyn and Peter Coy, "Airwave Wars: Too Many New Technologies, Too Few Bands," *Business Week,* July 23, 1990, pp. 48–53.

23. Susan Douglas, "Amateur Operators and American Broadcasting: Shaping the Future of Radio," in *Imagining Tomorrow: History, Technology, and the American Future,* ed. Joseph J. Corn (Cambridge, Mass.: MIT Press, 1986), p. 52.

24. In early 1991 Apple filed a petition with the FCC for 40 MHz of spectrum to be used in such a local network. Apple's request is more modest than the one proposed here, but it does point to the future. See "Apple Computer Files Proposal with FCC for Radio Spectrum," *Wall Street Journal,* January 29, 1991, sec. B, p. 7.

25. U.S. Congress, Office of Technology Assessment, *Critical Connections: Communication for the Future,* OTA-CIT-407 (Washington, D.C.: Government Printing Office, January 1990), p. 340. As this book goes to print, a new consensus is developing that the United States, with its proposed digital HDTV standards, may rapidly be becoming the world leader in HDTV.

26. *High Definition Television, Hearings,* October 8, 1987, p. 386; *High Definition Television, Hearings,* 100th Cong., Sept. 7, 1988, p. 320; William Schreiber, "Advanced Television Systems and Their Impact on the Existing Television Service," speech before the FCC, MM Docket No. 87-286, November 30, 1988, pp. 5–6; testimony of Fred Branfman, Director of Rebuild America, *High Definition Television, Hearings,* March 8, 1989, n.p.; Harold Krall, "Advanced Television Systems—Regaining the Competitive Edge," in *High Definition Television, Hearings,* March 22, 1989, p. 284; testimony of Dr. Craig Fields, Defense Advanced Research Projects Agency in the March 8, 1989, *High Definition Television, Hearings,* n.p.

27. *High Definition Television, Hearings,* October 8, 1987, p. 1.

28. See Robert Goldberg, "A Rosy, Rectangular View of the Future," *Wall Street Journal*, June 5, 1989, sec. A, p. 12; *Telecom 2000*, p. 623.

29. This assumes a screen with approximately 2,700 square inches, nine times the image area of a 25-inch TV's 300 inches, or a TV 67 inches horizontally and 40 inches vertically.

30. Andrew Lippman, "High-Definition Systems in the 1990's: Open Architecture & Computational Video," in *Extensible Television: View from MIT* (Cambridge, Mass.: MIT Media Lab, April 1, 1990), p. 1. See also *Public Policy Implications of Advanced Television Systems*, p. 555, and U.S. Federal Communications Commission, Advisory Committee, *Second Interim Report on Advanced Television Service* (Washington, D.C.: Government Printing Office, April 26, 1989). See also Handler, p. 81; *High Definition Television, Hearings*, Sept. 7, 1988, p. 312; Schreiber, p. 23; and Hugh Carter Donahue, "The United States Prepares for High Definition Television," in *Public Policy Implications of Advanced Television Systems*, pp. 311–313.

31. E.g., see George Gilder, "Forget HDTV, It's Already Outmoded," *New York Times*, May 28, 1989, sec. 3, p.2; Donahue, "Choosing the TV of the Future," pp. 40, 44–45; and letter from the Electronics Industries Association to the Federal Communications Commission, June 30, 1988.

32. *Public Policy Implications of Advanced Television Systems*, pp. 697, 699, 787, 794.

33. Sheila Kaplan, "The Powers That Be—Lobbying," in ed. Peter Woll, *American Government: Readings and Cases*, 10th ed. (Glenview, Ill.: Scott, Foresman, 1990), p. 335.

34. *High Definition Television, Hearings*, October 8, 1988, pp. 79–81, 190; *High Definition Television, Hearings*, June 23, 1988, p. 256; position paper of the Institute of Electrical and Electronics Engineers in *Public Policy Implications of Advanced Television Systems*, p. 528; Schreiber, pp. 6, 20; statement of Kenneth Phillips of the Committee of Corporate Telecommunications Users, in U.S. Congress, House, Committee on Science, Space, and Technology, *High Definition Television, Hearings Before the Subcommittee on International Scientific Cooperation*, 101st Cong., May 31, 1989, n.p.; Statement of Joel Chaseman, chairman of the Association of Maximum Service Telecasters in *High Definition Television, Hearings*, May 31, 1989, n.p.; U.S. Federal Communications Commission, *Tentative Decision and Further Notice of Inquiry in the Matter of Advanced Television Systems and Their Impact on the Existing Television Broadcast Service*, MM Docket No. 87-268 (Washington, D.C.: Government Printing Office, 1988), pp. 5, 10, 48.

35. *High Definition Television, Hearings*, June 23, 1988, pp. 258–61, 268.

36. George Gilder, *Microcosm: The Quantum Revolution in Economics and Technology* (New York: Simon & Schuster, 1989), pp. 311, 315; *High Definition Television, Hearings*, Sept. 7, 1988, p. 373; "Manning the Barricades for Free TV," *Broadcasting*, April 24, 1989, p. 27; position paper of the National Association of Broadcasters in *Public Policy Implications of Advanced Television Systems*, pp. 603, 607; *High Definition Television, Hearings*, October 8, 1987, pp. 79–81; "Prime Time Push for Free TV," July 24, 1989, p. 34; Ben Bagdikian, *The Media Monopoly*, 2nd ed. (Boston: Beacon Press, 1987), pp. 92, 134, 219–221; J. Abramson, F. Arterton, and G. Orren, *The Electronic Commonwealth: The Impact of New Media Technologies on Democratic Politics* (New York: Basic Books), p. 120; Ronald Hawkins, "Through the Future Brightly," *Cable Television Business*, March 1, 1989, p. 45; and *Telecom 2000*, pp. 501, 548–49; *High Definition Television, Hearings*, October 8, 1987, pp. 79–81.

37. See also "The Grace Under Pressure of Jim Mooney," p. 36.

38. *High Definition Television, Hearings*, June 23, 1988, p. 266, and *Second Interim Report on Advanced Television Service*.

39. Geller, pp. 328–330.

40. For discussions of media monopolies and limitations to free speech in today's media, see Brand, p. 207; Laura Landro, "Viacom Is Suing Time, Alleging Trust Violations," *Wall Street Journal,* May 10, 1989, sec. A, p. 3; Harry Shooshan, "Cable Television: Promoting a Competitive Industry Structure," in *New Directions in Telecommunications Policy,* p. 235; Pool, p. 102; Bagdikian, pp. 21, 236–237.

41. Pool, pp. 76, 84, 172, 183, 224–225, 236. Although writing largely of cable television, Pool clearly intends his remarks for both this medium and its inevitable successors. See also Anita Wallgren, "Video Program Distribution and Cable Television: Current Policy Issues and Recommendations," in U.S. Department of Commerce, National Telecommunications and Information Administration, *National Telecommunications and Information Administration Report,* NTIA Special Publication 88-233 (Washington, D.C.: Government Printing Office, 1988), pp. i, 37–39, 54–58.

42. Pool, p. 106.

43. In fact, such a common carrier system was proposed in 1970 for cable television, but critics felt that such a system "would not provide enough economic incentive to potential companies." See Pool, p. 169.

44. Dale Hatfield and Gene Ax, "The Opportunity Costs of Spectrum Allocated to High Definition Television" (New York: Center for Telecommunications and Information Studies, Columbia University, 1988).

45. E.g., see Joe Sharkey, "Newspaper Publishers Debate Pros, Cons of Allying With Phone Firms," *Wall Street Journal,* April 26, 1989, sec. B, p. 6, and Charles Mason, "Greene Rejects Bell Info Plans, Harshly Criticizes Companies," *Telephony,* June 19, 1989, p. 10.

46. *Telecom 2000,* p. 432.

47. A convincing argument can be made that in the short term the phone companies could help jump start the consumer-information services with their substantial financial clout. Unfortunately, once such rights are given, it's very hard to take them away. For example, in the 1970s many argued that cable companies should be given control over the content of their programming, but only until the cable business was well established. Today, the now well established cable companies would be outraged if anyone suggested they should lose their control of programming.

48. No one, in fact, is proposing that the phone companies should become our sole source of information. But if the phone companies are allowed to provide information, the temptation would be very strong for them to put competitors using their lines at a disadvantage.

49. Sheila Kaplan, p. 328.

50. E.g., See Robert Cohen and Kenneth Donow, *Telecommunications Policy, High Definition Television, and U.S. Competitiveness* (Washington, D.C.: Economic Policy Institute, 1989), p. 3.

CHAPTER 12

The Information Agent Ideal: Independent Consumer-Information Companies

Imagine a society without trust. Indeed, it is impossible to imagine. As one philosopher put it, "Trust is a social good to be protected just as much as the air we breathe or the water we drink. When it is damaged, the community as a whole suffers, and when it is destroyed, societies falter and collapse. . . . Trust [is] the foundation of relations among human beings."[1]

One of the primary roles of government is to provide institutions that foster trust among consumers and producers. This role partially explains why we have contract laws (for buyers and sellers), conflict-of-interest laws (for judges and politicians), and labeling laws (for foods and many other goods). In contrast, given ineffective legal systems and unenforceable contracts, buyers and sellers in parts of the Third World often have to spend weeks getting to know and trust each other before making even a simple deal. This inefficient system virtually precludes an advanced economy. Similarly, rules against bribery and conflicts of interest, and regulations that promote financial disclosure for bureaucrats, judges, and politicians, lessen the abuse of power. Governments that lack such legal requirements not only tend to be more corrupt but also tend to impede the development of efficient marketplaces.

Trust is also desperately needed in the exchange of information. In the future, third parties (I.C.I.C.s) that are truly independent will need to be able to distinguish themselves. As we have seen in Chapter 9, conventional media (newspapers, magazines, radio, TV) constantly assert complete objectivity despite well-documented advertiser-directed biases.

Not surprisingly, when someone who is truly objective makes such a claim, no one believes it. Thus, it doesn't pay to be truly objective in today's media, although it will always pay to appear to be objective.

Concern for the appearance of objectivity leads the truly trustworthy product-rating organizations, such as Consumers Union, to prohibit all commercial enterprises from advertising favorable ratings. Advertisers love to exploit favorable recommendations by so-called objective sources—they love to claim that their products were "recommended by the American Heart Association," "recommended by J. D. Powers," "recommended by *Consumer Reports*," or "recommended by the American Bar Association"—but such claims may suggest some direct or indirect payoff. Indeed, most of today's so-called ratings organizations are biased by the money they receive from their advertisers. An extreme example would be *Good Housekeeping*, which actually gets paid to give out its seal of approval but does not emphasize that fact to consumers. Fortunately, *Consumer Reports* persuaded the New York State legislature to pass a special clause in the New York Business Law statute barring unauthorized use of a non-profit's name in advertising. No such laws exist, however, to prevent similar abuse of a for-profit's good name. The very idea of "for-profit," in fact, suggests bias to many consumers, perhaps because until now the media corporations have been riddled with conflicts of interests—advertising, pay-offs, sharing of stock, overlap of boards, and the like.

Such unsavory links will make it very difficult to trust the recommendations offered by the independent consumer-information companies, the organizations described in Chapter 10. And if we don't trust these private, for-profit companies to share our interests, if we don't assume that they are unbiased and that they research their recommendations thoroughly, we won't want to buy their information. Conversely, if consumers knew that they could trust certain information companies, they would feel a lot more confident employing them.

To make it profitable to provide high-quality information, people must first be convinced that the information is in fact of high quality. If consumers are too confused or ignorant to assess the quality of information, however, they will tend to distrust all I.C.I.C.s. However diverse and unbiased our sources of information, if we don't trust those sources, no I.C.I.C., however honest, will be able to survive. For similar reasons, people generally welcome unexplained recommendations from friends, whom they trust, but require hard evidence to back the claims of today's media, whom they don't trust. Consumers will not be able to have the perspective they demand without a mechanism to instill trust in I.C.I.C.s, a mechanism which allows them to present unbiased and expert judgments without having to present all the overwhelming details.

Despite the enthusiasm throughout the computing and publishing industry today for intelligent "agents," of which our I.C.I.C.s represent one variety, the issue of credibility is usually overlooked. None of the technological forecasters have thought carefully about which type of companies or people will run these agencies, how such agencies will obtain their "expert" information, nor how consumers will differentiate unscrupulous or inept sources from trustworthy and competent ones. Here, therefore, we propose a possible mechanism: certifying those third parties (I.C.I.C.s) that meet financial-disclosure and conflict-of-interest requirements.

THE CERTIFICATION OF I.C.I.C.S

The designation of a certified I.C.I.C.—either through the government or an independent association—could be a useful marketing tool for companies and seal of approval for consumers.[2] A procedure to certify I.C.I.C.s would not only provide a minimum quality threshold for consumer information but also foster an important new consumer service. Such certification would not preclude companies with conflicts of interest from offering information but would show the public which information sources have strong incentives to present a systematically colored viewpoint.

Here's the type of plan that could help us achieve this goal. Congress could recognize a new class of company called "independent consumer-information companies" (I.C.I.C.s). To merit this classification, companies would have to satisfy certain criteria: (1) they must finance their information without any advertising dollars; (2) they must receive no money from the owner of any product they analyze; and (3) I.C.I.C. owners (anyone holding, say, 5 percent or more of stock) and any employee engaged in rating particular products must be free of conflicts of interest—specifically, none of these people or members of their immediate families could hold stock in a company that their I.C.I.C. assesses.

Many of these conflict-of-interest restrictions are simply extensions of what is already required from senior government employees.[3] Admittedly, a certain degree of government involvement is the price we must pay for improved consumer information. Fortunately, the small set of laws involved in the proposed certification process would allow us to eliminate the tens of thousands of pages of laws now governing virtually every aspect of advertising and promotion. In this way, the I.C.I.C.s can be compared to the computer, which allowed us to replace thousands of specialized machines with a few smart ones.

The idea of regulating product reviewers rather than product providers is not new. Economist Benjamin Shimberg, for example, has proposed that one way to deal with the gross abuses of the Byzantine occupational-licensing system by health professionals is to abolish such licensing and replace it with a system that licenses the hospitals that hire these people. With this approach, hospitals would hire doctors and other health professionals based on their skill and performance, and medical institutions that couldn't prove they have employed qualified practitioners would lose their license.[4] Applying the same concept to agents who provided consumer information would allow us to eliminate all selling restrictions on such groups as the funeral, eyeglass, consumer-electronics, clothing, and food industries. It would allow us to eliminate the archaic and ineffectual licensing and certification laws for more than eight hundred occupations. It would allow us to take consumer protection out of the hands of the lawyers and the politicians and put it back into the free-enterprise system. As I.C.I.C.s gain a foothold, moreover, many of the specific recommendations below will become unnecessary, or can be passed to just a few of the highest-level rating organizations, which, in turn, will ensure the trustworthiness of everyone else.

SPECIAL   EXEMPTIONS   FOR   I.C.I.C.S

In the interest of ensuring the full functioning of I.C.I.C.s, and, thereby, high-quality consumer information, companies might get certain privileges in return for the designation I.C.I.C., just as other regulated entities, such as banks, non-profit organizations, and licensed occupations, receive special government benefits (as well as special responsibilities) in the name of the public good.[5]

LIMITED LEGAL FEES.

I.C.I.C.s undoubtedly are going to say things that certain manufacturers and retailers and service companies—the low-quality or dishonest ones in particular—don't want to hear. Even though I.C.I.C.s will be expected to exercise due diligence in verifying their information, litigation that results from unfavorable product reviews may cost enough to set back seriously the growth of the I.C.I.C. industry. At least in its early years, I.C.I.C.s will not have the tens of millions of dollars that the large manufacturers and retailers will be able to devote to such judicial battles.

The government must protect the small consumer-information companies—ones operating in good faith and that have strenuously avoided conflicts of interest—from being harassed by the larger companies they evaluate. To do so, we must modify our conception of limited liability. Today, corporations are granted limited liability in that investors are liable only up to the amount of their investment. This principle is important for failing corporations because it holds that only the assets of a corporation, not the personal assets of its owners, can be liquidated to cover the corporation's debts. Independent consumer-information companies, by virtue of their freedom from conflicts of interest, might be granted a sort of limited liability, too. Courts could routinely force prosecuting companies to pay legal fees for the small consumer-information companies if their suits are found to be groundless. In addition, penalties for losing a suit should not be crippling. Just as retailers and manufacturers are only slapped on the wrist by consumer agencies for deceptive advertising, so too should the new consumer-information companies be able to survive a mistake or an indiscretion. In other words, just as the laws against deceptive advertising are designed primarily to stop deceptive advertising and get the truth out to the public quickly, rather than to collect punitive damages, so too should the focus of the libel law in regard to I.C.I.C.s be to obtain public correction of errors.[6]

REVISED POSTAL RATES.

As third-party information providers, I.C.I.C.s share many characteristics with today's media. They simply rely on an as-yet-unrecognized medium: the computerized, intelligent database and the reports and analyses it generates. Before the full implementation of Omnimedia, many of these are being sent through the mail like periodicals. Unlike periodicals as we know them today, however, these reports and analyses are customized to the individual consumer and are thus disqualified from the postal discounts afforded to second-class (high-volume, periodic) mailings. The rationale for postal discounts is that dissemination of information is an important value for society, and periodicals, especially those with minimal advertising, are thought to be particularly effective in this context.[7] But the criteria for second-class (and bulk) mailings are out of step with modern technology, once you consider that customized information is inherently of higher utility than high-volume periodical information. From this perspective, any information generated without advertising support merits the status of at least second-class and possibly even non-profit status.

REVISED RETAILER PROPERTY RIGHTS.

In many situations, the I.C.I.C.s envisioned here will serve as representatives for consumers. They will interpret manufacturers' literature for them. They will evaluate brands and features. And they will even shop for them by going into the stores and checking availability, prices, and sales practices.

Unfortunately, under current laws, I.C.I.C.s cannot represent consumers effectively because they can be asked to leave stores even if they are there to collect information for potential customers. Although it's illegal for retailers to evict people from their premises for reasons of race or sex, as private companies they retain every right to ask people to leave for any other reason—including disruptive behavior, inappropriate dress, or simple antipathy. Because some store managers and salespeople feel threatened by anyone scrupulously compiling pricing information—often suspecting that the collector represents a competitor—they often badger such people continually or ask them to leave. Representatives from our own consumer-information service were often escorted from stores merely for writing down prices and model numbers—ostensibly public information to which any shopper should have access.

A law which would allow consumers and their representatives, I.C.I.C.s, to gather model and pricing information freely, as long as this process does not disrupt stores, would substantially reduce the cost of gathering such information. Obviously, allowing I.C.I.C.s to do such work would also save the individual shopper tremendous amounts of time and energy.

STRENGTHENED INFORMATION PROPERTY LAWS.

At present our attitudes towards information are analogous to the attitudes toward usury and privately owned land during the Middle Ages. Can we imagine a society today where it is acceptable or even praiseworthy to usurp land? Can we imagine a society that considers it unethical and extortionist to charge interest on loans? Modern ideas toward private property and usury took hundreds of years to develop. For the sake of our society, we should make it a high priority to make sure that it doesn't take the same amount of time to develop modern attitudes toward information.

If the so-called information age is ever to near its full potential, we need to accept that information is both easily and frequently stolen unless, as with other property, there are penalties and social opprobrium for stealing it. Indeed, as long as information can be stolen as easily as it is, its quality will be unnecessarily low.[8] It is like the bane of socialism: take away property rights and you kill the desire to work and produce goods for everyone's greater benefit. If I.C.I.C.s are going to succeed, we need to structure a set of laws protecting information that allows the full motivating force of private property to come into play.

Although patent and copyright laws are designed to motivate those who develop intellectual property, these tools cannot, as they presently exist, provide adequate property incentives for I.C.I.C.s and others in the new age of easily copied and interactive information. This is not such a serious problem for time-sensitive data (such as those on fast-changing computers or consumer electronics) or data with clearly copyrightable components (such as test results) or data embedded in a complex database incorporating artificial intelligence (such as an on-line expert program that acts as an artificial legal advisor), but it's a problem for the data covering most of today's products and situations where these natural market protections are less applicable. New mechanisms must be developed to motivate entrepreneurs to provide a socially optimal level of information.

Other than strengthening the copyright laws, one such mechanism would be to limit the number of licenses granted to certain kinds of I.C.I.C.s. By restricting information providers in areas particularly prone to information stealing, the incentives for producing high-quality information could be enhanced significantly. For example, we might limit the number of I.C.I.C.s licensed to cover products with high upfront research costs and easy-to-copy research results. This principle is adopted in many other areas of the economy. For example, cities limit the number of medallions awarded to taxi drivers. Similarly, each metropolitan area limits to two the number of cellular-phone competitors.

I . C . I . C . S   A N D   T H E   B A L A N C E   O F   P O W E R

With all these special concessions, it seems reasonable to ask if we are making I.C.I.C.s too powerful. Such a concern, however, stems from a basic misunderstanding of the power imbalance that already exists. Today's seller-based product-information system is already quite concentrated, leaving tremendous power in the hands of very few. For example, most categories of consumer products are made by only a handful of companies.[9] Nor is this seller-based concentration an isolated phenomenon: for the entire United States—including industrial-product manufacturers—just six hundred companies own 75 percent of total manufacturing assets.[10] These companies not only manufacture their products: they are the prime source of information about their wares.

Other vital areas of information in our society are already highly concentrated. The few major national TV networks, for example, profoundly influence our attitudes toward national news and politics. The one or two newspapers that dominate most metropolitan areas similarly influence local events. And when colleges want to assess student abilities, they rely heavily on the judgments of the two independent educational testing organizations which administer the SAT and ACT. Despite this tremendous concentration of power, neither students nor colleges seem to object.

In contrast, we envision that in the future there will be many thousands of influential I.C.I.C.s, many of which will evaluate the same product. For example, we can imagine hundreds of doctors setting themselves up as independent consumer-information companies for pain relievers; contrast these to the less than six drug companies that provide most of today's pharmaceutical information.[11] Clearly, the power of I.C.I.C.s is likely to be less concentrated than the power of advertisers.

Of course, in certain areas we expect only a few competing I.C.I.C.s. But here note that many organizations that essentially serve as I.C.I.C.s to businesses today have scrupulously avoided abuse of power despite their lack of extensive competition. For example, companies that advertise on TV rely almost solely on Nielsen ratings to determine the size and quality of TV audiences. Arbitron and the Audit Bureau of Circulations, other highly concentrated information sources, provide similar information for magazines, newspapers, and radio, quite valuable to advertisers who would shudder to return to the days when the media reported its own circulation figures. Dun & Bradstreet (which rates corporate creditworthiness) and Moody's (which rates corporate bonds) also are single-source rating organizations which wield huge power within the business world and yet are viewed as indispensable. As long as information providers deliver good, objective, and reasonably priced information, companies don't seem to have any trouble with this system.

I.C.I.C.s could also lend important balance to government policy-making by providing an institutional mechanism by which the consumer's inherently weak and distracted voice in government is transformed into a potent force and effective check on producers. Such a balance between consumer and producer interests conceivably could also increase confidence in government and encourage new policy initiatives. There has been a lot of talk in recent years about the need for industrial policy in the United States, an idea spurred on by the success of Japan's policy of favoring and sometimes subsidizing specific industries such as supercomputers, semiconductors, and high-definition TV. The major objection in this country to industrial policy has been that companies and industries will be picked on the basis of their political clout rather than their merit. By providing a valuable source of expert and nonbiased opinion about companies' past performance, I.C.I.C.s could help screen out meritorious companies.

Finally, note that there should be less government protection of these information companies than might appear at first glance, because they will be regulating each other. This is the way it might work: Under the certifying provisions, I.C.I.C.s would be required to disclose their conflict-of-interest information. Certain companies, which we might call "I.C.I.C.s squared" or $I.C.I.C.^2$, would be certified solely to rate other I.C.I.C.s. They would notify the government if any consumer-information company seemed to be withholding information required by law. The government's primary enforcement role would be implementing conflict-of-interest regulations at the top of the information-company pyramid. The idea would be that if the top of the pyramid is in good shape, this would percolate down, through the principle of self-interest, to the lower levels. In fact, there could be three layers of independent consumer-information companies: I.C.I.C.s that rate actual products, $I.C.I.C.s^2$ that rate I.C.I.C.s, and $I.C.I.C.s^3$ ("cubed I.C.I.C.s") that rate I.C.I.C.s^2. In practice, I.C.I.C.s^2 would probably be limited to covering a single industry, whereas I.C.I.C.s^3 would simply be in the business of covering I.C.I.C.s^2, that is, information companies that don't directly cover products. As the system matures, when searching for advice, consumers presumably would start at the top of the pyramid. That is, they would focus their efforts on choosing I.C.I.C.s^3, which in turn would recommend more specific I.C.I.C.s.

Having different layers of independent consumer-information companies will reduce conflicts of interest between them. That is, I.C.I.C.s will be more inclined to recommend a consumer to another I.C.I.C.—one at a lower level—because none of these will be potential competitors. Different levels will foster the development of many smaller I.C.I.C.s. Otherwise, information companies might become like brand names and become very large when consumers lack the knowledge or trust necessary to support many different "brand-named" I.C.I.C.s.

In short, the purpose of the I.C.I.C. is to rectify the power imbalance—the knowledge imbalance—between consumers and sellers. The goal is to give each side of a transaction equal power by reducing the costs of searching for product information.

1. Sissela Bok, *Lying* (New York: Vintage Books, 1978), pp. 26–27, 31.

2. E.g., see Stewart Brand, *The Media Lab: Inventing the Future at MIT* (New York: Penguin Books, 1987), p. 205.

3. Jeff Gerth, *New York Times*, March 19, 1989, p. 5 and Jeffrey H. Birnbaum, "Lawmakers Have Become Supercautious as Ethics Obsession Sweeps Capital Hill," *Wall Street Journal*, May 18, 1989, sec. A, p. 18.

4. Benjamin Shimberg, "What's the Future of Licensing," address before the American Occupational Therapy Association Conference "1990 and Beyond: The National Agenda for State Regulation of Occupational Therapy," October 14, 1989, pp. 16–18. See also Clark Havighurst, "Practice Opportunities for Allied Health Professionals," paper prepared for the American Society of Allied Health Professions Critical Issues Conference, June 15–16, 1987, pp. 11, 17–18, 20.

5. This chapter presupposes the I.C.I.C.s will have at their disposal NIPI-like data. But in the event that I.C.I.C.s have to go into stores and contact manufacturers directly to collect such information, then the following regulations will be required: (1) clearly labeled model numbers and prices by stores, (2) the legal right to visit stores and gather such information without the threat of being asked to leave the premises, (3) equal access to all manufacturer information that is supplied to other I.C.I.C.s, (4) printed literature from manufacturers that describes (a) every model they currently sell, (b) the model's features, and (c) the exact method by which those features were measured. Given that NIPI-like institutions will probably take longer to develop than I.C.I.C.s, and that these simple rules will vastly improve the economic feasibility of I.C.I.C.s, we strongly recommend that they be implemented immediately. The consequence of not doing so will be that sellers continue to restrict access to vital information that impedes the efficient operation of the marketplace. For example, anyone who goes into a store to collect large

amounts of model and price information is highly visible. When we ran our own I.C.I.C.-like information service and attempted to collect this information, store managers often would expel us. They did not want their pricing information to become widely available. The result is that we had to hire specially skilled employees and surreptitiously collect this information at great expense to ourselves and our customers.

6. For a detailed discussion of the type of libel law reform we think is necessary, see "The Report of the Libel Reform Project" by the Annenberg Washington Program, Communications Policy Studies, Northwestern University, 1988. This report, put together by a blue-ribbon panel of lawyers, judges, and policymakers, argues that the emphasis of libel law should be on getting the truth out rather than on awarding punitive damages. Our view is that libel law regarding corporations and products should be the same as libel law regarding public figures. See also Richard Poster, "Truth in Advertising: The Role of Government," in ed. Yale Brozen, *Advertising and Society* (New York: New York University Press, 1974), p. 120.

7. E.g., see Ithiel de Sola Pool, *Technologies of Freedom: On Free Speech in an Electronic Age* (Cambridge, Mass.: Harvard University Press, 1983), pp. 17, 20.

8. Douglas Greer, *Industrial Organization and Public Policy,* 2nd ed. (London: Macmillan, 1988), p. 85.

9. Richard Lipsey, Peter Steiner, and Douglas Purvis, *Economics,* 8th ed. (New York: Harper and Row, 1987), p. 265.

10. Ibid., p. 310.

11. Today's pharmaceutical companies spend more than a billion dollars a year advertising drugs. If 250 doctors each earned $400,000 a year as pharmaceutical I.C.I.C.s, that would come to only $100 million a year. Clearly, given the thirty-second commercials which now dominate pharmaceutical advertising, such I.C.I.C.s would have little trouble providing a superior information product.

The Information Clearinghouse Ideal: The National Institutes of Product Information

Never before has it been technologically so easy and inexpensive to gather information about goods and services. Yet because our institutions have not kept up with changing technology, what should be easy and inexpensive is actually quite difficult and uneconomical. Without a government-sanctioned centralized authority, it is difficult to gather efficiently certain types of factual information, such as gross national product (GNP), company financial data, and census data. The situation is similar for certain types of product information. In this chapter we argue that a revolution in product-tracking technology makes it feasible to institute a new institutional structure: a government-sanctioned, quasi-private organization called the National Institutes of Product Information, or NIPI, from which I.C.I.C.s would purchase the raw factual data on which they'd base their shopping recommendations to consumers.[1]

Each major consumer industry—for example, hard goods, travel, health care, legal, or finance—would have its own institute responsible for collecting and disseminating data about that particular industry. Although these institutes wouldn't be the *sole* source of product information for I.C.I.C.s, they would constitute a vital component, offering facts about features and selling costs, reliability, and customer satisfaction as appropriate to the industry involved. On occasion I.C.I.C.s might still collect facts about products. But their more important role would be to provide perspective—to integrate and interpret NIPI and other data so as to develop specific recommendations. The efficiencies and otherwise unavailable factual information provided by the National Institutes of Product Information would allow independent consumer-information companies to both charge less and provide better information.[2]

NIPI meets a kind of need that sellers and buyers have already recognized for years: one-stop shopping. The ease and convenience of all merchandise and information about that merchandise under one roof has been a major reason for the widespread development of trade shows (for industrial buyers) and shopping malls (for consumers). Indeed, if corporate America's trade shows suddenly disappeared, the resulting difficulty of information exchange would cripple the economy. Centralizing shopping data particularly benefits industries characterized by a relatively large group of small, scattered companies or individuals (i.e., weak sellers) who are selling to an organized and knowledgeable group of consumers or I.C.I.C.-type agents (i.e., strong buyers). It's readily imaginable, for example, that young, unestablished professionals such as doctors, lawyers, or morticians would want to band together and make their rates and services publicly accessible. Indeed, once such a network is established, those that don't belong to it are significantly disadvantaged. Once a NIPI-like organization is created, and consumers start to use the organization to make product choices, all sellers that expect to stay in business will feel obliged to contribute their own product's specifications. Consumers reasonably assume that anyone who doesn't belong to the organization must have an inferior product. Thus, they don't feel like they're missing much when they don't even consider buying from such companies. Besides, those companies' products will be more costly because of increased search costs associated with finding them.

You can see this logic in action at any major trade show. At such shows fifteen vendors can be selling virtually identical products. Yet it is in the interest of such vendors, especially the ones with undeserved reputations for superior value, to make it as difficult as possible for customers to comparison shop. The reason they participate in the trade shows is that customers force them to. Making it easier for customers to comparison shop is the price they must pay to get any business at all.

A question now arises, however: what will happen to this principle of one-stop shopping in an electronic world? Most obviously, vendors will have an incentive to provide their product information via on-line computerized shopping systems (as many already do) to allow easier consumer access. But they will also have an incentive to have this information about their products gathered in a single national database because that will be most convenient for consumers seeking one-stop shopping. What will be created, in effect, are comprehensive, electronic, industrywide information clearinghouses.

We can already see these grass roots electronic information clearinghouses developing, and we can expect to see more of them as the logic of the new information technology works itself out. Some of these clearinghouses involve improving older collections of data, while others are brand-new clearinghouses that have been made possible by the ease of collecting, manipulating, and disseminating data on a computer. Perhaps the airlines provide the most vivid example of a newly established information clearinghouse using electronic technology: such NIPI-like systems as SABRE centralize all pricing and flight descriptions in a computerized database and then distribute them to the personal computers of travel agents via a modem. The real estate industry also relies on an advanced NIPI-like entity: the Multiple Listing Service (MLS). This service, available electronically to real estate brokers, has detailed specifications on all homes for sale in a given geographic market.

Unfortunately, though such private, centralized databases will proliferate, much information of great value will still not be collected. Many sellers with monopoly power will undoubtedly find it in their interest to withhold information from clearinghouses unless the government forces these sellers to participate. Furthermore, without government sanctions, even companies that voluntarily participate in clearinghouses may have an incentive for submitting false or misleading data. The private clearinghouses themselves could have a tendency to present data in a way that favors their most powerful members. Such considerations, along with the possibilities of the new information technology, have led government to develop increasing numbers of information clearinghouses.

Some of these government-sponsored clearinghouses have been around for many years. One of the most important is the Security and Exchange Commission's financial-disclosure requirements, which since 1934 have obligated all public companies in the United States to submit detailed and clearly defined financial statements. These statements, made available to the public, serve as a vital and credible source of information for individuals who recommend or purchase financial securities. In 1987 plans were put in place to completely automate the collection and dissemination of this information by the mid-1990s. In the late 1980s, another government agency, the U.S. Department of Transportation, began collecting from major airlines data about flight delay, lost baggage, and overbooking, data which the transportation department considered to be of vital interest to the flying public but which airlines would not provide voluntarily. Prior to embarking on this course, the transportation department had already imposed stringent regulations on the airlines' own private information clearinghouses (i.e., reservation systems), which generally present information in a way that favors large airlines. The transportation department now requires airlines to submit this information in a machine-readable format for every flight flown in the United States and then makes it available to the public in three forms: (*a*) a monthly written report which summarizes the findings about each airline, (*b*) a special code next to every flight in the airlines' on-line directory that reveals the on-time performance of that flight, and (*c*) a magnetic tape the government sells for $150 that includes all the information about every flight in the United States for any given month. A much smaller (and less successful) information clearinghouse established by the federal government is the Interstate Commerce Commission's collection of data about moving companies. The ICC requires that movers involved in interstate transport submit a performance report every year which includes such information as the total number of shipments, the percentage shipped on time, the percentage not exceeding the mover's written quotation, and the percentage not resulting in damage claims.

Perhaps nowhere is industry opposition to these government clearinghouses more apparent than in the health-care industry.[3] In April 1985 the U.S. Department of Health and Human Services instituted a rule requiring the public dissemination of its existing mortality data involving Medicare patients. The rule preserves the privacy of the doctor-patient relationship but makes it possible to identify grossly incompetent practitioners and hospitals. One particularly striking use of this data has been in comparing the relative success of different hospitals and doctors who perform open-heart surgery. In his book *Heart Failure*, Thomas J. Moore uses this data to show how in 1984 two hospitals, virtually identical in their patient demographics, differed in their mortality rate from open-heart surgery by a ratio of more than 15 to 1. While the one hospital, in New York, had a mortality rate of 15.2 percent, the comparable hospital, in California, had a mortality rate of less than 1 percent. After much investigation, the New York hospital replaced its primary open-heart surgeon, and the next year its mortality rate dropped to 1.8 percent, almost identical to the rate in the comparable California hospital. Without the NIPI-like data about surgical success rates, the New York hospital may never have spotted its own poor performance, and dozens of additional patients probably would have died unnecessarily each year.[4]

Physicians and hospitals have come up with dozens of plausible excuses as to why such data are inaccurate and subject to misinterpretation, but the glaring fact is that centralized collection and dissemination through a NIPI-like organization potentially saves thousands of lives each year. In addition, flawed as it may be, generally accessible data facilitates comparison shopping, and can reduce health-care costs for patients and their employers. Furthermore, such systems to help identify and reward hospitals and practitioners who have excelled and would otherwise go unrecognized.

Of course, to achieve such benefits, it's not enough to collect and disseminate data: users must analyze the data and then act. The trouble here is that individual consumers simply don't have sufficient time, ability, or even interest in any one product or service to sift through masses of data, however great that data's potential value. This fact may explain why the ICC data on movers, used primarily by people who are planning to move, receive relatively little use, while the SEC data on companies, used primarily by research analysts, brokers, and professional investors, receive relatively more scrutiny. This fact also explains why any information clearinghouses, whether in the forms existing today or in the form of the unified NIPI we propose, will work best in conjunction with independent I.C.I.C.s that have the competence and motivation to interpret masses of data.

The close connection between information clearinghouses and information agents (I.C.I.C.s) has led us to believe that the most effective clearinghouse should be neither public nor private, but a unique hybrid of the two. As a quasi-government institution, NIPI will be able to access much of the information that private enterprise has hitherto managed to keep proprietary. At the same time, as a quasi-private and self-supporting organization, NIPI will allow us to eliminate many of the problems inherent in a government agency discussed earlier in the book. Indeed, NIPI, a key part of the information infrastructure and consumerism of the future, could replace many existing government regulatory agencies and government-sanctioned self-regulatory organizations such as licensing boards.

The specific proposal below is for a hybrid government-private information clearinghouse covering retail transactions and manufactured hard goods. Whether or not all the details are practical or can be universally applied, the proposal hints at the vast possibilities now opening up for efficiently gathering the vital facts that consumers and even sellers have always dreamed of possessing.

THE TECHNOLOGICAL FOUNDATION FOR NIPI

The last decade has witnessed a revolution in product-tracking technology, which automates every transaction and every decision related to buying, selling, and distribution from manufacturer to retailer to consumer. It's impossible to pick up a retailer or manufacturer trade journal today, in fact, without finding some article about the "revolutionary" implications of this technology.[5] The message is clear: anyone who hasn't completely automated product-tracking technology by the mid-1990s is not going to make it in the competitive consumer-product markets of the future.

This product-tracking technology has a second side to it, however, largely unknown by retailers and manufacturers. It completely changes the cost-to-benefit equation for huge areas of consumer protection.

Some of the most important new product tracking technologies relevant to a national information clearinghouse include machine-readable universal product codes, computerized price lookup, electronic data interchange, and the computerized UPC catalog.

MACHINE-READABLE UNIVERSAL PRODUCT CODES (UPCs).

Perhaps the most fundamental change in product tracking today is "automatic identification," the most ubiquitous example of which is the preprinted bar code, a pattern of vertical lines, that can be "read" by point-of-purchase computers. Almost every large retailer in the United States currently sells products marked with these codes. In fact, it is difficult today to go into a store and find an item not marked in this way. Each coded model sold in the United States has a unique UPC number. The General Merchandise and Apparel Implementation Committee of the Uniform Code Council (UCC) first assigns each manufacturer a unique identifying number. The manufacturer is then responsible for assigning each of the models he sells a number of its own. It is only the combination of the two numbers—the manufacturer's ID number and the model ID number—that makes up a unique identifier for each product in the United

States. With UPCs, retailers can avoid adding a second number (a private number, known in the industry as a stock-keeping-unit, or SKU, number) to all their merchandise, thus saving ticketing and administrative costs.

Wireless automatic identification, also known as radio frequency identification (RFID), is the next logical advance, and one that will eventually replace printed bar codes. As one retail publication describes it, sellers place a small, totally passive tag or circuit on a product, which, when it passes through an electromagnetic field of a specific frequency, emits a radio frequency signal that can be read by a detection device. The information on the tag is read without any physical contact or line-of-sight access to the tag reader or detector.[6] This system allows customers the convenience of simply walking through a given space while all product-identification material is gathered automatically, and it allows sellers to eliminate the manual labor now required to add up products at the cash register.

COMPUTERIZED PRICE LOOKUP (PLU).

PLU is a computerized table used by virtually all stores that employ universal product codes. The table matches a UPC-marked product with its corresponding price so that once the computer reads the UPC it can automatically generate the price.

ELECTRONIC DATA INTERCHANGE (EDI).

UPCs and PLU make it easy to computerize sales and inventory information down to the level of the individual transaction. EDI makes it possible for sellers to transmit immediately this information to others throughout the distribution process, using a combination of computers and telecommunications. With EDI, chain headquarters can know on a daily basis exactly what is selling in every store. Vendors can order supplies and pay bills from outside suppliers and central warehouses without the slowness and cost of manual systems. Almost every major manufacturer and retailer in the United States today is using EDI. Says John Roach, chief executive officer of the Tandy Corporation: "Every morning I know how many products by model, by price, by gross margin were sold the previous day."[7]

THE COMPUTERIZED UPC CATALOG.

This is one of the newest retailer and manufacturer technologies, first implemented in 1988 on a relatively small scale but expected eventually to become a central part of every major manufacturer's and retailer's product-tracking strategy. This catalog, maintained by two major computerized information providers (QRS and GE Information Services), records every UPC on the market as well as key information about the item, such as whether it is still being sold. Today's large retailers stock tens of thousand of different items from different manufacturers. Manufacturers may sell to hundreds or thousands of different retailers and are constantly introducing new products and new variations on old ones (e.g., new sizes, flavors, and packages). Not only is it inefficient for manufacturers to send this information separately to each retailer, but it's also equally inconvenient for retailers to deal with separate information from all these manufacturers. The universal catalog makes life simpler for everyone, since manufacturers need only send out information once and retailers need only go to one source to update completely the status of all products they're selling or might want to sell. This catalog is supposed to be improved continually, eventually including not only detailed product features but also pictures.[8]

SCOPE OF INFORMATION

New technologies such as universal product codes, computerized price lookup, electronic data exchange, and the computerized UPC catalogs will make it easy and economical to collect extensive data about all sorts of selling practices. To prevent possible government control of public opinion, however, NIPI would be limited to gathering factual information such as dates, prices, store names, brand names, model numbers, serial numbers, and general customer satisfaction indices. Serving strictly as an information clearinghouse, it would sell and license this factual information to other institutions, such as I.C.I.C.s, which could then interpret, enhance, and resell the data as they saw fit. Specifically, using electronic means of collection, NIPI could gather and disseminate four basic types of information: (1) purchases, (2) customer satisfaction, (3) post-purchase service, and (4) features. Initially, it may only be feasible to gather a limited set of this information, increasing the amount as technology progresses and as stores and manufacturers increasingly automate order entry and inventory systems. For example, NIPI could start by simply collecting a limited set of purchase information from large stores. Alternatively, it could start by collecting purchase and customer satisfaction information concerning mail-order purchases.

Purchase information would include selling price, selling date, final seller trade name and location (i.e., zip code), and customer zip code (for non-cash transactions). For goods, it would also include manufacturer name, brand name, model number, and serial number. For services it would include service type (e.g., funeral, mail-order transaction, or life insurance policy). Such information, as well as customer satisfaction information, could be gathered for all consumer goods excepting those costing less than a token amount (e.g., $1) and nonstandard, nonpackaged, or one-of-a-kind merchandise such as produce, restaurant meals, and antiques. It could also be gathered for a small number of services such as funerals, life insurance policies, car insurance policies, and mail-order transactions to gauge customer satisfaction.

Service information would be particularly relevant for mass-produced products that run on electricity, battery power, or fossil fuels and have substantial (e.g., over $20) retail values or nonreplaceable components. Features information would be assembled into NIPI's universal product catalog, which records by code every product in the marketplace. This catalog would include information such as the product's current market status, general type (e.g., TV, men's shirt), and basic features.

NIPI'S STRUCTURE

Just as we have likened I.C.I.C.s to federally regulated banks, we liken NIPI to the Federal Reserve system. Besides bearing responsibility for certain data-collecting activities, it would function as an autonomous self-supporting agency required to break even. As we noted earlier, the proposed relationship between NIPI and I.C.I.C.s also resembles in many respects the relationship between the Federal Reserve and its member commercial banks. Banks pay fees to belong to the Federal Reserve system and in return receive special privileges. The administration and policy of the Federal Reserve is determined jointly by Congress and the thousands of votes of the private member banks. Similarly, representatives from licensed I.C.I.C.s could elect a chairperson for the institute, subject to Congressional veto. All rate and policy changes could then be subject to the veto of an independent commission whose members would be appointed by the president (subject to Congressional veto). As with members of the Federal Reserve's board of governors, these commission members could be elected to fourteen-year terms on a staggered basis, thus minimizing any one president's influence.[9]

To ensure that manufacturers and sellers comply with NIPI's data-gathering mechanism, Congress would need to pass a set of laws. NIPI would then be responsible for enforcing them, just as the Securities and Exchange Commission is responsible for gathering financial information and policing its accuracy.

INDEPENDENT DATA GATHERING

Data gathering could be handled largely by independent manufacturers, sellers, and consumers, with NIPI simply serving as administrator. To ensure collection of purchase information, NIPI could require manufacturers to encode each qualifying product with basic information: manufacturer's name, brand name, model number, and serial number. The final seller (manufacturer or other) would then decode this information using a mechanism such as a bar-code reader, and then supplement it with the selling date, selling price, seller's name, seller's zip code, and customer's zip code. They would then electronically transmit this information to NIPI on a regular (e.g., weekly) basis.

For all goods qualifying for customer-satisfaction information, NIPI might also require manufacturers to enclose one or more machine-readable postage-prepaid business reply cards (addressed to NIPI), which customers have the option of returning. In addition to the same basic product information already encoded on the merchandise itself, this card would ask customers if the product met all claims made for it by either manufacturer or retailer. Replies would be valid only if given during specified times—for example, more than a week but less than two months after purchase. Of course, if we had already implemented a fully functioning Omnimedia infrastructure, cards would be unnecessary: customers could transmit all vital information electronically at their convenience.

For service information, manufacturers might be required to send a second machine-readable postage-prepaid business reply card (addressed to NIPI) with every qualifying good, which customers could return after any servicing. In addition to the manufacturer's name, brand name, model number, and serial number, this card would ask customers when the product first broke down, how much the first repair cost, how much time the repair took, whether the product was under warranty when repaired, and if the manufacturer paid for parts and/or labor.

To gather features information, NIPI might require notification from manufacturers introducing a product. Then manufacturers would simply enter into a computer the model's UPC along with its features—which could include pictures, simulations, and user documentation—and transmit this information automatically into NIPI's universal product catalog. This system is much more efficient and equitable than asking manufacturers to deal separately with each I.C.I.C. covering their product category (as many primitive I.C.I.C.s now ask manufacturers to do).

We recommend that committees of I.C.I.C.s (one for each product category) determine which features should be recorded for each product type—subject to NIPI's veto. Today, manufacturers include in their product descriptions only features that make their products look good, making comparison very difficult. Requiring standardized information regarding features would level the playing field. Of course, I.C.I.C.s will be very interested in learning about new features and variations on old ones as well.

The committees of I.C.I.C.s could also determine universal standards of measurement for reported features. Manufacturers are notorious for measuring specifications in ways most favorable to themselves, thus making them little more than rough guides. Universal standards would ensure that certain features are measured comparably. Where such common and pre-established standards were lacking, manufacturers would describe exactly how they measured the feature in question. NIPI's universal product catalog (made up of many related files) would keep track of these measurement techniques, and then the committees of I.C.I.C.s, subject to the veto of NIPI, could establish new universal standards. In practice, we envisage that such a system would rapidly eliminate inconsistent standards of measurement.

THE COST OF NIPI

Expected to break even, NIPI would involve no additional costs to taxpayers. Like the Postal Service, it would be a government organization that generates its own revenue: it would sell and license its factual information primarily to I.C.I.C.s, while sellers would pay what amounts to the negligible cost of most of the data collection. And because an information clearinghouse like NIPI would offer benefits outside the shopping realm, the data it collected could easily be sold to many other groups, including insurance companies, marketers, academics, businesses, and the U.S. Census Bureau. For example, in the realm of health and nutrition, NIPI would make it possible to relate the health of the nation to its food consumption. Combining sickness data with NIPI data could provide unparalleled tools for determining which foods are harmful to people, allowing us to see, for instance, whether people who eat relatively high quantities of sirloin steak are more prone to colon cancer or whether people who eat relatively low quantities of salmon are more prone to heart disease. In the realm of economics, too, NIPI would provide a treasure trove of data for economists and government officials studying the workings of the economy and making policy recommendations. Business people, furthermore, could get from NIPI very low-cost and high-quality data on competitors.[10]

As far as manufacturers are concerned, NIPI's function could be achieved cost-effectively, given the continued advances in information technology that have dramatically reduced the cost of gathering such information. Once the cost of these technologies reaches anticipated levels for labeling each eligible product, NIPI's requirements should not cost the manufacturer more than negligible sums. Consider a few examples. Since most manufacturers are already printing bar codes on products (identifying the model number), incremental costs for supplying purchase information would only include adding to this code a unique serial number for each item. In fact, computer hardware and software manufacturers already have a special code to keep track of serial numbers for warranty and technical-support purposes, so perhaps the easiest first step would be to limit the requirement of a serial code just to expensive products such as automobiles and computers, many of which will already be uniquely coded.

Manufacturers would also have to add the cost of printing and reply postage for the response cards, but again, these costs are minimal. Printing the customer satisfaction and service business reply cards should run to no more than a few cents for each card, and return postage should be in the range of 15 cents per card.[11] Moreover, since only a small fraction of consumers would be expected to mail their cards, the costs on a per product and per card basis should be significantly less than postal costs would suggest.

Even providing features information directly into NIPI's universal catalog would not represent a burdensome expense. The current computerized UPC catalog already maintains the status and type of product. Where we would add the most significant enhancements are in the features information. Furthermore, having one centralized product catalog for I.C.I.C.s is cost- and time-efficient in much the same way as having one centralized UPC catalog. Similarly, NIPI's universal catalog will save manufacturers the time it currently takes them to fill out features charts for various consumer publications and the time it would have taken them in the future to fill out charts for each I.C.I.C.

Finally, since retailers and other sellers already have automated order-processing and inventory systems, the incremental cost to retail businesses due to NIPI requirements would be negligible, simply involving the cost to transmit information electronically to NIPI. Once systems are in place, the cost to transmit such information would probably be under a penny per thousand orders.[12]

METHODOLOGICAL   PROBLEMS

Several serious criticisms can be leveled at the above proposal. Perhaps most obvious is the possibility of a biased sample regarding customer satisfaction and service information. Because consumers have no obligations to return their postage-paid response cards, chances are high that most people won't complete or return them or, more significantly, that only certain types of people will do so. Another problem would arise if many consumers distorted their answers, perhaps exaggerating repair times or attributing their own mistakes to the products. One might also question the simplistic way in which the customer satisfaction and service questions distinguish between different types of breakdowns and dysfunctions.[13] All of these are legitimate concerns. And yet any statistically significant distortions could be reduced simply by knowing a customer's demographics (via the zip code or possibly even a social security number) and by differentiating product data by final seller, manufacturer, and customer.

As for the problem of getting manufacturers to send the features data required for the UPC catalog, we anticipate little need for legal or monetary sanctions. Once we assume that consumers will have good information at their fingertips (the old idea that "the customer is king"), then manufacturers should have a sufficient incentive to get features and measurements in line with reality. It will be the job of the independent consumer-information companies, not the National Institutes of Product Information, to alert consumers to fraudulent or deceptive manufacturer specifications. The market mechanism will itself clean out deception, but only if the deception is detected and significant numbers of consumers are informed about it.

Certainly there are other imperfections in the NIPI proposal, but the key to remember is that, flaws and all, this system still would generate far better data on products than is gathered anywhere today. The concept that a method doesn't have to be perfectly accurate or fair, but just an improvement over a present situation, is already well embedded in public policy and in private research. For example, "no-fault" auto insurance is a far from perfect method for allocating responsibility and insurance costs, but because the overall benefits outweigh the problems, many states have chosen to implement such a policy. Perhaps the best example involves the way today's leading gatherer of reliability data, *Consumer Reports,* operates. Contrary to popular perception, most of this magazine's reliability data comes not from independent testing but from polling its subscribers, a method which is not only less expensive than testing in a laboratory but also generally more accurate. Even so, data are often at least a year old and limited primarily to reliability, type of product, brand, and year that there was a problem. Moreover, the sample size is much smaller and undoubtedly even more biased than the one proposed for NIPI.

In short, most people would grant that this much more limited approach now used by *Consumer Reports* generates very useful data. And by the same token, it should be recognized that the data-gathering effort envisaged here would be superior to the more primitive methods now used. Furthermore, NIPI would add price, features, reliability, and trustworthiness of product-claims data to what anyone now gathers.

1. The value of centralized information clearinghouses has been recognized and extensively discussed in many fields of endeavor. For example, industry (usually through trade associations) and government (through such departments as the Bureau of the Census and the Securities and Exchange Commission) have already sponsored many such organizations. In contrast, the need for consumer-information clearinghouses has largely been ignored. One area where this issue has at least received some attention is in the general discussion of the need for a localized consumer-information system. Specifically, a number of scholars have recommended the advantages of a local *Consumer Reports*-type organization—in effect, a clearinghouse for the type of information NIPI would gather, combined with the synthetic abilities of an I.C.I.C. Indeed, in the mid-1970s a former director of Consumers Union started publishing *The Washington Consumers Checkbook* with just this purpose in mind, and in late 1990 New York Attorney General Robert Abrams proposed a NIPI-like organization to provide information to consumers on the insurance industry. See F. M. Scherer, *Industrial Market Structure and Economic Performance* (Boston: Houghton Mifflin, 1980), pp. 490–491; "Abrams Seeks Ways to Better Inform Auto Insurance Consumers," press release issued by New York State Office of the Attorney General, September 25, 1990; E. Scott Maynes et al., "The Local Consumer Information System: An Institution-To-Be?" *Journal of Consumer Affairs* 2 (Summer 1977):17–33; Hans Thorelli, "The Future of Consumer Information Systems," in ed. David Aaker and George Day, *Consumerism*, 4th ed. (New York: Free Press, 1982), pp. 115–126; Donald Dunn and Michael Ray, "A Plan for Consumer Information System Development, Implementation, and Evaluation," in Aaker and Day, pp. 127–133; and Patrick Murphy and Steven Ross, "Local Consumer Information Systems for Services: A Test," *Journal of Consumer Affairs*, Vol. 20, No. 2, Winter 1986, pp. 249–262.

2. Most writers who have argued that we should strengthen consumer-information services have made no such distinction between I.C.I.C. and NIPI-type functions (i.e., between the provision of perspective and the collection of data). We propose this separation for two reasons: One is that fact-collecting businesses and perspective-generating businesses have very different economics. Fact-collecting businesses are subject to huge economies of scale (i.e., are natural monopolies), whereas perspective-generating activities rely on individual human judgment. As we have seen, similar reasoning led us in the past to separate common carriers (e.g., the post office and telephone companies) from content providers (e.g., publishers). The other reason is that the "public goods" (i.e., something private enterprise cannot or won't generate on its own) associated with the two types of businesses are very different. In the case of I.C.I.C.s, the key public good is trust, whereas in the case of NIPI it is universal and mandatory cooperation.

3. For a striking account of the lengths to which doctors and hospitals will go to prevent the dissemination of this type of data, see Thomas J. Moore, *Heart Failure* (New York: Simon & Schuster, 1989), pp. 222–269.

4. Moore, pp. 11–12. In recent years there have been many proposals for more ambitious medical-information clearinghouses. See, for example, Paul Ellwood, "Outcomes Management: A Technology of Patient Experience," *New England Journal of Medicine* 318 (June 9, 1988):1549–1556.

5. See, for example, "A Decade of Change: 1978–1987," *Chain Store Age Executive*, November 1988, pp. 60, 63.

6. "Radio Frequency Identification," *Stores*, September 1989, p. 11. See also "Smart Cards Are Getting a Lot Smarter," *Wall Street Journal*, June 26, 1989, sec. B, p.1.

7. Manning Greenberg, "Tandy Sees Changed Roles for Management in '90s," *Home Furnishings Daily*, December 18, 1989, p. 134.

8. Gary Robins, "Using the UPC Catalog," *Stores*, February 1989, pp. 61–64. This article cites a March 1987 study sponsored by IBM, Carter Hawley Hale, and Levi Strauss and Company which

concluded that "the most efficient way to handle the vast amounts of electronic traffic was to focus it in a single data base managed by an independent third party."

9. As with the Federal Reserve, the actual structure of NIPI could be far more complicated and reflect greater input from other interest groups, such as sellers. To carry the Federal Reserve analogy further, each of the regional "Federal Reserve banks" (i.e., NIPI institutes) could represent a particular industry rather than a geographic region. The nine directors of each of these institutes could be elected in the same fashion that directors are elected to the Federal Reserve banks. The member banks (i.e., I.C.I.C.s) could vote for six of the nine, three of which would be fellow I.C.I.C.s and three of which would have to be unaffiliated with an I.C.I.C. The remaining three would be appointed by the "Board of Governors" (i.e., the Congressionally appointed commission members) and could represent producer groups. The I.C.I.C. "member banks" could also be divided into three voting blocks, one each for large, medium, and small I.C.I.C.s. This highly complex system of checks and balances, combined with elements of centralization and decentralization of power, has worked spectacularly well for the Federal Reserve.

10. Whether all the information collected by NIPI should become publicly available is an entirely separate public-policy issue. See Chapter 14 for our discussion of this privacy issue.

11. If the U.S. Postal Service would set up a special postal rate for such product-information cards, as it has for other socially desirable businesses, this cost could be reduced substantially. This rate would reflect lower variable postal costs (but higher fixed costs because of added machinery) because the post office would not have to sort or deliver the cards. The Postal Service would feed the cards into a machine that would automatically process all the machine-readable information and then dispose of the cards. The specific mechanism could work in one of two ways: (1) each local or regional post office could be given a special machine which could read the cards and transmit their contents electronically to NIPI, or, preferably, (2) the post office's existing sorting and bar-code-reading machines could be given this added function.

12. See "A Decade of Change: 1978–1987," p. 63.

13. This claim is not as compelling as it may seem, in that most consumers are primarily interested merely in knowing whether something tends to break down, how much it costs when it does, how long it takes to get repaired, and whether they can trust a manufacturer's or final seller's claims.

The Failure
of the Imagination

Proposals for reform . . . begin as seemingly eccentric and implausible suggestions. Gradually they gain adherents; in time they emerge as grave needs; and then they become fundamental human rights.[1]

—John Kenneth Galbraith

Whenever we describe the problems of consumer confusion, people always seem to nod their heads in agreement, often jumping in with their own examples of frustration and anger. As soon as we mention that there's a solution to these problems however, their faces fall. Apparently, suggesting a solution to a problem is a sign of either naiveté or evil. In fact, whenever we even hint that there may be a way around consumer confusion, we are accused of promulgating either some childish fantasy or some societal nightmare, whether it be elitism, communism, or fascism.

We haven't been alone in noting this cynicism. A film critic recently observed that the latest generation of film noir "depicts a world in which bigotry, corruption and greed have gone out of control—a world in which any broad discussion of the public good—how all human beings can improve their lives, their communities and share the benefits of progress—has been ruled out of order." A couple of decades ago films reflected the still-common belief that individual and collective action could change the system and redress societal corruption and greed.[2] Today, however, we see all around us an implicit credo that if there really were an acceptable solution to societal problems, it would already be in place; the cynics themselves surely would have found an obvious way to implement it. Any proposal for reform must be inherently flawed.

A look at history, however, suggests that great institutional innovations are never obvious. None of the great institutions of the West came without a fight. Democracy, the banking system, the separation of church and state, fiat money, the system of governmental checks and balances, and the rule of law all were opposed by powerful forces representing antiquated institutions. At every step of the way, vivid imagination was required to dream up and implement new and better ways of doing things.

The cynicism about consumer confusion represents nothing short of a failure of the imagination. People seem to assume that by criticizing the current regime we are also advocating another existing or a previous regime. They fail to see that we are arguing for a new order, one that has never before existed.

Futurist Alvin Toffler puts his finger on the problem:

> Most people—to the extent that they bother to think about the future at all—assume the world they know will last indefinitely. They find it difficult to imagine a truly different way of life for themselves, let alone a totally new civilization. Of course, they recognize that things are changing. But they assume today's changes will somehow pass them by and nothing will shake the familiar economic framework and political structure. They confidently expect the future to continue the present.

Toffler goes on to say that this "straight-line thinking," whether it appears in the form of unexamined extrapolations or sophisticated statistics, "adds up to a vision of a future world that is essentially 'more of the same.'"[3]

In the case of consumer confusion and the changes we propose to help alleviate it, people forget that advertising, brand names, and department stores are little more than one hundred years old. They forget that radio, TV, and VCRs have been around for less than a single lifetime. God didn't ordain that the electromagnetic spectrum be given away to the broadcasters. Nor did God ordain that more than eight hundred occupations had to be licensed, certified, or registered because consumers would forever be too ignorant to judge the basic competence of people who provide common services. None of these systems are written in stone, and if they are more costly to the consumer than they need be, as is often the case, then something has to be changed.

To facilitate these changes, however, we need more than anything a new mindset toward our country's information infrastructure. Progress, not tradition, must be our guiding vision.[4] We must recognize that, figuratively speaking, we are in the Dark Ages. We must recognize that our basic information policies were developed when the information technologies available to us were vastly more primitive. The way we determine our information policies today is like building a military strategy around the bow and arrow when the gun has already been invented. Admittedly, most countries learned the hard way that a world of guns is very different than a world of bows and arrows. But a few countries had the vision to recognize the change and adjust their policies—and they benefited accordingly.

For an information infrastructure to genuinely work in the consumers' interests, consumers cannot continue to abdicate their responsibility to monitor their elected representatives. Dominated by special interests, awash in tribute from government-sponsored media monopolies, and oriented toward maintaining the traditions of its own fiefdoms, the government is unlikely to lead us into the Information Age without pressure from constituents.

Part of this process involves acknowledging that almost all technological and institutional changes, however beneficial overall, hurt some people. Certain countries, in fact, seem to progress much slower than others because entrenched interests always seem to find some way to block beneficial changes. By contrast, the United States, with its democracy and free market, has shown a remarkably robust capacity for change.

Nevertheless, the kind of innovative infrastructure that will maximize our social welfare may greatly strain the political system. Many entrenched interest groups will undoubtedly find grounds for opposition: retailers, consumer-products manufacturers, advertisers, salespeople, licensed professionals, and, above all, the giant media conglomerates. But the public should be wary of those voices who would have them favor these powerful special interests at the expense of the economic and social health of society as a whole. Here it helps to remember the conflict that emerged two hundred years ago when the rising industrial classes threatened the power of the reigning agricultural classes. In England, for example, it took thirty years for the industrial classes to gain enough economic and political might to overturn the monopolistic Corn Laws, which were designed to protect the agricultural classes from foreign competition, and which severely damaged the health of England's economy.[5] Let us strive to make sure that the analogous conflict between the reigning information monopolists and the rising merit-oriented companies resolves itself more quickly.

We also must recognize that our individual knowledge as consumers can fundamentally affect the economy. We must think less about production costs and more about the time, effort, intelligence, and money (collectively representing part of what economists call "demand") spent by consumers as they search for products. This emphasis on demand is part of a larger intellectual tradition. Early economists observed the workings of the economy and assumed that supply always creates its own demand.[6] The twentieth century's Great Depression, however, presented striking evidence to the contrary. John Maynard Keynes, often considered the greatest economist of this century, observed "Poverty Amidst Plenty," the phenomenon of empty factories surrounded by unemployed workers who not only desired to work in the factories but to spend their own wages on the products they were producing. In mulling over this seemingly strange phenomenon, Keynes realized that the problem was one of inadequate demand. He realized, specifically, that both supply and demand determine a society's wealth. He also realized that most of the business cycles in history had come from swings in demand rather than swings in supply.[7] Consequently, much of modern monetary and fiscal policy now focuses on controlling how much demand there is for products and controlling which segments of the economy demand them. The new tools made possible by burgeoning information technology, however, have given our society a new priority: to maximize not only the quantity and allocation of demand, but, above all, its *quality* and *efficiency*.

Our problem is not that the supply of products don't exist, it's that this doesn't do us any good if we cannot find them. In a modern society, information is becoming as crucial to personal happiness and prosperity as are food and clothing. Information is the glue which shapes our lives; it is the means by which we choose a better life. The time has come for the public and the politicians it elects to recognize the full import of this—that whenever we complain about the problems of finding a spouse, a doctor, a job, or just about anything else, we are usually, at least in part, talking about the difficulty of obtaining information.

WILL INFORMED CONSUMERS
MEAN COMMUNISM?

Many Americans become immediately suspicious whenever a reformer suggests a new set of responsibilities for government, even when the net effect may be to reduce overall intervention. These people seem to forget that government, despite its drawbacks, does indeed have a purpose: to harmonize the otherwise divergent interests of the individual and the public at large. Unfortunately, many issues of telecommunications policy—and information policy more generally—have an important government component. Large and efficient telephone networks, for example, don't spring up without a host of government regulations. The government must be involved in building up a modern nation's information infrastructure. But it's also important to recognize that government regulation of industry is not the same as government control of industry— e.g., communism—and that what we're suggesting is merely an extension of a policy that has been in place for over a century in America.

This call for government regulation to foster competition and maximize social and economic welfare is in keeping with American tradition. As we have seen throughout this book, over the last two hundred years more and more aspects of the marketplace have emerged in which private interest and social welfare diverge, thus requiring a constant rewriting of the "social contract" to bring the interests of private individuals back in line with the public good. We have already seen in Part II of this book how a completely unregulated marketplace tends to generate monopoly imperfections and how we've instituted consumer-protection laws to moderate these imperfections. Similarly, we often take steps to reconcile private and public costs and benefits, which tend to diverge in a strictly laissez-faire marketplace. For example, a polluter in a laissez-faire system bears no cost for fouling the air and water. Thus, we have instituted laws to bring the polluter's interest in line with that of society. By the same token, the government supports many useful services—such as road construction and public sanitation—because private enterprise has found no mechanism with which to charge for these services economically or efficiently. If we left private industry to provide all goods, roads would never get built, the military would never be funded, and common utilities such as water and electricity would be far more expensive.

Similarly, unless we institute the right government-sponsored infrastructure, it's going to be quite difficult for consumers to gain access to good information. Imagine, for example, that you are an entrepreneur in Russia. You cannot get phone service. You cannot send faxes. The little phone service you get makes voices sound virtually inaudible. The postal service takes two weeks to send mail to the next city. The trains and planes are unreliable, often holding you and your clients up for days on end. Lastly, the bureaucracy holds you up for months for even simple permits, such as for installing a copying machine.

The difficulties that attend normal business transactions in the USSR today are analogous to the hardships in store for individuals who seek to create I.C.I.C.s in America today. The infrastructure required to make I.C.I.C.s work doesn't yet exist. Without this infrastructure it is uneconomical to gather such data as pricing, model features, and customer-satisfaction indices. The Soviet Union may lack the infrastructure for industry to flourish, but the United States, two steps ahead, has done virtually nothing to lay the infrastructure necessary for the development of the consumer-information sector. Specific policies to promote the development of such an infrastructure have nothing to do with communism; they are aimed instead at keeping the free market alive.

WILL INFORMED CONSUMERS MEAN FASCISM?

At the same time that Omnimedia, I.C.I.C.s, and NIPI suggest communism, they seem paradoxically to suggest fascism as well. A single source of information? A single institution hording every bit of product information? A decision by a so-called expert that everyone should eat the one and only "best" spaghetti sauce or use the one and only "best" soap? Informed consumers or not, this sounds like a nightmarish technocracy in which drab consumers obey the dictates of Big Brother.

Some of these fears represent nothing other than a misunderstanding of the society we envision. For example, the fear that I.C.I.C.s will dramatically reduce product differentiation, offering just one or two brands of soap, rather than fifty, is incorrect. Instead, we foresee many different I.C.I.C.s selling many different opinions. Experts often disagree, especially about personal items such as soap. One thing that we certainly do anticipate I.C.I.C.s helping to bring about, in fact, is far greater product diversity. We expect that we'll have 350 different types of soaps to choose from, not 50 as today. The crucial concept here is that instead of differentiating soaps primarily by meaningless brand labels, we'll see more real product differentiation, and soaps will come in hundreds of additional sizes, colors, and scents.

Other critics of the I.C.I.C. concept might argue that dealing with multiple viewpoints (in this case, of various salespeople in contrast to a single information agent) is the best way for the marketplace to work. This argument is analogous to the argument that we should live in a direct, not a representative, democracy. Ideally, each citizen should become knowledgeable about and vote on every issue, but today's huge populations and complex issues make such a system impractical. Thus, we elect representatives who we feel will best represent our interests, and let them worry about the details. The advantage of the I.C.I.C. is very similar. Today we're given the impossible task of having to vote intelligently about every product in the marketplace. A far more efficient system would be to "elect" representatives—I.C.I.C.s—to do this voting for us.

Admittedly, the proposals we make for a single information network like Omnimedia or a single institution like NIPI will lead to a concentration of information. Information connotes power, which can be abused. To avoid fascistic tendencies, then, we'd have to set up an Omnimedia system in which control of *content* (that is, information) would be separate from control of the *conduit* (that is, the ways of conveying that information to consumers). The (multiple) providers of data would be separated from the providers of information technology—as discussed in Chapter 11. The National Institutes of Product Information, with its comprehensive and easily accessible data, is indeed the type of institution that a dictator would love to possess. But so are the existing means of mass information distribution: TV, for example, can be used to improve the quality of information people have available to them. It also can be used, in totalitarian societies, as a vehicle of propaganda. As with TV and radio, the potential for abuse exists, and appropriate precautionary measures must be taken.

In evaluating the risks that would accompany the vision of consumerism presented in this book, it's important to recognize how much "fascism" and invasion of privacy already exists in American society—and how such control resides mainly in the hands of the sellers. Businesses already have the same information about consumers that we are proposing that NIPI should collect, and this information is already highly centralized. For example, there are only three major credit bureaus in the United States. Similarly, American Express and major banks which offer credit cards maintain and sell huge amounts of information regarding credit card purchases. Government agencies, too, already have lots of information about the public that is stored in NIPI-like institutions. Although most people consider their income to be a very private matter, the IRS already has a huge amount of data on the income of Americans. We've managed to work out a system where we can have the advantages of an efficient tax-collection system without the abuses that this centralized information could entail. From this perspective, NIPI would simply even out the scales, allowing the consumer access to the information that businesses and government already have. It seems reasonable, as a starting point, that if we object to NIPI gathering such information, we should also object to these other companies gathering this information. If it's acceptable for retailers and others to collect and use the transaction information relating to consumers, it should be equally acceptable for consumers to do the reverse.

THE NEED FOR A NEW CONSUMERISM

There is one more failure of the imagination that could do even more damage to our vision than fears of communism, fascism, or the interference of special interests. That failure involves consumer leaders themselves, many of whom are unable to imagine how a high-quality information infrastructure could benefit the American consumer. Many of these leaders, in fact, maintain that proposals for bettering our means of communication would be positively harmful to consumers.[8]

The public-utility commissions (which regulate the phone companies) and the Consumer Federation of America, for example, have all come out against allowing the telephone companies to install home fiber-optic networks (replacing still viable copper wires), which, as we've seen, are essential to the development of cost-effective Omnimedia networks. Their justification is that this installation will raise consumer rates with minimal benefits.[9] These so-called consumer representatives can't seem to understand that the huge cost to the social and economic welfare of having such a poor information infrastructure makes this cost reasonable. Their argument is akin to saying we should preserve horse travel because it's less expensive than automobile travel.

The consumer leaders today are also blinded by a narrow and antiquated notion that suggests that wrongs against consumers can be best rectified via the legal system. Today just about every consumer scam leads us to look to lawyers and legislation for a solution. We want to haul deceptive storeowners into court; we want to pass laws barring price-fixing; we want to license barbers and morticians to make sure they are competent. It's no surprise, incidentally, that Ralph Nader has a law degree or that many of the leaders at Consumers Union have legal backgrounds. Newer technology will allow us to replace this mindset with one more in keeping with the values of the free market: instead of relying on a series of Byzantine and unenforceable rules to keep the marketplace moral and efficient, we'll be able to rely on independent consumer watchdogs, who will profit by providing the best information they can. Consumer advocates have to be farsighted enough to see that this new consumerism cannot work effectively until the marketplace has the technological and institutional infrastructure to revolutionize the economics of providing consumer information.

Consumer advocates also have to convey this insight to the country's key decision makers, who right now just don't seem able to visualize the significance of the new information technologies despite the glowing speeches they give about the wondrous new Information Age. When pressed about specifics, something like this is likely to come out: "The Information Age is for the elite. The average citizen, the average consumer, does not and probably never will want better information. The average person is lazy, stupid, and irrational. People do not want electronic banking, they do not want electronic shopping, they do not want electronic news, they do not want electronic education. Companies already have tried to get consumers to use these services, and they have failed. Yes, a small number of Americans are willing to purchase PCs and sit in front of their screens to use these services. But we just can't imagine that the vast majority of Americans ever will."[10]

The error underlying such a judgment is the assumption that anybody has actually ever provided anything close to high-quality information services. Naysayers believe that because consumers have not wanted to use inconvenient, expensive, and low-quality electronic information, they will never want *any* electronic information. Moreover, these visionaries-turned-critics forget that if you have a lousy medium, you can't help but have a lousy message. Not following technology closely, they may not be aware of how sadly dated our TV technology or our telephone networks have become over the last forty years. They may not know, at least in a concrete, vivid sense, that a vastly superior medium is at hand, and without that medium in mind, their imaginations rot over obsolete possibilities.

Let's give some examples. In the first two decades of this century, radio was transmitted in Morse code. Hobbyists traded news and information over this primitive radio, but for the most part Americans ignored it. Once it began transmitting spoken voices, however, radio became very popular. It wasn't that Morse code couldn't transmit news; it was just that getting such information by such means was more bother than convenience. In retrospect, we see the problem of acceptance was ultimately one of inadequate technology.

Computers, too, have been around for a long time. But early applications were so expensive, complicated, and ineffective that very few people bothered with them. Today, as the underlying technology of computers has improved, so too have the applications that employ them. Not surprisingly, people are switching en masse from manual to computerized tasks.

The skepticism toward high-tech information services is reminiscent of the way ancient Persian kings once killed messengers who brought bad news from the war front. In this case, we regard flawed applications as the messenger boys and fail to realize that the applications we so mercilessly doom to oblivion can do no more than the technology they are built upon. In other words, the problem with interactive telecommunications services is not that people don't want them; it's that people don't want lousy services based on lousy technology. The failure of such services should be taken as a mandate to improve our clearly inadequate information infrastructure rather than as an excuse to maintain it in its current state of obsolescence.

The fact is that many uses for technologies have emerged only over time. The entire electric-utility network, for example, was built in the last quarter of the nineteenth century to run Thomas Edison's electric light bulbs with no concept at all of the thousands of electric appliances destined to appear down the line. Soon factories started using electric machinery, and by the 1920s the use of electricity for light bulbs began to be dwarfed by its use for heating and running appliances. It is indeed doubtful whether many if not most of today's appliances—including microwave ovens, refrigerators, TVs, alarm clocks, stereos, personal computers, hair dryers, and blenders—would have been developed if they had to run on separate gas-powered engines rather than the electricity infrastructure that preceded them.

Yes, the future is hard to predict. Thomas Edison also thought that his phonograph would be used largely to mail letters as records. Guglielmo Marconi viewed his radio as a wireless telephone, best suited for communications with ships at sea, never guessing that it would be used for broadcasting—the Italian government thought the whole idea so impractical that it wouldn't even grant him a patent. Even more amazingly, when Alexander Graham Bell's business partner and future father-in-law offered Western Union all rights to the telephone patent for a mere $100,000, the then powerful company refused, reportedly asking, "What use could this company make of an electrical toy?"[11]

On the other hand, many people do successfully forecast the development of future technology. Bell, for example, is credited with envisioning very clearly how the telephone system would evolve over the hundred years following this invention. Likewise, to make investments, venture capitalists forecast three to ten years into the future—often successfully. And the government, in long-range programs like the development of the atom bomb or setting a man on the moon, must make precise forecasts. In fact, whether as corporations or individuals, we all must forecast constantly. The question is not whether forecasting can be done successfully, but rather what types of forecasts are most reliable and what types of individuals are best able to make them.[12]

But the goal of the new consumerism is not so much to forecast the future as to create it. And, as we have seen, the greatest obstacle to this vision is that many of the key decisions necessary to implement it will have to be made as a nation. How will our politicians make those decisions? Will they be guided by the narrow factions that our country's Founding Fathers so feared? Will they be guided by the inertia of the past? Will they be guided by the negative impulse of beating foreign rivals such as the Japanese or Europeans? Or will they be guided by the more noble impulse of creating a better future for the American people?

America has built great societal infrastructures in the past—the Constitution, the school system, the monetary system, and the highway system, to name just a few. We didn't build these infrastructures without a fight and a leap of imagination. But we did build, and as opportunity beckons, we can build again.

1. John Kenneth Galbraith, *The New Industrial State* (Houghton Mifflin: Boston, 1967), pp. 287–288.

2. Suzanne Gordon, "Why 'Film Noir' Dominates Our Movie Screens," *Boston Globe*, May 27, 1990, sec. A, p. 22.

3. Alvin Toffler, *The Third Wave* (New York: Bantam Books, 1980), p. 11.

4. Ronald Stowe makes similar pleas in his "Free the BOC's: The Time Is Now," *Telematics and Infomatics* 6 (1989):9.

5. Robert Heilbroner, *The Worldly Philosophers*, 3rd ed. (New York: Simon & Schuster, 1967), pp. 71–75, 89.

6. Paul Samuelson, *Economics*, 10th ed. (New York: McGraw-Hill, 1976), p. 842.

7. The demand idea isn't really new, at least not as far as businessmen are concerned. Stuart Ewen, in his *Captains of Consciousness: Advertising and the Social Roots of the Consumer Culture* (New York: McGraw-Hill, 1977) quotes an editorial from *Printer's Ink* on p. 53 which expresses the conviction of the early twentieth-century advertisers that "the future of business lay in its ability to manufacture customers as well as products." That sentiment is true today more than ever. But it needs to be examined afresh, recast in light of today's technological possibilities.

8. The one significant exception to this stance is the Alliance for Public Technology in Washington D.C., whose stated goal is to "[f]oster access to and the availability of useful and affordable information services and communications technology to all people." This organization is particularly concerned with extending the benefits of the information age to groups that have not traditionally been included, such as the poor, the elderly, and the disabled.

9. Julie Lopez and Mary Carnevale, "Fiber Optics Promises a Revolution of Sorts, If the Sharks Don't Bite," *Wall Street Journal*, July 10, 1990, sec. A, p. 1.

10. E.g., see Tom Valovic, "The Rewiring of America: Scenarios for Local-Loop Distribution," *Telecommunications*, January 1988, p. 31; U.S. Federal Communications Commission, Office of Plans and Policies, *Through the Looking Glass: Integrated Broadband Networks, Regulatory Policy and Institutional Change*, by Robert Pepper (Washington, D.C.: Government Printing Office, 1988), p. 12; U.S. Department of Commerce, National Telecommunications and Information Administration, *Economic Potential of Advanced Television Products*, by Larry Darby (Washington, D.C.: Government Printing Office, April 7, 1988); Joel Dreyfuss, "The Coming Battle over Your TV Set," *Fortune*, February 13, 1989, pp. 105–106; and Roy Rosner, "Can Packet Switching Survive ISDN and Fiber?" *Telecommunications*, April 1988, p. 84.

11. Ithiel de Sola Pool, *Technologies of Freedom: On Free Speech in an Electronic Age* (Cambridge, Mass.: Harvard University Press, 1983), p. 27; *Public Policy Implications of Advanced Television Systems*, p. 564; Harold Sharlin, *The Making of the Electrical Age* (New York: Abelard-Schuman, 1963), pp. 95, 123, 195, 209, 211; Sidney Aronson, "Bell's Electric Toy: What's the Use?" in ed. Ithiel de Sola Pool, *The Social Impact of the Telephone* (Cambridge, Mass.: MIT Press, 1977), p. 15; Arnold Mandelbaum, *Electricity: The Story of Power* (New York: G. P. Putnam's Son's, 1960), pp. 140–141; and William Meadowcroft, *The Boys' Life of Edison* (New York: Harper and Brothers, 1911), pp. 2–3.

CHAPTER 15

The Death of the Promotional Society

The ideas of economists and political philosophers, both when they are right and when they are wrong, are more powerful than is commonly understood. Indeed the world is ruled by little else. Practical men, who believe themselves to be quite exempt from any intellectual influences, are usually the slaves of some defunct economist.

—John Maynard Keynes

What this book predicts is nothing less than the death of the promotional society—the death of the promotional companies and personalities which now thrive in advanced industrialized countries. Promotional systems have become so deeply woven into the fabric of our lives that they seem a part of the natural landscape: we can't even see them or imagine a world without them. Moreover, the experience of the last two hundred years suggests that these systems are becoming more robust than ever. Nevertheless, the trend is about to reverse. As independent consumer-information companies use next-generation information systems to fill the gap between the knowledge of consumers and sellers, the promotional world engendered by this gap will become obsolete.

Today few people doubt the pervasive impact of promotion on American life. Consider advertising, for example, which is undoubtedly the most obvious and most often analyzed form of promotion. It's been said that today, by age seventeen, the average American has seen 350,000 television commercials. One writer has called advertising "the propaganda arm of American culture," while another, noting advertising's pervasiveness, has called it the "burning brand on the crest of our civilization."[1] Since its first struggling days in the nineteenth century, however, the conventional wisdom about advertising has reversed. Originally it was considered a novel, universally repugnant, and economically questionable means of conveying information about products. Remarkably, although it has existed for less than 1 percent of human history, today no one questions the status of advertising as an economic necessity.

Advertising's overall moral and social effects remain controversial.[2] One school holds that in a world without religion or other guiding ideologies advertising gives people hope, a set of goals. Theodore Levitt, former editor of the *Harvard Business Review,* sums this view up nicely by explaining that "civilization is man's attempt to transcend his ancient animality." He explains that advertising is a laudable attempt in our secular age to find significance and security, to transcend our primal insignificance and escape hostile and unpredictable nature:

> Many of the so-called distortions of advertising, product design, and packaging may be viewed as a paradigm of the many responses that man makes to the conditions of survival in the environment. Without distortion, embellishment, and elaboration, life would be drab, dull, anguished, and at its existential worst. . . . [We] expect and demand that advertising create these symbols for us to show us what life might be, to bring the possibilities that we cannot see before our eyes and screen out the stark reality in which we must live. . . . Thus, the issue is not the prevention of distortion. It is, in the end, to know what kinds of distortions we actually want so that each of our lives is, without apology, duplicity, or rancor, made bearable.[3]

It can be safely said, however, that the critics of advertising's social effects vastly outnumber its boosters. John Kenneth Galbraith, generally recognized to be the most illustrious critic of advertising, views promotion's distortions in a very different light:

> To ensure attention [advertising] must be raucous and dissonant. It is also of the utmost importance that this effort convey an impression, however meretricious, of the importance of the goods being sold. The market for soap can only be managed if the attention of consumers is captured for what, otherwise, is a rather incidental artifact. Accordingly, the smell of soap, the texture of its suds, the whiteness of textiles treated thereby and the resulting esteem and

prestige in the neighborhood are held to be of highest moment. Housewives are imagined to discuss such matters with an intensity otherwise reserved for unwanted pregnancy and nuclear war. Similarly with cigarettes, laxatives, pain-killers, beer, automobiles, dentifrices, packaged foods and all other significant consumer products. . . . The educational and scientific estate and the larger intellectual community tend to view this effort with disdain.[4]

Robert Heilbroner, arguably America's most popular economic historian, has expressed similar sentiments: "If I were asked to name the deadliest subversive force within capitalism, the single greatest source of its waning morality—I would without hesitation name advertising. How else should one identify a force that debases language, drains thought, and undoes dignity?"[5]

Meanwhile, Americans, in contrast to citizens of many other countries, have for all practical purposes considered the debate over advertising's social effects to be irrelevant. Americans are a pragmatic people, and studies have shown that they almost universally accept that advertising has contributed greatly to our national wealth. If Americans generally dislike the social effects of advertising, this has been a relatively small price to pay for the higher standard of living it has helped to bring about.[6] We suspect, however, that if advertising and other forms of promotion ever became economically obsolete, as we have suggested they will, the American public would not be unhappy to see them disappear. And we certainly cannot imagine the American public going so far as to subsidize advertisers for the moral content of their messages.

One consequence of the obsolescence of promotion is that what Daniel Bell calls "the cultural contradictions of capitalism" may well resolve themselves. Bell has observed that companies teach a hedonistic ethic to consumers while preaching an altruistic ethic to their employees. They tell the consumer "relax, enjoy yourself, consume" whereas they tell their employees "discipline yourselves, work hard, live frugally. . . ."

"On the one hand, the business corporation wants an individual to work hard, pursue a career, accept delayed gratification—to be, in the crude sense, an organization man," notes Bell. "And yet, in its products and its advertisements, the corporation promotes pleasure, instant joy, relaxing and letting go. One is to be 'straight' by day and a 'swinger' by night."[7] The decline of promotion should eliminate much of this hypocrisy.

For similar reasons, we can expect a shift in the balance between consumption and investment. One of the most basic messages of promoters is the virtue of immediate consumption over savings and investment. As this message recedes, Americans may decide either to work less (because they'll have fewer items they'll want to purchase) or to invest more in the future (which will ultimately allow them to consume more). In the former case the economy will decline; in the latter it will grow faster than ever. We suspect that in the future people will do a little more of both.

Given the right information infrastructure, we also can expect the promotional personality to lose its utility—and therefore its social repute. The defining characteristic of this personality, nurtured by a complex society in which people know little about the capabilities of their contemporaries, is a premium on appearance rather than substance. As more transactions are made between people with equal knowledge, the value of "persuasive abilities"—and the temptation to display them—will diminish radically. More generally, honesty and competence as real and practical (not just espoused) values will receive more respect. There will be, so to speak, a genuine cash value to truth. And once ethics pay, as night follows day, we must imagine that people will adjust their characters and values accordingly. In fact, we can readily imagine that, given good consumer information, the deceptive selling practices taken for granted today will seem barbaric—perhaps viewed with the same disgust with which we now view many practices of the past such as punishment by stoning, the eighty-hour child work week, and the fraudulent advertising of patent medicines.

Of course, we are not suggesting that if people were all more knowledgeable consumers, promotional personality traits would completely lose their value. Ignorance of our fellow person, particularly in a complex social environment, will never disappear entirely. And as long as human beings remain tender and vain creatures constantly in need of praise and affection, we'll probably never completely eliminate the payoff for at least modest deception. On the other hand, the level of ignorance between buyers and sellers in our financial relationships undoubtedly influences our personalities significantly. We suspect that as these personality characteristics lose their usefulness in our business life, this change will rub off onto our general personality structure and the general esteem with which we judge such talents of misrepresentation.

Instead of a promotional society, then, we envisage a much more honest, diverse, and affluent society, one characterized by the harmony of ethics and economic success, of traditional religious values and the exigencies of everyday life. Ours is a vision of a reinvigorated invisible hand spurring us on to this harmony of self-interest and the social good. It's a vision of the past, of a time before the Industrial Revolution when both consumers and producers had equal knowledge about products. It's also a vision of the future, of a time when this knowledge power will be put back into balance. Finally, it's a vision about both the moral and economic significance of information, a vision that good information— whether it be consumer or almost any other type of information—will play a vital role in leading us to the type of society we have always desired but never thought practical.

We conclude with a series of predictions about what the new consumer-information systems will mean for our economy and our society. Admittedly, we are basing all of these predictions solely on a theory, not on historical trends. But when it comes to predicting the future, historical trends have their limitations, especially under conditions of major technological change. In other words, if you accept that new technologies will alter fundamental economic realities, extrapolating historical trends will get you nowhere in anticipating what those new realities will be for consumers and for the rest of the economy.

Power will shift from knowledge distributors to knowledge creators.

Heretofore, groups such as television, radio, and newspaper companies, which controlled the means of distributing information, dominated the media business. But in the future the people who provide the actual content or information will dominate. Whereas today's media are characterized by monopoly, forthcoming information technologies will revive competition. Beaming bits and bytes over the future information network will be like farming today, a business characterized by relatively small entrepreneurs. The giant media conglomerates—who have grown solely because of their control over distribution rather than their ability to generate quality information—will become a dying breed. The experts, researchers, and independent sources of consumer information (independent consumer-information companies) will be the center of the media. What this means is that whereas today authors get 10 percent of a book's revenue, and newspaper writers even less of newspaper revenue, future "content providers" will get 90 percent of the revenue. Whereas today a city has only a handful of influential publishers, tomorrow it will have tens of thousands. The expert on consumer-electronics stores—or plumbers, funeral homes, banks, builders, and a million and one other fields of expertise—will have ready access to the public. We will have a diverse, free, and affordable press unlike any dreamed of in all of history.

We'll see the arrival of quality goods and services that could never make it to market in the past because of exorbitant consumer-education costs.

Anything which reduces the costs of informing the consumers about products leads to more product diversity and innovation. Historians often discuss how past growth in our monetary, transportation, and communication systems all increased both the quantity and diversity of goods and services in the economy. The onset of Omnimedia, I.C.I.C.s, and NIPI will have similar effects. Thus, we can expect the variety and utility of consumer products sold in the marketplace to increase dramatically. Some of the exciting new product opportunities will be (1) products whose geographically dispersed markets can't be reached through traditional direct-marketing methods, (2) products for which consumer demand is very sensitive to small changes in price, and (3) products with significant economies of scale in which the amount produced could be significantly increased once consumers have easier access to information about the product.

The variety and utility of information and entertainment products will improve dramatically.

Product information not only helps consumers evaluate goods and services. It also helps them to evaluate "information products" such as entertainment, news, and education. Today few people have the time, energy, or ability to wade through all the existing TV channels, books, magazines, newspapers, or videocassettes to find what they would consider to be the optimal entertainment or information. The problem here is not so much that viewers neglect some great TV show or news broadcast but rather that there aren't too many great TV shows or news broadcasts at all. Unless people can conveniently and affordably recognize high-quality programming, there's no economic reason to create it. We might expect this situation to worsen in the future, since video on demand will only broaden our choices and make it even harder to reward quality. I.C.I.C.s using new information technology will make all the difference here, however, by recognizing and thereby promoting the information and entertainment that viewers desire.

The meritocracy achieved through better informed consumers and more rigorous competition will lead to a more volatile business environment.

Merit tends to be an unstable attribute. One year's tennis champ succumbs to next year's young lion. One year's revolutionary VCR succumbs to next year's revolutionary VCR. When promotion and reputation give way to merit, no company will be able to count on past success to carry it along. Small innovative companies will rapidly become large companies, and large conservative companies may decline as quickly. Entrepreneurs will have a much greater incentive to start new firms.

Brand names will lose their market value.

Ignorant consumers rely on brand names to encapsulate the cues that tell them about products. With better information, consumers will no longer need to rely on such cues. We can therefore predict that in the next generation, more than $1 trillion of goodwill assets—assets based on name recognition—are likely to disappear from corporate books.

As selling costs become intrinsically inefficient, savvy sellers will focus energy and resources on producing or distributing superior products.

As independent consumer-information companies (I.C.I.C.s) take over the consumer-education function, sellers will suffer as a group, but some will suffer more than others. The biggest losers will be those companies whose primary strength comes from their marketing power rather than their product value.

These companies can be spotted by their large promotion budgets, their heavy reliance on brand names and reputation, and their relatively small production or physical-distribution expenses. Such companies can expect brand names to lose substantial value. A company like RJR Nabisco, for example, which, on the strength of its brand names, sold for $25 billion in the late 1980s, might sell for only a small fraction of that—the value of its hard assets—once a competitive marketplace is established.[8]

Such companies can also expect a shift in the internal balance of power. Corporate structure, and the power blocks that constitute it, will reflect the loss of monopoly power and the information-providing role. There will be far fewer marketing-oriented heads of companies. In fact, anyone associated with the selling function—whether in establishing a brand or a store's image or actually selling products—will lose out. This includes marketing-oriented purchasing agents, especially those who buy products that will ultimately be sold to consumers. Many of their currently esteemed skills, such as negotiating for derivative models, working out bait-and-switch product strategies, and ordering superfluous models to circumvent laws preventing constant sales, will become obsolete.

Business talent will follow the rewards. Smart companies and investors will sell off their image and brand assets and invest in superior talent and production facilities. Smart employees will make sure that their careers focus on managing production rather than consumption.

In-home selling increasingly will replace in-store selling.

The growth of electronic retailing and improved telecommunications mean that we'll be purchasing more and more products without leaving home. At the same time, we can expect less need for in-store retailers and the wholesalers that supply them. Of course, we'll still buy certain products outside the home, particularly (1) those that can be sold more conveniently in stores, (2) those that can be sold less expensively in stores, and (3) those sold by stores with an atmosphere more pleasant than the home. Correspondingly, the major types of future stores will be warehouse clubs, local convenience shops, and enclosed malls. The big losers will be specialty stores, such as consumer-electronics chains, toy chains, and sporting-goods chains, that attain their power from their prowess at marketing a specific type of product and by providing information that is currently unavailable elsewhere. Groups of consumers such as working mothers with young children, as well as the elderly, sick, or disabled, will benefit the most from the advent of in-home shopping.

*Manufacturers as a group will gain at the expense of retailers
as a group.*

Massive concentration of the retail channel over the last few decades has significantly shifted industry power away from the manufacturer and towards the retailer.[9] However, the growth of in-home shopping, combined with the growth of I.C.I.C.s, will give manufacturers relatively more market power, although retailers that get into electronic shopping will show great strength at first. A new breed of consumer products manufacturer that bypasses conventional distribution altogether and sells directly to the public will begin flourishing. Now able to sell directly to consumers or through retail brokers such as Comp-U-Card, with relatively little marketpower, manufacturers will begin to see retailers as inefficient and disposable middlemen.

Smart manufacturers may want to abandon the retailers they cultivated in the past. In the short term, they will appease demands to avoid "channel conflict," but in the long term they will usurp that channel when the time is right. Smart retailers, in turn, will focus on the convenience, low-cost distribution, and entertainment functions that will keep drawing consumers into their stores.

Mail-order retailers will be hurt more than local retailers.

Contrary to popular belief, national electronic retailers—mail order, TV shopping, and videotex—do not represent the "future of retailing" or even a long-term growth market. In fact, better-informed consumers signal the death knell for retailers who want to sell long-distance. The reason is that once I.C.I.C.s take over the information role, such retailers will lose their superior ability to disseminate certain types of product information and thus lose their competitive advantage over manufacturers. For example, if you're buying a camcorder, you'll get the information about it from an I.C.I.C. and then purchase it directly from the manufacturer. Of course, local retailers will still offer better distribution than manufacturers offer for many cheaper, perishable, or single-purchase products. If a California orange juice producer wants to sell to New Yorkers, for example, it's a lot more economical to ship five thousand cartons of juice in advance and store it in a warehouse or retail outlet than it is to send a single carton through the mail to a single customer.

Local retailers will have to provide in-home shopping services.

Given the information available to them, many future retail shoppers will want to browse and purchase from the convenience of their home. They won't be satisfied by the paltry information they can get in a conventional newspaper or yellow pages ad. They will want the additional conveniences of (1) previewing the store before entering it, (2) pre-ordering merchandise and having it packaged and ready for speedy pickup, and (3) having merchandise delivered to their homes directly from the store. Home delivery will probably work best for giant local hypermarkets (combination supermarkets and discount stores), which will be able to offer lower-cost deliveries than smaller stores doing less business in a given geographic area and unable to combine as readily different products in a single delivery.

Package-delivery companies will grow tremendously.

If consumers start ordering more and more directly from manufacturers, it follows that package-delivery companies can expect booming business. In-home electronic shopping will massively increase package deliveries. Consumers make small purchases thousands of times more than do businesses, and for the first time it will be economical to send a significant percentage of those through the mail.

Professionals will have to undergo repeated testing and retraining during their careers.

Although most workers in the United States are held accountable for the work they do, licensed professionals, who are largely independent and do work which consumers cannot readily evaluate, are allowed to let their skills slip with little if any loss of earning power. Doctors, dentists, and morticians, for example, rarely if ever get fired. Once they are licensed, the quality of work they later perform has only a modest relation to their income. As the technology of testing and disseminating test results improves, however, professional testing and retraining should increase. It follows, too, that if I.C.I.C.s become fully functional as independent evaluators of skill and performance, the need for government licensing of so many occupations, with all its inherent limitations, will disappear. So too should the notion of a "professional ethic" or "sense of duty," replaced by more concrete measures of performance. As the line between professional and nonprofessional is blurred, moreover, we can expect to see nonprofessionals, such as paramedics and paralegals, taking over many of the tasks now restricted to licensed professionals.

Consumers and their representatives, the I.C.I.C.s, will drive the growth of the computer industry.

Today, producers are the prime drivers of the information sector, but consumers and I.C.I.C.s will replace them in this role. At the moment, computers can do very little for the average consumer. But the number of tasks for which the average person can use computers is about to increase exponentially and will produce a huge growth for computer sales. To put this in perspective, in the 1980s approximately 30 million PCs were sold in the United States, primarily for business. With the right information infrastructure and information services, this number could easily increase to 250 million—one for each man, woman, and child in the United States—by the first decade of the twenty-first century. As a shopping tool, the PC will be considered as important as the car and credit card are today.

Information services, not applications software, will be the primary application of personal computers.

Americans spend more of their free time shopping (for intangibles such as entertainment, mates, and doctors, as well as for physical goods) than in any activity other than entertainment. Thus, it wouldn't be surprising if today's bread-and-butter computer applications—spreadsheets, data bases, word processors, telecommunications programs—evolved into minor utilities as consumer-information services burgeon and become the primary use of computers.

Traditional telephone companies and cellular telephone companies will both flourish.

Given that many people spend more time shopping than talking on the phone, the new shopping applications could even outweigh today's existing phone applications. One segment that should do particularly well may be providers of wireless information services, such as cellular-telephone companies, since I.C.I.C.s will let shoppers carry their unbiased advisors wherever they go and with utmost convenience.

Businesses will seek more government intervention in the marketplace, consumers less.

Businesspeople pursue profits through the cultivation of monopoly power. They may like "competition" in the abstract, but no businessperson likes competitors. True competition means selling a "commodity" product, a product readily understood and comparison-shopped for, and no businessperson wants to be in such a situation. Of course, "competition" is a value no one would deny overtly. As Galbraith has observed, "[The businessman] must aver that in his industry the 'truest, finest form of competitive pricing exists.' For competition, with us, is more than a technical concept. It is also a symbol of all that is good."[10] Whatever they may say about "competition," however, companies that have already achieved significant monopoly power are not going to benefit by giving it up.

Increased competition will force them to do so, however. Information is power, and independent sources of consumer information—I.C.I.C.s—will force these manufacturers and retailers to lose exclusive control of strategic business information. Increased competition will hurt businesses with substantial monopoly power, primarily large corporations with significant brand-name awareness and control of distribution channels. Many industries today are dominated by a relatively small number of companies that have struggled to differentiate their products and win whatever monopoly power they could for themselves. They will not be at all pleased to see this power threatened by the formation of a more competitive marketplace, and we can therefore suppose that they will do everything possible to oppose it.

Large and powerful businesses, of course, have always railed against anything that might take away their monopoly power. They've traditionally fought bitterly against antitrust and consumer-protection laws, for example, and have protested excessive government intervention. Ironically, however, the new nemesis of monopoly power shouldn't be government intervention but the laissez-faire market itself, the same laissez-faire that once fostered monopoly power. The old antigovernment ideology that business has used to justify monopoly imperfections will no longer be relevant in an economy which largely has overcome the historic incompatibility of laissez-faire and competition. Thus while businesses increasingly turn to government to preserve and enhance their monopoly powers, consumers may attain new confidence in the genuinely competitive nature of the laissez-faire marketplace.[11]

In industries where market leaders currently benefit from promotional economies of scale, small companies will succeed as never before.

Today, in many consumer-product industries, there are huge promotional economies of scale. Fighting against an established brand name, for example, can cost a small fortune, even if that brand name represents an inferior product. This seriously inhibits the small company with the superior product from competing. Similarly, the advertising industry favors big spenders. For example, the cost of taking a full-page ad in a metropolitan newspaper is the same whether you have one store in that region or twenty. This precludes small stores from competing in many industries. For example, one of the reasons that major consumer-electronics superstores enter a metropolitan market with at least four and sometimes many as twenty stores at once is so they can achieve advertising economies of scale, something that has become vital in the consumer-electronics business with its heavy reliance on advertising.

In the future, no companies will have promotional economies of scale, because promotion will become uneconomical. All companies will be on a level playing field. The influence of I.C.I.C.s will almost instantly allow superior products to achieve national recognition. The only economics the small company will have to worry about are the economics of producing and distributing its product. Any efficiencies that currently exist in terms of building demand for a product will become irrelevant.

In industries with economies of scale in production, large companies will succeed as never before.

Not everything about the information age will favor the little guy. In many industries the little guy only exists because confused consumers can't distinguish between competing claims. In these industries, companies have been able to survive without taking full advantage of economies of scale, but better information will change this situation. For example, we won't have forty companies selling camcorders but instead just a handful of large efficient companies. Similarly, in many of the service businesses, such as funeral parlors, jewelry stores, eyeglass vendors, plumbing businesses, and auto dealerships—currently dominated by many inefficient, underutilized operators within each market—better consumer information about quality and price will favor fewer but more efficient stores or even national chains.

Information will be seen as an increasingly important moral resource.

Deceptive selling by the unscrupulous few in the business underworld is, in fact, our most serious form of theft. It cheats Americans of . . . more than is lost through robbery, burglary, larceny, auto theft, embezzlement, and forgery combined. Unlike the con men of yesterday who were often so heavy-handed that they offended the law, today's modern bandits of the marketplace are the masters of the light touch. . . . [T]hese men can reach even deeper into our pockets without producing a rustle to disturb the law, or often the victim himself.[12]

As Senator Warren Magnuson made clear with these words, there is a profoundly moral element to information. In a secular world, a world in which communication is the central fact of political, economic, and cultural organization, high-quality information becomes the key to a moral society. While the *appearance* of morality always pays, the significance of high-quality information is that it can separate the master impostors—the shrewd and practical companies and individuals—from those whose sustenance comes from real hard work and achievement.

We have always recognized the importance of high-quality political information—a vigorous and free press leading to an informed electorate—as essential to thwarting totalitarianism, corruption, and incompetence in government. Even in our day-to-day lives, we see information about products, companies, and people as vital to preventing exploitation. But we don't always appreciate this abstract and increasingly important relationship between information and morality.

We foresee the emergence of a new product-information system, a system in which high-quality information about persons, products, and companies dramatically reduces the payoff for distortion and deception. In an Information Age, it is information crimes, not physical crimes, that most widely harm society. We have seen throughout this book the high price of our ignorance, not only to our pocketbooks but to the moral fiber of our society as well. Anything that can help improve the information infrastructure of our society so that such abuses are harder to perpetrate will be hailed as a moral triumph. We won't tolerate those that wield monopoly power over information—whether they be politicians, companies, or media. The independent information companies will be seen to play as important a role as the police of today, making freedom from information abuse just as important as freedom from physical abuse.

*   *   *

We're about to enter a period in which new information technology will fundamentally alter the world in which we live. The way consumers go about gathering information and making decisions today is closer to the eighteenth century than the twenty-first century. As the twenty-first century progresses, the consumer's growing information power will transform the marketplace and many of the values currently associated with it. Individuals and nations who don't recognize the emerging obsolescence of their old ways of thinking and acting will surely suffer. The future will belong to those with the vision to anticipate what the new information technology will bring and the courage and resources to take appropriate action.

1. Ben Bagdikian, *The Media Monopoly*, 2nd ed. (Boston: Beacon Press, 1987), p. 185, citing Billie Wahlstrom, "Sex Stereotyping in Advertising: Geritol Days and Aviance Nights," *Interface*, 1980, p. 39; Daniel Bell, *The Cultural Contradictions of Capitalism* (New York; Basic Books, 1976), p. 68.

2. For a typology of advertising criticism, see Richard W. Polloy, "The Distorted Mirror: Reflections on the Unintended Consequences of Advertising," *Journal of Marketing*, April 1986, pp. 18–36.

3. Theodore Levitt, "Advertising and Its Adversaries," in *Advertising's Role in Society*, eds. John S. Wright and John E. Mertes (Boston: West Publishing, 1974), pp. 248–250.

4. John Kenneth Galbraith, *The New Industrial State* (Boston: Houghton Mifflin, 1967), p. 218.

5. Robert Heilbroner, "Demand for the Supply Side," *New York Review of Books*, June 11, 1981, p. 40.

6. Raymond A. Bauer and Stephen A. Greyser, *Advertising in America: The Consumer View*, (Boston: Harvard Business School, 1968) pp. 105–107.

7. Bell, pp. 70–72.

8. Mark Landler, "What's in a Name? Less and Less," *Business Week*, July 8, 1991, p. 67. See also David A. Aaker, *Managing Brand Equity* (New York: Free Press, 1991).

9. *1988 Nielsen Review of Grocery Store Trends* (Northbrook, Ill. A. C. Nielsen Company, 1988), p. 11.

10. John Kenneth Galbraith, *The Affluent Society*, 3rd ed. (New York: New American Library, 1976), pp. 33–34; Idem, *American Capitalism* (Boston: Houghton Mifflin, 1956), p. 94. See

also F. M. Scherer, *Industrial Market Structure and Economic Performance* (Boston: Houghton Mifflin, 1980), p. 22.

11. Galbraith, *American Capitalism,* p. 51.

12. Warren Magnuson and Jean Carper, *The Dark Side of the Marketplace: The Plight of the American Consumer,* 2nd ed. (Englewood Cliffs, N.J.: Prentice-Hall, 1972), p. 13. See also Edwin Sutherland, *White Collar Crime: The Uncut Version,* Gilbert Geis and Colin Goff, eds. (New Haven, Conn.: Yale University Press, 1983); Marshall Clinard and Peter Yeager, *Corporate Crime* (New York: Free Press, 1980); and Paul Blumberg, *The Predatory Society: Deception in the American Marketplace* (New York: Oxford University Press, 1989), p. 206.

Index

Printed in the United States
207056BV00002B/247-294/P

9 780595 503636